P9-DZP-116

O P E

A S I A

North

Pacific

Ocean

C A

andaka • Kampala • Muqdisho *Maldives* • Singapore

EQUATOR

• Nairobi Bukittinggi • Pontianak • Samarinda

zzaville • Kigali

inshasa

Indian

AUSTRALIA

Ocean

R C T I C A

EQUATOR

A Journey

THURSTON CLARKE

EQUATOR

A Journey

William Morrow and Company, Inc.

New York

Copyright © 1988 by Thurston Clarke

All rights reserved. No part of this book may be reproduced or utilized in any form or by any means, electronic or mechanical, including photocopying, recording or by any information storage and retrieval system, without permission in writing from the Publisher. Inquiries should be addressed to Permissions Department, William Morrow and Company, Inc., 105 Madison Ave., New York, N.Y. 10016.

Library of Congress Cataloging-in-Publication Data

Clarke, Thurston.
    Equator : a journey.

    1. Clarke, Thurston.   2. Voyages around the
world—1951 –   3. Tropics—Description and
travel.   I. Title.
G440.C6C6   1988   910'.0913   88-5197
ISBN 0-688-06901-0

Printed in the United States of America

First Edition

1 2 3 4 5 6 7 8 9 10

BOOK DESIGN BY MARIA EPES
MAPS BY VIKKI LEIB

016
Flagstaff Public Library
Flagstaff, Arizona

910.0913
C 6112

FOR EDWINA AND PHOEBE

EQUATOR

A Journey

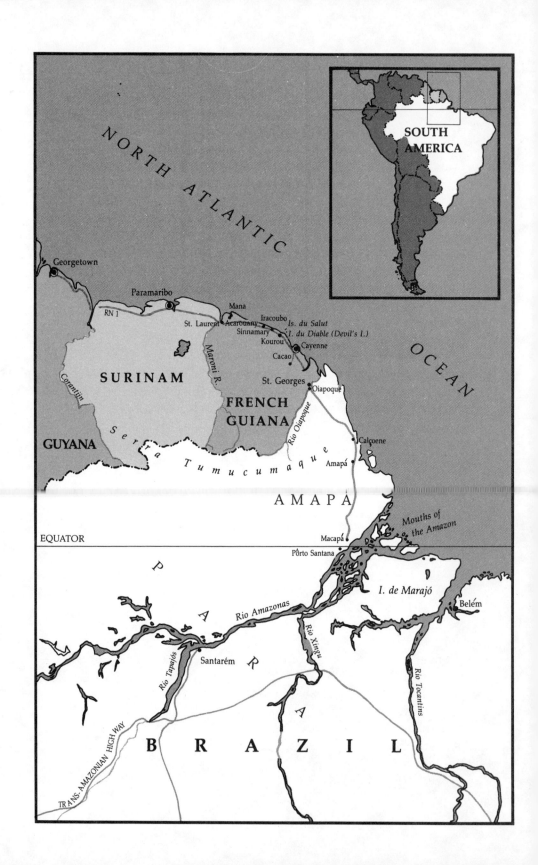

MY CLOTHES ARE EXHAUSTED, THIN AS SILK FROM BEING slapped on rocks and scorched by irons heated over charcoal. I slip them on and smell, I think, the equator: sweat, charcoal, and low tide.

Souvenirs litter my rooms. There is a paper clip from Albert Schweitzer's desk, a box with a pop-out snake, and a chunk of propeller from a plane crashed on a Pacific atoll by Amelia Earhart, or so I was told. I have a T-shirt saying Happy Trails, in Indonesian. I won it racing Baptist missionaries up a Borneo hill. I keep pencils in a soapstone box from Somalia, as white and square as the houses of Muqdisho. I weight papers with a gold-flecked rock from a Sumatran mine. My wife says it is fool's gold.

I have become a connoisseur of heat. There is the heat that reflects off coral and scorches and softens the face like a tomato held over a fire. There is the greasy heat of a tropical city, a milky heat that steams a jungle river like a pan of nearly boiled water, a blinding heat that explodes off tin roofs like *paparazzi*'s flashbulbs, and a heat so lazy and intoxicating that all day you feel as though you are waking from a wine-drugged nap.

Letters still come from the equator. Those from the Africans, my best correspondents, have two themes: "Remember me?" or "Remember me!"

A postcard from a Pygmy starts, "Do you recall . . ."

Yonda writes, "Greetings from Mbandaka, Zaïre!! How are you doing? I'm sure you're gonna be surprised to receive a letter from somebody you really do not know that well. I don't know if you still remember when you passed by Mbandaka; you met a young man . . ."

Edward has found postage to remind me he is "an Orphan and alone. There's no job for me here. I have tried a lot but No Way Out so please don't forget me. . . . Remember I'm sleeping on a street in front of Bar #6 which operates for 24 hours. Imagine what life I am leading now."

Imagine I can. I have seen where Edward lives, and the word "Orphan" ignites memories—just as someone smoking Benson & Hedges reminds me of tides racing through a Pacific channel while George, king of Abemama, chain-smokes this brand and struggles to reconstruct a family tree, borrowed, but never returned, he says, by a noted anthropologist.

A boy kicks a ball, and I remember the soccer-crazy governor of Macapá and his plan for an equatorial stadium. The equator will be at midfield, with each team defending a hemisphere.

A satellite dish in a suburban yard reminds me of larger equatorial ones, oases of technology encircled by jungle, glowing ghost-white at night and marking the line as surely as crumbling obelisks and rusting signs.

Lazy northern sunsets bring back fast equatorial ones flashing like color slides across a screen. Click: The sun quivers above the horizon. Click: Quick as a guillotine it falls into jungle or ocean. Click: Stars glitter bright and close in a planetarium sky.

Some memory pictures flash without warning: A tornado of bats circles a French war memorial in the jungle; crabs scuttle through the collapsed blast towers of ground zero, Christmas Island; and a spider web of cracks surrounds a bullet hole in the windshield of a Ugandan taxi.

I can order these pictures by consulting my maps. Before a journey a map is an impersonal menu; afterwards, it is intimate as a diary. Before, I had stared at my maps and wondered if there was still a Jardin Botanique in the middle of Zaïre. Did passenger ships sail between Sumatra and Borneo? Tarawa and Abemama?

And what should I make of the black dots signaling a "difficult or dangerous" road? Now I know, and these maps have become as comfortable as my canvas boots. I enjoy touching them, imagining I can feel, as if printed in Braille, the mountains, rivers, roads, and railways, all the familiar contours of the longest circular route on earth.

Why do maps attract the finger? Who has not—well, who nearing middle-age has not—run a finger across a page in an atlas and imagined traveling to the end of this highway or that river, sailing to every island in a chain or climbing every mountain in a range? What child has not traveled by spinning a globe? I owned an illuminated one. I switched it on and darkened the room and it became the glowing, revolving planet that introduced travelogues and newsreels. Then I closed my eyes, stabbed at it with a finger, and imagined going wherever I landed.

My journey began this way on a snowy February evening in New York when I grabbed a globe off a friend's bookshelf and spun it into a whirling bouquet of continents and oceans. Then I held it in front of a frosted window and watched places I might never see race past. It stopped and I saw a box in the South Pacific, saying W.A.R. Johnson Ltd., Edinburgh and London, 1898. On a modern globe, Africa and Asia are a patchwork of colors, but on this Victorian model they were piebald, British red and French blue, and my eye was drawn to lines instead of colors: wavy ocean currents throwing tendrils around continents, thin isothermals swooping from Cancer and Capricorn, and a date line zigzagging down the Pacific. Longest and most prominent was a triple-thick, brown-and-yellow-checkered line coiled like a snake around the middle of the earth. The equator.

I traced it with a finger, imagining for the first time a trip along its path. It sliced Borneo and Sumatra in half. It cut across Mount Kenya and the mouth of the Amazon. It brushed Singapore, Nairobi, and Quito, and threaded through the Maldives, the Gilberts, and the Galápagos. There was desert in Somalia, a volcano in Ecuador, savanna in Kenya, and, most of all, jungle.

Along the equator, I learned in the library, you find superlatives: the largest atoll and heaviest rat, the widest river and longest snake, the highest volcanoes, heaviest mammals, biggest flower, stinkiest fruit, and greatest expanse of virgin forest ever destroyed by fire. It is a reassuring line, geometry imposed on nature's seeming anarchy, evidence of a divine intelligence at work in creation. Even the earliest flat-earth cartographers believed in the earth's symmetry and drew equators across the Danube, the Mediterranean, and the Nile. If the earth were stationary and perfectly spherical, any circle would divide it into equal halves, and by now an international conference would have chosen an artificial equator to standardize maps. This is what happened in the case of zero degrees longitude, which can theoretically be any vertical line connecting the poles. For centuries chauvinistic map-makers drew it through Rome, Paris, Washington, Stockholm, and Peking, until finally, fatigued by this chaos and bowing to British sea power, the world agreed at the Washington conference in 1884 that zero degrees longitude, the prime meridian, ran through the Royal Observatory, in Greenwich, England.

But since the earth is an imperfect sphere, rotating about the poles and bulging in the middle, the equator, like a river, desert, or mountain range, can only be exactly where it is: equidistant from the poles and perpendicular to the earth's axis, at 24,901.55 miles the longest circle that can be thrown around the earth. It divides the world into climatic and vegetative mirror images. On the equator at sea level, gravity is weakest, barometric pressure is lowest, and the earth spins fastest. To its north, winds circulate clockwise around zones of high pressure; to its south, counterclockwise. Where it crosses oceans, placid seas spin unpredictable hurricanes into the hemispheres; where it crosses land, predictable temperature and rainfall nurture life in sensational abundance and variety. The Amazon, the Congo, and the Nile rivers have been charted and explored, the Sahara and the Empty Quarter crossed in every direction, but the equator remains a virgin, known in part but not in sum, the longest but least visited, least appreciated, natural feature on earth.

When I proposed the equator as a natural feature, I heard a lot of "Bah, humbug!" It was nothing but a line on a globe, the only line on those little maps fastened to zoo cages that show the habitat of exotic animals. Because no one could "see" the equator, it was unworthy of exploration. Some people, remembering the Coriolis effect from high school physics, said it was where water changed direction as it flowed from a sink or a toilet, clockwise north of the line and counterclockwise to the south, and they saw me traveling around the world, flushing toilets to discover in which hemisphere I stood. Well, "Bah, humbug" to all that. A blind man cannot see mountains, but his ears sense the change in altitude and he becomes light-headed. In a swamp, his pores open and he senses humidity. He feels his nostrils drying in a desert and his skin catching salt from the ocean. We can none of us see the equator, but we can sense it, and feel its effects.

Mariners consider it a dangerous line. At sea, rising warm air produces the belt of lazy winds and dull seas known as the doldrums. The history of tropical trade and exploration is full of ships becalmed for weeks near the equator, of crewmen dying from thirst under drooping sails. Because of the doldrums, a successful crossing of the equator came to be celebrated by a "crossing the line" ceremony, one with strong overtones of rebaptism and thanksgiving. And because of the doldrums, French slavers carried barrels of lime so if they were becalmed in the equatorial "middle passage," they could poison their cargo before tossing it overboard—a more humane solution, they argued, than the despicable Anglo-Saxon practice of throwing live slaves into the sea.

Underneath the oceans' surface, the powerful equatorial countercurrent forces the captains of even the supertankers to adjust their steering as they cross the line. In the Pacific, this current stirs up a feast of plankton that attracts whales, and their killers. The first American whaleboat to reach Honolulu was named *The Equator*. Captain Ahab tracked Moby Dick into these equatorial hunting grounds, and Melville wrote of his own journey there: ". . . we spent several weeks chassezing across the Line, to and fro, in unavailing search for our prey. For some of the hunters believe, that whales, like the silver ore in Peru, run in veins through the ocean. So, day after day, daily; and week after week, weekly, we traversed the self-same longitudinal intersection of the self-same Line; till we were almost ready to swear that we felt the ship strike every time her keel crossed that imaginary locality."

On land and sea, the equator is characterized by a consistent absence of twilight and daybreak. Nowhere else do you have less time to adjust between day and night. Nowhere is the sun so high in the sky at midday for so many days of the year. Europeans have traditionally found these extremes of quick darkness and overhead sun unsettling. Into the twentieth century, Europeans living near the equator feared that even a moment's exposure of their bare heads to the sun might cause sunstroke or fatal brain hemorrhage. In a book published between the wars, Doctor Albert Schweitzer wrote, "A white man, working in a store, was resting after dinner with a ray of sunshine falling on his head through a hole in the roof about the size of a half-crown: the result was high fever with delirium."

You cannot feel the lessening of gravity at the equator, but you can see the results. A scale would show you weighing less at sea level in Borneo than in Belgium. A pendulum clock calibrated to mark time at a temperate latitude will slow down if moved nearer to the equator. In 1673, the French astronomer Jean Richer journeyed to Cayenne, in Equinoctial France, to observe the movements of sun and planets near the equator. By chance, he noticed that a pendulum clock he had carried from Paris lost time at the sea-level city of Cayenne. He had stumbled on proof of Sir Isaac Newton's theory that the earth bulges in the middle and flattens out at the poles. Since Cayenne was nearer the equator than Paris, it was further from the center of the earth, and thus gravity exerted less pull on the pendulum.

Like other natural features, the equator has given its name to the places it touches. Just as there is an Atlantic City and a Pacific Palisades, and just as the cities of Erie, Geneva, and Como border their namesake lakes, so too is there an Equator railway station in Africa, an Equator Town, founded by Robert Louis Stevenson, in the Pacific, and an Equatorville (since renamed), where the line crosses the Zaïre River. In South America, there is Ecuador — "equator" in Spanish — and in the Pacific, the Line Islands. Open an atlas or pick up a globe and run your finger along zero degrees longitude. What do you find named after the prime meridian? Nothing.

Nations have tried to profit from the equator, as from any natural resource. One reason the French built a space center in their Guiana colony is because the weaker gravitational pull of the earth there enables missiles to be launched with a quarter less fuel than those of identical weight shot from Cape Canaveral. For centuries, Norwegian packets bound for the southern hemisphere have carried sherry casks filled with aquavit. Connoisseurs of aquavit believe some alchemy occurs at zero latitude that improves their favorite beverage. Multiple voyages make it still more prized and expensive. I tracked down a bottle of this "Linie [or Line] Aquavit." Its label certified that on January 19 and July 5, 1985, it had crossed the equator on the M/S *Tourcoing*.

Countries touched by the equator have tried claiming national sovereignty for 22,300 miles into space, from their land equators to the necklace of communications satellites hovering exactly overhead in geostationary orbit. These satellites relay telephone calls and television pictures and are positioned over the equator so they can travel at the same rotational speed as the earth. In 1977, some nations attempted to form a cartel to regulate and charge rent for the satellites sitting above their equators. The Colombian delegate to a United Nations conference on broadcast satellites argued that since "parking places" above the equator are limited, the equatorial orbit is a "natural limited resource" over which the equatorial states have "inalienable rights of sovereignty."

Evidence that the equator is a natural feature is so convincing that some people are fooled into "seeing" it. For centuries, sailors have pasted a blue thread across spyglasses offered to shipmates for "viewing" the equator. One nineteenth-century traveler reported cabin boys being "sent aloft to see the line." They came down describing a "blue streak." The missionary pilot who flew me across it in Borneo threw his Cessna into an amusement-park dip and said, "There! You feel it? The equator!" His pretty wife laughed. "He can't resist. Last month the passenger threw up. Most folks believe they're feeling the equator. Some take pictures." And Mark Twain wrote, "Crossed the equator. In the distance it looked like a blue ribbon stretched across the ocean. Several passengers Kodak'd it."

If you found yourself in Colombian or Ugandan airspace, 22,300 miles above the earth and among the equatorial satellites, you would be closer to "seeing" the equator than from any other vantage point. From here you could "Kodak" the gray doldrum clouds that smother the equator at sea and the green band of jungle that marks it on land. Satellite photographs show this terrestrial equator to be slightly moth-eaten, broken by mountains in central Africa and Ecuador, a high plateau in Kenya, and desert in Somalia. There are also human intrusions: slash-and-burn agriculture, cattle ranches, plantations, and logging.

In 1974, American astronauts orbiting the earth in *Skylab* no-

ticed fire lines flaming across the tropics. At night the fires twinkled; by day, canopies of smoke and dust swirled over eroded
land, obscuring burning forests. In Africa, a fire line ran north and
parallel to the equator through Cameroon and the Central African
Republic; to the south, one cut through central Africa. They had
been set by farmers clearing land and herders desperate for pasture, by hunters flushing game and loggers destroying "garbage"
trees. Trapped between them were the tropical forests that strad-
dle the equator.

Within this shrinking green band are African Pygmies, Ama-
zonian Indians, and Asian aborigines, the last survivors of a cen-
turies-old war waged against tribal peoples by civilized man.
Trapped as well is an irreplaceable library of genes: two thirds of
all living species and several hundred thousand plants, animals,
and insects as yet undiscovered and unidentified. Consider that
the British Isles contain fifteen thousand species of trees and
shrubs, while in a single square mile of Colombian rain forest
botanists have identified a thousand, some unique to this square
mile. When it is burned, they will be lost forever.

Since 1974, the tropical fire lines have advanced on the equator, consuming every year forests half the size of California. So
where astronauts once saw fires, they would now see dust spiraling upward from eroded fields. Where they saw rain forest, they
would see fire lines. Even the most optimistic scientists predict
that during the next century the jungle fires of the northern and
southern hemispheres will meet almost everywhere, and then
anyone looking down at the equator will see a continuous band of
smoke and flames.

I was in London before leaving for the equator, so I traveled
to Greenwich to scout the opposition. At the National Maritime
Museum, a curator showed me early equatorial maps. One of his
favorites was a sixteenth-century Portuguese chart on which the
Linha Equinoccial was correctly shown to hit the African island of
São Tomé. Its only fault was in portraying this slaving entrepôt as
too large, and the Linha as so fat you could imagine the slaves,
the only product of consequence ever traded between equatorial
regions, walking to Brazil. Long after I had extracted every possible lesson from this map, the curator was still moving his finger

back and forth along the equator, saying "Around the equator is it? I do envy you . . . well, in a way."

Up the hill, at the Greenwich Observatory, an astronomer stood straddling a brass line marking the Greenwich Mean while he was interviewed by a Portuguese television crew. I had arrived just after Meridian Day, the hundredth anniversary of the conference establishing Greenwich as the international standard. The Duke of Edinburgh had come to "inspect" a huge jelly, colored like the Union Jack and molded in the shape of the British Isles. Seven thousand schoolchildren ate it, then passed from hand to hand "an important message from the Governor of Fiji." Judges chose a Miss Meridian, and celebrants jumped through hoops stationed between the western and eastern hemispheres. Pubs baked "meridian pies" and offered commemorative ales. A family discovered their home was on the meridian and painted a white line across a couch. A Meridian Day committee printed maps depicting its path, and a spokesman was amazed so many Britons did not know that the famous line intersected their property. (I did not think anyone living on the equator would need to be told, and I was right.) The meridian celebrators had even stolen the crossing-the-line ceremony from the equator. Their Neptune crossed a duck pond in a dinghy.

This was fitting hoopla, as contrived as the line it commemorated and in keeping with the command of one postwar British politician to "Let the Empire go if you must but cling fast to the Prime Meridian." I detected an inferiority complex. Was it because zero latitude beats zero longitude on distance? Or because, although the prime meridian also crosses France, Spain, Algeria, and several African countries, the British were celebrating alone? Until 1978, the stubborn French had set their watches to Paris Mean Time, a fifth of a second behind Greenwich, and they were readying l'Institut de l'Heure to measure atomic time and seize glory from Greenwich.

The observatory gift shop sold commemorative buttons, pens, and key chains stamped with a distinctive emblem: a red-and-white world map, divided into hemispheres by a prominent white meridian and surrounded by the inscription Longitude Zero. Greenwich 1984. The world map was the Mercator projection, on which the flattening of the globe distorts every line and feature except one, the equator. I bought a button and hired a graphic designer to copy it, rotating the meridian ninety degrees so it became the equator. He changed the words to The Great Equatorial Expedition and added a third color so my button was more eye-catching. I would hand them out en route. It was time someone celebrated the equator.

Back in New York, I found a clinic that prepared travelers for the tropics. It was inexpensive and offered free follow-up visits. The young physicians nursed secret hopes we would return with challenging ailments. The man I saw recommended a diet of canned fruit and overcooked meat. He agreed it would cause constipation and suggested a laxative. He said the most dangerous tropical beast was the mosquito and wrote prescriptions for two anti-malarials, Aralen and Fansidar. He prescribed antibiotics "in case you catch typhoid. The symptoms are like malaria, but you'll know it's typhoid when you don't improve." What about my typhoid vaccination? "Not foolproof," he said, and suggested another regimen of pills in case I contracted malaria. But wouldn't the Aralen and Fansidar protect me? "Perhaps not. Some of the places are cooking new strains." Then he traced the equator on his wall map and said, "Boy! I really envy you . . . I suppose."

In the late nineteenth century, the British explorer Mary Kingsley received medical advice that was less complicated and expensive but scarcely less encouraging: "Abstain from exposing yourself to the direct rays of the sun, take 4 grains of quinine every day for a fortnight before you reach the Rivers, and get some introductions to the Wesleyans; they are the only people on the coast who have got a hearse with feathers." I found myself surrounded by people with stories belonging more to her century. Someone's friend had returned from Asia with hepatitis, yellow as a traffic light. A Foreign Service officer described colleagues who, decades after tropical postings, had yet to regain their health. A Peace Corps volunteer had come back from Africa exploding with itchy rashes. The son of my pharmacist had caught schistosomiasis in Kenya. "They told the kids not to swim. But it was so hot they dangled their feet in the lake and thought it was OK because they weren't swimming. Now he's got it for life. Good luck," he said, ringing up seventy dollars' worth of prescriptions.

I needed twelve visas. Brazil and Kenya took a day, but

Somalia and Gabon each wanted a week. The Ugandans said a month. "We must send your application to Kampala," a diplomat said, "so our computers can be sure you are not an enemy of the Ugandan people." Their real enemies were probably in Kampala programming these sinister computers, but I did not say this. Applying for a difficult visa turns any traveler into a coward.

The old slaving center of São Tomé had become a people's republic where, according to a woman answering the telephone at their UN mission, "tourism is forbidden." Visas were only issued to those who swore they were not tourists and presented invitations from the foreign minister. I wrote a crawling letter and nearly a year later, long after returning from Africa, received a reply addressed to my telephone number. Octavio do Nascimento, the chief of cabinet, saw "no inconvenience to my visit if I obeyed all the laws of São Tomé." But did this include the law against tourists? I solved other visa problems by engaging a Mennonite travel agency so my applications arrived at embassies surrounded by those of Mennonite missionaries, who seemed welcome everywhere.

Like a pilot using a flight simulator, I made a test run at the Bronx Zoo. There were snow flurries outside the World of Tropical Birds, but inside, tame birds fluttered close as butterflies and water dripped from glistening leaves. The longer I stared into this tame jungle the more I saw, and the more I realized that even here I could not see everything. A small beast, a snake, for example — particularly a snake — could easily hide itself.

Besides snakes, I have never been that fond of tropical nights, an antipathy shared by many temperate-zone people. We romanticize the tropical day for its dazzling colors, sunlight, and leisure, for its Technicolor butterflies and afternoon sex under slow-moving fans. At night we appreciate a star-filled equatorial sky or the moon shadows of palm trees, but from the safety of a veranda or walled garden, from within a circle of light or stone. Outside, snakes are wiggling, wild dogs roaming, and mosquitoes biting. We wonder, Are the roadblock soldiers drinking? Are the servants, obsequious by day, gathering at secret bonfires with their machetes? We lock ourselves in and sleep poorly, waking to find paths spotted with chicken blood and slogans ending in exclamation marks. Since the equator is at the dead center of the tropics, might it not also be at the dead center of our tropical myths and fears? Balancing them as perfectly as its twelve-hour days and twelve-hour nights?

If I am sensitive to these temperate-zone fears, it is because the nearest I have come to losing my life was in a hot country at night. It happened in southern Spain when I was eighteen. Hardly the tropics, but there were palm trees, humidity, and poverty. At a poorly lit rural station I was almost hit by a train. A whistle blasted and I turned and froze, stunned like a deer by the huge eye of light. At the last second a soldier grabbed me, throwing me backward into the stationmaster's garden and knocking me out. I woke sweating, smelling blossoms and ringed by soldiers in strange uniforms.

After visiting the Bronx Zoo, I bought a backpack that converted into a canvas suitcase, ideal luggage for a thirty-nine-year-old. I strapped it to my back and felt like a student. I zipped up the shoulder straps, grabbed the handle, and was ready for policemen in places where backpacks mean drugs and debauchery.

Ten years before, I had traveled to Niger, in West Africa, to write about the Tuareg nomads. I had taken only a notebook and clothes. Since then a new industry has grown up, manufacturing lightweight travel and camping gear. Seduced by the catalogues, I ordered a miniature flashlight, a plastic washbasin that folded to fit into a shirt pocket, foil-wrapped vitamin bars, and a snake-bite kit that employed a huge syringe to suction venom out through the fang marks. Each gadget was light and marvelously well-designed, but when I tossed them together into a nylon sack they assumed the weight and shape of a cannonball.

Dr. Livingston believed sumptuous provisions and excessive native bearers encouraged theft and extortion. But this ascetic Scots philosophy reduced him, to use his own words, "to a skeleton," condemned to wait for help "in beggary." Stanley's expedition to rescue him included two hundred bearers, collapsible boats, Persian carpets, and champagne. "The American flag at the head of the column told of the nationality of the stranger," Livingston wrote. "Bales of goods, baths of tin, huge cooking pots, tents etc. made me think, 'This must be a luxurious traveller, and not one at his wit's end like me.'" At the last minute I reduced my cannonball by a third, slightly favoring luxury over wit's end.

I decided to move from west to east, following the prevailing winds and the earth's rotation. To find a starting point I traced my New York latitude south to the equator. I was in the middle of the Colombian jungle, surrounded by those one thousand species per square mile but far from any road or village. I was looking for an adopted home, somewhere I might be remembered when I returned. I followed the equator across South America until, at the mouth of the Amazon, it hit the port of Macapá. My South American map letters towns in five sizes of print. Macapá was third darkest, neither an overwhelming city nor an obscure backwater, a good place to begin. But then I tried to buy a ticket there and found it was accessible only through Belém, which meant flying over the equator to Belém, then doubling back to Macapá. I wanted to start *on* the equator, not commute over it.

I had neither the money nor the inclination to set off overland with trucks and traveling companions, grimly determined to follow everywhere the equator's exact path. The famous overland routes—Cape to Cairo, and the Pan-American and Trans-Saharan highways—run longitudinally, cutting the equator at right angles. Most lesser roads and railroads also run north to south, since they were built to ship tropical products to the temperate zones. I would have to weave back and forth, using whatever transportation I could find. I pictured my route curling around the equator like a strangler fig.

I could not afford to wait months for the rare passenger-carrying freighter to take me between the continents. Passenger ships cruise the tropics but rarely sail between them. The only way to travel among the equatorial zones of Africa, Asia, and America is by plane. Even so, it is virtually impossible to fly between equatorial regions without going through a temperate-zone city. To travel from Macapá, in South America, to Libreville, in Africa, involves flying through the United States and Europe. Somalia to Singapore requires a detour to Rome, and reaching South America from the equatorial Pacific means flying through Los Angeles. I decided to break the journey into continents, stopping after each one in Europe or America to collect more visas and money and leave behind my notes. I would visit the continents in order, traveling east, going from South America to Africa and Asia and then back to South America, stopping off at the equatorial islands of the Pacific either before or after Asia. But I still intended to be as much a purist as one man with only so much money can be, so I resisted the idea of arriving in Macapá by airplane after having already twice crossed the equator.

I bought more maps and discovered I could reach Macapá through French Guiana. Its capital, Cayenne, was 350 miles north of the equator but accessible from New York through the French Caribbean island of Martinique. I could travel by ship from Cayenne to St. Georges, cross the Oiapoque River to Brazil, and continue by road to Macapá. On some maps this road was dotted, meaning "unpaved road under construction," but an employee of the Brazilian consulate swore it was finished and promised "luxury buses, running on schedule from Oiapoque to Macapá." With equal pride and conviction a Frenchman said, "All the river towns of la Guyane française are linked by ship to the capital. And no visa is necessary because, monsieur, when you are there, you are in France!"

In the days before my departure, the equator began appearing in overexposed daydreams, not a blue streak shimmering across the doldrums but a hairy rope, woven from sisal and thick as a tugboat's line. I saw it draped over volcanoes, bleached white in the desert, and smothered by orchids in sun-flecked forests. Plankton and well-fed whales choked equatorial currents. Norwegian packets with barrels of aquavit lashed to their decks pitched through typhoons. A wreath of satellites hummed and clicked in equatorial skies, and water paused over sink drains, uncertain which way to flow. Aborigines crouched in smoldering forests, their eyes pinwheeling as bulldozers carved roads to Macapá. Then I saw snakes as thick as a wrestler's thighs and jerked awake, wondering how any journey can match the daydreams that precede it, or the extravagant memories that follow.

2

IT WOULD BE DARK WHEN WE LANDED IN FORT DE FRANCE, Martinique. Even so, when we left Miami, passengers slipped into the toilets and changed into bathing suits. The woman behind me painted her nails pink, and my neighbor Barbara shouted down the aisle, "Hey! Are you going there too? And you guys? You, and you? Wow! I guess everyone's going." To the Club Med in Martinique, it turned out. The others were paying, but Barbara had earned a diploma from Club Med University in the Bahamas. She said, "I'll be teaching you guys aerobic dancing!" She turned to me. "In six months they'll send me to another one. They're everywhere: Bali, Senegal—that's in Africa—Tahiti, Morocco . . . I'm going to see the world!" She tossed her glistening hair and described the Club Med hardships: "a piddly living allowance," "pain in the bee-hind rules," and a training program that sounded like the Peace Corps. She opened a box of new stationery and underneath a cluster of colored balloons with smiling faces wrote, "Hi Mom!! I guess I'm a little scared . . ."

When we arrived, Barbara and the others climbed into a Club Med minibus, and I won an argument with a taxi driver who in-

Flagstaff Public Library
Flagstaff, Arizona

sisted Monsieur would prefer a beach hotel to the commercial center of Fort de France. At nine on a Sunday evening the city had the exhausted, faintly sinister feel of the last night on a carnival midway. Gunshots and squealing tires leaked from cinema doors. Ramshackle taxis tooted horns, and boys in tapered shirts struggled to wring a last pleasure from the weekend. They jammed dark bars where television sets sat on pedestals like lighthouses. They clicked tongues at whores and rocked on heels before a huge movie poster, lit by stuttering bulbs and showing an orange-faced woman screaming, *"La terreur commence! . . ."* They drank beer and pissed on palm trees in a park where their cigarettes danced like fireflies. They moved with the grace of barefoot nomads, stepping carefully over the blue plastic garbage bags that lay ripped open on the sidewalks as if someone had rummaged for a hidden cache of fun.

My hotel had sticky bar tables, a jukebox of scratched records, and a *patron* scowling behind a metal cage. I walked around the corner, stopping in a dim bar where teeth and fingernails glowed phosphorescent. Nearby, in the well-lit La Rotande, a man showed off a scar to his friends. It was drawn horizontally across his neck, so angry and fresh they brushed it with their fingertips, as if it were hot. A waiter filled their glasses from a bottle of brandy fetched from high over the bar. It was collared with dust. They clinked glasses. They were celebrating the scar.

The next morning the bars were closed, and stores shuttered the night before displayed color postcards, straw hats, and sun oils in fifteen shades. Gendarmes in Paris uniforms whistled and waved at compact cars beetling around a park exploding with blossoms. Lines of smiling women sold baskets and tourist carvings. Ferries, yachts, and windsurfer sails dotted the harbor. The air was dry, the sky impossibly blue, the breeze perfumed with bread and coffee. I could not believe I would find better weather anywhere, and I was right.

I had the names of several people said to know French Guiana. One said, "Above all, never call it a colony in front of the French, at least the white Frenchmen. It's an overseas department of France, and its people are French citizens." Apparently, though, it could be a "colony" when speaking with black Frenchmen, if I thought they were among the minority wanting independence.

But with everyone else I must be careful to say, for example, "Is it true Cayenne is the fifth largest fishing port in France?" rather than, "Is it true that French Guiana is the largest mainland colony in the world?" Otherwise I might be reminded that Frenchmen had landed in Cayenne before the Pilgrims in Massachusetts, and that Cayenne was closer to Paris than Anchorage was to Washington, D.C., and since we Americans had our Alaska, how could we deny France its resource-rich frontier where, after all, their Indians were better treated than our Eskimos? And didn't I know that France bordered more foreign countries in the western hemisphere than the United States? Yes! You Americans have only two foreign frontiers, Canada and Mexico, while la France borders Surinam, Brazil, and the Netherlands. What? I didn't know France and Holland shared the Caribbean island of St. Martin? Shame.

I was told France hung onto Guiana out of habit, for glory, because she had always been irrational about her colonies—who else would have colonized the Sahara?—and because France was still a colonial power, ruling several million people in its island colonies in the Caribbean, Pacific, and Indian oceans, and worried that de-colonization was contagious; because France was loath to surrender any outposts of French culture and language in an increasingly Anglo-Saxonized world; and because who could say when France might not need the timber and whatever other riches lay in the unexplored interior?

I learned that the Guianese received more "foreign" aid per capita than anyone on earth, and that they had the highest standard of living but the lowest level of productivity of any country in South America. Cayenne's cost of living was half that of Paris, but the French government generously indexed Guianan social-welfare payments to a Parisian scale. So, in a country with less than five hundred miles of paved roads, there was a car for every two citizens. But no traffic jams, because although Guiana is the size of Maine, it has a population of only seventy-five thousand, making it the second least densely populated country in the world, after Mongolia. But the Guianese might soon move into first place, because no country in the world had more unmarried middle-aged men and women. Half the Guianese between the ages of forty-five and fifty had never married. I began to see the point of the French Guiana aficionado who argued it was the most fascinating country in the world. "Or, depending who you're talking with," I said, showing I had taken my lessons to heart, "the most interesting department in France."

I took a ferry to one of the beaches, drank too much Muscadet at lunch, and fell asleep wondering why French Guiana had so many bachelors and spinsters. When I drove to the airport at dusk, the blue garbage bags had reappeared. Ragged children tore into them as if it were Christmas morning.

The departure lounge was a humid atrium humming with bugs. A frog hopped inside a locked duty-free shop, and jet-lagged Frenchmen off a connecting flight from Paris stood opposite a refrigerated food stall, the French Farm, staring with zombie eyes at sweating Camemberts. Few wore wedding bands. In three hours, French Guiana would widen its lead in the bachelor category. They sat far apart on the plane, memorizing labels on miniature wine bottles and reading books with titles like *Putsch à Ougadougou*. They greeted their dinner trays with little French raspberries of displeasure. Convicts had sailed to Devil's Island with more joy.

The Cayenne airport resembled an aircraft carrier at sea, a blazing rectangle of lights floating in darkness. There were no lines of streetlamps, no city glowing on the horizon. We were met by Creole chauffeurs chewing toothpicks and waving placards scrawled with the names of arriving bachelors. I searched for my name and was irrationally disappointed not to find it. At a strange airport, everyone likes to be met.

On this moonless night my taxi driver wore reflecting Tonton Macoute sunglasses. When I asked him to slow down, he argued it would not be *"juste"* to the other passengers. There were not enough taxis at the airport, and if he hurried he might return for another fare. I had been in France less than an hour, and already I had received a lecture in etiquette from a Frenchman. And if I doubted this was France I had only to look at signs announcing the RN 4 — Route Nationale 4 — to Cayenne. In the Metropole, the RN 4 connects Paris and Strasbourg. Here it was a thin black tongue rolling into dips and curving around jungle mounds. We swerved to miss a disabled truck and my Tonton cursed. *"Scandale!* A week he has parked there."

I heard a gunshot.

"Hunters."

"But so close to the road?"

"Monsieur, here within a hundred yards of the road you can find *anything*."

"Anything?"

"All manner of game."

On the back page of a notebook I had collected descriptions of Guianese animals. The pingo: a savage pig that weighs over sixty pounds, travels in two-hundred-strong packs, and eats everything in its path. The capybara: at a hundred and twenty pounds the largest rat in the world. The bushmaster: the biggest poisonous snake in the Americas. The black caiman: "the fiercest and noisiest of all crocodiles." My favorite was the matamata turtle. It resembled "a repulsive clump of debris" and sucked up its dinner "with a powerful vacuum device in its long snakelike throat." According to one authority, "Hunters who have ventured into the Guiana interior say that the problem is not to find game but to avoid being eaten by it." And, sure enough, we sped around a curve, and trapped in our headlights was the fattest, longest snake I have ever seen in the wild. The Tonton swerved to hit it. There was a considerable bump. He smiled, displaying a gold tooth bought with his Parisian dental allowance. *"Un serpent méchant!"*—"An evil snake!"

"Venimeux?"

"Oui, mais seulement un bébé."

I learned later that wild dogs were the most dangerous animals prowling this stretch of highway. As French functionaries drove to the airport for the last time, they opened their car doors and booted their pets into the jungle. The animals had clubbed together into man-hating packs.

We slowed for an empty crossroads with blinking lights set on yellow and a billboard advertising flights to Paris. We turned away from the streetlights leading to the center and climbed a steep hill under a tunnel of trees. Dead leaves fell so fast the Tonton switched on the wipers. I had forgotten this, how every tropical evening is an autumn of dying leaves, and every night a winter of dead insects piling into snowdrifts.

The hotel was shrinking. The restaurant was closed and the pool drained, and a spotlighted birdcage stood empty. Instead of local handicrafts, glass cases in the lobby displayed dead wasps and moths lying on catafalques of dust. The clerk said I was lucky to find a room. Cayenne was hosting an "international medical convention," impressive-sounding until you learned the "doctors" were mostly faith healers, vitamin quacks, and chiropractors.

In the bar, the air conditioning was broken and the foliage grew dense and close to the windows. Two Germans with the raw, bony faces I associate with chiropractors sat with an African, who was shouting, "Why, if they wish to kill me, they'll simply blow up the hotel! Perhaps they will try tonight. It would give them great pleasure." He smiled, imitating their joy.

"They have tried to get me in your country, Germany, and in yours," he said, turning to me. "So why not here? That's why I won't sleep tonight. You can't trust a hotel. Someone pays the clerk and he doesn't wake you, so you're stranded until the next plane, and they have more time."

"More time?" echoed the Germans.

"To plot against me. So tonight I'll go to the discos, drink punch, write another chapter of my autobiography, then off to the plane without sleeping."

Why not buy an alarm clock, I wondered and then made the mistake of asking. He glared at me and drained his beer, slopping some on his white dashiki. He was a neckless man with a perfectly round head and body, a cue ball glued to a bowling ball. As he talked, he rolled across the couch. "Whenever people recognize me in airports or hotels, why, it's funny to see them because they just can't believe their eyes. 'My God!' they say, 'it's you!!'" His eyes flew open, mimicking a reaction composed equally of surprise and terror.

One of the chiropractors asked, "So you were a very big, how do you say it, a big manager?"

"No, not a manager, a *leader*, until the problems of seventy- . . ." His voice trailed away and, missing the date, I interrupted to ask where he had been a leader.

"You must excuse me but I'm busy with these German gentlemen. I'll get to you later. You know, of course that your government is responsible for my situation." He turned his back and said, *"I love Germany,"* making it clear he did not feel similar affection for America. "I have many German friends in Hamburg. I can arrive anytime and if they're away, why, they just leave me the key. No bother. I go alone to the discos. And there everyone knows me. They say, '*My God! It's you!!*'"

"Then why are you in French Guiana?" one of the Germans asked.

"But my friends, *I . . . love . . . it . . . here!* I come for a holiday because even in the discos, *no one knows who I am!* No one stops me in the street and says, '*My God! It's you!!*' Aha, here we are . . ."

A pouty Creole tottered into the bar on stiletto heels and, from a great height, dumped a file of newspaper clippings onto the Leader's table. He grabbed an article from the top of the pile. It crumbled at the edges, showering him with yellow confetti. "Look! There I am in front of the Foreign Ministry. Go on, look at it." The Germans held it to the light like cashiers examining a suspicious bank note.

"Here I am again, the following year, a conference in Geneva. See, I'm standing next to the president." His finger stabbed the photograph; more confetti fell. "And here's Rome, three years later."

"Yes, *it's you!*" one of them said, at last entering into the spirit of things.

"Yes, *me!* Wait, here's one in German. Keep it. Go on, it's a copy, I have more. Wait, here's Miami. He's my friend. Very big. Recognize him? Of course you do."

"Yes, yes, you were important, that's for sure," the Germans chorused. The Leader sighed and rolled back, exhausted by the exile's struggle to explain himself. How many times a week did he perform this act? Many, judging by the Creole's expression. She gave a cruel, exaggerated yawn, then walked across the fallen clippings, ripping as many as possible with her heels. "Such a silly girl," the leader said. "But she loves to 'dance.' You understand?" The Germans leered. I tired of waiting for him to get to me and went upstairs. The core of an apple I had eaten an hour before was already black with ants.

The next morning I paused with my hand on the curtain, enjoying the anticipation and imagining a small version of Fort de France. This is the advantage of arriving at night in a strange city and staying in a room with a view: The following morning you see everything, suddenly and at once. I pulled the sash and the sun exploded into the room. The ocean was flat calm — the doldrums — and brown to the horizon with Amazon mud. To the south, jungle rose from mangrove swamps to a dragon's-back of woolly hills; to the north, it stretched unbroken into the interior. The hotel sat on the highest coastal hill. Cayenne was below, a rickety jumble of palms and low buildings, trapped between unswimmable ocean and unexplored forest.

I opened the door to my narrow balcony. A wasp big as a sparrow motored into the room, and two lizards darted between my legs. Outside, a lone fishing boat sliced the water, leaving ripples lapping back half a mile to the mud flats. Mist filled the hollows of nearby hills, and puffy cannon-shot clouds floated over the jungle. The air was still and silent. I had landed myself in a coastal city without beaches, breezes, or boats, a city without the clatter of traffic or industry, an antique embalmed in a formaldehyde of jungle and mud. I was spooked, tempted to pull the curtains, darken the room, call the airlines, and join the Leader on the next plane out. I told myself that the first hour of the first morning in the first strange city had to be the most difficult of all. I needed somewhere to start — for instance, that rectangle of land that glittered like a field of diamonds.

I walked there and found a cemetery. The glitter came from sunlight bouncing off crosses, ornaments, and tin roofs protecting the graves of Euphrasius Joseph, Algae Amoise, and others. The deceased lay aboveground, buried under mounds of earth, concrete, or bathroom tiles. Puddles of wax, feathers, conch shells, and one-armed virgins decorated graves surrounded by spiked fences and gates fastened with new padlocks. I had never seen a busier cemetery. Pickaxes and shovels rose and fell like metronomes. Women arranged flowers and turned the earth with spades. They whitewashed mausoleums, re-mortared bricks, and scrubbed tiles. Their children played peekaboo. A party of gravediggers leaned on shovels, arguing over the dimensions of a new trench. A hand, moist with dirt, touched my arm and a low voice said, "Monsieur, the toilets are closed." He pointed to bolted public conveniences at the entrance, the only reason, apparently, for a European to visit this place. Then I remembered that All Saints' Day fell in a week and that the Guianese, like other Caribbean and South American peoples, celebrate by camping on their relatives' graves and feasting.

Cayenne was the perfect setting for this holiday. Its houses looked haunted. Shutters missing slats swung off their hinges. Gingerbread balconies sagged over narrow streets, rust speckled the New Orleans ironwork, and mildew spotted statues and monuments. In cavernous stores, hammocks and mosquito nets hung like grapes over Chinese and Lebanese traders. But since this was France, the public buildings were in good repair. The seventeenth-century prefecture was a colonial fantasy of white balconies and colonnades, and more than a hundred rare forked palm trees, the tallest in the world, cast long morning shadows across the Place des Palmistres, providing the only relief from a limitless white sky.

But where was the usual bustle of a tropical city? The rattling buses and crowded vans? The persistent shoeshine boys and pirouetting madmen? And where, for that matter, were the pedestrians? Schoolboys zipped around on mopeds, and French and Creole housewives stared suspiciously over the wheels of Japanese sedans. I bought a street map promising a *plage municipale* at the end of the Avenue Pasteur. I found mud flats studded with gray rocks and driftwood. Birds wheeled out over the mud, then changed their minds and darted to shore. A boy in a colorful shirt sat weeping on a bench. He looked out to sea, crossed himself, and shook with sobs. I hurried to find a travel agent.

I was told that on Wednesdays a boat left Cayenne for St. Georges and other settlements on the Oiapoque River. Today was Thursday, and the following week's service was canceled. There were no roads to St. Georges. I could wait here thirteen days for the next boat, or take the small propeller plane that hopped over the 125 miles of jungle between Cayenne and St. Georges.

The clerk at Air Guyane was astonished when she checked the flight manifests. For the next six days, the daily plane to St. Georges was fully booked. Apparently the Brazilian workers were going home to celebrate All Saints' Day on the graves of their ancestors. I bought a ticket for the following week and went to Cayenne's only sidewalk café, the Café des Palmistres, to read about French Guiana in a guidebook touted as "winner of the first ever Thomas Cook Best Travel Guide Award." Because I had assumed my stay in French Guiana would be brief, I had only skimmed this chapter, which was too bad because now I read in fine print that in St. Georges I would find "Immigration ½ km from docks — only French spoken and normally only French and Brazilians are allowed to cross this frontier." Any comfort I took from "normally" vanished when I turned the page. "Transport to Brazil by motorized dugout from St. Georges to Oiapoque is only for Brazilians, no customs or immigration post, and foreigners are returned to Guyane."

I bought a "Tourist and Road Map of French Guiana" to search for another route into Brazil. There was none, and on this authoritative map, published in 1980 by the National Geographic Institute in Paris, there was no such place as Oiapoque on the Brazilian bank of the river of the same name, only a village identified as Martinique.

The clerks at the Brazilian consulate had never heard of this Martinique that French cartographers had placed where Oiapoque belonged. They said I was welcome to enter Brazil, but only through the real Oiapoque. But they always flew between Cayenne and Belém. They had never visited this border, did not know the regulations for crossing it, and could not imagine why I wanted to, since there was a weekly jet to Belém. When I asked to speak with the consul, they shot worried looks at a closed door and said she was busy.

At a second travel agency, a young Frenchwoman thought I would be happier touring Indian villages with a party of German doctors who had stayed after the medical convention for this adventure. But the villages were even further from the equator than Cayenne, and I did not fancy a week in a canoe with the chiropractors. She thought only French and Brazilians could cross from St. Georges, but perhaps I would be lucky. If not, I could always "holiday" in St. Georges, which was a *ville merveilleuse* with much folklore and a *restaurant gastronomique,* the famous Chez Modestine. And if I did not believe a jungle outpost could boast such a fine establishment I need only look at my map, where — to my surprise — a box next to St. Georges promised 1,051 inhabitants, a mechanic, gas pump, hotel, post office, a *communaute indien,* and *gastronomie.* She herself had not yet had the good fortune to dine Chez Modestine, but she looked forward to the day when —

"So you've never been to St. Georges?" I asked.

"Sadly, no. Perhaps next year . . ."

"But it's only a hundred and twenty-five miles."

"In French Guiana, monsieur, that can be a considerable distance."

And how long had mademoiselle lived in French Guiana?

"Eight years."

I telephoned Modestine. She said I was not to derange myself. I could stay and eat Chez Modestine, crossing to Brazil whenever I wished. If I had a Brazilian visa I would encounter no difficulties, provided of course I spoke good French and resembled a Frenchman. She hung up before I could ask how a good French vocabulary would fool immigration officials as they examined a visa in my American passport. I called back but no one answered.

There was no American consul in Cayenne, but the British had an honorary one, a Lebanese named Georges Nouh-Chaïa, who owned a busy department store. His office was a convivial mixture of commerce and consulate. Yellow balloons advertising Établissement Nouh-Chaïa bobbed on a desk covered with the passports of Hong Kong Chinese hoping to finagle their way to London via Cayenne. Underneath dated photographs of the royal family, one of the zombie-eyed businessmen from my flight was fingering samples of women's underwear.

Mr. Nouh-Chaïa tried to convince me that my unexpectedly long stay in French Guiana was the luckiest of accidents. Now I had time to drive along the coastal highway—the Route Nationale 1, visiting Devil's Island and the space center at Kourou. The space center's fuel-thrifty rockets reminded me of Jean Richer and his pendulum clock. Perhaps I could give my unexpected week here an equatorial spin by visiting whatever monument the French had erected to celebrate his discovery. But Mr. Nouh-Chaïa had never heard of the famous astronomer. I asked about the astonishing number of bachelors in the department, and Mr. Nouh-Chaïa was also astonished. These were all questions best answered by French Guiana's unofficial historian, a Monsieur Masse, whom I would find at the National Museum. "Leave plenty of time for Mr. Masse," Mr. Nouh-Chaïa advised, "because he will talk your ear off."

I asked Mr. Nouh-Chaïa about the chances of crossing the

frontier at St. Georges. "I have never been asked that," he said. A
Mr. Condé Salazar who managed the tourist office would know,
but he was on holiday. Dr. Claude Ho-Ha-Chuck, the noted doc-
tor-politician, might also know, but he was a hard man to find. "I
am his very good friend," Mr. Nouh-Chaïa said, "and he won't
even see me. But you can always try." The Brazilian vice-consul
was also notoriously reclusive. She had arrived months before,
but Mr. Nouh-Chaïa and the rest of Cayenne's diplomatic corps
were still waiting to meet her. But I could trust Modestine. If she
said I could cross to Brazil, I had no worries. Mr. Nouh-Chaïa
envied me. In less than a week I would be in St. Georges enjoying
her legendary kitchen.

"Then you've eaten Chez Modestine?" I asked.

"To my misfortune, no, but everyone knows her reputation."

"But you've been to St. Georges."

"Not yet. But it is a very agreeable village, and very soon I
hope to be fortunate enough to—"

"Mr. Nouh-Chaïa," I said gently, "how long have you lived
here?"

"My father brought us in the 1930s, so it's about fifty years."

The ground floor of the National Museum was a public library where, under slowly turning fans, an assembly line of black
and white girls flipped through Asterix picture books at the same
thoughtful pace. The second-floor museum was a dead zoo of
stuffed animals and jarred fetuses, laid out on long wooden tables, buffet-style. I counted 150 jars. The largest imprisoned a cat-
sized frog, the Crapoud Bœuf. The murky waters of other jars
embalmed tortoises, wild pigs, fish with horrifying teeth, sea
slugs, a boa constrictor's skull, and a poignant baby armadillo.
Each had given something of itself to the liquids, and someone
had arranged them by color rather than species. Displayed along
the walls were the relics of 350 years of France's *mission civil-
isatrice:* a diorama of a gold mine that had flourished during the
nineteenth-century gold rush that had depopulated the coast; a
canoe the size of a bassinet that a Devil's Island inmate had hammered together for a successful escape; a huge canvas depicting
the dedication of a municipal monument to the six fallen heroes
of the Franco-Brazilian war of 1895; and a working scale model of
Cayenne's second ice-cream machine (1913). The first had burned

during the great fire of 1888, leaving the city without this treat for twenty-five years. A portrait of the rapist and mass murderer D'Chimbo was mounted between the headstock and blade of the guillotine that had beheaded him. A card under the exhibit explained that at dusk D'Chimbo would burst from the jungle surrounding Cayenne, hacking up his victims with a rusty saber. He had tattooed his face and chest. He was "prodigiously muscled," possessed of "herculean strength" and "incredible agility." He also had a sense of humor. When the priest at the guillotine described the delights of heaven, D'Chimbo said, "If it's so great, why don't you take my place?"

Mr. Masse worked at a desk tucked behind a dusty flamingo and a black caiman arranged snout on floor, like a vacuum cleaner. He was a shy sparrow of a man, and instead of talking my ear off, he seemed to think there was nothing to say about French Guiana that was not already in his book *La Guyane Française. Histoire (de 1604 à 1975), Géographie, Possibilités.* Everything I might wish to know about St. Georges was in this book, and I would find there as well a full account of the Franco-Brazilian war, although Mr. Masse was shocked that I was ignorant of this conflict, the only one between a European and a South American nation until the Falklands war. He produced a copy of his book and quickly inscribed it to me. As I put it in my bag he said, *"Prix réduit,* only eighty francs."

"Does it have an account of Jean Richer's famous expedition?" I asked.

"I have never heard of him. Who is he?"

I said Voltaire had celebrated him for his astronomical discoveries in French Guiana.

"That may be," Mr. Masse said. "But he is not in my book."

"Does your book explain why there are so many single people in French Guiana?"

"No, but I will think about that and tell you before your departure. For the moment you must excuse me—" A Frenchwoman and her daughter were patting the flamingo. He asked their names and wondered if their visit to the museum would not be enriched by the official guidebook. They agreed it would, and Mr. Masse produced *Le Musée de Cayenne. Ses Richesses. Ses Merveilles . . .* The author was Daniel Masse. He scrawled their names on the title page. "A souvenir of your visit, dear lady," said Mr. Masse, who had courtly manners. "For a *prix réduit,* only twenty-five francs."

By late morning the tables at the Café des Palmistres had filled with Europeans drinking Alsatian beer. The alcohol opened their pores, staining shirts with perspiration and giving them the appearance of having come from heavy labor. I took the last table, opened Mr. Masse's book, and read about St. Georges. Its notable structures were a radio tower and a water cistern. It was difficult to reach, conceded the author. The plane was small and places scarce. "But to put an end to this isolation the authorities have decided to build a road." It was difficult to predict when this road would be completed, or, for that matter, started. In the meantime, concluded Mr. Masse, "one cannot help but appreciate the calm of the place."

Mr. Masse explained that the Franco-Brazilian war had started over a hundred thousand square miles of disputed jungle between the Amazon and Oiapoque rivers, a territory that is, coincidentally, shaped like a fleur-de-lis. France claimed the Amazon as its southern frontier, whereas Brazil claimed the Oiapoque as its northern one. Neither country pressed its claims until 1894, when prospectors found gold. The following year France dispatched soldiers to the port of Amapá. During a skirmish — "the battle" — six Frenchmen and sixty Brazilians died. France won this engagement but lost the war. Five years later, Swiss arbitrators awarded the entire fleur-de-lis to Brazil. The French retreated north of the Oiapoque River, but a century later official French maps still identified the Brazilian settlement of Oiapoque by its prewar French name, Martinique.

A hollow-cheeked young man sat at the next table. Lines of dirt were sealed into his hands and the sun had peeled his face, leaving him with the complexion of a Dalmatian. He was Ruurd, a Dutch exile from neighboring Surinam. "This suitcase," he said, pointing to a cheap box gripped between his knees, "is heavy with my problems."

Then why not leave it on the sidewalk? I suggested. Perhaps someone would steal it.

He laughed and shook his head. "That would not help. In a

minute, more problems. I have a big mouth." He pointed to it. "I cannot help myself."

He had emigrated to Surinam in the early 1970s, when it was a Dutch colony congenial to Europeans with big mouths. He had married an Indian and started an engineering company and a rice farm. His problems began in 1980, when a military junta over-threw the democratic government that had ruled Surinam since independence. Two years later, the army rounded up leading journalists, businessmen, and opposition figures in the middle of the night. They were murdered in their pajamas.

"After that everyone is pleading with me to keep quiet," Ruurd said. "But I can't. My big mouth again." He made the mis-take of attacking the junta in public and, because the killings had poisoned Surinam's economy, attempting to dismiss five of his workers. "If you pay off the big men and then fire workers, it's OK. I say no to this because then I am corrupt too. So I hired a lawyer and tried to fire those men the legal way and this was what happened." He opened his suitcase to show me manila files bulging with a tattered correspondence, his "problems."

Seeing these papers again enraged him. "All this to fire five men," he shouted. "Can you believe it!" The other mid-morning beer drinkers edged away. Ruurd shuffled his papers, thrusting forward choice ones. No wonder he had problems. Engaging in a legal battle with the murderous Surinam junta had to be spec-tacularly stupid, or brave.

"Just when I am winning my case, everyone gangs up," he said. "Suddenly everyone who owes me money says, 'We pay later.' But my creditors all say, 'Pay now!' The government was behind it and it worked! I lost everything. I knew this would hap-pen when I refused to bribe but I did it anyway. See? My big mouth! And I cannot stop myself.

"I showed my problems to a Dutch journalist. Ten minutes later the police arrested him. Then the police beat me, so I took my family to French Guiana before I have *real* problems. Know what I mean?" He drew an imaginary knife across a prominent Adam's apple.

"Look at what I left behind!" His envelopes bulged with photographs, all grease-smudged and faded. Here were Ruurd's former warehouses, rice paddies, and faithful employees standing rigidly at attention. Flowering shrubs and sprawling verandas surrounded his enormous house. I praised these snapshots and he dealt out another dozen, fanning them like a winning card hand. "These are the best part, taken last month by my wife's relatives. They cross the border and no one notices because they're Indians."

His house had became a puddle of rust and wood, melting into a weedy yard. Ruurd smiled. He stabbed one picture with a finger, exclaiming, "This is my favorite!" His tractors were tilted at crazy angles, like exploded tanks on a battlefield. "See what happened after I left? And in only a year too!"

It seemed to me Ruurd had sent his in-laws on a perilous mission. Surely an Indian caught photographing tractors and railway stations in Surinam was an Indian in trouble. Had he weighed their danger against his pleasure in collecting evidence of the ruination of his home and business? After all, these snapshots would not awaken the world to some great injustice. At least the Leader had placed no one in danger to gather his exile's portfolio.

"You can see this makes me happy," Ruurd said. "But I would be happier living in the house I built with these hands."

"But you must be happy to have escaped to French Guiana."

"Oh, my God, no! Here are the laziest people on earth. More lazy, even, than Surinam. I complain about this and everyone, even my wife, tells me to shut my mouth. But I cannot help myself, and so . . ."

"More problems?"

"And more beatings."

"Beatings?"

"Yes!" Ruurd had found work at a rice farm in Mana, near the Surinam border. From here his wife, Lillian, could slip across the river and visit her family. And everything had been fine in Mana, he said, until the beatings. But who in French Guiana would beat up a skinny Dutchman? The fat Dutchman, it seemed, who managed the Mana rice farm. Ruurd pulled down one lens of his sunglasses. A bruise circled his clouded left eye. "I write letters to the prefect and the police, protesting this beating. I petition the labor office for disability payments. I hire a lawyer. Everywhere I protest!" He showed me his French Guiana file, already as thick as the ones from Surinam. Now that Ruurd was the wronged worker, he had embraced the same bureaucratic harassment that had undone him in Surinam. He was here to show himself to the French functionaries before his bruise faded. He hoped to win enough compensation to buy land in Mana and cultivate melons. "I arrived in Surinam with nothing. I built my business there and then I left with nothing. So now I will do it again. Big deal. Ha-ha. Ha-ha-ha." But he spoke these ha-ha's, unable to turn them into a genuine laugh. And no wonder: He had no money, home, or job. His capital was a black eye that might or might not persuade the authorities to award him enough money to grow melons on reclaimed swamp.

"What if you lose?" I asked.

"I won't." He gave a sly smile. "Not when they see this." He removed his sunglasses. His right eye was blacker than the left. Ruurd's trump.

"The Dutchman again?"

"No, the other boss, an Indonesian. He knocked me down but I fought back."

"Why does everyone hit you?"

He rose to leave. "I can't be late for my appointments. Come to Mana and I'll tell you everything."

Visiting Ruurd seemed as good a way as any to pass the time until I flew to St. Georges. Mana was 130 miles up the coast from Cayenne, past Kourou and Devil's Island. Because so many Guianese own automobiles, there is no public transportation. I rented a car and left the next morning, starting before sunrise and driving through banks of jungle mist without meeting another vehicle. The Devil's Island convicts forced to build the road from Cayenne to St. Laurent called it the *route zéro*, or "road to nowhere." It took fifty years for the first twenty-four miles out of St. Laurent to be completed, at a cost of ten thousand lives. The construction machinery sent from France was sold by prison authorities to Dutch farmers in Surinam, forcing convicts to clear the jungle quite literally with their bare hands. Men hanged themselves with vines and slashed their wrists with axes. Every few yards of road mark an agonizing death.

As I arrived in Tonate, the only town for sixty miles between Cayenne and Kourou, the sun jumped over the horizon, blazing through the slats of a tumbledown church and illuminating like a miracle a line of women kneeling for mass. Outside Kourou I passed a hunting party of Indians riding bicycles. They wore straw hats and had rifles slung across their backs. Around the next curve a pair of bearded space technicians jogged in silver track suits. Then came a squad of Foreign Legionnaires, shouting cadence as they ran. Ignoring a turn for the center of town, I drove toward a rocket that rose like a skyscraper from the jungle. It was surrounded by scaffolding, almost ready for its fuel-efficient equatorial launch. The space center was a sad little glass-and-plastic box, a budget motor inn. Its guards waved me away. Because of the launch, it was closed to visitors.

Outside the gate I picked up two Peruvians in jazzy shirts. They had built the scaffolding and now the French had expelled them, part of pre-launch security. They were bitter. Alberto said, "The French are racist dogs and we spit on them."

"Which French?" I asked. "The white or black ones?"

"They are all racist against Spanish people. They hate us because we work hard. I have been in Miami, Brazil, and Chile. Wherever there is work you will find Alberto." His favorite city was Belém, followed by Macapá. When I told him I would be visiting both, he squeezed my arm and said in the tone of a man at prayer, "Mucha mujer — many women . . . mucha, mucha, mucha mujer." The other Peruvian giggled and sucked his fingertips, as if savoring the last juices of a chicken dinner. Alberto sang, in a lewd Hispanic whine, "Ah-h-h, Belém; ah-h-h, Macapá . . . Mucha mujer."

But the scene as we drove back toward Kourou called more for the gently mocking soundtrack of a Jacques Tati movie. Going in the other direction was a procession of tiny white French cars, evenly spaced, traveling at identical speeds, each driven by a single space technician making his morning commute from Kourou to the space center. When I dropped the Peruvians at a crossroads, Alberto leered at lucky me, soon to be in this paradise of mujer. "So many whores they do it for 'love.' They hope we men will take pity and give them a present. They are cities of desperate women," he said, smiling.

Kourou looked like a city of desperate women: hot, dusty, ugly, and circled by jungle and mud-streaked water, an incubator for alcoholics and wife-beaters. The space workers lived in the same stark apartment blocks that border the freight yards and motorways of European cities. The concrete was stained, the tiny balconies used to dry laundry and store bicycles. Boys trudged to school heads down, scuffing the weedy parks and empty building sites. Women shoved strollers over unshaded sidewalks or sat bolt upright on benches, staring with shock-treatment eyes as their children amused themselves in playgrounds slapped together from whatever scraps remained after the construction of this model city.

The Foreign Legion had its own playground, where recruits in red gym shorts climbed ropes and jumped hurdles. Their "fort" was a group of concrete apartment blocks surrounded by cyclone fencing. The guards at the gate wore the boxy white hats that call up camels, Beau Geste, and white-washed Saharan castles. What a cruel joke Kourou must be for recruits seduced by this glamour. Here they were, swinging on their adult jungle gyms, watching the space technicians and functionaries putt-putting past in their Monsieur Hulot cars, quartered in just the dreary social-welfare housing they had probably joined the Legion to escape.

Kourou made the misery of Devil's Island more understandable. After all, this little concentration camp of a town was meant to be a pleasant place, with amenities to compensate for its heat and isolation. Perhaps climate and geography would defeat any attempt to build a model European community in Kourou. In 1763, fourteen thousand colonists had come from France to settle here. They arrived in a gigantic flotilla: tradesmen, farmers, doctors, blacksmiths, priests, even actors and musicians — in all, the largest tropical settlement ever attempted by a European power. The organizers had misled them about conditions at their destination and, thinking they were sailing to a more temperate paradise, they had brought ice skates, and tools to keep them sharp. They landed during the rainy season, without food or fresh water and in a swamp laced with quicksand. They died by the thousands of typhus, malaria, and malnutrition. Two years later the government evacuated the survivors and imprisoned the organizers. French Guiana's reputation as a tropical hell was assured.

Some survivors of the Kourou debacle sailed for three islands they christened Les Îles du Salut — the "Healthy Islands," because on them no one caught the fatal fevers. (Ocean breezes repelled the mosquitoes.) They named one island Île Royale, another St. Joseph, and the third Île du Diable—"Devil's Island," because of the treacherous channel separating it from Île Royale. A century later the Healthy Islands became the most notorious part of a penal colony which, although scattered across the mainland and islands of Guiana, was known collectively as Devil's Island.

The penal colony was founded in 1852, four years after black slaves in Guiana were emancipated. It pretended to be a noble experiment: Rather than being confined in metropolitan dungeons, incorrigible criminals would be given an opportunity to settle in Guiana. Its real purpose was to import white slaves to replace the black ones. Naturally only the most corrupt and sadistic volunteered to be administrators and guards, prompting Napoleon II to concede that prisoners were supervised by "criminals far worse than they." The prison authorities sold the convicts' rations in Cayenne, and malnourished inmates died of tropical ailments. To increase their chances of surviving, convicts hid valuables in a *plan,* a metal tube inserted in the rectum. The battle between guards and prisoners for these anal treasures caused much of the suffering and brutality. Of the eighty thousand men sent to the island between 1852 and 1938, seventy thousand died before completing their sentences.

I sailed from Kourou to the Healthy Islands with a dozen French forestry students. As we left the dock, their leader distributed spades and plastic sandwich bags for collecting samples. Near Île Royale, the soup of Amazon mud and twigs vanished, and the wife of a space engineer stopped rubbing herself with tanning oil for long enough to tell me that these islands were the only place in Guiana with clear, swimmable water, if you didn't mind the sharks. Burying convicts at sea had supposedly given the sharks here a taste for flesh. They were summoned and excited by the church bells tolling each death. They circled the rowboats carrying corpses to sea, snapping at bodies even before they hit the water.

We docked on the Île Royale, where an entrepreneur had converted the former guards' quarters and administrative buildings into a holiday camp, the Relais of Devil's Island. Here the space technicians could escape Kourou, eat huge French lunches, and swim in clear water, although the few I saw only waded up to their knees in the lee of a crumbling shark barrier. The thick-walled tomb of a room where the guards once dined was now a restaurant and bar. I ate a stale croissant and watched Foreign Legionnaires, who looked the type to have been Devil's Island guards, shoot pool and breakfast on beer and Gauloises. Their arms were pockmarked by the telltale circular scars left by a game of chicken popular with prisoners and bored soldiers. The "chicken" was the first man to pull a lit cigarette off his forearm. The *patron* sold novelty postcards and souvenir T-shirts showing a cartoon Devil's Island inmate bowling his ball and chain. At a neighboring table, two boys with drugged eyes argued over a per-spiring apple, all the time chopping it into smaller slices with a switchblade. In the doorway a little girl threw stones at a limping chicken, laughing when she hit it. The Relais of Devil's Island gave me the creeps.

As I walked the circumference of Île Royale, I had a sensation of déjà vu. Somewhere else I had seen these damp stone walls green with fungus and clutched by vines, seen rotting ceilings open to the sky and fingers of hibiscus slithering through iron bars. I had walked through cellblocks busy with lizards, watched black men in straw hats raking endless leaves, and heard cicadas screeching like subway brakes.

They screeched loudest in the children's cemetery. Its trees had attracted the French forestry experts. They knelt underneath, turning the earth with spades and dropping plant samples into plastic bags with the care of detectives collecting evidence. The headstones were rather large and ornate for such small corpses, erected by parental guilt. Of the thousands who died here, these children were surely the most wronged. The inmates had com-mitted a crime, although often not a serious one. The guards had volunteered, and many wives were drawn from the waterfront brothels of Marseilles and Toulon, although even they had a choice: prison, or marriage to a Devil's Island guard. But the chil-dren killed by this place were blameless.

The neighboring island of St. Joseph held the *réclusion,* where inmates condemned to solitary confinement were locked into "bear pits," underground dungeons aired and lighted by hand-kerchief-sized grates. Prisoners lived months and years in these coffins, handcuffed to a bed, never speaking or seeing the sun, and dying in conditions similar to those suffered by Frenchmen in Gestapo prisons during the Second World War, perhaps explaining why France closed this penal colony in 1946.

It was on St. Joseph that I realized what memories these islands had provoked. There was an identical French-built slave island three thousand miles across the Atlantic, also constructed to supply cheap labor to the Americas, although in its case the labor was black. It was the Île Gorée, an island off the coast of West Africa where slaves from the interior were imprisoned in suffocating barracks while awaiting transportation to the Americas. The government of Senegal has left the ruins undisturbed, creating an open-air museum as eerie as Devil's Island. I had visited it fifteen years before, and I remember thinking that its crumbling stone walls, like those of Devil's Island, were still releasing a noxious, long-stored gas of suffering and despair.

I drove north from Kourou toward a mountain range of blackening clouds. Lightning strikes danced around the rocket. Rainstorms swept the jungle like black brooms. I stopped for the night in Sinnamary with Jack Morin, gold prospector, art dealer, former chief petty officer in the United States Navy, and now bartender and owner of French Guiana's only "motel," the Eldo Grill and Motel. "Welcome to the ass end of nowhere," he said. "Welcome to the most fucked-up country in the world. The people here are the laziest fuckers in the world and they're supported by a people even lazier and stupider, the fucking French."

He had the leathery skin of a sailor and the shrewd smile of a turtle, Popeye come to life. His tattoos were old and so blurred that, depending on the angle of his arm — depending on whether he was opening a beer, drinking it, or reaching for another — they could have been serpents, geisha girls, eagles in flight, anything.

"Why are the French such fuckers?" I asked.

"Because they're so eff-ing cheap." He had stocked the refrigerators in his seven motel units with beer and soft drinks. Most hotels charge customers for drinking from these mini-bars, but Morin did not, because "fuck me if I can be bothered to creep around, counting how many beers they've drunk." The French

had abused his generosity. "I catch them in the morning, tiptoe-
ing to their cars with their arms full of my beers.

"And the eff-ing French bureaucrats are ridiculous. See all
these big telephone towers in the middle of every town? Shit, you
can dial Paris direct, but for two weeks we haven't been able to
call down the road or anywhere else in French Guiana because of
some French fuck-up. At least in Cape Canaveral the fucking
phones work."

Jack Morin's complaints really came to this: French Guiana,
with its unpopulated, potentially wealthy land, was as authentic a
nineteenth-century frontier as you could find. Yet France had burdened it with a twentieth-century European welfare state, administered by civil servants sent from Paris. Conflicts between them
and freebooters like Morin were inevitable. Still, he was lucky to
have chosen French Guiana over the former British or Dutch
Guianas. There are few tropical countries left where a European
can start his own business, curse the authorities, and slip into the
bush to mine gold at secret tips, which he did to give a zing to his
cash flow. His mines were five days up the Sinnamary River, and
he wanted me to know he had come here for gold-mining, not
bartending.

He must have enjoyed some strikes, because after eating one
of Madame Morin's fricassees, patrons of the Eldo Grill often
slipped into his office to buy nuggets. Others went upstairs to the
family living quarters, which doubled as what he called "the largest Haitian art gallery in France." And displayed for sale in the
restaurant were Indian jewelry, blue-winged butterflies in Plex-
iglass boxes, stuffed baby caimans, and, an item enjoying inex-
plicable popularity, black beetles the size of turtles, mounted in
family groups. For someone so fond of damning the French,
Morin had a very French wife. Madame Morin cooked, welcomed
guests with the usual brittle politesse of a French restaurateuse,
and watched Jack with a frozen smile both loving and fearful. She
had been married to a Frenchman in Kourou and had a grown
son named Edie who helped on weekends. She and Jack had
opened a small café in Sinnamary. They had saved their money
and bought this patch of jungle, cleared it, and built the Eldo
Grill, and for all Jack's bitching, it was their dream come true.

Madame Morin's smile became more pained as the bar filled

with uniformed Legionnaires. The older veterans were afflicted by minor yet visible imperfections. I saw a harelip, a chicken neck, acne scars, and crooked teeth. The man taking the next stool removed his kepi to reveal a head shaped like a pyramid. Jack greeted them with handshakes and French pleasantries. Then he turned to me, saying in English, "The famous Foreign Legion. Ha! Ten years ago they had the old veterans, and if anyone crossed them . . . *wham!* But these scrawny fuckers aren't in their league."

The Legionnaires stared straight ahead, apparently not understanding, although neither I nor Madame Morin could be certain this was so.

"Encore, la même chose?" Jack asked, opening more beers and joining in ritual complaints about the lazy Creoles. He shifted to English. "Just look at them, coiled and ready to go at the blacks. Mention a black riot and they get so excited they breathe fire. Argh-h-h!!! They're so fucking bored they'd love an excuse to bash them."

Still no reaction, but I began to suspect that Pyramid-head understood, because at this talk of black-bashing he smiled, flicking out an unnaturally long tongue. It may have been forked.

"Poor fuckers." Still no reaction. "Nothing to do but build roads and hold exercises in the jungle. Plenty of desertions . . . *Une cigarette, monsieur?"* He offered around a pack. *"Je vous en prie . . .* Most are Yugos or Krauts, and fuck me if half the lot aren't queer."

Suddenly Pyramid-head pushed back his stool and asked in French if I had ever been a Legionnaire.

"No, never!" I said, wondering if this was a prelude to a fight.

"But you have a fleur-de-lis, a common tattoo for us."

I babbled out the story of my tattoo. I was a teen-ager alone in Copenhagen. I met a French girl, and the fleur-de-lis was in her honor. This brought me several uncomfortable minutes of Legion camaraderie. I did not admit to having been paralytic with aquavit and vomiting into a canal after leaving Tattoo Bob's. The disgusted French girl ran away and I never did sleep with her.

The next morning, Madame Morin invited me upstairs to see the largest Haitian art gallery in France. She wore a leotard, and her rooms smelled of her morning exercises and the cologne she had sprayed to disguise her odor. A dozen snake-filled aquariums sat underneath the Haitian paintings. In one, an emerald tree boa lay draped over a branch like Christmas tinsel. Another aquarium wiggled with a snake family; inside a third, which was covered with plywood held down by bricks, a dirty brown serpent lay coiled inside a cinder block. "My son is a snake fancier," Madame Morin explained. "And this . . . well, this is his collection. That brown one next to the television, he is very, very venomous." She hugged herself. *"Deux instants!"*

"Two seconds! You mean . . ."

Yes. She meant precisely that.

"But accidents are infrequent." She gave a wan smile. She was scarcely more fond of snakes than I, yet every morning she saw a snake with every sit-up, and when she looked up from one of the thick romances stacked on the coffee table, there they were. She climbed upstairs after an evening of sautéing paca and anaconda, and they were waiting. She fell asleep next to her foul-mouthed American sailor, and they were a foot away. Could she — could anyone — have imagined such a life?

"Where does he find them?" I asked, picturing expeditions up remote rivers.

"Monsieur, he finds them everywhere." She shook her head helplessly. "Many he catches at night, with a flashlight and less than a hundred yards from the motel."

Jack suggested I forget Mana and stay at the Eldo Grill. The road was dangerous, and French Guiana had the second worst automobile fatality rate in France. He had not visited Mana in years. "Why bother? All these fucking towns are the same. Seen one, seen them all." He thought Ruurd's story was "a crock of shit." He knew the fat Dutchman. "Gentle as a teddy bear and wouldn't harm a fly.

"You be careful now," he said as I left. "All kinds of weird shit-bags get washed up here."

Jack was right about everything. With their peeling roofs and sagging warehouses, the other towns did look alike. Each had a radio tower, a war memorial, a PTT (post office), and a town hall. They were all near the mouth of a river and had served as trading centers during the last century's gold rush. Elsewhere they would have become ghost towns, but in tropical France they were empty gourds, rattling with civil servants and traders.

And he was right about the dangerous road. It explained the wavy skid marks meeting in the middle, the shattered glass on the shoulders, and the automobile cadavers hugged by pink orchids. RECHTS HOUDEN! said a frequent sign I first took to be a warning in a Creole dialect. It was Dutch for "Keep Right!" In Surinam they drove on the left, and collisions between French-speaking Creoles keeping right and Dutch-speaking ones hugging the left were frequent.

Jack was even right about the "weird shit-bags." In forlorn Iracoubou, I stopped for a hitchhiker who defined the term. He jumped in front of the car, windmilling his arms and making me skid to a stop. His black beard and hair were matted with dirt, and he had the high, sunken cheeks of a starving Indian. "You must help us!" he shouted, grabbing my open window. "Two days we're here and no one has stopped." He spat on the ground. "These people, they are true pigs."

"We?"

"Yes, I have a friend." It was the old hitchhiker's trick, one I had used myself. The pretty girl throws out her thumb while the boy hides behind a tree with the filthy backpacks, except this weird shit-bag was the girl, the bait. His friend dashed from behind the church. He was a wilder, dirtier man with blackened teeth and a Pancho Villa moustache. Two machete handles poked out of his backpack.

A crowd assembled, curious to see the idiot who had stopped. "Yesterday they stoned us," the man with the machetes said. "Two days here and no one fed us. We slept in the church." He smelled like two weeks in Iracoubou. "OK. Let's go!" he shouted, jumping up and down in the back seat like an impatient child.

"But I'm only going as far as Mana. In less than an hour I'll be turning for the ferry. I'd be dropping you in the middle of nowhere."

"Good! That's where we live."

"'Nowhere' is better than Iracoubou," the decoy said. "Will it derange you if we smoke?" I hate cigarettes, but I said, "Sure! Go ahead."

The decoy lit a small cigar and said they were French surveyors. The machetes were for hacking through jungle as they
mapped boundaries. They slept in a surveyor's shack or lived wild
in the jungle. "We think we've been a year in the forest, but we
don't have calendars, so we wonder about the date. It is October
tenth today?"

"It's the twenty-sixth."

He shrugged. "We would prefer to speak English with you. It
is good practice for us. When we leave French Guiana we will go
to Beverly Hills and marry rich women. It will be difficult to leave
because we love our work, and we have enjoyed a year of magic
mushrooms." He leered like Alberto.

"Where do you find them?"

"My God, they are everywhere! They jump from the cow
shit."

"So you eat them often?"

"Whenever I see them."

"What happens?"

"Man, I see everything. Crazy, man. I — how you say it? —
'dig' that craziness."

"Why are you so keen on Beverly Hills?"

"Well, I do like my independence. And here, lots. But can
you live forever in French Guiana? I think not."

"But why that place?"

"Because it is a capital of rich American women and in the
'hills,' and we must always be escaping from the big cities. They
are too much for us."

"Beverly Hills is pretty big."

"We had to leave that other city because the noise was making us crazy."

"You mean Paris?"

"No, Cayenne."

Cayenne? Cayenne! I remembered chopsticks clicking in
Chinese restaurants and shutters banging shut for the afternoon
siesta.

"Yes, all the noise was driving us mad! But now we are sick
of the woods too. We stay only to earn money for California. We
will need it to impress the rich women and make them marry us."
He was not smiling; he meant it. Fifteen years before, these

weird-looking shit-bags would have wanted to bomb Beverly Hills. When I left them in the middle of nowhere, the decoy said, "Don't worry, we know a short way to our tent." They pulled out their machetes, and when I checked my rearview mirror, they had disappeared.

From across the river, Mana resembled Sinnamary and Iracoubou, a hodgepodge of tin roofs and wooden houses lurching in every direction. I waited for the ferry with two families of Creoles. To amuse their children, the men swooped their hands through the air, clapping them together with a bang. I thought they were imitating the flight of exotic birds, but then I overheard them describing automobile accidents on the Route Nationale 1.

Ruurd's house was in better repair than any in Mana, and his Indian wife, Lillian, was a demon housekeeper, a skill she must have perfected during a frequently described trip to the Netherlands to meet her mother-in-law. She didn't relax until I removed my muddy boots, allowing her to line them up outside with the others. Keeping a Mana house Dutch-clean entailed a perpetual battle with ants, and during the several hours I was there she twice swept the ground-floor living quarters and wiped the kitchen counters. Whenever she looked up from her housecleaning she saw a strip of wallpaper running at eye level around the kitchen wall. The pattern was delft-blue windmills.

Lillian was proud of her refrigerator, and when Ruurd opened it to fetch beer, she insisted I marvel at its ice-maker. Ruurd said, "We had the same model in Surinam, so I bought it to remind her of home."

While Ruurd and I talked, she flipped through a Dutch-English dictionary, finding words to compose a sentence. She was learning French, and English too, in case of another hurried exile. Several minutes after we had moved on from that conversation, she said, "Yes, there we enjoyed a beautiful home. Here not nice, but I work to make it good." She swept up some more ants.

"And look at our books!" Ruurd pointed to ratty paperbacks and ripped comics belonging to his daughter, Elisabeth, who had inherited his long Dutch face and her mother's full-moon eyes. "A disgrace. Why, in Surinam we owned a whole library."

"Yes, there we had everything," Lillian said, erasing a column of ants from the windmill wallpaper.

"Let me tell you about my blue eyes," Ruurd said.

"You mean black eyes."

"Yes, blue eyes." He did not have Lillian's patient dictionary approach to language. "The Dutch boss is a man with big money and big ideas. But he never works himself and his money is from his father, so he knows nothing. I build a farm in Surinam; he gets money from his father. You see the difference? But still I have to work for him. A disgrace! I tell him to do things my way. He says, 'No, my way.' His way is stupid so I do it my way. He punches me down, then hits me again. Pow! I have a blue eye."

He jumped up, reenacting the fight: two Dutchmen standing in a flooded paddy in French Guiana, punching and screaming about an arcane aspect of rice farming. He became so agitated in the retelling he nearly punched himself again. "The second eye happens the same way. I tell the Indonesian boss his way is stupid—See? my big mouth again—and he hits me. Pow!"

Lillian looked up, worried he might re-injure himself. She had constructed another sentence to fit our last conversation. "I go back to Surinam and look at our beautiful home. But he cannot because . . ." She covered her mouth and giggled. Ruurd forgot his boss and joined in this old family joke. "Because I'm a white man!"

Ruurd looked at her fondly. "Soon we will have another home, better than Surinam." He had returned from Cayenne triumphant. The labor office had promised a cash award, and his attorney had prepared a lawsuit against his boss. He was negotiating to buy the melon farm and planning a vacation in Holland. "Yes, the French are being generous with me," he admitted. "But I am working too. Before Holland I will work mining gold." He had contracted for several months of heavy labor at a jungle mine south of St. Laurent. It sounded like punishing work, but he was bored sitting here, waiting for his eyes to heal and raising his legs for Lillian's sweeping. He was going, as the French say, *pour le sport.*

"What if the melon farm fails? Or French Guiana becomes independent, like Surinam?" I asked. "What then?"

"No problem. I take my family to the United States. I think you can be independent there. You can say this for damned French Guiana. At least here you can be independent and—"

He ran to the open door. "Hey! Stop! *Arrêtez!*" Two bare-chested Creoles were walking up from the river, carrying the headless, blood-dripping carcass of a wild animal. "Hey, I want to buy meat." They ignored him. "I'll pay a lot for meat!"

One man shouted *"Non!"* and spat. Ruurd was not popular in Mana. The veins in his neck bulged and he gripped the door frame. "See what I mean about these people? Lazy! Impossible! You'd think they would sell me meat, they have plenty, but no —"

Lillian touched his arm. Her face was frozen in Madame Morin's worried smile, and I thought she must find her life here equally surprising. First she was an Indian in Surinam, then an Indian living in a glorious house with a huge refrigerator, a VCR, and a mother-in-law in Holland who kept a bug-free kitchen. Suddenly she was an exile in Guiana, learning French for this country and English for the next, although not so much an exile she could not go home when she wished. But her husband, because of his white skin, the same skin that had once seemed such an advantage, had to stay here. And after a difficult year in Mana, they might have money because another white man had hit her husband. But now his big mouth might lose them this windfall.

I decided to leave. There was no room for me. Ruurd had rented only the ground floor, and I could hear his children buzzing in the tiny bedrooms. He said there was a small hotel in Acarouney, a few miles off the road leading to the border town of St. Laurent. Before I left, Lillian insisted on cleaning my boots, and in ten minutes she had extracted from their treads every piece of dried dirt.

In Cayenne I had heard the Relais de Acarouney described as a "fine country inn," but no one had mentioned that it was in the middle of a leper colony not entirely abandoned by its patients. The Relais itself, which had once housed the administration, was a weather-beaten, two-story building fronted by a long screened porch. It sat within a partially walled courtyard, facing garages and workshops and surrounded by overgrown paths and the lepers' rotting cabins. The *patron* was named Michael. He had the round head and stuck-out ears of a French peasant and the manner of a master sergeant. He had gathered an extended family comprising the younger children of his second wife and the married children of his earlier marriage. There were several husky men in their twenties and a blond boy carrying a pet monkey on his shoulder. They were all having a grand jokey time, hammering up the collapsing roofs and gathering in the evening to eat big meals and watch American soap operas on a cloudy television. Michael told me that until last week he had been the hotel handyman, and I was his first guest.

"For eighteen years we've lived all over French Guiana," he said. "But this is our last displacement. Here my family will make a success of the Relais. Already we have made great improvements." Across the courtyard, one son stood on a ladder, nailing boards over a hole in the garage. The sky was darkening. Wind rattled the buildings. Michael made expansive gestures. "We will expand into the colony, converting the lepers' cabins into holiday cottages for families. Most of the former occupants have decamped. A few elderly ones remain for sentimental reasons, but since they are cured they will not derange my guests. You might even say they are an attraction."

The afternoon rainstorm sounded like an avalanche of pebbles hitting the tin roof. I woke from my nap — there was nothing else to do — and found Michael sitting on the screened porch, whistling military marches while adding columns of figures from a ledger. He gave me a thumbs-up, but an hour later it was still raining. He had stopped whistling and was furiously erasing and re-adding. He stubbed out cigarettes half-smoked, tapped his pencil on the table, and stared outside. The palms funneled waterfalls onto the ground. The courtyard was a swamp. Every minute the road to the Relais became more impassable, the jungle thicker, the weeds higher. Rising water had trapped one son in a jalopy. In the garage his youngest boy was swinging in a hammock, alone and bored. Michael rubbed his eyes and returned to the ledger, searching for the equation that could turn a ruined leper colony into a holiday resort.

The Relais was doomed. There was nothing to see but ruined buildings, no attraction but the elderly lepers, and nowhere to swim, although a child might enjoy the buggy puddles. The terrain was flat and, being inland, missed the breezes that sometimes freshened Kourou. The next morning I asked Michael who had patronized the Relais of the leprosarium before. Who would rent his renovated cabins?

He was offended. "You forget that I worked here. I saw the previous *patron* turning away guests. Why, this hotel is always full during the tourist season."

"When is that?"

"May."

"Just May?"

"Yes. In May the turtles lay their eggs at the mouth of the Maroni, and tourists come from Cayenne and Kourou to witness the spectacle."

On the way back to Cayenne I stopped at the Eldo Grill. The tables were filled with mixed parties of black and white Frenchmen stretching Sunday lunch into a day's outing. They lingered, chins in hands, considering the mounted insects and stuffed animals. They dawdled over coffee and gazed at the pasture bordering Jack's terrace as if it were the Mediterranean. A man waiting for a table played frantically with his golden-haired daughter. He placed her fingers in the stuffed crocodile's mouth, unwrapped sweets, kissed her cheeks, and dangled toys. I asked if he had visited Devil's Island. He said that last month his family had passed *le weekend* there, but before I could inquire if he had seen the children's cemetery, Madame Morin led him to a table.

Madame Morin seated patrons, took orders, and helped in the kitchen. Her son Edie, the snake lover, bussed tables and brought drinks. Jack stood behind the bar, pouring drinks between gulps of beer. For someone fond of complaining about French work habits, he was, as he himself would say, "doing fuck all."

When I told him I had spent the night in Acarouney, he said, "That poor son-of-a-bitch Michael. I think he owned a bar in Kourou once, a restaurant somewhere else, and a business in Cayenne. Lost them all. A sweet guy, but his head's in the fucking clouds. Now he's got a new wife, so maybe . . . Nah, he'll work hard but fuck it up somehow."

"I think he's done that by buying it."

"Nah-h-h, you crazy? That place is a fucking gold mine! The last guy did a helluva business."

"I don't believe it. Who wants to holiday in a leper colony?"

"What do you mean, 'holiday'? That was the best cheaters' hotel in the Guianas. Everyone'd go for the weekend with their girlfriend. No chance of running into the wife there. But that Michael, he'll find a way to fuck it up."

He already had. By renovating and promoting it as a family resort, he would lose the lovers but keep the turtle enthusiasts. But what a place for a tryst! What kind of love flourished among the elderly lepers and their crumbling barracks?

When I returned for dinner, Edie was tending bar. "Have you heard of the new snake-bite kit?" I asked. "It looks like a big hypodermic. You put it over the fang marks and—"

"Sure, I've got two of them. Hey, you interested in snakes?"

"In a way . . ."

"The Bronx Zoo. You know about it?"

"I know it has a big reptile house."

"I'm talking about the prize, the Bronx Zoo prize. Even the Indians know about that prize: ten thousand dollars for the first ten-meter-long anaconda. [I checked with the zoo, and to my surprise there *was* a prize, originally donated by Theodore Roosevelt, for anyone catching a live snake over thirty feet. The sum had once been $10,000 but had long ago increased to $50,000.] Everyone in Sinnamary has been looking like crazy for such an anaconda. I've been weeks on the river looking. I've found fat anacondas, but none that long."

"How do you measure them?"

"Easy. A tape measure. But I am beginning to think that prize is a big joke, like the prize for the first man to be pregnant. An anaconda that long is impossible, but everyone here is still looking, hoping to hit *le jackpot*."

"How about that snake upstairs?" I described *Deux Instants*.

"He is very evil. The worst. Look here . . ." Edie pulled from behind the bar, where it was as handy as a corkscrew, a copy of *Snake Venom Poisoning*, by Findley E. Russell, M.D. He flipped to a photograph of a dirty brown reptile. Dr. Russell identified it as a South American rattlesnake (*Crotalus durissus terrificus*). It was "large, stout, badly-tempered. . . . The patient bitten must be treated quickly and diligently."

"Edie, why are you so interested in snakes?"

He shrugged. "If you live in French Guiana, they are the thing to be interested in."

"Why is that?"

"Because they are everywhere."

He led me slowly, lovingly, through the book. Color photo-graphs illustrated the fate of victims who had not reached in time someone as informed as Dr. Russell. I saw withered hands, legs as black and swollen as blood sausage, Indians with droopy eyelids and death-mask grimaces and bubbly fingers that looked bar-becued.

Edie said, "Like ignorant peasants everywhere, the people here are terrified of snakes. It is because of the bad serpents in the Bible. But you and I know differently. We know snakes are only dangerous during their season of love."

"And when is that?"

"To be honest, it is always the season of love for some snake in French Guiana. There are so many species here, at least eighty-two, and new ones are being found all the time."

He insisted I admire his scrapbook. It was similar to the kind my wife and I fill with vacation snapshots. I saw a two-headed snake, an albino snake, a snake eating a wild dog, and a caiman munching a stew of bone and tendons. There was a coral snake — "Hangs on and chews for thirty minutes," he said. And a *Lydphis cobella* — "Very gentle and good for *les enfants*." Edie had a story to go with each snake, and there was no stopping him. Not many Eldo Grill guests shared my fascination with snakes, he said. It was too late for me to admit to being one of the terrified peasants, so he continued taking my questions as signs of interest, and when I asked how he decided if a previously unknown species was safe or venomous, he said, "Easy. I count the teeth."

Teeth were the big clue to a snake's species. Edie had just mailed the skin and head of a serpent to the Pasteur Institute, in Paris, and was nervously awaiting a reply. "If it is a new species, they may name it after me. That would be *le vrai jackpot*."

As he went on, absorbed by his scrapbook, I wondered when it was his "season of love." He was a small-boned, rather hand-some man, and certainly enthusiastic about whatever happened to interest him, but there could not be many women, even in spinster-rich French Guiana, eager to share this hobby. Finally I interrupted to ask if he ever dated the women of Sinnamary.

He said, "Whenever I can, I go to Belém. The women there, fantastic!" He insisted I take the card of an acquaintance who owned a disco. I must stop and convey his regards. "Understand, they are not whores, but they are very fond of foreigners. Go to the right place and they are nine to one. Ah, Belém! I wish I could accompany you. Perhaps I will go for Christmas."

Jack came back to the bar and said, "You don't have to go to Belém for women. Line up all the women I've had here and you could walk to Cayenne on their tits. But watch yourself in Belém, Thurston. Check for Adam's apples."

"Why?"

"Man, don't you know anything? Because it means the she's a he."

I said that at this rate I might never get to Belém. After a week in French Guiana, I was no closer to the equator than when I arrived.

"Shit, what's a week when you're floating like a butterfly? If you don't like one place, go to another or come back here. Hell, you're starting here, you must be coming back, right?"

"I might, if you took me to your gold mines."

"Fuck me, why not? But the way this fucking place is going, I might have to move to Paraguay, maybe Costa Rica, anywhere I can mine a little gold and do what I fucking well please."

3

I HAD THREE MORE DAYS IN CAYENNE BEFORE MY PLANE LEFT for St. Georges. I found myself spending them in the company of exiles and refugees for the same reason Edie collected snakes: In French Guiana they were everywhere. You could not say this about the indigenous inhabitants. Assimilation and European diseases had reduced the Indian population to three thousand, and those south of St. Georges lived in a "restricted zone," theoretically protected from European culture and germs. I had written to the French authorities, asking for permission to visit, but my letter was ignored. The Creoles were hard to meet, perhaps because government jobs and social payments had freed many from engaging in daily commerce. Like remittance men everywhere they were charming but insubstantial, and less interesting than Cayenne's exiles and refugees.

French Guiana was a colonial Berchtesgaden, a tropical last redoubt that attracted people like Jack Morin who wanted to live in a hot country, not as a technical expert on a two-year contract but forever. There were Chinese and Lebanese traders, Brazilian and Haitian laborers. There were *pieds noirs*, driven from Algeria a quarter of a century earlier, and the descendants of Devil's Island

inmates. There were Eurasians who had emigrated from Indonesia to Surinam at independence and then left Surinam when it
too became independent. There were French who had fled from
Indochina in 1954, and Indochinese who fled in 1974. The newspaper *France-Guyane* reported the election of the new leaders of
the Young Farmers of Guiana. Their names were Jean-Rock
Hourau, Jean-Albert Chong Pan, Cleante Poco, and Tsa Tsiong,
and they came from Vietnam, Madagascar, Réunion, and Laos.

The biggest and most recent waves of refugees had come
from Guyana and Surinam, formerly British and Dutch Guiana. It
is tempting to apply a domino theory to the Guianas, particularly
since they are shaped like three dominoes slotted into the northeast coast of South America. When British Guiana became independent, in 1966, it was one of the richest countries in South
America. Now, twenty years later, it has become one of the
poorest, on a par with Haiti and Bolivia, and its disintegrating
economy has spilled refugees southward into Surinam and French
Guiana. Surinam became independent in 1975; ten years later, it
has become a nightmare state, losing a third of its population and
spilling more refugees into the last domino, French Guiana.

When I dined with the Nouh-Chaïas, Georges blamed a rash
of robberies on the new immigrant workers. He had reluctantly
surrounded his home with a fence. Madame Nouh-Chaïa, a beautiful Lebanese who spoke French and Dutch but not Arabic, worried for her parents, still living in terrifying Surinam. As we left
there was a power blackout. It locked the Nouh-Chaïas's electric
security gate, trapping their guests in the darkened driveway.
"These failures are becoming more frequent," Madame Nouh-
Chaïa said in her Dutch-accented French. She took them as an
omen of political turmoil. "If there is trouble here we will have to
move," she whispered in the dark. "But where? Perhaps Brazil,
but I cannot speak Portuguese."

"But this is France," I said.

She sighed, shook her head, and in a we're-not-children-
here-thank-you-very-much tone of voice said, "And honestly
now, how long do you think that can last?"

After sunset, when you could no longer see the dirt-stained
ocean or the columns of menacing clouds that rose every afternoon from the jungle, you could almost believe Cayenne was a
pleasant town in southern France. Olive-skinned men in under-

shirts sat on second-story balconies drinking *pastis*. Gendarmes circled the Place des Palmistres, hands behind backs, while little girls cartwheeled under the double palms and their fathers played boules. A carnival had decamped, leaving behind its bumpercars. Underneath strings of colored bulbs, black, white, and Oriental Frenchmen slammed into one another, throwing up their arms in mock agony. A burly ex-Legionnaire sold shish kebab, and in a neighboring wagon a long-haired blond couple cooked crêpes. I dined twice at a restaurant offering cutlets and stews made of snakes, crocodiles, and armadillos. I ate what I feared most, discovering that fricassee of anaconda had a delicate taste, like blanquette de veau.

Another evening I accepted Mr. Nouh-Chaïa's invitation to join members of the Rotary Club for drinks at the bungalow of a doctor from the Pasteur Institute. The Cayenne Rotarians were so shy and gentle-mannered it was hard to imagine them enjoying commercial triumphs anywhere else. They passed dainty canapés, never raised their voices, and gave the appearance of being slightly asleep. They were in whole or in part Arab, Asian, African, French, and South American, but usually in part, so a Creole had an Asian slant to his eyes, and a Frenchman had the sallow complexion of a light-skinned Creole, and when they drew their chairs into a circle to attend to Rotarian business I was reminded of those UNICEF Christmas cards showing the "children of all nations" holding hands and dancing in a circle. They all knew exactly where the equator was, and when they heard I was returning to Macapá at the end of my trip, they insisted I come up to Cayenne and give them a report. Gin and tonic had numbed whatever corner of the brain stores French vocabulary, and I finally stopped searching for words to fashion an elegant refusal and simply said, *"Oui."* They toasted my return, pulling out pocket calendars to fix a date, and I thought, These are just the men who, had they happened to live a few hundred miles north of here, would have been found murdered in their pajamas.

French Guiana's largest enterprise is PIDEG, a shrimp-fishing and -packing operation owned by Americans and Japanese and employing mostly immigrants from other South American and Caribbean countries. The manager was a curly-haired American in his late twenties from Minnesota named Michael Corser, who ran his treacherous-looking Caribbean captains with the firm hand of a good high school football coach. As we walked along the dock, inspecting the fleet, several men asked for a salary advance. Corser was slight and boyish, but they accepted his decisions without complaint. He had won several fights and once sailed a burning boat into the harbor to extinguish the flames. "Man, was I scared," he said. "But I had to do it. It showed them I give the orders *and* take the risks." After graduating from college, he had pulled out an atlas and searched for a warm country where he could make a living. He chose the Guianas, because "No one knew anything about them and they were a long way from Minnesota." He started as a deckhand in Surinam. Seven years later, he spoke English with a Caribbean lilt, managed the largest enterprise in French Guiana, and battled the Brazilian navy.

A large sign in his dockside office warned, YOU ARE NOT UNDER ANY CIRCUMSTANCES TO FISH IN BRAZILIAN WATERS. IF YOU DO, THE BRAZILIAN NAVY WILL SINK AND DESTROY YOUR BOAT. He said, "Whenever the shrimp are across the frontier, my captains can't resist the temptation. They sneak across, and that Brazilian gunboat machine-guns them or seizes their boat, and I have to get them back. I go to Belém all the time to ransom our boats and bail out my captains. We're always patching up boats riddled with bullets. But my captains think it's worth the risk, and they enjoy the game.

"Usually they put the boat on automatic pilot and hit the deck when the Brazilians open up. Some of my captains are real wild." He was secretly proud. "One likes to pull down his trousers and moon the Brazilians. They shot up his boat and rammed it. One crewman died and two others went into the drink. That's why I bought a plane and learned to fly: so I can ride herd on my captains, keep them out of Brazil, and fish them out when they go there anyway."

He also had problems with the local politicians. "Whenever they want money for their pet projects, they squeeze us, because we're the biggest, most profitable enterprise going. They also complain I only employ immigrant laborers. We've tried hiring locals, but they aren't interested because the French welfare is so generous. But people are still mad. I've had threats to kidnap me to Surinam, and they've even called me a slave. Yeah, it's a real common curse here. When one of the local blacks gets pissed off he sometimes calls me a 'slave,' or 'son of a slave.'"

This bizarre curse had its genesis in the *doublage,* a cruel law requiring the few Devil's Island inmates who survived their imprisonment to remain in the colony for a period equal to their sentence. They had to work for whoever would shelter them, or risk being arrested for vagrancy and returned to the penal colony for a life term. Some Guiana Frenchmen were descended from convicts who had labored as virtual slaves for Creole farmers.

At the end of Corser's dock, muddy currents swirled around the pilings. "The Brazilian mud has never been worse," he said. "It's risen ten feet in a year and blocked the channel so bad we only leave at high tide. I can see it from my plane, a big blob moving along the coast. Something's disturbing that river for sure, and the weather too. Funny things are happening. Lightning storms on the coast that should be inland. No rain in the rainy season but lots in the dry. Worst shrimping in years. I flew over Macapá last year. I wanted to land, but the airport was ringed with forest fires. All I saw was smoke."

An American woman whom I will call Peggy, who worked as a secretary in Corser's office, invited me for a drink on the yacht she shared with her two children and French husband. I imagined a red sunset, bobbing boats and nautical flags, swooping gulls and a rum punch in one of those thick plastic glasses you always find on yachts. Perhaps Peggy and her husband also imagined this when they quit their jobs in France, sold everything, and bought their boat, the *Cowabunga.* It had been named, although not by them, for an exclamation of surprise made popular by a children's television program of the 1950s, *The Howdy Doody Show.*

The Cayenne municipal pier looked more Scandinavian than South American, more hippie colony than marina. The boat children were beautiful, untamed towheads. Their parents had dark tans, sun-bleached hair, and a determined, practiced serenity. I arrived during the brief tropical twilight, when the boat children were returning from school and their parents from whatever jobs they had scrounged in Cayenne. I found Peggy and her two small boys in front of the same crêpe truck I had seen in the Place des Palmistres. I had since noticed it in several unlikely locations —

near the cemetery, at the unswimmable beach—and always with bemused Creoles staring at the blond crêpe-makers.

"Do you think the shrimp captains would eat crêpes for lunch?" the crêpe lady asked Peggy. Mike Corser's pirates did not strike me as crêpe types, but Peggy, who had a freckly, button-nosed, optimistic American face, said, "Sure!" There was nothing they would like more than a crêpe for lunch. However, as we left, she admitted selling crêpes in Cayenne was not such a hot idea. But the couple had just arrived from Brazil and sold their boat, which represented their life savings, to buy the truck, so why, you know, depress them, right?

The harbor, she admitted, was not at its best. The rainy season had come early, and the sky sagged with black clouds. Women and children in yellow rain slickers lined up for a single cold-water shower. It was low tide, and mud flats surrounded the beached dinghies of the boat people. Most would have to wait several hours for the tide to rise so they could reach their yachts, but Peggy had cleverly anchored her dinghy to the second of two docked Venezuelan fishing boats. She skittered over a slippery plank to the first boat, carrying her two-year-old in one arm and almost losing her balance in the middle. Twenty feet below, the boat ground against the side of the dock. The Venezuelans greeted us with sullen stares. The port authorities had ordered them to allow the boat people to transit their decks at low tide. We climbed down to a lower deck, broad-jumped to a second fishing boat, skated across a deck slippery with fish guts, swung over the side, and landed in a puddle of water in Peggy's rubber dinghy. The boys fought and splashed. Rain fell hard and heavy. As we putted across the muddy harbor, Peggy searched for the *Cowabunga* with a dim flashlight. It was a good name for a boat anchored in Cayenne. Cowabunga!

Peggy said, "The government threatened to build a marina and force everyone to dock there and hook into water and electric outlets. But all the boat people protested so much they dropped it."

"But why? Then you wouldn't have to climb over the Venezuelans or line up for a cold shower."

"But we would have to pay. The government promised to keep the fees low, and most of us—you know we have jobs in Cayenne—could have afforded it, but that's not the point. It was the principle." The principle was this: The boat people had left France to escape taxes and functionaries and were in Cayenne because they could anchor here, in this muddy inlet, for free.

The *Cowabunga* smelled of spilled milk and mildew. Peggy found a lemon and mixed its juice with rum. We drank this under a leaky tarpaulin while she fed her boys a supper of cold cocktail frankfurters. Was this what she and her husband imagined when he dissolved his architectural firm and bought the *Cowabunga*? Every reason for living on a boat was missing. The sea was too muddy for swimming. Day sailing was difficult, since they could only enter and leave the harbor at high tide. ("We never go for sails," Peggy admitted. "I guess we just live here.") The view was mud, swamp, and warehouses. Breezes were rare, sunsets short, nights long, and soon it would rain every day. Every month they had to beach the *Cowabunga*, sinking to their knees in mud while scraping filth from the hull. "Yeah, it's kind of a pain in the ass," she said, smiling as her boys fought and water dripped on their homework. "But it's all worth it, I guess."

Worth it to escape France. "So petty, the French function-aries. And after the Socialists, everything became a hassle: the insurance, the taxes. We sold out, and we've been sailing for two years. We stopped in Dakar but hated it, so we only stayed two months."

For all the boat people's professed love of independence, they sounded rather herd-like. According to Peggy, many of the seventy yachts moored in Cayenne had arrived within the same two weeks, simply because they had all sailed to Brazil last spring for Carnival and their six-month visas had expired simulta-neously. And next spring they would sail into the Caribbean, ar-riving when the tourist season ended and prices fell. Most boat people were French, and many had read the same best-selling book extolling the joys of round-the-world cruising. Its publica-tion had coincided with the electoral triumph of the Socialists, an added incentive to leave home. But now they had sailed thou-sands of miles only to find themselves floating in a fetid harbor, not only still in France but in the most bureaucratic of all French departments, a place where three quarters of all salaried workers worked for the government. Peggy's husband had found a job as an architect in a government office in Cayenne. Other boat people labored as schoolteachers, typists, and clerks. Because their supervisors knew they would quit within a year, they were given menial positions and poorly paid. They had sailed into the arms of what they were escaping.

Peggy swept her flashlight across the neighboring yachts. "We have a dentist, two doctors, two architects besides my husband, a professional photographer, a hair stylist, an engineer . . ." On she went, presenting the boat people as a diverse, interesting community by listing the very educations and professions they had fled. Not everyone was enjoying the life promised by that best-seller. Peggy's flashlight fell on a darkened hull. Its owner was in the Cayenne prison, charged with murder. He had purchased a contracting business, piled up debts, and shot his most persistent creditor. She pointed out another yacht. "Her husband once worked for IBM, but he's back in France now, in an insane asylum." His wife had deserted him for another boat person. In despair, he set fire to their yacht and set out in a dinghy without food or water. The other boat people saw him silhouetted against his blazing boat and brought him back. His wife committed him, salvaged the charred boat, and started, according to the optimistic Peggy, "a new life," which sounded like the old life with a new partner.

Like most exiles, the boat people could not easily return home. Those tiring of the life sailed to Miami, slipping into the United States as illegal aliens. "My husband could never go back," she said. "French society disapproves of our irresponsibility, and his colleagues would never take him back. They are jealous."

Her oldest son tugged on her shirt and cried *"Regardez, maman! Regardez!"* He had used every crayon to draw his picture. Peggy complimented him absentmindedly, but he continued pleading until she clicked on the flashlight. There, circled by its beam, was a large suburban house. Huge trees shaded a yard scattered with bicycles, and smoke curled from a chimney.

French Guiana's most successful exiles are the Hmong, a tribal people from the mountains of Indochina. I saw them in the markets, checking sums on pocket calculators, consulting digital watches, unloading basketball-sized cabbages, and selling fish from white vans. In the markets, their bountiful stalls were coiled around the shabby Creole ones like boa constrictors.

The spectacular success of the Hmong in French Guiana is

made more extraordinary by the equally spectacular failure of Hmong refugees elsewhere, and by the spectacular failure of every other nationality of immigrants — Portuguese, French, Chinese, and Javanese — to settle and farm French Guiana. The most recent French settlement scheme had occurred in 1975, when the minister for overseas territories, Olivier Stirn, called for thirty thousand Frenchmen to emigrate to Guiana. Sending this number of whites to a multiracial tropical country with a population of only seventy thousand, fifteen years after most tropical countries had become independent, was a plan only French colonial circles could have entertained. Stirn announced a budget of $160 million to promote the white colonization of Guiana, saying, "Everything indicates that Frenchmen from every region of France and the overseas territories will come in sufficient numbers. . . . In the last few days hundreds of letters and thousands of telephone calls reaching me have shown that the French are still builders and pioneers." Thirty-six thousand "pioneers" applied to Stirn's office, eager to escape modern France for the comfort of its former penal colony. Four months later, all but thirty had been disqualified because they lacked minimal financial resources or skills, or because they were too young, too old, or physically or mentally deficient. Within several years, most of the remaining thirty had left the interior for Cayenne, where they opened restaurants and boutiques.

As the Stirn Plan collapsed, the Hmong arrived. After the Communist victories in Indochina, they had fled to camps in Thailand, where the world divvied them up. A people who revered village, family, and the graves of ancestors suddenly found themselves in France, the United States, Argentina, Canada, or Australia. Families were separated, and everywhere the Hmong became notoriously unhappy refugees. They learned languages slowly. Capitalism confused them, and criminals victimized them. In Chicago and Seattle, healthy Hmong men died in their sleep. Physicians theorized that nightmares had literally scared them to death.

A French priest led a thousand Hmong from Thailand to French Guiana. Seven hundred traveled sixty miles inland from Cayenne to Cacao, cleared the jungle, and planted vegetables and fruit trees. They were so successful that the French wanted to admit several thousand more, but the Creoles, fearing they might soon monopolize the commercial life of the department, such as it was, rioted in Cayenne. The government capitulated, suspending further Hmong immigration. But the Hmong remain a sore subject for the Creoles, and one not helped by the French, who are hysterical in their praise of the plucky Hmong. Again and again I was told I must visit the Hmong at Cacao. They were the only people in the country who really worked. In seven years they had built a Shangri-La of orchards, paddies, and long houses.

The heavily laden Hmong market trucks had carved such deep ruts in the road to Cacao that the thirty-mile trip took two hours. I drove through a hilly jungle concealing birds that wolf-whistled like truck drivers. The terrain was so steep, the forest so thick, it seemed impossible anyone could farm here, and when from a distance I saw a herd of Hmong cows, standing in jungle mist as they grazed an emerald pasture, udders heavy with milk, I suspected a mirage. But then I saw Hmong women walking single file and stooped under the weight of baskets piled with children and cabbages. An old man bicycled past with a banana seedling balanced in one arm, waving so furiously he tumbled into the ditch. Because the Hmong had built their houses at the same time and out of the same materials, Cacao resembled a prosperous suburban development. The roofs had the same Oriental pitch and the houses sat on stilts, leaving space underneath for the Hmong to park their Toyota Hi-Lux trucks.

The nuns at the church passed me on to the nuns at the dispensary, who took me to a hill overlooking the village where the mayor was showing Cacao to his younger brother, a Mr. Yang Va, from Montreal. The mayor was a smiling, sinewy little man with a crew cut who resembled the happiest Marine in boot camp. Mr. Va was intense, long-haired, and sallow. He had drawn Canada in the Hmong refugee lottery and was visiting Cacao for the first time. His relatives had welcomed him with so many banquets that, after a week, today was his first opportunity to tour the village. He had a degree in business administration but worked in Montreal as a male nurse. He did not mind. His real avocation was preserving Hmong history and culture. During his vacations, he traveled throughout Canada and the United States, photographing and interviewing Hmong refugees about their former lives and current misfortunes. He was collecting this material in a book that would teach future Hmong about their homeland. Was this not a more worthy profession than Canadian businessman? Mr. Va wondered. The situation was desperate. The old men who remembered Hmong history were sickening and dying of sadness. "Here in Cacao," he said, "are the only happy Hmong in the world."

The mayor explained why the Hmong of Cacao were happy. He spoke in French and Hmong, which Mr. Va translated in an urgent, hushed voice, like a sports announcer in the final minutes of a game. "He says when the first hundred and twenty families came from Thailand, this was jungle. The French dumped them here. The land was free, but that is all the Hmong got. The first six months they cleared three hundred acres with hand axes. They did this to rid themselves of mosquitoes, and so they could grow crops. During the clearing, serpents bit the children, but they survived. Then they planted mango trees, bananas, coconut palms, and wild eggplants, all our favorite Hmong foods."

"Do you understand how hard the Hmong worked?" Mr. Va feared his brother was being too offhand. "Everyone was bent double cutting away jungle, even the children. Can you imagine?" He searched my face for signs of appreciation. "At first, the Hmong live in tents and walk to their fields. Then they make their houses and buy bikes, then trucks. You must write down this truth: In Cacao, no one gives the Hmong anything."

He watched my eyes taking in the television antennas and streetlamps. "That's right, you can see it all: television, electricity, filtered running water, and flushing toilets. In their houses the Hmong have video-cassette recorders and electric washers. When the air is fresh, they sleep under duck-feather comforters. But remember: no gifts! All this the Hmong earn for themselves."

"We Hmong have only one problem," the mayor said in French. "Not enough Hmong!" After the Creole protests, only the Hmong already residing in France could emigrate to Guiana. No more from the Thai camps, no freezing, nightmare-ridden Hmong from the United States. The Hmong of Cacao were devastated. They had hoped to be reunited with their broken families and gather the Hmong diaspora here. The mayor and Mr. Va were two of seven brothers scattered across the globe. "We could not choose our country or go together as a family," the mayor said. "It was *sauve qui peut.*"

The immigration restrictions were also a financial setback.

The Hmong had planted crops and purchased cattle and equipment in expectation of their relatives joining them. Now there were not enough Hmong to harvest and market the produce. Hectares of food were rotting, and instead of welcoming Hmong immigrants, the Hmong of Cacao were hosting French ones. The mayor found this amusing. "When the French left us here, they thought we would come back to Cayenne begging for help. But now they want to live here with us." A hundred French had already settled in Cacao. There were priests, teachers, and functionaries, and men who had formerly served in these posts and married Hmong women. Cacao's houses and fields had a raw, unfinished look, but it was easily the most pleasant village in French Guiana.

I was told the Hmong prospered because the climate and countryside were similar to their homeland, and because they had come directly from Thailand without being exposed to what they considered the enervating climates of North America and Europe. I asked the mayor to compare Cacao to Indochina. He said, "The countryside looks similar, except our home was more fertile and the rains more predictable."

"And the village?"

They stared down at Cacao. For the first time, Mr. Va fell silent. The mayor pinched the bridge of his nose and blinked, as if trying to bring what he saw into focus or superimpose it on his memory. At last he said, "Yes, it looks the same, but it's not the same at all. Here, we lack the graves of our ancestors."

We climbed into the mayor's truck and toured what Mr. Va called the Hmong miracle. He insisted on seeing everything. After years of interviewing wretched Hmong, he wanted to gorge on this feast of Hmong success.

We marveled at the plump Hmong ducks, honking and waddling around a shack. Mr. Va took me aside. "The mayor wants you to know that before the Hmong, the restaurants in Cayenne bought frozen ducks from France. And the Hmong did not build that ugly house. It belonged to gold prospectors and was the only structure they found here."

We paced the circumference of the spring-fed Hmong crawfish ponds. Mr. Va held his hands wide apart. "The Hmong crawfish are like this, the biggest ever." The mayor gently pushed his brother's hands closer together and said, "We ship them frozen to the U.S.A. Perhaps you have eaten Hmong crawfish."

We slogged through a grove of trees heavy with green berries. I was told the French call these wild eggplant and like their bittersweet taste. The Hmong airfreighted them to Parisian delicacy shops, where they commanded big prices.

We admired the Hmong cattle and chickens, the sawmill that cut planks for Hmong fences and homes, and the tractors that carved Hmong rice paddies; the groves of Hmong mango, orange, and lemon trees; and the red flowers the Hmong sold to the florists of Cayenne. There was even a Hmong fast-food stall — *Frites, Glacés,* Kebabs — catering to French weekend tourists.

I mentioned that in many tropical countries the fragile jungle soil became eroded and exhausted after several harvests. The mayor pointed to several empty fields. "We know to rotate crops, leave our land fallow, and scatter fertilizer. When we couldn't afford fertilizer, we tied our animals to the fruit trees."

Whenever we passed other Hmong they slowed their trucks, smiling and throwing little toodle-oo waves. Just beyond the boundary of Hmong land, we came upon the old man who had waved so furiously when I arrived. He was packing down the earth around a banana tree. "My uncle," the mayor said. "This land is not ours, but we cannot stop him planting bananas. He says they will make Cacao as beautiful as Laos."

Back in the village, tiny Hmong men split wood and shrunken Hmong women prodded trees with forked sticks, harvesting fruit. Hard work and sun had blurred distinctions between young and old, male and female. Everyone looked brown and shriveled, as if they had poured their fluids into these fields. "What do the Hmong do for fun?" I asked.

Mr. Va shook his head. "Hmong have no time for fun! They are too busy building Hmong future."

"We like to fish and hunt," the mayor said.

The Canadian saw me scribbling a note. "You should write, 'The Hmong never relax. They grow things and work. That is all.'"

Much as I admired the Hmong miracle, I was just as glad I was not a Hmong in French Guiana. They were energetic and desperate, a potent combination. No wonder the Creoles took to the streets at the prospect of another thousand of them. The mayor complained that most Creoles had ignored his invitations to visit Cacao. I could see why. Compared to their tumbledown villages, this was paradise. It was hard to blame them. After emancipation, they found it was easy to live off the land, and soon after that gold was discovered in the interior. Some Creoles became suddenly wealthy; many abandoned their farms to become prospectors. Then the gold petered out, and white convicts arrived to do the heavy labor. When the penal colony closed, French social-welfare payments drew the Creoles to Cayenne, depopulating the countryside again and making farm work even less necessary. Given their history, the Creoles could not compete with the Hmong, and, to their credit, they knew it.

At a Thanksgiving-style lunch, the mayor and assorted children, grandchildren, and relatives attacked the Hmong food surplus. We passed platters of chicken, stews of Hmong beef, and a puree of the gourmet eggplants. "Clean! No human dirt," the vigilant Mr. Va shouted when he caught me hesitating over the salad. I sat next to the mayor's twelve-year-old son. He was going back to Montreal with Mr. Va to attend high school. The mayor said, "He is very bright, and the schools in Guiana are too limited."

During lunch, it struck me that for all this talk about the Hmong loving hard work, the mayor was doing precious little himself. I asked if he would be heading into the overgrown lettuce patches after lunch. No, he would not. Or the crayfish ponds? No. The duck farm or rice paddies? No again. Mr. Va whispered, "He is not working because he just had an operation."

"What kind of operation?"

"Hernia."

So the little Marine Corps mayor had worked so hard he had, quite literally, busted a gut.

"Who organized the riots against the Hmong?" I asked Mr. Masse when I stopped at his museum on my way to the airport.

"The politicians!" Mr. Masse spit it out like a piece of bad meat.

"Which politicians?"

"The local ones. They hate the Hmong because they work and the politicians are lazy."

"Why did the leprosarium at Acarouney close?"

"The politicians! French nuns had managed the institution,

but the left-wing politicians are anticlerical so they eliminated the government subsidy."

Why did Mr. Masse think there was so little economic development in Guiana?

"The politicians! They insist on such generous labor benefits no one invests here."

I searched for a question that could not be answered by Mr. Masse's favorite word. "Have you developed a theory to explain the extraordinary numbers of single people in Guiana?"

He had. "There are many single immigrant workers, and many single men at the space center. More important, the women of Guiana do not care to marry. They don't need husbands because the state meets their financial needs. So the reason for the *célibataires* is, in a word—"

"The politicians."

"Precisely."

If the politicians had their way, the future of Guiana was not bright, according to Mr. Masse. And since he seemed to lump together all politicians, and since it was difficult to imagine who but the politicians would run the country—well, then, from Mr. Masse's perch among the stuffed caimans and flamingos, the future was bleak.

"And what will happen if French Guiana becomes independent?" I asked.

"My dear sir, then French Guiana is fucked."

Mr. Masse checked his watch. Now that I understood his country, he must, regrettably, end the conversation. He had a rather long shopping list today and the stores closed at noon. It was already ten-thirty.

As we parted in the street, I said I was flying to St. Georges. Had Mr. Masse ever visited this town?

"In the course of my researches I have visited every village in the department."

"Then you know Modestine."

"Ah, one of our best chefs. What takes you to St. Georges?" I explained, and he looked up in astonishment. "But I have never heard of *anyone* crossing *that* border. Is there even a Brazilian customs post? I doubt it, but perhaps it can be done."

I decided French Guiana was the opposite of most other

countries on my equatorial itinerary. Their populations had increased; in more than a century, French Guiana's had scarcely grown. They were clearing their tropical forests; in French Guiana, 99 percent of the forest was untouched. They were independent; French Guiana was the largest mainland colony in the world. They had struggled for their freedom; most Guianese preferred to remain "French," and were so worried the Socialists might thrust independence on the overseas departments that they voted against Mitterrand in the last election. Other tropical countries wanted to develop their natural resources; French Guiana did not, because, although no one would admit it, the French knew development would require English-, Spanish-, and Portuguese-speaking immigrant laborers who might soon demand independence. Other tropical peoples struggled for adequate food and shelter, but the Guianese enjoyed total literacy, a good diet, and good health care. They had the highest standard of living in South America, and the lowest level of productivity. It came to this: What had been the first mainland European colony in the Americas, and was now the last, had become a bizarre curiosity, the mad dog out too long in the midday sun, the idiot savant portraying the true face of colonialism, its paternalism and destruction of initiative. And finally, and ironically, it had become the Socialist paradise promised by so many third-world leaders at independence. French Guiana was the photographic negative of their countries, a place where black was white, and whites — well, whites were "slaves."

4

THE WOLF-WHISTLE BIRDS FLITTED THROUGH THE RAFTERS OF the Cayenne airport. Lizards darted, and some large animal, perhaps one of the cruelly orphaned French pets, had left a turd among the plastic chairs. The room was empty except for the other passengers for St. Georges. A tall, redheaded woman and a short, bug-eyed man snuggled and giggled. A skinny Creole girl spoke endearments into a cage holding the only untuneful bird I had heard in Guiana. Two Vietnamese boys in matching safari suits fluttered their hands and whispered.

We took off through a necklace of thunderclouds. I sat next to a chain-smoking Frenchman. A tropical ailment had ballooned and frozen his right hand, which he had sensibly converted to a cigarette holder. He extracted the butts with his good hand, replacing them immediately with a lit cigarette. The bird squawked, the Vietnamese loaded their cameras, and I spread out my map and stared down at the least explored and least populated jungle in the world. The map said the riverbanks were dotted with Indian villages, prospectors' cabins, and "remarkable rocky peaks," located at a point described as approximate. The richest gold strikes had occurred between Cayenne and the Approuague

River, but I looked in vain for Lieu-Dit Tintin—"a place called Tintin," "a place called Dubol," and Jean-Jean Remission. I saw only jungle, cut by brown rivers, rippled with misty hills, and covered by a tree canopy so seamless it was said monkeys could swing across it for hundreds of miles without touching ground— meaning that if a monkey had set out from Cayenne a week ago, he might have beaten me to St. Georges.

The airfield was a bumpy strip carved from jungle. The other passengers stood among their luggage, waiting for what the Vietnamese described as transportation to the center of town. The bug-eyed man and his redhead slipped into a concrete bunker belonging to the telephone company. Somehow they had a key. I converted my bag to a backpack and walked to St. Georges on a one-lane asphalt road. I passed a stop sign, a one-way sign, and another warning motorists of CHILDREN AT PLAY. A directional sign of a style common to French autoroutes said TO THE SUBURBS. To what suburbs? There were scarcely a hundred buildings in this frontier village, most of them crude shacks grouped around a tick-tack-toe grid of streets. I stared down each intersection. The paved streets quickly became dusty footpaths, then jungle. And where were the motorists to obey these signs? No roads led to St. Georges, and the handful of automobiles had arrived on the deck of a riverboat.

Chez Modestine was a two-story wooden house facing a riverfront park where a bleached flag hung over a war memorial and a litter bin imported from France—*Papiers s.v.p.* I sat on the steps of Chez Modestine for several minutes before she emerged from a neighboring building, the Bar Modestine. She was a stout Creole with a fey smile, as if still amused by a joke told long before. She had forgotten I was coming, but no matter, I could still have her best room. "Remember to speak French to the Brazilians and you will have no problems at the frontier," she said, wagging a finger.

"But they'll see my passport!"

"Surely you have a French passport."

"No, American!" I studied her round, cheerful face. I had been told she was also the postmistress, the agent for Air Guyane, and the city's leading trader. How could such a woman think a Mr. Clarke with an accent like mine could possibly be French?

"If you are American, who knows? But foreigners have

crossed without incident, I think." She excused herself. Tonight the Foreign Legion was dining Chez Modestine, and they insisted on fried river fish.

St. Georges's three bars followed a crafty schedule. Instead of competing for scarce patrons, they observed complementary hours, so only two at most were open at the same time. At 4 P.M., the Oiapoque Café, where pictures of Brazilian soccer teams decorated peeling pink walls, was a busy coffee shop with cassettes blasting Brazilian music. Then, at 5:30, the shutters of the Hotel Damas flew open. A boy set tables out on the porch, and the clientele of the Oiapoque drained their glasses and moved en masse. I shared a table with three Japanese-Brazilians in red bathing suits who did so many un-Japanese things — shouting, drinking excessively, pounding each other's backs, and mouthing the slushy lyrics of Brazilian love songs — that I wondered if they were Brazilians wearing Japanese masks. One said, "We have come for the shopping."

"The shopping?" I had not spoken Portuguese for fifteen years. Perhaps I had misunderstood.

"Yes, the shopping!" They had come up from Macapá on a twice-weekly flight to Oiapoque, then crossed the river to St. Georges. They opened airline flight bags, showing off champagne, Scotch, and perfume. The Damas doubled as a store, selling canned beef, knives, and pots to Indians, and duty-free swag to Brazilians. The champagne had a familiar orange label. It was Veuve Clicquot, the kind served at my wedding, and seeing it here made me suddenly and unexpectedly homesick.

Some Foreign Legionnaires returned single file from maneuvers, their arms and legs splotched with Mercurochrome applied to jungle cuts. They sprawled over the Damas's chairs, ordering a fizzy French soft drink called Orangina, and I saw they were all teen-agers, resembling baby robins with their fuzzy crew cuts and spindly legs. Their straws made childish sucking noises as they vacuumed up their Oranginas. What crimes or secrets could possibly have prompted their enlistment?

They left, and the mothers of St. Georges allowed their daughters to stroll around the war memorial. They wore long, gingham missionary dresses and made only one revolution before the Japanese-Brazilians scattered them with whistles and dirty words. Then two hunters walked out of the jungle carrying plastic pails filled with bloody chunks of meat. "Capybara," the waiter said, as they disappeared into the back door of Chez Modestine.

The sun set, the jungle blackened, and on clicked the yellow autoroute streetlights of St. Georges. Bats swooped around the war memorial in perfect circles, as if attached by invisible cables. Families who had been preparing for All Saints' Day returned from the cemetery with muddy shovels. Then the mosquitoes attacked, and the Damas's patrons moved to the Bar Modestine.

Here I sat with the tall redhead and her bug-eyed boyfriend. We had eyed one another while playing musical cafés, and since there was only one unoccupied table at Modestine's bar, we would have to share it. He said he was a telephone engineer in Cayenne. She was a teacher, and they were both in Guiana on two-year contracts. "We have come here for a vacation from Cayenne," he said.

"And to pass *le weekend gastronomique chez* Modestine," she added.

And to make love in that concrete telephone bunker, I thought.

He voiced the usual complaint: Social welfare had made the people of Guiana impossibly lazy — almost as lazy, in fact, as the typical French functionary.

"But you are French and you work for the government," she said gently. "So you are a French functionary."

"But . . . well, I suppose I am!" His eyes bugged out even further, and he slapped his forehead in amazement.

We crossed the street to Chez Modestine. They too had heard her kitchen praised extravagantly. Next to us a table of Foreign Legion officers speared crispy fillets of fish from a platter. We dined on a different menu: soapy broth studded with raw carrots, a tureen of cold canned peas in their brine, and a sinewy stew, perhaps the capybara. The redhead spat it back. "It is truly disgusting, this cuisine. It is almost raw, but cooking would be no help. Three days here. I cannot believe it."

"The Legion is eating delicious fish," the functionary said. "Tomorrow we will demand fish and eat well." We craned our necks, watching as the Legionnaires nibbled at their fillets, then shoved them uneaten into the middle of the table.

"How lucky you are," the redhead said, looking fierce. "Tomorrow you will be in Brazil, eating their delicious meat. I adore their steaks and sauces." For the next half hour we talked about food. They recounted memorable dinners, course by course, and wanted to know: Was it true we Americans ate the salad first? Had I eaten those big crabs in San Francisco? And anaconda, had I tried that in Cayenne? "So delicate." He kissed the air.

"Like blanquette de veau," I offered.

"Oh no, much better," she said. "But not as good as the crab beignets at . . ."

I went upstairs to make a meal of my Hmong oranges. Modestine's room was as near to a prison cell as I ever hope to come. The toilet sat in one corner on a pedestal, like a sculpture. It reeked of urine and flushed itself every six minutes, all night. Smashed mosquitoes and roaches polka-dotted the walls, and the air buzzed with aggressive insects. The sheets were damp, smelling of cheese, and a shower of curly black hairs covered the pillow. Iron rings had been hammered into the walls. They were too small to hold clothing or towels but perfect for anchoring a prisoner's chains.

I closed the shutters and the room became stifling. I opened them, and the autoroute streetlamps surrounding the park bathed the room in a concentration-camp light. There was a rooster below one window, a howling dog tethered to a post beneath another. It was impossible to fall asleep in the six minutes between toilet flushings. It was impossible to angle the bed so it avoided the lights. I turned to my South American guidebook and soon read, "Remember that rabies is endemic throughout South America so avoid dogs that are behaving strangely, and cover your toes at night to foil the vampire bats, which also carry the disease."

I studied the bats outside Modestine's windows, wondering if they were vampires. I had not forgotten a vampire passage in a book about Devil's Island: "These little bats, rarely more than a foot in wingspread, would make contact with him [the convict] only while he slept and they were in need of blood. . . . The vampires would hover over his bare feet, never touching him until their teeth made the painless needle-sharp incision so they might suck a minute quantity of blood; the fearful thing was that they injected simultaneously a noncoagulating agent into the bloodstream, which would leave the wound flowing until the convict awoke in the morning with a quart or more of his own blood drained onto the floor."

I left Modestine's shutters wide open and lay on her awful bed, dozing fitfully, perspiring, and naked except for a towel draped over my toes. My ankles itched all night, from bedbugs rather than vampires, I hoped; from jigger fleas, I discovered later. I had caught them by walking in sandals. The female jigger burrows into the foot, ovulates, grows to the size of a small pea, and lays eggs, which she passes through a hole in the skin. The itching caused by these fleas is so annoying it has led to the expression "I'll be jiggered." My jigger gave birth when I stopped in New York on my way between Macapá and Africa. The eggs hatched in our bed, leaving my wife well and truly jiggered.

The next morning I found the Creole gendarme sitting in a bathing suit on his front porch, dunking chunks of baguette into his café au lait. "You must tell me the date," he said, as unsure as the French surveyors. I said November first, and with a toothpick he moved the date in his exit stamp from October 6, the last time he had had occasion to use it. He pounded my passport and wished me *"bonne route."*

Back at the hotel, a new character was sipping Modestine's oily coffee and scowling into a dictionary-thick French novel. He was dressed for the beach with white trousers, a shirt open to the navel, and plastic sandals. Everything was spotted and wrinkled, and his earring was tarnished. He said, "I have been four days in St. Georges." His name was Gé.

"Is it your first or last name?"

"It is how my audience knows me."

"Your audience?"

"I am host of a radio program in Cayenne. You might say I am the Johnny Carson of French Guiana. Since French Guiana is absolutely the asshole of the whole world, I am keeping busy on my program, sifting the *merde.*"

But why live here if it was such an asshole?

"Because where else could I have such independence? Broadcast whatever I want on a French channel? My God, even the Socialists don't give a damn what I say. They ignore me. No one cares, but I say it anyway."

I told him I was going to Macapá today, and he gave a pitying laugh. Every morning for three days he had crossed to Oiapoque, hoping the bus would leave, only to be told that heavy rains during the night had made the dirt road impassable, postponing the departure another day. "There was no rain last night, so maybe today the bus will go, but maybe not. Maybe it will go tomorrow, or next week. This coffee is truly disgusting." He pushed it away. "My God, I am really *trop âgé* ["too old"] for this business." He was several years younger than I.

"What time is the bus supposed to go?" I asked. It was the same bus I planned to take to Calçoene, where it connected with another bus to Macapá. Everyone in St. Georges had been vague about the timetable.

"The schedule says seven A.M.," Gé said.

"But it's already eight-thirty!"

"Yes. I'm counting on a late departure because of the roads, and because that bus never leaves on time."

"Why not telephone Oiapoque and ask?" A huge telecommunications tower shadowed St. Georges.

Another pitying laugh. "That would cost at least twenty dollars. And the connection would take several hours, perhaps days. The call goes to Cayenne, then to Paris, then to Rio, and from there to Oiapoque. It is an imbecility that delights the Indians. The functionaries say to them, 'Why do you resist our marvelous French civilization? The benefits of French technology?' The Indians point to the radio towers of St. Georges and Oiapoque and say, 'What benefits? To call between those takes hours. In less time we can paddle a canoe between our villages and exchange news with our relatives, and it costs nothing.' Then the Indians have a big laugh at us."

"Why didn't you sleep in Oiapoque?" I asked. "Then you'd be sure of catching the bus."

"You have never seen Oiapoque."

"It's better here?"

"By comparison, here is paradise. My God, I am really *trop âgé* for this business."

I threw everything into my bag and paid Modestine. She was slicing carrots into a familiar soup. "A pity you leave so soon, Monsieur Clarke," she said. "Tonight I am offering a bouillabaisse."

The Legionnaires were leaving too. Led by a sleepy Indian guide who held his rifle by the barrel and dragged the stock in the dust, they marched to the memorial for a flag-raising ceremony. The air was so still and humid their flag drooped like a wet sheet.

They put on orange life-vests and headed upriver in motorized canoes. "They will rendezvous with Brazilian soldiers and map the frontier," Gé explained. "Ever since the war, that boundary is in dispute." The war, of course, was the Franco-Brazilian one of 1895.

As Gé and I pulled away from the municipal dock in a canoe, loudspeakers, fed by microphones trained on the cemetery, came to life, so that long after St. Georges had disappeared behind a bend we could hear the All Saints' Day mass, booming out across the headstones and rolling up the river after us.

A canoe full of Indians passed in the other direction. A striking figure stood in the stern, dressed in a kimono and turban and towering over the Indians. "The queen of the Indians," Gé said. "Or perhaps the king. No one knows for sure. His name is Paul, or her name is Pauline. He/she, Paul/Pauline, you may choose. I have spoken with it. The accent is upper-class Parisian, but I cannot decide the gender. It arrived about ten years ago and has lived ever since with the Indians of the protected zone. It has become secretary to the Indian mayor and, I'm told, makes many decisions for the Indians, even considering requests to visit the protected zone." I said I had applied for permission without success. "Yes, myself too, and always he/she gives the same answer 'Non! Non! Non!' I think Paul/Pauline is afraid of competition for the affections of the Indians.

"I am also fond of the Indians. Last year I attended a Common Market conference in Europe and showed photographs of them to the other delegates. I said, 'Look! *Regardez!* Here they are, your fellow Europeans!' The Italians were stupefied. 'What is this? How is it possible? Europeans? Like us?' They thought I was playing a joke. My God, I enjoyed that conference."

On the French bank of the Oiapoque, some darkskinned children were hanging laundry over the rail of a beached steamer. When they saw us they jumped up and down, waving both hands like shipwrecked sailors. "A family of Pakistanis, maybe two families," Gé said. "One day they appeared. No one speaks their language, so it is a mystery how they arrived, or why. They have been six months on that boat, eating fish and jungle fruit. They lack the documents for France or Brazil, so they stay here, trapped between St. Georges and Oiapoque."

Even without the Pakistanis, this length of jungle-bound

river felt like a purgatory. You left one frontier post and completed one set of formalities long before the next flag came into view. Uncertainty surrounded bus schedules and immigration requirements, even the proper names of the towns. It was a serious frontier. Like the Rio Grande, it separated wealth and poverty, an underpopulated country with too few children from an overpopulated one with too many. According to Gé, the federal district of Amapá, which we were about to enter, had the youngest population in Brazil: 80 percent were under twenty-five.

We slid into a mud beach beneath Oiapoque's main street, and immediately the heads of children popped up behind a concrete parapet, like targets in a shooting gallery. Oiapoque's dusty roads were a school yard at recess. Children ran in every direction, stamping in puddles, climbing hills of refuse, dodging trucks, and disappearing into potholes like ships falling into the swell of a heavy sea. A crowd of boys attached themselves to us, following closely as bodyguards while Gé asked about the bus.

A man led us to a rectangle of dry earth surrounded by mud. The bus had stood here for four days until this morning, when it had departed at seven, exactly on schedule. Gé paced the perimeter, studying it like an archeologist, pulling at his earring and muttering, "We are very, very unlucky."

A new Chevrolet pickup truck with oversized tires was parked down the street. "Now I think we are lucky," Gé said as we approached it. Two boys in blue bathing suits leaned against the tailgate. Their arms were folded and they wore confident smiles. "We are lucky, maybe," Gé corrected.

The boys were cousins, both named José, and the truck belonged to José One's father. They had collected cargo in Oiapoque and would leave soon for Calçoene. They expected a four-hour trip. Gé negotiated a price, but when José Two motioned to us to climb into the back with the boxes and empty gas cylinders, Gé shook his head. "My God, can't you see we are professional men, not students? We are *trop âgé* for the back of the truck."

I hoped that by avoiding public transportation I might also avoid the immigration officers, who, if my prize-winning guidebook was correct, would send me back to St. Georges. But the two Josés insisted I stop at the federal police. The police knew their truck and would be angry if they carried illegal immigrants to Calçoene.

I found a plainclothes officer dressed in a tapered pink shirt and gold chain, stuffed behind a child's desk, drumming his fingers and humming a pop song I had heard on the radio while shaving on my last morning at home. He looked at my passport and, without opening it, shook his head. "No good."

"But inside," I pleaded in my execrable Portuguese. "Inside, a visa."

He summoned an older officer, who examined it and said, "The visa is genuine but your passport is counterfeit. It is much too small."

"But all American passports are this size!"

The younger man flipped it across the desk without losing a beat. "*Much* too small. A real American passport is bigger. We know because we have seen them. You must return to St. Georges."

"Why would the Brazilian consulate put a visa in a counterfeit passport?"

Silence. They looked confused, and I understood the problem. Several years before — could it be as many as four? — the State Department had changed the size of our passports. In Oiapoque they had yet to see the new model.

The younger policeman took out a pocket calculator and asked, "How much does it cost?"

"Fifteen dollars."

"Not your passport. We accept that. You are right: If our consulate has stamped this small document, it must be valid. No, how much did you pay to fly to Oiapoque from New York?"

I named a figure in dollars. He converted it to cruzeiros, and the sum brought whistles. The older policeman waved his fingers as if burned by a hot stove. "How much from Miami? It's cheaper from there, yes?" I invented a price so ridiculously low I worried it might depopulate Oiapoque.

"Too much for us." The younger one shook his head and stamped my passport. Now that I had reminded him how difficult it was to escape Oiapoque, he wanted rid of me.

José One was humming the same song. "Donna Summer," he said. Brazilian television had just broadcast a "Donna Summer Special." He pointed to me, to a slot on the dashboard built for a cassette tape recorder, and again said, "Donna Summer." He pointed to Gé. "Jackson Browne." He had saved for a tape deck, and our fares were buying the first tapes.

Amapá is so underdeveloped that it has yet to become a state and is ruled by a governor sent from the national capital. The dirt road we drove from Oiapoque to Calçoene had been completed only two years before and had pushed the frontier of this frontier district to its northernmost limit. When Oiapoque was accessible only by boat or plane, this jungle had been as untouched as the interior of French Guiana. But in less than two years, thousands of landless Brazilian pioneers had traveled north up the road, set-tling like trolls alongside crude wooden bridges and sifting jungle creeks for gold. They slashed and burned, threw up crude shacks, and farmed on squares and semicircles of newly cleared land. Since there were miles of jungle separating their pioneer home-steads, and no schools, villages, or neighbors holding them to a particular place, they lost nothing by farming one parcel of land, then moving up the road to clear another. Jungle soil is fragile, easily exhausted by grazing and slash-and-burn farming. Circles of eroded and abandoned land already flanked this new highway. Population pressure and land hunger were sure to send more families here. They would set their farms closer together, until finally these little battlefields of blackened stumps and churned earth would merge and become overgrown with the scrubby growth of a secondary forest. This strand of virgin jungle was doomed by the energetic, desperate pioneers who traveled up the road. It was that simple.

For Americans, the words "frontier" and "pioneer" evoke im-ages at odds with the shrinking equatorial frontier. There are sim-ilarities between our frontiers: the boomtowns and ghost towns; decimation of tribal peoples; plentiful free land; opportunities for independence and profit; and the misfits, escapists, and "weird shit-bags" drawn to them. But overshadowing these is one essen-tial difference: the poverty of the soil on the equatorial frontier. A hundred years later, land in the former temperate-zone frontiers of the United States, Canada, and the Soviet Union is still green, its farms still productive. But on the equatorial frontier, land that was the dark green of primary forest for centuries has become, after a decade of grazing or cultivation, a wasteland.

We picked up a barefoot farmer with a tubercular cough. He

carried a bottle of moonshine and a shotgun that José Two made him empty before climbing aboard. Here, wrapped in a single package, were all the pioneer imports that prove so fatal to tribal peoples: liquor, disease, and firearms. We stopped at his cabin, and its windows filled with the faces of children. He insisted we come inside, meet them, and drink moonshine. The invitation was direct and sincere, an offer of hospitality from one man to his equals, and I was sorry when both Josés refused.

Gé was mysterious about the purpose of a trip involving such inconvenience. He said he planned to visit a "friend" in Amapá, a town several hours south of Calçoene, but when I probed for details he changed the subject to the equator, saying he had visited many of the African countries touched by it in the 1950s, when his father was governor of one of the departments of French Equatorial Africa. He particularly remembered the Eala Botanical Gardens, at Coquilhatville (now Mbandaka). "They are fabulous, a paradise of blossoms and flowering shrubs and specimens of every tropical plant. You must not miss them."

We came over a hill, almost slamming into the back of the Oiapoque bus. An axle had broken, and the bus listed like a floundering ship. The passengers were realistic. They had tied blankets between trees to make sunshades. A man whittled sticks into spears. Boys gathered wood, and a woman had started a fire. They expected to camp here several days. We were the first vehicle to pass in four hours. The etiquette of an Amapá bus disaster resembled that of a shipwreck. The back of our truck became a lifeboat for women and children, while the driver delivered a speech promising to remain with his vehicle until everyone was rescued.

Twenty miles from Calçoene, the jungle vanished and the land, so frequently planted, grazed, and scorched by fires, had become desert. Dust devils spun in the distance, and frail cows stood under palms ripping at weedy grass. There was a single plastic sandal, a plastic bottle, then a pile of charred plastic and tin, a derelict truck, an acre of rusting cans, and, finally, Calçoene.

It was dustier and cruder than Oiapoque, even more a frontier settlement. Unshaven, bare-chested men fired rifles at beer-can targets. Signs said We Buy Gold!, and Gé showed me a bar where on weekends miners sold nuggets and murdered each other while their nimble children swept up gold dust with whisk brooms. Down every street, dirt-smudged children kicked soccer balls, scrawled pictures in the mud, and stared, naked bellies thrust out and mouths open, as we dumped the survivors of the Oiapoque bus disaster at the only hotel.

"This is a simply terrible hotel," Gé said. "They fired the last manager, but still it is terrible." It looked like an asylum managed on a stingy budget. Stranded travelers wearing nightshirts shuffled through a garbage-strewn yard. They slapped dominoes, threw dice, or sprawled asleep in smashed lawn furniture. The bus from Calçoene to Macapá had not run for days, and due to the holiday there would be no bus tomorrow or over the weekend. Already scalpers had cornered the tickets for the following week. Calçoene was bursting with stranded travelers. The hotel and boardinghouses were full, and hammock hooks on porches rented for five dollars a night. New hammocks were sold out. Travelers expected to be stranded and fleeced in Calçoene, but only for a day or two. The rainstorms had quadrupled their agony. Guests at the hotel had hoped to persuade the Oiapoque bus driver to continue to Macapá. Now this was impossible, and we had just increased Calçoene's stranded-traveler population.

"It is always something like this in Calçoene," Gé said. "But never have I seen it so bad." I wondered if the bus-ticket scalpers and hammock-hook renters scattered tacks on the road. "That is not an impossible idea," he said.

"How much to drive to Macapá?" I asked José One.

He considered his imaginary tape deck and said, "Four hundred thousand cruzeiros."

"But we only paid a tenth of that to travel from Oiapoque, and we're at least a third of the way to Macapá."

"True, but now you are in Calçoene." The survivors of the bus disaster were jockeying for sleeping space on the hotel's concrete patio. "If you wish to bargain you may speak with my mother, but frankly you would be wiser to pay me four hundred thousand."

"For five hundred thousand cruzeiros my son will drive you to Macapá," José One's mother said. She sat behind the counter of the family store, a sly, mountainous woman jangling with bracelets and necklaces and surrounded by signs offering to buy or sell gold, silver, anything of value.

"Your son just said four hundred thousand."

"He did not know the conditions here. But since you are already a customer, I will make you a discount of fifteen percent. He will drive you to Macapá for four hundred twenty-five thousand cruzeiros."

"My God! We only paid a hundred francs each from Oiapoque," Gé said, tugging so hard on his earring he risked ripping his lobe.

"But now you are stuck in Calçoene. Maybe my son does not wish to drive to Macapá. Maybe he is tired and wishes to watch the television."

"I'll pay in dollars," I said. She yawned. How could she? The dollar was strong, the cruzeiro weak, and there was a black market.

"I don't know the rate. Maybe you pay in francs. Those I know. She played the keys of her calculator like a pianist. "OK. You pay me eighteen hundred francs."

"That's more than four hundred twenty-five thousand cruzeiros."

She laughed. "Then sell something." She twisted my wrist, examining my watch. "Sell me that."

"I need it."

"Maybe you need to sell it to leave Calçoene. OK. Sell me something else—your shirt." She rubbed it between her fingers. "Take it off, I buy it!" She leaned over the counter to check my shoes, scowling when she saw the canvas boots. "Open your bag. Let's see what you have. Here, have a Fanta." A small boy slammed a bottle in front of me. "For you, our friend, it is free!"

"There's nothing in my bag—"

"Everyone has something to sell. But no T-shirts please. Let's see your camera. Cigarettes? You could buy gold from me with your dollars. Then we calculate a discount, in francs. Throw in your camera, and then we'll convert it all to cruzeiros." Her gold bracelets banged against the calculator keys. She pushed them up her arms and started again.

"I thought you didn't know the rate for dollars."

"I'll find out." She flicked her wrist and the boy disappeared. Finally she proposed a deal involving an almost total swap of my luggage for gold and currency, and the exchange of several currencies. Then I would buy back my own luggage with cruzeiros. The truck became more expensive by the minute.

"This is too complicated. I'll find another truck or take a taxi."

"Ha! Look out there." On cue, a shuddering, low-to-the-ground, unmuffled wreck of a Volkswagen crawled past the open door. "That is the best taxi in Calçoene," she said. "He will do his best, but you will never reach Macapá."

We agreed on twelve hundred francs. I would drop Gé in Amapá, collecting a fare from him, but José One could keep whatever he extorted from whoever rode in the back. In ten minutes he had recruited eight passengers. Several were wrapped in blankets, flushed and shivering with Amapá's legendary malaria. They hoped to be saved at the Macapá hospital. When we left Calçoene, they hugged like immigrants at the Statue of Liberty, then passed around a tin of butter cookies, sang, and pounded on the sides of the truck with joy.

When the lights of Amapá appeared on the horizon, Gé said, "Everyone here catches malaria and suffers. This territory is the worst place in Brazil—maybe in the world—for malaria, and this city is the most malarious place in the territory. It is bad because it is built on a swamp and there are many canals and channels. My friend lives on a canal."

Arriving in Amapá after sunset had disoriented Gé. Several times we stopped for directions while the cab of the Chevrolet filled with mosquitoes. We circled a graveyard filled with picnicking relatives and coasted down a hill lined with lamplit shacks throbbing with music. We stopped at one shaped like a mobile home, and Gé said, "My friend lives here. He is one of France's most celebrated novelists." He mumbled a name I did not recognize. "Every year he escapes his admirers to live anonymously in Amapá. The atmosphere inspires him. He is something of a saint."

We parked, and a fog of mosquitoes settled around the truck. An ascetic-looking man in his fifties greeted Gé. A halo of insects buzzed around his saintly bald head. He shook my hand absentmindedly but did not ask me inside. I considering inviting myself, but it was already seven o'clock and José was anxious to leave. We were still six hours from Macapá. I was tired. I had eaten almost nothing last night, and nothing today but coconut cookies and an orange. Perhaps hunger and exhaustion dulls curiosity, perhaps I was *trop âgé* for all this, but I left without learning who this saint was and what inspiration he drew from this place. I told myself that staying was unfair to the malaria patients, but I really worried that every minute in Amapá shortened the odds on joining them.

José's truck ran on an alcohol fuel that was scarce along this new road. We had left Calçoene with half a tank, and after Amapá we had to stop at the larger settlements to beg for more. We bumped for a mile down a side road to purchase several gallons from a farmer. We siphoned fuel from a drum behind a grocery. One of the malaria patients emerged from underneath a blanket and whispered, "We fear it is the first time this boy takes this road." They worried not that he would lose his way but that he lacked the connections to buy fuel. José cheerfully admitted it was his first time on his own. He was eighteen and had always before driven to Macapá with his father. But I was not to worry, he said, "because I like the voyage." And I liked it too, liked the feeling of accomplishment that comes from a long night journey over rough roads, the distant shacks lit by kerosene lamps and twinkling like stars, and the bats swooping through our headlights — white-tipped bats gliding like sea gulls, nervous fluttery bats, and daredevil bats diving at the windshield.

I liked our stops for fuel and beer. We paused in a courtyard where three generations of a family swung in identical hammocks, singing in unison with the radio. We threw dice in a country store that filled with children who begged sweets and swung on my legs. We blinked our headlights to summon a ferry. It carried us across a black river that upstream, the captain said, ran thick with gold. He unknotted a handkerchief, displaying a "nugget" the size of a peppercorn. We ate omelets in a candlelit bar where José filled one yellow plastic jerry can with beer and the other with alcohol fuel and insisted it did not matter if he confused them. He and his truck could run on either. He told everyone our story: He was driving in a single day from Oiapoque to Calçoene to Macapá, then back to Calçoene without sleep or rest, but he was not tired because he "loved the voyage." He wove the day's events into a narrative that, like the "Twelve Days of Christmas," gained a new verse with each telling. His listeners whistled their appreciation. José was a hero.

The malaria patients stayed in the back, shivering and hugging each other. "Come on, hurry up! Let's go!" they begged as

José drank more beer and added verses, enjoying his celebrity. I offered my seat to one couple, but they refused. They were more comfortable stretched out, and besides, they had not paid for the cabin; it would not be *justice.*

I woke to a whistle blast and found José racing a train running on parallel tracks. The passengers were framed in square windows and silhouetted by yellow bulbs. The train suddenly turned right and disappeared over a hill. I blinked, thinking I had seen a bus or a distant village. But when I checked my map, I saw that for a distance the road followed the railway connecting Macapá to the phosphate mines of Icomiland.

José shouted "Macapá!" and I woke, again unsure of my eyes. We were in the midst of the kind of fanatical Olympic training camp I have always imagined finding in East Germany. Every empty boulevard ended in an athletic field lit by spotlights; everywhere, boys in colorful jerseys kicked soccer balls, punched volleyballs, or shot basketballs. The games were official, played without spectators but refereed by adults. I remembered Gé describing the soccer-mad governor of Macapá: Autographed pictures of stars covered his office walls, and meetings with him revolved around soccer anecdotes. He had converted the city's squares and parks to playing fields for his youthful constituents. Still, there were so many young in Macapá that weekend games were played after midnight in these blazing rectangles of light and sport.

In front of the hotel I shook hands with the malaria patients and paid José in francs, adding a tip that made him smile. It had brought the total to the equivalent of 400,000 cruzeiros, his original price. He drained the beer and said he would return to Calçoene. No, he was not tired; in fact, he might try joining one of the games.

The next morning I pulled open the curtains of my room and saw the Amazon River. It was just across the street and reflected the harsh white light I associate with a nuclear test. Brown waves slapped at a pier. Green poker-chip islands floated on a smoky horizon. The river was fifty miles wide, yet still a hundred miles from the Atlantic. Its mouth had been discovered by a Spanish sea captain who, in the custom of the sixteenth-century navigators, fixed on one latitude and tracked it west across the Atlantic. Since he chose the equator, he arrived at the mouth of the

Amazon, although he imagined himself in the open sea until a crewman noticed the water was fresh.

It was low tide, and barefoot boys were kicking a soccer ball across the mud flats, aiming for a goal marked by driftwood. They sank into soft patches and headed the ball, only to have the wind punch it back. They juggled it off mud-caked ankles and flicked it with graceful hips. They ran downfield in a conga line, copying one another's moves as perfectly as shadows. At first I thought they enjoyed the challenge of wind and mud, but then I saw that on this Saturday morning every lot in Macapá swarmed with boys kicking balls. The next day these same boys were back, sitting on the seawall, impatiently kicking their legs and waiting for the tide to ebb and uncover their field.

As I moved south from Oiapoque, an invisible hand seemed to be turning up the volume. First there was the policeman humming pop music, then the tinny radios of Calçoene and the joyful whoops of the malaria patients. Now speakers in my Macapá hotel were booming out slushy songs. The Japanese waitress wiggled and mouthed the lyrics, and I had to shout my order. This same tape could be heard in the bar, hallway, patio, and, if you flipped the right switch, your room. It drove me out into what my guidebook described as "the formerly decrepit Macapá."

The town had a skyline of steam shovels, cranes, and skeletal buildings wrapped in scaffolding. Billboards tottered over excavations or stood like scarecrows in empty lots, announcing SITE OF FUTURE CULTURAL CENTER, or FUTURE SPORTING PARK TO BE ERECTED HERE. They all carried the governor's name and said Amapá, Future Brazilian State. Elsewhere the Brazilian construction boom had slackened, but in Macapá it continued, fueled by the magnesium mines and the soccer-loving governor's legendary energy.

The streets were gripped by a children's crusade. Uniformed soccer teams marched to playing fields while supporters blew horns, banged strips of tin, and waved pennants. Winners shot their arms into the air and raced about wildly. In a square opposite the cathedral, Macapá's adults hammered together carnival rides and stalls to amuse their children. When I returned at dusk, screaming youngsters packed the seats of a small Ferris wheel. A few lonely adults stood underneath, waving. Boy Scouts had jammed into the cathedral for a special mass, and at outdoor cafés older children served soda pop to younger ones. In a kitchen, a woman cooked while rocking a hammock of children nestled close as kittens. Children sat piled on each other's laps in the miniature planes of the *avião infantil* — the "infants' airplane." The toy planes swung into the night and reappeared seemingly even more overloaded, as if out in the darkness the children had multiplied.

Nowhere in Macapá did I see the clouds of smoke rising from burning forests described by Michael Corser. But I could see that more land-clearing fires were inevitable. This youthful population was the kindling. It was only a matter of time before they outgrew soccer and exploded up that road into the interior.

And nowhere did I see the legions of willing women celebrated by Alberto — although, to be fair, Macapá had figured as an afterthought, and he had lavished the most praise on Belém. Instead of the beautiful and desperate *mucha mujer,* I met Sondra, the best English interpreter in Macapá, I was told. She looked slightly battered, a woman in her thirties who had not had a happy time with men and who had a habit of cringing and hugging herself when I asked a question. Perhaps she was wary because I was a man, or perhaps she wondered why I had hired an interpreter when I could speak a smattering of Portuguese (a question I soon asked myself, since her English was not much better than my college Portuguese). Perhaps she suspected I wanted an "escort," since, as we drove south toward the equator, she said, "For me the marriage is finished. Enough. Enough men too, I say. No more marriage. Never! Understand?" She hugged herself tighter, as if chilled by the words "men" and "marriage." She was twice-divorced, with a teen-age daughter from one marriage and two children from the other. Her second husband had brought her to Macapá from São Paulo, and now she was stuck. "To be a woman in Macapá," she said, "is to be no one."

She was counting on English to change everything. She was six months from her diploma, and she expected to earn a fine living soon as an interpreter and translator. "We must make a treaty now," she insisted. "Next year course is finished and I'm ready. All your books I make into Portuguese. Yes?" She presented a smudged business card.

My interest in the equator to the exclusion of Macapa's traditional attractions unsettled her. "But you must see the zoo, is beautiful. And the beach, is fine, and the village of blacks. Yes?" We compromised, and after the equator I toured these sights. Her "village of blacks" was a clutch of shanties inhabited by the descendants of freed slaves who had preserved some African customs. They hawked handicrafts and entertained visitors with folklore staged in a bar built for this purpose.

Macapá had the Devil's Island of zoos. Its gate swung open on one hinge, and its ticket kiosk was abandoned. We were the only visitors. It was of recent construction, but flashier projects had since claimed the governor's attention. A tree had toppled into a cage, freeing some animals. Seedlings sprouted in the gravel paths and creepers clutched concrete walls. It was a cruel place because the neglected animals lived so near their natural habitats. If the wild boar had escaped from his slimy pit, he could have lumbered into the jungle, joining other wild boars. A monkey swung in a cell within sight of monkeys swinging in trees. Parakeets were jammed in a cage the size of a handbag, chirping at wild parakeets fluttering above. Imagine locking a man in a filthy cage in his own backyard and feeding him scraps, all within sight of his family and neighbors, and you are imagining the Macapá zoo.

Sondra praised the beach at Fazendinha until we arrived, when she admitted she rarely swam here. The sand was dirty and the water too muddy. Instead, we sat in a café managed by children. A boy of fourteen cradling an infant in one arm brought us a Beer Antarctica. She said, "He could be her brother or her father. Her father I bet." She leaned across the table. "But *my* daughter is virgem."

Had she really said that?

"Virgem, *virgem!* You understand?"

I did. But what to say to this announcement?

"Fifteen years old and still virgem." She looked hurt. I was not being appreciative. She held out a picture. "Look! Here she is. Alessondra, still virgem."

I mumbled a compliment.

"You don't understand. All the boys—the black boys—want to make love all the time. They give the girls children and then—whoosh!—they are after another virgem. It is not like that in São Paulo. Listen: It is very hard work keeping a virgem in Macapá."

I had imagined the equator in Macapá celebrated by a sign or line across the road, or perhaps a souvenir stand. But when the asphalt road running south from Macapá to Porto Santana hit the equator, it divided and flowed around a circular Park of the Equator. A foot-high concrete wall cut through the middle of the park for twenty-five yards, marking the equator. It was faced with blue tiles and carried an inscription fashioned from pieces of magnesium. It said: EAST * LINE OF THE EQUATOR * MACAPÁ * BRAZIL * LATITUDE 00'00'00 * WEST. Around the wall was the Garden of the Equator. This featured aloe plants sprouting from the center of automobile tires painted yellow.

Sondra stood straddling the line, with a foot in each hemisphere. "When I arrived in Macapá, I came here the first day and feel a big emotion. I still come often and still it is big emotion." She hugged herself and stared up at the sky. "I think, Here I am, Sondra, standing on the middle of the earth. I close my eyes and see the whole world. Understand? Because I am standing here I can see myself, Sondra, alone on the equator."

She pointed to lines of whitewashed stones I had taken for ornaments. "Look, it is the earth. You don't see?" We crossed the road and climbed a flight of circular stairs to a concrete observation platform. The white stones were arranged in the shape of a world map. The actual equator doubled as the map's equator. I could not believe I would find the equator more extravagantly marked anywhere. This was my Greenwich Observatory.

Two concrete obelisks flanked the wall to the east and west. By lining them up I could sight the equator's path. To the west it crossed a recently cleared field. "There our governor is building a football field," Sondra said with little enthusiasm. "Its middle will be the equator. One team defends the northern hemisphere, the other the south. Is good idea?" I stood behind the western obelisk, sighting to the east, in the direction I was going. A dirt track ran east into the jungle, straight along the equator. I asked where it led.

"Is nothing."

"Is not nothing, it's a road."

"OK. Is road. Let's go to the zoo."

"And I'd like to see where it goes."

She shrugged. "OK. But is nothing interesting there."

Two hundred yards into the jungle we came upon the garbage dump of the southern hemisphere. Sondra smiled. "We go now?" A mile further, workmen bulldozed acres of northern hemisphere jungle. The road crossed a bridge, passed a tumbledown cabin straddling the equator, and disappeared into a swamp of mud. Someone had painted a number on the door of the cabin. I asked why this abandoned house, the only one on the equatorial road, needed an address. What mail had its former residents hoped to receive?

We had turned to leave when a dog barked and a young man opened the door. He wore tattered shorts and the cracked smile of a hermit. He was not surprised to find me on his doorstep, and when Sondra began a laborious explanation he waved his hand and said it was unnecessary. He accepted the celebrity that came with the location. He led us through the first cabin, through a courtyard of pecking chickens, and into a larger shanty to meet his family. He was José Maria, and here was his wife, her sister and her sister's two children, an infant boy and a six-year-old girl wearing a ripped white tutu ringed with pink ruffles.

José Maria had great presence for someone living in a warren of tumbledown shacks on the equator. He squared his shoulders and stared in my eyes even while Sondra translated. This was his "country house." He also had a cabin in Macapá, which he seldom visited. The city was too crowded and noisy. Here on the equator it was calm and cool. "That's right, cool. No one knows why, but in Macapá the equator is cool." It did seem cooler here. I noticed a drop in temperature and a mysterious breeze swirling through his cabin.

"And the equator is lucky," added his wife.

"Yes. Everyone in Macapá would live on the equator if they could."

"Then why don't they?"

"There were others near us." He motioned in the direction of the bulldozers. "But the governor purchased their land and destroyed their cabins. Squatters were evicted without compensation. The governor wishes to build a big solar clock here. He has gone to the courts, but I am lucky, so I will win. Of course, I could buy another house, but it would not be on the equator."

He was a holdout, the only man in the neighborhood refusing to move at any price, the kind of stubborn eccentric who takes up residence underneath a roller coaster, at the foot of a runway, at the edge of a ravine, or on the equator.

He was embarrassed by his Phillips twenty-one-inch color television. He switched it on and apologized for the quality of the picture. It was only three years old, but they watched it all the time. They were saving for a new one.

"You watch it all the time?" I asked.

"Yes, it is always on for someone to watch."

But how could they afford it?

"We are lucky."

The screen filled with a children's ballet, and I was forgotten. Everyone's eyes, Sondra's too, clicked to the picture. The dreamy little girl twirled in clumsy pirouettes, imitating the dancers on the screen. José Maria turned it off, and she fell back into a chair like a spent wind-up toy.

My surprise at finding such grand appliances pleased José Maria and put him in the mood to catalogue his other possessions. He owned twenty hectares planted with banana trees and watermelons. He kept ducks, chickens, a pig, and a cow. They all flourished on the equator, and his friends were jealous. He could even afford pets. His sister-in-law came from the kitchen carrying their monkey, Chico. They also owned four dogs named Here, There, Everywhere, and Cinderella. Last week Cinderella had stolen a shoe, so they had named her after that character in the cartoon. They had seen it on television. Before that, she had another name, and names before that, and they would change her name again, just as soon as she did something noteworthy. They were always changing the names of their pets. It was fun.

Sondra was laughing. "We are lucky to find him. He is a very nice man," she said, astonished such a creature existed.

I had brought a roll of Kennedy half-dollars. When I traveled to Africa for the first time, they had been popular. But as I handed one to José Maria, I realized they were an absurd and dated gift. He had been a child when Kennedy was shot. But he surprised me by saying that yes, of course, they knew about that president, from a movie on television. He was murdered. The bullet went into his head, leaving an ugly wound. The blood gushed out, ruining his wife's clothes. "And we know about the sad history of the murdered family: his brother, another bullet in the head, but not as much blood."

My wife is British and had given me several Jubilee Crowns, also to distribute as presents. I handed one to José Maria and asked what he thought of the Queen. "We know all about her," his sister-in-law said. "She was riding her horse and someone tried to shoot her."

José Maria offered me a gift I could take to the next family I found living near the equator. When I rejected the framed posters of racehorses and a Pakistani wall hanging, depicting the visit of the Magi, as too large, he pulled a small picture off one wall that was so improbable I could not resist taking it on to Africa.

As I left, he collected the women's half-dollars. I had put him a dollar-and-a-half closer to his new television. We shook hands just inside the southern hemisphere, and he asked if I would be returning.

"Of course I'll be back," I said. I was starting here, so I had to return to complete the circle. Then I looked at his shanty, the rutted road, and the governor's busy tractors, and tried to imagine myself returning to Macapá. I would hire Sondra again (would her daughter still be virgem?), walk down the center line of the Soccer Field of the Equator, and find the governor's solar clock, or José Maria with a larger television and the same dogs with new names. I would give him whatever the last equatorial family had given me, and by then I hoped to have learned more than that the earth is round.

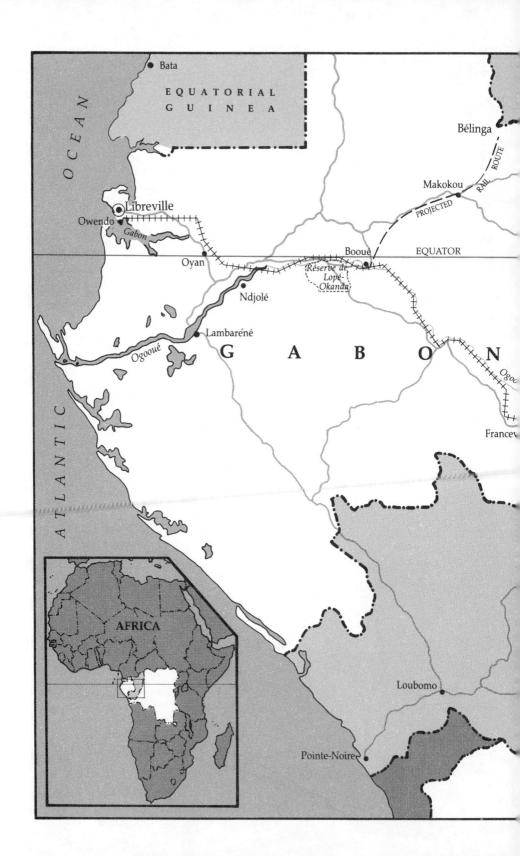

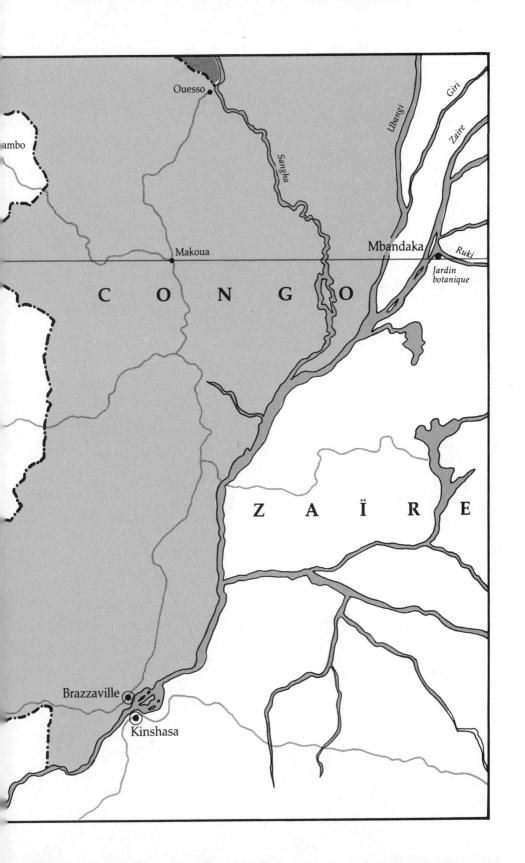

5

THREE MILES EAST OF JOSÉ MARIA'S FARM, THE EQUATOR CUTS across the Amazon for the first time, at its mouth. For the next 2,500 miles it divides the Atlantic into north and south. During this transatlantic passage it just misses St. Paul's Rocks, a cluster of volcanic rocks, ugly, uninhabited, and dangerous. Few sailors go ashore, but Peggy had, and during that rainy evening in Cayenne she had spread photographs across the deck of the *Cowabunga*, showing me rocks frosted with guano rising fifty feet from a boiling sea. The guano was glacier-white, the rocks coal-black, the ocean crayon-blue: the colors of science fiction. I wondered if it was the film or the camera. What photographic tricks had made these colors so stark and vivid? No, Peggy said, they were like that, exactly.

The rocks were an aquatic jungle, with creatures as unaccustomed to humans as those in any tropical forest. Peggy could have easily touched nesting boobies and terns. Sea gulls dive-bombed the *Cowabunga*, slamming into its sails. "I guess they thought my boys were big fish," she said. "They wanted to rip them apart and eat them." She had a picture of a white bird, its open beak pointed at the lens. It was askew and slightly out of focus, like the photograph of a Kamikaze taken by a terrified sailor.

They went ashore, and sharks circled the dinghy. At night, sharks banged into the hull. At sunset, sharks knifed through whitecaps, chasing the terrified flying fish who skittered across the *Cowabunga*'s deck and beached themselves on the rocks, where swarms of crabs devoured them. Her family saw more sharks at St. Paul's Rocks than in months of Atlantic cruising.

Peggy fished and caught a salt-water piranha, snapping its needle teeth even in death. She dropped a lobster trap. It came up pulsing with claws and tails — thirty lobsters, "which was eerie, because we wanted them to celebrate my thirtieth birthday."

They had not anchored there for fun. An Argentine scientist working for Columbia University had chartered the *Cowabunga*. The university had installed an unmanned radar device on St. Paul's Rocks to measure the equator's unpredictable winds, data that might improve the accuracy of global weather forecasts. The computer transmitting this information via satellite was broken. The Argentinian had been sent out with a replacement and had met Peggy's family at a Brazilian marina. They were the only boat people willing to go. "Sure, we needed the money," she said. "But we also wanted an adventure, and we sure got it."

After St. Paul's Rocks, the equator travels two thousand miles across open sea before making landfall at the former Portuguese colony and slaving center of São Tomé. I heard it described as a beautiful island of jungle mountains, volcanic beaches, waterfalls, and cocoa plantations. It also sounded like a good link between Brazil and Africa. Perhaps José Maria's African ancestors had waited there for slavers to ship them to Brazil. And it was a curiosity: the smallest, least-known nation in Africa, a place where plantation slavery continued into the twentieth century, although technically illegal. During the First World War, a São Tomé plantation was offered for sale "complete with bearing trees, buildings, and its Negroes," described as having a value of so much per head. Knowing all this makes it less surprising that after gaining independence from Portugal in 1975, São Tomé became a xenophobic people's republic.

In New York I had spent several days collecting information to use in my letter to the foreign minister. I came upon the account of one traveler who described being befriended by a Senhor

Amorim, "the only white man on the dock, [who] . . . warned us
that so long as we stayed on the island we must never, at the risk
of losing caste, perform any labor more strenuous than pulling up
a chair for a lady. . . . Life on the equator, he said, could be made
agreeable if one were ingenious. He clapped his hands for a
beer."

After a week on São Tomé, this traveler had learned that "In
São Tomé the older workers cross their forearms on their chest
and bow when a white man passes. While maintaining this extraordinary air of subservience, however, the plantation blacks
seemed the happiest, busiest, best-kept set I had seen. They were
all grinning teeth and laughing dark eyes. They were always gay."

The photographs accompanying his article told a different
story. In one, an emaciated man lay on a concrete floor, while an
even thinner man in a tattered undershirt swept the ashes of a
dying fire. The caption was: "For Ill and Weary Workers the Administrator Provides Comfort." In another, a line of barefoot girls
wearing patched rags stood in puddles, balancing bundles of dripping fodder on their heads: "Even the Native Children Have Their
Chores After a Day in the Forest." These were not the photographs or narrative of some Victorian traveler. They appeared in a
1946 *National Geographic.*

In Gabon, the African nation nearest to São Tomé, I met several amateur São Tomé watchers. Much of their information was
second- or third-hand. They said it was too bad I had just missed
São Tomé's first major international conference, a gathering of the
foreign ministers of Portuguese-speaking African countries.
(There are more of these than you might think — five, to be precise.) To entertain them, the government had chartered a plane-
load of eggs, a luxury food in São Tomé. Upon arrival, each
minister was assigned his own antique sedan, and at dinner each
man sat alone at a small table decorated with his national flag.
They stared across the room at one another, silently eating
omelets. In their bedrooms, microphones dangled like snakes
from holes in the wall. After bugging the delegates' rooms, São
Tomé's KGB had discovered a shortage of plaster.

The São Tomé watchers said the country's currency was too
worthless to support a black market. People ate the mangoes they
picked, the manioc they grew, and the fish they caught. Cigarettes
were the best currency, although there was nothing to buy but

more cigarettes, or the plastic sandals sent from East Germany to pay for the island's cocoa crop. Some whites had stayed on. They included the private secretary to the last king of Portugal. He was rumored to be almost a hundred, although he had not been sighted for several years. But it was my opinion, based on talking to an ex–Peace Corps volunteer who had married a São Toméan, that he was long dead. While visiting the island to meet her in-laws, she had stumbled on an abandoned plantation that sounded like the sort of place where a deposed Portuguese king's retired private secretary might have lived. Its veranda was sagging, its ornate ceiling collapsing. Squatters had planted manioc in the or-namental gardens and set cooking fires in the parlor, breaking up antiques and portraits for kindling. It was on an islet, the Isle of Turtles, just off the southern tip of the main island of São Tomé, precisely where the equator first touches land after Brazil.

Since the Isle of Turtles is small and the abandoned Por-tuguese plantation was described as large, it is not unreasonable to assume the equator intersects the property, if not the house itself. I liked this: that on one Atlantic coast, the equator was an-chored by a Portuguese-speaking descendant of slaves, living an independent, television-rich life in a ramshackle cabin; and on the other coast, it first hit the Portuguese-speaking descendants of Africans who, having escaped slavery in Brazil, now lived in the ruins of the civilization that had enslaved them, enjoying their victory.

The equator begins its journey across the African continent thirty miles south of Libreville, Gabon, at a deserted beach backed by swamp and accessible only by sea. The spot is marked by a small, weather-blackened concrete obelisk that has become, in a country with few attractions, a destination for weekend excur-sions. I was told visitors toast the equator with champagne, smashing their empties against the obelisk, and from offshore you can see the shards, twinkling in the sun and marking the line. At first I thought the champagne was celebratory, a treat for the mid-dle of the earth. But after arriving in Libreville, I discovered it was a mundane beverage. The commercial and functionary classes took it to beach picnics as a Briton might pack a thermos of tea, and every year the Gabonese account for more bottles per person than any nation on earth.

Libreville is the capital you would expect of such a country, a city best seen from the backseat of an automobile, preferably an air-conditioned one with tinted windows to dull the sunlight ricocheting off glass-faced buildings. Unlike Dakar or Saigon, it was never a handsome colonial capital, never called the Paris of anything. Still, in a book scarcely out of date, I read about shuttered wooden bungalows buried behind bougainvillaea, a handsome government house shaded by mangoes, forested hills, and a palm-shaded corniche running along an estuary, separating the stores of Lebanese traders from a beach littered with oukome logs that had broken loose from the port during the war. Only the logs, now backrests for French sunbathers, remain from this description. The rest has been bulldozed, cleared, and paved. This occurred when petroleum prices and Gabonese production rose simultaneously to record levels in the mid-seventies, just before Gabon was to host an OAU (Organization of African Unity) conference. Borrowing heavily against future revenues, the government built a fifty-million-dollar, hexagonal Palace of Conferences. It is, boasts an official publication, "a project of prestige," with "the best facilities this side of Paris." There is a banquet hall seating two thousand, forty-five villas for visiting dignitaries, a small zoo, and parking spaces for one fifth of the private cars in Gabon. This ratio is something of a theme. A stadium built for the 1976 Central African Games seats fifty thousand, one fifth of Libreville's population.

Divided highways connect the airport to the Palace of Conferences and to a presidential palace said to have cost $800 million. It stands on the former site of Government House and the cathedral. Other new buildings are scattered higgledy-piggledy along the autoroute, facing the corniche, and across the eroded hills. They are ugly, but not dull. One ministry resembles a porcupine; another is a grain silo. There is a wall of television sets, an Aztec pyramid, and half the Colosseum. The National Museum is a glass ski jump; the Ministry of Energy is an air conditioner. The Chamber of Commerce appears to memorialize General De Gaulle, with a box protruding like a nose from its second floor. One ministry missed the boom. Its functionaries work in a shabby building that doubles as a filling station. An island of working gas pumps sits at its front door, shaded by the same peeling concrete awning that shelters visitors from the rain. This is the Ministry of Justice.

When I first arrived, I wrote in my notebook, "Libreville = Las Vegas?" The buildings were certainly as aggressive and vulgar as casinos. Later I dismissed the comparison as farfetched, but later still I read an interview with the president of Gabon, His Excellency El Hadj (né Albert Bernard) Omar Bongo, and certainly an authority on what had inspired modern Libreville, in which he said, "When you see Las Vegas, it's wonderful; it would be even more wonderful if a small city like that could be created in Gabon."

A large bronze statue of President Bongo stands in a circle at the end of the Boulevard Triomphal de Omar Bongo. One of the president's arms is raised, palm outward in the classic gesture of a traffic policeman. It was a gift, "To the Gabonese People," from the Koreans. North or South? No one seemed to know. The only certainty was that it had been crafted by artisans skilled at bronze Buddhas.

"No! No! Forbidden to photograph," my taxi driver shouted when I asked him to stop. The president was no fool. He knew Europeans would photograph this statue only in order to ridicule it.

As African despots go, President Bongo is a benevolent one, but he bruises easily. He is under five feet tall, although how much is a state secret. He wears high-heeled boots and has banished the word "Pygmy" from Gabon's lexicon. He is also sensitive about the size of his nation. He insists its population exceeds a million, but United Nations and World Bank studies put it at less, so President Bongo forbids their circulation. When a French publisher brought out an unflattering biography, he retaliated by banning for six weeks any news from or about France in the government media. Even the word "France" was prohibited. Since Gabon is a former French colony, with considerable commercial and military ties to that country, these decrees tested the skills of the Gabonese censors, who were, I was told, overseen by expatriate Frenchmen.

The unwritten canons of despotic etiquette pronounce it unseemly for a leader to win an "election" by a perfect score, yet few can bear to tally less than 99 percent. In 1973, President Bongo triumphed by 99.6 percent. In the most recent election, held by custom every seven years on his birthday, he bettered his margin to 99.85 percent. Even so, leaving nothing to chance, he later attached an amendment to the constitution of Gabon's only legal political party restricting candidates in future elections to thé Secretary General–Founder of the Democratic Party of Gabon — in other words, President Bongo.

In most African markets, you can purchase cloth bearing a portrait of the country's leader. And you can turn on the television or buy a newspaper and see this leader reviewing singing women, cheering crowds, and schoolchildren, all sporting garments cut from this material. It is not thought odd for a man to salute or applaud hundreds of his own dancing, singing, or marching portraits. But President Bongo had improved on this. A magazine in my hotel room showed him dressed in a shirt decorated with his own picture. You had to wonder: What kind of man finds joy in wearing himself?

If I stayed in Libreville several days I might find out. My arrival coincided with the annual conference of the African-American Institute (AAI), a nonprofit organization that sponsors scholarships, exhibits, lectures, conferences, and performs other good works. For a week, American academics, politicians, bureaucrats, and businessmen invited by the institute would be meeting in Libreville with politicians from African nations to discuss the usual topics: apartheid, economic development, foreign meddling in African affairs, and famine. I could be an "official observer" at this conference, a prospect that became more appealing when I learned that official observers were included in the opening-night banquet at President Bongo's $800-million palace, scheduled to begin two hours after the famine symposium.

Had I considered carefully two facts of life in Gabon, I might not have sought out Mr. Emile Mandoukou, counselor to the minister and director general of tourism and leisure. Fact one: Gabon has fewer than a million people; fact two: It has about fifty government ministers and secretaries of cabinet rank. In this way, each of Gabon's forty tribes has its man in the government, a system that may be politically astute but that has created a tribe of idle senior functionaries with a small, but sometimes sharp, appetite for work.

An African in New York recommended Mr. Mandoukou as a

man who could answer any question, resolve any problem. I hoped he might suggest a way of reaching the beach-side equatorial obelisk. I also wanted to ask how far I could follow the equator into Gabon's interior, and if it was possible to cross the Congolese frontier. The new Transgabonaise Railway and the main road from Libreville both meet the equator near the village of Oyan. Then the railway runs parallel and a few miles south of the equator until Booué, where it forks into a "projected" northern branch and a southern one under construction. The road forks before Booué. Its northern branch is an "improved" dirt road as far as Makokou, where my map said it becomes an "earth road," "liable to be impracticable in bad weather." After a hundred and fifty miles of impracticability it crosses into the Congo, becoming "recognized or marked track." On this map, all the official African border posts are marked by colored flags, but there are none on this isolated crossing. After Booué, the equator runs through tropical forest, staying just south of this dirt track and not touching another significant road or town until Makoua, in the Congo. Then it disappears into miles of forest and swamp before crossing the Zaïre (formerly the Congo) River at the city of Mbandaka, in Zaïre. The government of Zaïre insists that Europeans enter only through Kinshasa, and my visa was stamped to that effect, meaning that even if I succeeded in crossing into the Congo by land, I would still have to travel south to the Congolese capital of Brazzaville, then cross to Zaïre River to Kinshasa, taking a riverboat north to rejoin the equator at Mbandaka. So I wanted to know from Mr. Mandoukou if there was any traffic — trucks, bush taxis, anything — on that dirt road between Gabon and the Congo. And did the road really exist? Several Peace Corps volunteers doubted it. I feared spending a week or more reaching the frontier only to find it impassable, either for political or practical reasons. I had given myself eight weeks to cross equatorial Africa, but I might easily waste half of these if I traveled deep into Gabon only to have to retrace my steps to Libreville.

The walls and door of Mr. Mandoukou's office were padded in an expensive leather that matched his sofa and chairs. He closed the door, and the leather muffled the sound of his secretary pecking at her typewriter. He stopped fiddling with an expensive desk set to ask, "Are you an official tourist?"

I did not like the sound of "official tourist." What was an

unofficial one? Probably me. And a hundred miles west, in São Tomé, a tourist was automatically a criminal. On the other hand, Mr. Mandoukou was counselor to the director general of tourism, so perhaps he would be pleased if I described myself as "tourist."

He looked incredulous. "Do you have a tourist visa?" Later I learned that most "tourists" in Gabon were resident expatriates and European businessmen taking weekend excursions. Package tourists or individual travelers from anywhere but France, which owned the country almost as surely as it did French Guiana, were rare.

"Of course I have a tourist visa," I said, for the first time in my life demanding to be labeled a tourist. I changed the subject to the equatorial obelisk. Had Mr. Mandoukou heard of it? And who had put it there? Was there an inscription?

"That is an affair for the minister of culture and arts."

Well, then, could Mr. Mandoukou tell me about excursions to this marker? Could the Ministry of Tourism recommend a boat?

"For that I would suggest the minister of transport and merchant marine."

I spread out my map, pointing to the track entering the Congo. Could I cross this border?

"The minister of the interior would know about that."

"And the condition of the roads? How many days would it take . . ."

"The minister of transport." Mr. Mandoukou stared at his leather walls. "Are you sure you have a tourist visa?"

I looked in my passport. The visa said *Affaires* —"Business." When I applied to the Gabonese embassy, I explained I was following the equator and would write something. "Actually, it's a business visa."

"Aha! What is your business?"

"I told you. I'm following the equator." I was beginning to dislike Mr. Mandoukou.

"Why?"

"Because it's there. And I plan to write —"

Mr. Mandoukou shot forward like a missile. His eyes, before hooded and sleepy, glistened with excitement. I was going to provide him — or, more precisely, his secretary — with days of paperwork. "Then you are a journalist, and you must consult the minister of information, immediately. Naturally you cannot leave

Libreville until you have received the proper authorizations. The prefects and subprefects in every region on your itinerary must be alerted to your visit. This is only common courtesy.

"First write a letter explaining the precise nature of your research and what you wish to learn about Gabon. Attach it to a letter of introduction from your ambassador. Then write covering letters introducing yourself to the minister of the interior, the minister for culture and arts, the minister of information, the minister of transport, and, of course, to us, the Ministry of Tourism. Come to think of it, you should write to all the ministers."

"All! But I thought there were fifty."

"Less than that, but don't worry." Mr. Mandoukou waved a hand. "I will help you cut the list. That is why we are here, to help visitors."

I felt like a rabbit snared in a trap, but I was not entirely without sympathy for the hungry hunter. Mr. Mandoukou was starved for work. "I may not be an official tourist," I said, suddenly inspired, "but I am an official observer to the African-American Institute convention." I pulled out my official letter of welcome, written by his Ministry of Tourism and encouraging us to "see as much of Gabon as possible, travel and meet the people." Checkmate to you, Mr. Mandoukou.

He fell silent, studying this letter for several moments before saying, "Yes . . . I suppose you can travel anywhere as an AAI delegate. But . . . but you cannot travel as a journalist! So what does that mean? Well, yes, you can go places, but no, you cannot take notes, or remember your experiences for publication. Yes, you may travel as a conference delegate, but not as a journalist. But that is impossible since you are a journalist. So you see, you must still write to the ministers and receive the necessary authorizations." He slumped in his chair, exhausted by this performance.

"I don't have a typewriter," I said weakly.

"Not to worry. There is a good secretarial service in town. It is owned by a friend. I will make certain they do not overcharge you." He jumped up to find a telephone directory. "Here! Take down this number. And your letters must be in French, so you will need help with the final translation. I know of an agency that will do that cheaply. Be sure to mention my name."

He picked up my letter of introduction and summoned his

secretary, saying, "Here, copy this immediately for Mr. Clarke. Ten copies—no, better make it twenty-five." I could not decide what to think of Mr. Mandoukou. He really believed he was being a tremendous help.

In fifteen minutes I had negotiated the ministers down to five. As a further gesture of goodwill Mr. Mandoukou agreed to write letters of introduction. As I left, he said, "Please do not worry yourself. I will expedite everything. I promise you all the necessary papers to leave Libreville, within two weeks at the latest."

"Do you think Gabonese journalists in the United States must obtain these permissions before visiting the American countryside?"

"But of course!"

There was nothing more to be said. Mr. Mandoukou was sincere. I changed hotels, telling the first I was leaving for Paris, but I had not heard the last of Mr. Mandoukou.

Libreville discouraged walking. There were few sidewalks, and shoulders were dangerous because the Gabonese drove with the intensity of the French—following closely, swerving suddenly to pass—but without their skill for avoiding catastrophe by millimeters. To be on foot in Libreville was to be in peril, and during the weekend I saw a Peugeot in a store window and a taxi that had dived into a house, first crushing a woman's legs. The climate was also hard on pedestrians. Every day the weather was different, but only slightly so: cloudy and humid, or sunny and still, or stormy and gray, but with so much heat and glare that I soon felt like a small roast in a large microwave, cooked to the bone.

But walking was the best way to see the African city behind the European facade. In many African capitals, the European center is miles from the African slums. But in Libreville, the huddles of shanties, creeks stewing with sewage, and ragged children were just behind the downtown banks, hotels, and government palaces. Libreville's slum dwellers, many of them immigrants from neighboring countries, distinguished themselves from those in countries far more wretched by the quality and quantity of the garbage they used to construct their homes. They had the Styrofoam blocks that had cradled Asian electronic marvels, the cinder blocks and steel reinforcing bars left from the

OAU boom, wooden refrigerator crates big as outhouses, and the heavy cardboard boxes that brought Granny Smith apples from South Africa. In fact, Libreville was bursting with more choice refuse than its people could build into their lives. It piled into drifts behind ministries and beside highways. Scoured for their valuable treasures, these heaps moved, mysteriously and at night, growing more putrid as they reached ever poorer neighborhoods.

It was not by chance that Libreville was a city of hovels behind modern facades. A city ordinance required structures facing paved streets to be constructed in concrete. And there seemed to be another code requiring the offices within these concrete facades to be staffed by a facade of Gabonese. I changed a hundred dollars in a bank, and for twenty minutes a floor of Gabonese clerks, tellers, and managers of increasing seniority checked my passport and traveler's checks, until finally someone took everything into an office where I saw a bald Frenchman recompute the calculations and approve the transaction. Gabonese occupied desks in the outer office of an African airline, but when I asked about changing a ticket, the clerk disappeared into the rear to consult a Frenchwoman. And so it went: a front office of Gabonese made sullen by their obvious humiliation, and behind every frosted glass door the squiggly silhouette of the Frenchman-in-charge.

About thirty thousand French lived in Gabon, most in Libreville, where they approached 10 percent of the population, far more than when Gabon had been a colony. They managed the airport and the army, advised government ministers, taught in the schools (where there were more French teachers than Gabonese), and were involved in major commercial transactions. They liked to be behind things: behind hotel receptionists, cashiers, air-traffic controllers, and ministers—and, for all I knew, behind President Bongo too. They were vigilant when their health or comfort was involved, so you saw them watching the salad being washed in restaurant kitchens, fixing air conditioners, and measuring the bacteria in swimming pools.

Gabon's fabled wealth was also, like its independence, something of a facade. Behind the glittering per capita income of over four thousand dollars a year, four times greater than the next wealthiest black-African country and forty times greater than the poorest, were statistics as squalid as the hovels behind the Las

Vegas architecture. Gabon had health and welfare indexes equivalent to a country with a tenth of its wealth, with the ninth highest death rate and the second worst infant-mortality rate in the
world. The statistical survey I consulted said, "Despite apparent
prosperity, the educational and health indicators are uniformly
negative."

Gabon is not the first place where sudden royalties from an
oil boom have been poorly distributed or squandered. What made
it unusual was that the champagne and foie gras, the bowling
alleys and windsurfers, were making people sullen rather than
gay. Everywhere I stumbled across fights, exploding as suddenly
and violently as the city's rainsqualls. Two market women slapped
each other, ripped dresses, and rolled in the dirt. Two men
bumped fenders and threw punches. I had never seen Africans
so tightly wound. While I waited to attend the post–famine–
symposium banquet at the palace, I tried to discover just who,
besides the leggy Frenchwomen long-jumping open sewers to
reach the boutiques, was having a jolly time with all this money.

Certainly not the students at Omar Bongo University, where
I gave an informal lecture. My audience of future Mandoukous
stared back with dead eyes. Their professors prodded them to ask
questions. Silence. Finally a boy wondered if I did not feel terrible
when receiving a poor review. He knew there were many newspapers in America, so the possibilities for embarrassment struck
him as huge. The others warmed to this theme. They wanted to
know if I kept my family from reading poor reviews. Did I pick
subjects that minimized the possibility of losing face? Writing
anything struck them as extraordinarily risky. Afterwards, their
French professor told me not to be upset. "It's always that way
here. No excitement. No curiosity. They're here to sit at their
desks for several years so they can have a job in the government.
That's it. The university is dead." His colleague disagreed. "No,
not dead. That implies it was once alive. This place was stillborn."

Nor did the Gabonese shopping in Libreville's markets seem
to be enjoying their money. At the municipal market of Mont
Booué, where I went to buy a pair of sandals, the shoppers were
apathetic and the merchants surly. Those on the upper level sold
silk ties, narrow Italian shoes that must have pained most African
feet, perfume, and leather bags, all marked with the symbols of
famous designers but poured into heaps, like onions. The "Ital-

ian" shoes had cardboard insoles, the stitching on the "Vuitton" handbags was unraveling, and the "French" perfume smelled like the free cologne in an airline toilet. The only items labeled correctly were the plaits of black hair wrapped in plastic and stamped Product of Korea.

One flight below this bogus luxury was the filthiest food market I have seen in Africa. The concrete floor was slippery with fish guts, rotted produce, and offal. Pyramids of garbage flanked the stairway. Much of the food was imported: mushy Spanish oranges, bruised apples, and blackening tangerines, with little stickers saying Maroc. Everyone had dumped their spoiled produce on Gabon. A few hundred Hmong refugees would have made short work of this place.

I finally bought my sandals in the largest supermarket in Africa, the Hypermarché M'Bolo ("Welcome"). It was evening, and in the parking lot frogs croaked in puddles and two boys trained flashlights on a dead snake. A confetti of box tops and Styrofoam squiggles littered the ground, the refuse of a people impatient to taste or touch the novelties inside. Once, temperate-zone peoples had gorged on tropical products like pepper, mangoes, and avocados, so who was I to stand in the Hypermarché parking lot, watching with disapproval as Gabonese families streamed out of this huge floodlit store, grimly pushing their overloaded shopping carts?

The M'Bolo had 3,800 square meters of imported food and gadgets, clerks trained in Europe, and thirty check-out counters. It was brightly lit and hot. Customers streamed with sweat. The French shopped from lists, tipping boxes to check prices. The Gabonese shopped with the detachment of sleepwalkers or the frenzy of looters. One family hurried down the aisles, seizing whatever they touched: a crock of paté, a child's toy, a toaster, Benedictine, and boxes of that dried toast from France that crumbles when you smear it with anything. They filled two baskets, stopped abruptly, and wheeled for the cashier. An elegant woman walked with the jerky gait and blank expression of the risen dead. She chose at random, handing her purchases to a servant. At the end of one aisle she stared at her cart, only half full. She retraced her steps, adding enough frozen fish fillets, canned coq au vin, and wine to fill it.

I remembered a description of the early "silent trade" between Europeans and coastal Africans. The Europeans piled up guns, beads, tobacco, and rum, then stepped back. A few yards away, Africans set out the equivalent in gold, ivory, and slaves. Each side dickered by adding and subtracting to its heap. Slaves were measured against beads and silk and moved like poker chips. When everyone was satisfied, they gathered up the booty and left, wordlessly. And despite the ringing cash registers and clattering shopping carts, there was something of the silent trade about the Hypermarché M'Bolo.

I was told that Glass was Libreville's most traditional neighborhood. It had the city's oldest buiding, the Baraka church, also known as the American church, since Presbyterian missionaries from Boston had built it in 1845. They mistakenly believed the Gabon estuary to be a mighty river that would take them to millions of unreached heathen in the interior. Instead, it is a tease, leading nowhere. The British and French were also interested in Glass, the British as a trading center, and the French as a port for their anti-slavery patrols. While the Yankees were building their mission, a French naval officer was persuading the king of Glass to sign a treaty giving France the exclusive right to found a settlement. The missionaries accused the French of filling the king with rum, and the people of Glass protested, raising American and British flags over the mission compound. French troops fired into a crowd of protesters, leaving bullet holes in the Baraka church. The *tricouleur* went up in place of the Stars and Stripes, but the American pastors remained, and for decades Glass was anti-French. The Baraka congregations stubbornly conducted their services in English, ignoring French missionaries and carving English epitaphs on their gravestones.

Glass resembled the back streets of a small Caribbean city. There were random breadfruits, lively children, and sagging cabins. The Baraka church was locked, but I found its pastor asleep on the rectory porch. He was a watery-eyed old man who had preached here fifty years. Pointing down the hill to the estuary, he said, "There! Precisely there the Portuguese cut their damned stairs. When the slaves climbed down to the ships, it was their last walk in Africa. And in this very spot, fifty families would pass their final evening in Africa." His house sat on the same foundation and was constructed from the wood of the Portuguese slave barracks. "Baraka" comes from the Portuguese *baracao*—"barracks."

He struggled to his feet. "Look, I'm an old man, tired all the time, but I'll open the church for you because you're American and it's your church." He descended from the porch on an iron staircase, "built in London but installed by you Americans in 1845." He gripped the railing, wincing as if this were his last African walk. If he fell, his legs would have gone snap.

The church was a wooden rectangle sitting on stone pillars above the insects and damp, like a back-road Baptist church in the American South. The floor was swept clean, the altar adorned by a simple wooden cross. The pastor said, "They cut our floorboards in Boston and brought them to us in 1842." He sighed. "But I have forgotten the day. The American missionaries Wilson and Griswold also arrived in 1842, on June twenty-second. We don't know the date of these benches because they came from the barracks. The slaves, they sat on them. Every Sunday we sit where they sat."

He eased into a rickety chair behind the pulpit. "Made in Madeira and brought by the Portuguese slave-traders. I forget the day, but it is an object for a museum."

"Is there a written history of the church?" I asked.

"No, our history is not in a book." He pointed to the ceiling. It was low and made from plywood panels strengthened by a steel cable. "In 1927 the roof split open and we made those repairs. In 1962 our church split open, and that has never been repaired." He gestured across the street to a one-story concrete building that resembled a car wash. "The other Baraka church. After 1962, half our congregation left and built that church. It was not a question of religious doctrine, merely a scandal."

"What kind of a scandal?"

"Of a personal nature. It is delicate," he said.

"Do your young people know?"

They did. Oral history, with its fondness for detail and vivid imagery, kept the wounds raw, just as elsewhere in Africa it keeps disputes between villages and tribes simmering for generations.

"On the fifth of January 1982 a French evangelist came to mediate," he said. "Some people became reconciled and worshiped together, but when he left they fought." And now the two

Baraka churches, one wood and the other concrete, faced each other across a dirt lane.

The pastor led me to the cemetery. Time had blurred some inscriptions, but he remembered the epitaphs and whom they commemorated. He knew the stones were "Vermont marble, cut in Boston just for this church," and that the original missionaries lay "shaded by the breadfruit trees they planted." Flowers decorated even the earliest graves. Not many nineteenth-century clergymen, buried in their own parish cemeteries, are as well remembered or lie in plots as well tended.

Pointing to one, the pastor said, "You see, 1954, and we are still using English. This really *is* your church." He wanted to know why Americans did not visit more often. The congregation was disappointed. The American ambassador came only on Thanksgiving. "Go tell your Americans they will feel at home in the Baraka church. They would do us a great service to worship here." He lowered his voice. "Monsieur, we need the Americans. Our congregation, it shrinks and shrinks."

Real American parishioners might lure back the young. Faith healers, Krishnas, and fundamentalist sects practiced in exploiting the unease that accompanies sudden wealth in a poor land had descended on Libreville. "Our young follow the foreign healers, saying that before they felt bad and now the healers make them feel good again." He looked around furtively, as if preparing to utter a dangerous heresy. "Our young people are troubled by the riches." He shook his head. "Monsieur, there is simply too much money in Gabon." But still I pressed money on him, a donation for the church. "I would prefer you come to our service," he said.

When I returned on Sunday, the taxi dropped me between the old and new Baraka churches. People arriving for the ten-o'clock services stared. Which church would this strange white man choose? I would like to report disliking this attention, but in truth I sometimes enjoy the drama of "the white man in Africa." I teased my audience, hesitating and pretending indecision, sticking my head into the new Baraka church before crossing the road to enter the old, where the congregation was smaller and more elderly.

Our service began first. We shouted a hymn, and during our Bible reading I heard its echo, the same hymn sung even louder across the street. And so it went. We prayed and they boomed out a Psalm. We recited the same Psalm and they prayed. Our liturgy was spare, in the spirit of the Boston Calvinists. They had drums, amplified instruments, and whoops of joy. Our sermon, "How to Live in Jesus Christ," condemned idleness, riotous living, and the pursuit of earthly riches. It was delivered by a middle-aged man in a banker's pinstripe to a counterpoint, from across the street, of drums, shrieks of pleasure, and hymns sung to a disco cadence. Two girls in front jiggled to the seductive beat. The pastor was right. Without some novelty, some real American parishoners, this church would lose its young.

But afterwards, standing on the front steps, I wondered if either church would survive. The Americans had chosen a fine site for their mission, a breezy hill with a view of the estuary. Perhaps too fine. At the bottom of the hill, cranes hovered over the new Sheraton. Other buildings were rising along the road from Libreville to Glass. The next boom would bring an autoroute, government offices, and hotels. Six more Hypermarchés were promised, one somewhere in Glass.

On the afternoon preceding the banquet in the Presidential Palace, delegates and observers to the African-American Institute conference met in the auditorium of the Palace of Conferences to hear welcoming speeches from President Omar Bongo and his cousin, Foreign Minister Martin Bongo. Afterwards we would adjourn to a meeting room to discuss the African famine that was at this moment on the front pages of American and European newspapers, prompting rock stars to throw concerts, congregations to fast, schoolchildren to donate lunch money, and starving Chadian peasants nine hundred miles north of Libreville to whack the tops off anthills searching for edible seeds.

The main auditorium of President Bongo's conference palace was, in size, between the United Nations Security Council and General Assembly. We sat underneath a towering dais and around a five-sided, felt-topped conference table. There was a spectators' gallery with rows reserved for "Members of Government," "Senior Functionaries," and "The Diplomatic Corps." Lines of women wearing red or yellow T-shirts bearing portraits of President Bongo filled the last rows. They were rival teams. The reds stood to one side of the center aisle, the yellows on the other. The guards shut the doors and they started.

The reds shouted "Ya-ya, ya-ya yiddy-yiddy, biddy-biddy-bo-bo *Bongo!*"

The yellows came back with "Sooo-soo, sock good, so good, bohohohoho. . . . Bongo!

It was a competition, with each side trying to clap and sing President Bongo's praises louder than the other. The team captains blew whistles into microphones, and the sound came screaming back from speakers suspended from the ceiling.

This praise-singing of African politicians is known as *animation* and is usually performed outdoors at independence-day parades, on airport runways, or before reviewing stands. It is high-spirited, and it is often the best part about the arrival or departure of any VIP. But here, the noise was trapped in a windowless, frigid, acoustically perfect hall, and the dancers' movements were restricted by the rows of padded chairs, their feet mired in a swamp of thick carpeting.

Having heard President Bongo's name sung at ear-splitting volume, seen his picture on posters and shirts, and read his name in every headline (today's was PRESIDENT KOUNTCHÉ OF NIGER WRITES TO PRESIDENT BONGO), driven down his boulevard, and lectured at his university, I had begun to think of myself as being not so much in Gabon as in the "Nation of President Bongo." I felt a curious intimacy with him, so that, as the band crashed once more through the national anthem, the Bongo women shrieked his name, and he emerged through a door, my heart pounded in anticipation.

The contrast between his size and the pyrotechnics preceding his appearance was out of *The Wizard of Oz.* He wore the polished, high-heeled black boots and the droopy moustache of a Mexican villain. His smile was weary, a smile that said, "It is tiresome for me to hear my name shrieked and see my picture worn, but I allow it because it gives my people pleasure." More impressive was what President Bongo did *not* look like: He did not look cruel, sadistic, or stupid. His country's wealth had allowed him to become a good-natured despot, and he looked it.

His bodyguards were Moroccans, thin as whippets, with busy eyes. They blocked the exits, arms folded, their faces lit by a red glow from illuminated signs saying SORTIE. Gabonese security men stood nearer the president, but the Moroccans had the exits. The message was: You can kill him, but you'll never leave alive.

President Bongo spoke about nuclear arms control. Only at the end, in passing, did he mention the famine, and then only to say, "We would particularly welcome more contributions from the United States." This even though in Gabon, the richest country in black Africa, there was no special appeal. He wished us "great prosperity," and we filed upstairs for the famine symposium.

The African participants quickly steered the discussion to more comfortable subjects: South Africa; the need for an African perspective on the nuclear arms race; and colonialist meddling in African affairs, all subjects scheduled for meetings on the following days. A Sudanese diplomat charged the major powers with forcing African countries to make costly arms purchases. He said, "Resources needed for other things are put into armaments and the military . . ." A trumpet fanfare drowned out the rest. Beneath our windows, President Bongo's military band was pounding out the national anthem.

"Military expenditures forced on Africa by the powers . . ." Another crashing of cymbals and tooting of trumpets as the band, dressed in elaborate comic-opera costumes, launched into a stirring French march. An honor guard of motorcyclists gunned engines.

I looked around the room. The wife of one American congressman had sucked in her cheeks to keep from laughing, but no one else saw any irony in this. They leaned forward, cupping ears to hear "Global interdependency has became dependency."

Apparently these words meant everything; the context in which they were spoken was irrelevant. How else to explain that a conference whose stated concerns were South Africa, famine, economic underdevelopment, and European meddling in African affairs had chosen to gather in a country where the president was guarded by Moroccan mercenaries and the notorious mercenary leader Bob Denard was permitted to operate a private security company? A country whose stores sold disguised South African produce and that had more French now than when it was a colony? The delegates had brought their worries about African overpopulation to a place where exotic strains of venereal disease had sterilized a good portion of the population, and the government paid bonuses to women having more than twelve children. They were meeting in a "palace of conferences" that was a paradigm of the wasteful prestige projects everyone now condemns. Many were staying in the hotel that had been the headquarters for the Rhodesian pilots who had delivered clandestine shipments of Rhodesian beef to Gabon, and for white mercenaries who had raided Marxist Benin. President Bongo's military band had almost drowned out their discussion of wasteful military expenditures. And they would follow this famine symposium — at which famine was hardly discussed — with a banquet in an $800-million presidential palace.

The only palace that President Bongo's resembled was Caesar's Palace, Las Vegas. Both had grandiose fountains and entrances and the same ugly massiveness, and inside both you found mirrored walls and security men with fake smiles. A table ran down the center of the banquet hall, splitting into two branches along the far wall. I paced it off. There was a hundred yards of food, tightly packed: platters of chickens and cold meat, heapings of rice and plantains, stews bubbling in chafing dishes, slabs of fish, and pink-frosted cakes sitting above it all on pedestals, like angry boils. The hall was arranged for five hundred, a yard of food for every five guests.

Each table had a centerpiece of vintage Bordeaux and French mineral water. Gabonese dignitaries filled the front tables. The men wore suits or tuxedoes, and their wives wore plaits of Korean hair and too many jewels, as if they had been magnetized and shot through Madame Bongo's new atrium of boutiques.

The presidential party arrived in a flying wedge of Moroccans. Everyone jumped up and applauded. Food was set before the Bongos. An impatient, insect humming came from the crowd. Men pushed back chairs and leaned toward the tables. A bell sounded and an amplified voice said, "The president has been served." The guests shot from their chairs, rushing the buffet. I stood looking down the table. A chorus line of hands lifted serving spoons dripping with food.

I sat next to the Reverend Stanley Mogoba, a Methodist minister on the board of the South African Council of Churches. During the famine symposium, he had said Africa's problems could only be solved by a spiritual renewal, particularly among its leadership. "We must ask ourselves what kind of a man allows himself to be a tool of foreign interests, rather than put his own people's interests first," he had said. "What kind of a man steals from his own people who are starving? These men must change from the inside before Africa changes on the outside."

Now he shook his head over the small fish fillet he had selected. "There is too much, simply too much food here," he said. "And this place, there is too much of it too. To be discussing famine and then come here on the same day . . . I don't know."

On my other side was Mr. Mwamufiya, a Zaïrian with the African Development Bank. He was quiet and serious, an expert on African highways and transportation systems. "It is a great shame," he said in his precise English, "that we cannot fly all this food to Ethiopia." He looked around the table. There was no reaction. "I'm serious. Perhaps Mali would be a better destination. It's closer, and you could land this food in Bamako in three hours. It might still be hot."

With dessert came bottles of vintage champagne, Dom Pérignon 1976. The tables of delegates received one or two bottles, the tables of Gabonese functionaries three or four. Afterwards we filed downstairs to the president's theater for the after-dinner show, past a bar where a mob of functionaries chugged champagne from beer mugs. In the theater, a handsome young Frenchwoman whom I shall call Patrice placed herself next to me. As she spoke she touched my arm lightly, holding her face inches away with her eyes fixed on mine. She was easy to like.

I asked what she did in Gabon.

"I work here in the palace." She waved a delicate hand. "I had left my husband and was in Paris looking for work and then, luckily, I found this job."

And what was it?

"Oh, I help the president solve his problems."

And what kinds of problems were her specialty?

"Oh, I advise him on social problems." She wanted to know how long I was staying. She knew Gabon well and could help me. Perhaps I could come back to her apartment tonight? I hesitated. Well, how about lunch tomorrow? Or dinner? Drinks? I agreed to dinner, but only if I returned to Libreville on my way to the Congo.

The show was billed as an evening of Gabonese folklore.

There was a nervous emcee in a ruffled shirt, a band in red tuxedos playing electric guitars, clumsy square dancers dressed like South American peasants, and more chanting and whistle-blowing from the red-shirted Bongo women. Patrice put her head in her hands. "This is terrible. I've never seen these dances before. Where did they find them? It's all made up. The president is doing it for you. He thinks this is what you Americans like."

"It is what we like," I said, thinking of a Las Vegas floor show. "But perhaps this is the wrong American audience." But I was mistaken. As we left, one of the delegates, keen to admire anything African, said, "That was great, good as any Broadway show. In fact, we should raise some money and bring them to Broadway."

"Pretty good party for a Moslem country," said another.

"It's actually ninety-five percent Christian," I said.

"Then what's all this 'El Hadj Omar Bongo' business?" He had not known that the president's conversion was motivated more by realpolitik than by religious fervor. It had occurred in the mid-seventies, a ploy to curry favor with the Arab oil countries. Other American delegates shared this misconception and, fearing the banquet would be dry, had gathered beforehand at the bar of the Intercontinental for double martinis.

"So what did you think of Patrice?" asked a diplomat from the American embassy. I said she seemed uncommonly curious and friendly. "That's her job. She's an intelligence agent. She spies for France on the American community." I started to laugh. "No, I'm serious. She specializes in the Peace Corps."

"She must be a very junior spy." It was too fantastic — a pretty French agent watching the Peace Corps in Gabon. On the other hand, during the sixties the Peace Corps had been expelled from Gabon, and it was rumored that the French, always jealous of American influence in their former colonies, had engineered it.

An Ethiopian who worked for the Gabonese information office in New York stopped me in the palace lobby. He was the man responsible for sending me to Mr. Mandoukou in the first place. "Mr. Mandoukou is very upset," he said. "He is still waiting for your letters."

"I'll be dropping them off first thing tomorrow."

"Good. I will tell him." A train left Libreville early the next morning, and now I would have to be on it.

6

THE WESTERN TERMINUS OF THE TRANSGABONAISE RAILWAY, one of the most costly civil-engineering projects anywhere, is a concrete blockhouse bordering a rutted parking lot. The main purpose of this railway is to move Gabon's rich mineral and forest reserves from the interior to Libreville's port of Owendo. Passenger service had started five years earlier, but already the toilets were closed and the walls smeared with dirt, and the clock was missing a hand. ACCÈS AUX QUAIS said a sign pointing to the only platform. Another, copying a regulation enforced in large French stations, cautioned that this access was forbidden to those not holding tickets or "platform tickets." The clerk claimed to have exhausted his change, and a prominent sign threatened a large fine for boarding without a ticket. This was a good racket. The station was isolated, and there was nowhere to change large bills. I paid with several small ones. The clerk slid them into his drawer and demanded exact change from the next passenger. This was the only train of the day, and some were so desperate they allowed him to keep their change. Those with small notes sold them to other passengers at a premium. Several women bargained for change with arriving taxi drivers. A loudspeaker played, again and again, the chimes that precede an announcement in a French station, whipping up a low but profitable level of hysteria. As we pulled out, several men were cursing and waving large bank notes at the ticket window.

We ran through thick forest or deep cuttings and I saw mostly green curtains of foliage or red walls of soil. Deeply tanned Europeans supervised work crews. The identical concrete stations had ACCÈS AUX QUAIS signs and warnings about platform tickets. First class carried Gabonese functionaries and European engineers engaged in building the line beyond Booué. Back in second class, people hugged baskets, suitcases, and children. They looked terrified, like grandparents taking a first plane trip.

According to my map, the Transgabonaise crossed the equator about a mile from Oyan. I asked one of the functionaries, a school administrator, if he knew the precise location. And was there a marker by the tracks?

"Of course I know where the equator is," he said. "I travel all the time. I've been to educational conferences in Paris, Abidjan, Dakar . . ."

"Then where is it?"

"South of Oyan." He polished his glasses carefully. "There is no sign, but I know when we cross it. I feel it in here."

"In your heart?" Like Sondra, I wondered.

"No, in my stomach." But before he could explain or point out the equator, we stopped at Oyan and he left.

A functionary named Gaston had overheard me. He promised to point out the equator. We leaned out the windows. Five minutes after Oyan, the diesel tooted its horn and Gaston shouted, "*Voilà*! The equator!" Just then we crossed a deserted jungle track that could have been the twin of Macapá's equatorial road.

"Where does it go?" I asked.

"Nowhere." The same thing Sondra had said, except now I could not jump off the train and explore for myself. Public transportation was fine when the equator touched a sizable town, but in the countryside I needed my own vehicle so I could stop.

To celebrate my first African crossing, I offered José Maria's gift to Gaston. It was a Swiss Alpine scene painted on a wood plaque. There were two perfect snowy peaks, a log cabin, a rushing stream, and, written in Portuguese, "God Is Our Strength and

Refuge." Only a man who renamed his dogs weekly could consider this a good equatorial present.

Gaston shrank back. He did not want this present — in fact, he did not even want to touch it. With his hands behind his back and his eyes darting to his bags, he said he had nothing to give me in return.

"But it can be something without value, anything."

"Everything I have is very valuable."

"Take it anyway."

"No, it is a religious object. You must keep it yourself. Anyway, I'm not certain that road was the equator."

Our train terminated at Ndjolé station, two thirds of the distance to Booué. There was no through train for two days. I had known this, but I was eager to escape Libreville and Mr. Mandoukou. Ndjolé was ten miles south of its station, and I shared a taxi with five other passengers. Halfway there, we came over a hill and swerved onto the shoulder to avoid a barricade of oil drums. A policeman our driver addressed as Chef Noël examined his license, even though this must have been a daily ritual. A cheerful commercial suburb had grown up around Chef Noël's roadblock. Women sold bananas and roots, boys hawked gum and cigarettes. A mechanic offered to pound out dents. In the bar a radio blasted "Ya ya Bon-GO!" and I shook hands with Chef Noël's fetchers and acolytes, most were missing a finger or two.

The other passengers presented identity papers and opened bags. African nations have roadblocks for the same reasons African colonies had them: to control emigration into cities, to discourage smuggling, and to collect taxes (the bribes are almost as predictable as the colonial-era taxes). As in the colonial era, roadblocks testify to a government's obsession with internal security, and as in the colonial era, white people driving private cars are usually waved through. So if you want to see a kind of neo-colonialism that torments millions of Africans every day, stand near one of these roadblocks and watch busloads of people patiently unpacking their luggage at the side of the road, standing for hours in the heat, digging out their tattered papers, and paying "fines." In Uganda, travelers are murdered at roadblocks; in benign countries like Gabon, roadblocks are like an obligatory truck stop, where travelers are forced to buy refreshments and stretch their legs.

"Papers!" Chef Noël said.

I hoped Mr. Mandoukou had not issued an all-points bulletin.

"Sit!" He pointed to the highest stool in the Michael Jackson bar. I perched there while he copied information from my passport into a school exercise book. A boy behind the counter asked what I wanted.

"Nothing."

Chef Noël's head shot up. "Aren't you hungry? Thirsty? This will take time."

I ordered a large beer, with two glasses.

"Father's name?" I answered, and watched the name of my father, dead for two decades, appear in Chef Noël's elegant script. Then his date of birth. I had almost forgotten it.

"His birthplace?" I hesitated. Was it Boston or Brookline?

"You do not know your father's birthplace?" Chef Noël was shocked. "You must ask your father." I said he had died when I was sixteen. Chef Noël pulled off his sunglasses and said, "How tragic." So I was an orphan. Well, half an orphan. Had my mother remarried, and did I have many brothers and sisters? How had they taken this loss? It was years since anyone had shown interest in my father's death.

A pickup truck sped over the hill and slammed into the barricade. But since Chef Noël was a kind man, the drums were empty, so damage was minimal. Still, it brought another client for the man with the hammers. Chef Noël did not look up. He was busy writing down my mother's maiden name.

"Are accidents frequent here?" I asked.

Chef Noël smiled. "Yes, trés fréquent." A boy led in the driver, who paid without protest a small fine for "injury to government property." Quick as pinboys, the other boys rolled the drums back into position. Chef Noël bought a round of beer for all of us, including the driver, with the fine.

Chef Noël was curious about my itinerary. I said I hoped to travel by boat down the Ogooué River to Lambarené and visit Dr. Schweitzer's hospital, returning to Ndjolé two days later to take the train to Booué. He promised to help me find a boat, then bought us more beer and asked, "How much does it cost to fly here from New York?" He wanted to know if one airline was cheaper and if my government had paid my expenses. He converted the fare from dollars to local currency and, unlike the Oiapoque policemen, found the final sum encouraging. "You must give me your card," he said, "so I can call you when I arrive in New York."

We drank more beer. I perspired, and my head throbbed to the Bongo songs. The boys came inside, leaving their drums unguarded. Several trucks slowed and, seeing the roadblock unmanned, accelerated around it. The taxi driver and the other passengers joined us. They did not mind the delay. We drank still more beer, and I handed out equatorial buttons. The women remained in the taxi, and the market women stayed with their manioc and bananas. Our impromptu beer party was only for the men.

I arrived in Ndjolé tipsy; soon I was drunk. Chef Noël had ordered the taxi driver to find me a pirogue. We stopped at a riverfront bar where three toothless pirates emerged from a back room scratching and yawning. One wore a captain's cap with an anchor. First they insisted on beer. After three liters, they admitted their sons had taken the boats and would not be back for days. When I left, they stood in front of the bar, pointing their arms different ways to direct me to the nearest pirogue. One lay overturned and rotting in a driveway; the others had been loaned to friends. The taxi driver gave up, leaving me at a gas station in the center of town.

While I soaked up Chef Noël's beer with sardines and butter cookies, two teen-age boys sidled up, offering to take me to Lambarené in their powerful speedboat. I would be there in three hours. But they were vague about the location of this boat and demanded an advance for gasoline.

A white-haired man crossed the road with the leisurely gait of the retired. He was Robert, former mayor of Ndjolé, and he would take me to Lambarené in his pirogue, he said, "because Chef Noël has instructed me to help you." The boys protested. They had offered a better price, and their boat was faster. Robert took me aside. "These boys are in a hurry—that's why they're cheaper. They will never show you the hippo pools, the ruined Catholic mission, or the Protestant church at Samkita. And look at them. Do you trust them?" I did look at them: sullen and secretive about their boat. "And has Chef Noël recommended them? No. He has confidence only in me."

I waited in a bar while Robert collected his wife and filled wine casks with gasoline. More people drifted by to demand equatorial buttons. I drank more beer. My head buzzed and my shirt dripped with perspiration. A man gave me some oranges for the journey. Another bought me a beer and congratulated me on choosing Robert over the boys. I wondered if Robert had coached him. I was offered still another beer, "compliments of Robert," and I had the traditional European response to generosity from an African employee: I am paying that bastard too much.

Robert lived ten minutes south of Ndjolé on the southern bank of the Ogooué. We stopped to unload his wife's marketing and siphon our gasoline from the wine flasks into safer plastic *bidons.* There were two houses in this riverside clearing, a dilapidated two-story brick house where Robert lived, and a concrete ranch house belonging to his brother. The ranch house was bolted shut and its new patio furniture covered with plastic sheeting. An aluminum boat lay upside down. The lawn was groomed and planted with aloe and miniature palms. "My brother is a big man in Libreville," Robert explained. "This is his vacation home, and only yesterday he returned to the capital after spending the weekend with us. He comes often and helps us." How he did this was not apparent. He certainly did not let Robert commute to Ndjolé in his aluminum boat, sit on his porch furniture, or enjoy frigid blasts from his air conditioner.

Perhaps these pleasures did not appeal, since Robert was fiercely proud of his tumbledown house. It resembled the homestead of a hillbilly family. Gutted refrigerators and rusty engine parts littered a backyard, and tattered laundry hung from a line. Children chased animals through the dust, and a goat ate scraps of paper. On the porch, two grannies with swollen ankles sat in exploded armchairs knitting sweaters.

"What does your brother do in Libreville?" I asked as we motored out into the river, and the contrast between the neighboring houses became more stark.

"My brother"—he paused for effect—"is a very big man, a government minister."

"Which one?" I asked quickly.

Robert puffed himself up. "He is the minister for culture and arts. A pity you did not arrive yesterday. You might have met him."

The beauty of the Ogooué River is a matter of dispute. The nineteenth-century British traveler Mary Kingsley saw "scenes of loveliness whose component parts are ever the same, yet the effect ever different. . . . It is full of life and beauty and passion as any symphony Beethoven ever wrote; the parts changing, interweaving and returning." Albert Schweitzer's Ogooué was a river where "each new corner, each new bend is like the last. Always the same forest and the same yellow water. . . . You shut your eyes for an hour, and when you open them you see exactly what you saw before." Trader Horn remembered it as "full of strange life and sounds at early dawn, in fact it was a veritable zoo let loose."

I leaned to Kingsley's description, although the Beethoven comparison was stretching. The gentle curves and hilly terrain made the Ogooué pretty, but not remarkably so. From the middle, its steep banks were a dark-green hedge, but when rocks and currents forced us to hug the shore I could see the insect clouds, strangler vines, and ghostly white trunks.

The Ogooué was never the important commercial route to the African interior imagined by early explorers, but it attracted Schweitzer, Horn, and Kingsley, and their lives and books shaped Europe's view of Africa in the early twentieth century. Their Ogooué was my boyhood Africa: the Tarzan Africa of Trader Horn, with its "dawn cry of the gorilla," white men becoming "blood brothers" with cannibals, and the "white woman goddess of Isorga"; the missionary Africa of Schweitzer, with its needful people and possibilities for sacrifice and good works; and Kingsley's exotic Africa of rare animals and friendly peoples.

If they traveled the Ogooué now, they would recognize only the forest. Poachers have decimated the elephant herds, selling the ivory to traders like Horn, and, like a once-bustling highway bypassed by an expressway, the river has been largely abandoned. People have left for Ndjolé, Lambaréné, and Libreville, and the scattered riverbank villages each had a single cooking fire, and a child who fled as we came into view. The Ogooué was once "the bastion of Christianity," the most converted stretch of water in Africa. But I saw only rotting steeples and a Catholic mission drowning in jungle.

We stopped at the Samkita Protestant mission, where Robert had promised we could spend the night. A century before, Horn had described a thriving trading center whose blacksmiths were famous for copper-handled swords, "splendid weapons at close quarters." Fifty years later, when Schweitzer visited, it was "the leopard station," infested with leopards who devoured the goats of Alsatian missionaries. We found the pastor's house shuttered and the mission deserted, except for an old woman who pointed to a line of narrow benches and said we could sleep on the rectory porch.

Hoping to find the pastor, we climbed a hill to the Samkita church. It had peaked tin roofs and a tall wooden steeple. Robert said services were held every Sunday. I wondered if this was true. The bell was frozen in a net of cobwebs, and bats had punched holes in palm mats stretched across the belfry. Inside, it was dark as a cellar. The forest had grown close, and branches scratched at the outer walls. Dead leaves and insects covered the floor. Months before, someone had tied palm fronds to the wooden pillars as decorations. They had turned white, coming to resemble skeletons in the dim light. We decided to continue to Lambaréné.

As we motored into the setting sun, the river turned copper. Fish jumped and birds swept ahead of us, screeching like a motorcycle escort. I quartered some limes and sucked them, imagining a daiquiri. Sitting in the prow of Robert's pirogue, speeding with the current into this brilliant red sky and whizzing past the lonely villages with their fires spiraling smoke, I could not suppress that feeling of superiority that comes from moving fast and in relative luxury through a poor countryside. And because this river appeared so empty, it was easy to imagine that whatever I saw belonged to me. Who else would want it? Simply by traveling so far, did I not have some special claim?

Garlands of lights twinkled across Lambaréné's hills. As we docked, they flickered and died. A boy with a flashlight led me up a hill to the hotel, past a shed blazing with kerosene lamps. Inside, shirtless men waving wrenches attacked an old generator. A sign boasted that my hotel had received a medal from the Aero Club de France in 1955. The clerk insisted I pay now, "and none of those traveler's checks or dollars. Cash only!" Too many Europeans making a pilgrimage to Schweitzer's hospital had screwed her on the exchange rate or skipped the bill.

Two dozen tables were set for dinner, but only one was occupied, by a pair of Frenchmen who explained that at every meal the guests — and they were the only ones — moved from table to table, circling the room until they exhausted the settings. Then the staff put out clean plates and they started again. Tonight they had completed their first revolution. They hated Lambaréné. They were making an educational survey for the government, too boring to bear discussion, but the hotel food was good, if you liked eggs. Dinner tonight was egg mayonnaise, then omelet, and for dessert, custard. They sat diagonally at a table for four. When they looked up, their moustaches dripping yoke, they did not have to look at one another. They each had a carafe of red wine — "Because we drink different amounts," one explained. They were so bored with fighting each other as they circled the room eating omelets that they immediately attacked me. I was an idiot for taking a pirogue, and I had paid too much. Didn't I know there was a road? And didn't I have a government car at my disposal? They did.

My beer was warm, and they had cornered the only ice. It sat heaped in a bowl between them, melting fast. I asked for two cubes. "No!" they chorused. "We need it for our wine." Then they let it dissolve into a puddle. In five minutes we had become enemies.

The Albert Schweitzer documentaries I saw as a boy portrayed Lambaréné as a pestilential place shunned by other Europeans. To my surprise, it was a beauty spot. Its hills rolled away to a smoky horizon, and the river widened dramatically to flow around an island containing the town. But the documentaries had been right about the damp, smothering heat. Even at eight in the morning, as I walked downhill to find a taxi to the Schweitzer hospital, I felt as if I were wrapped in hot towels. There is a scene in one of the documentaries where Schweitzer is making his rounds, perspiring into one of his droopy white short-sleeved shirts, and the interviewer asks if the heat doesn't bother "le Grand Docteur." Schweitzer answers that the heat never bothers him, because he doesn't permit himself to think about it. I tried this. It was impossible.

By mistake, the taxi left me at the new Lambaréné hospital. I had assumed, this being Gabon, that these modern buildings had replaced Schweitzer's hospital. The new clinic was lavish and antiseptic, with high ceilings and tiled walls that echoed. Tall European doctors were bending down like giraffes, planting their stethoscopes on the chests of Gabonese who wore the anxious expressions of passengers on the Transgabonaise.

Dr. Schweitzer's original hospital and living quarters were a quarter of a mile away, on a hill overlooking the Ogooué. Madame Suzanne, a Gabonese nurse who had worked with Schweitzer, showed me around. Her father was the Protestant pastor who had greeted him in 1913, and now she was the curator of le Musée du Grand Docteur. His operating theater and consulting rooms had been faithfully preserved, his scalpels laid out on a counter and his surgical gloves draped over the neck of a spotlight. Madame Suzanne had borne three sons here. "They are now," she said with pride, "all three of them, high functionaries in the government."

Mental patients and the abandoned elderly filled le Grand Docteur's wards. In Africa, the old are considered treasures of wisdom and experience. To abandon a parent is a disgrace. But here were whole barracks crammed with grandparents booted from home and village. They shuffled in their pajamas, like starved POWs, or lay curled up, staring at the walls. Their eyes were watery, and few met my gaze. They were ashamed of themselves.

"Some of their families died, but others moved to Libreville, leaving them behind," Madame Suzanne said. "There is an epidemic of abandoned old people. Some walk into the forest to starve. For us this is a new horror."

She had kept Schweitzer's bungalow—la Case du Grand Docteur—exactly as it was on the night of his death. Every calendar lay open to that date: April 9, 1965. Music on the piano showed he had last played a Bach organ composition, and his Bible was open to the final Scripture he had contemplated. "All the housekeeping chores," she said, "are performed on the schedule set out by le Grand Docteur." It had been hard work, protecting his possessions from twenty years of ants, termites, and humidity. His white smocks had to be laundered and checked for mold, his microscope and surveyor's instruments oiled, and his pith helmet touched up with white shoe polish. She polished his shoes, pressed his trousers, and dusted his books. Every week she changed his sheets. His bed was turned down, waiting.

I saw he had slept under a white cotton mosquito net on a hard bed, too short for a man of his height to stretch out. On damp nights he snuggled a red hot-water bottle. He woke to a Westclox alarm, brushed his teeth with a pure badger-bristle brush from Harrod's, and sharpened his straight razor on a Hoffritz strop. He sometimes wore a silk clip-on bow tie. His droopy shirts were always white (to repel tsetse flies). He owned two pairs of Bally "Vill-Aire" shoes, in black and brown, and preferred the brown. He wore white smocks with his name stitched in red thread. He anchored his khaki trousers with a leather belt from Swank.

He marked his days on a calendar illustrated with a painting by Frédéric Roux. He wrote prescriptions on small squares of brown wrapping paper. He took Rexall aspirin for headaches, and Persatum and Cardenia for his heart. The aspirin bottle was full, the heart-medicine bottles almost empty. He needed a magnifying glass to read the theology and biographies of statesmen filling his bookshelves. He had wood samples arranged by color, and, like Mr. Masse, he collected jars of snakes and fetuses. Some had leaked, leaving his rooms smelling, ever so faintly, of formaldehyde.

After this, it was a shock to see his grave. His wishes had been respected: The headstone bore a cross but no epitaph. (In jest, he had once suggested that if he fell victim to the cannibals of the Ogooué, his epitaph should read: We have eaten Doctor Albert Schweitzer. He was good to the very end.) Every day Madame Suzanne decorated his grave with trumpet flowers. "But you must not imagine I am the only one who remembers le Grand Docteur," she said sternly. "Every year, many Gabonese made a pilgrimage here from Lambarené, Libreville, and villages on the river, just to mark the anniversary of his death." They included former patients and young people who owed him their lives because he had saved their ancestors. They were more interested in his bungalow than his grave. "They always whisper to me, 'Le grand docteur, il est là-dedans' —'He is in there.'"

If he is là-dedans, I thought, the man who wrote "Christianity . . . assures [the African] that he is not in the power of nature-spirits, ancestral spirits, or fetishes" must not be pleased. In the end, Africa had beaten even le Grand Docteur. His admirers had turned his medical articles into fetishes and his home into a shrine, imagining that his spirit hovered overhead, watching.

I returned to his bungalow and stole a rusty paper clip from a pile on his desk. This is a theft that still puzzles me. My only explanation is that I was infected with the spirit of la Case du Grand Docteur, imagining there was something of him *là-dedans* the paper clip. I consider it more a lucky charm than a souvenir, and I have it tacked to a bulletin board where, from time to time, I can touch it.

At his desk, I rummaged through files of his correspondence. Important handwritten letters had gone to an archive, but hundreds of letters addressed to him were still here for anyone to read, or steal. One file bulged with communications from American philanthropists. Le Grand Docteur had organized their chaotic charity, clipping together letters with a typewritten note summarizing who gave what: "Ties: Mr. Alan Hut, Hut Neckwear / Blankets—Fieldcrest / Swank Jewelry for wristwatches / Wamsutta for sheets."

I read a letter from the president of an American company I shall call Union Metals, dated December 28, 1961: "It gives me the most heart felt satisfaction to inform you, on the occasion of your eighty-seventh birthday, that Union Metals, Inc., has arranged to present a unique, fully-equipped, and self-contained hospital to further your great humanitarian service to the people of Africa.

"As the photographs and drawings suggest, however dimly, the hospital is a unique product of the technology of the 20th century. It is our hope that it is a worthy and practical—though perhaps mundane—contribution to your expression of brotherly love." The president asked Schweitzer to send details of any modifications he wanted and said he waited "anxiously for word of your desires." He closed, "Until we hear from you we remain your most humble and sincere admirers." It was signed, "In the interest of mankind."

What an accompanying photograph showed, and not at all dimly, was a glass box on concrete stilts. A sports car, presumably belonging to a doctor, was parked underneath. The "hospital" had been designed to house a medical practice in an American suburb. I could not imagine anything less suited to Lambarené than an air-conditioned glass box with shaded parking for Corvettes. Neither could le Grand Docteur, who had written across the letter in his cramped handwriting: *"Impossible: Le terrain n'offre pas de place convenable pour ces dense grands bâtiments"*—"Impossible: The land cannot support these big heavy buildings."

My first reaction was, Misguided philanthropy, but a generous offer nevertheless. Then I read the next letter. It was addressed to "M. Leon M'Ba, Premier [sic], The Gabon Republic," and signed by the chairman of Union Metals. Most important, it was dated December 26, 1962, two days *before* the letter from the company president to Dr. Schweitzer. Apparently it had been forwarded to Schweitzer by someone in President Mba's office. "Your Excellency," it said, "we have the honor to extend to you, as the elected representative of your country, an unusual opportunity to provide your people with complete and modern educational and medical facilities. As you know, [we have] presented Dr. Schweitzer with a unique hospital, the first structure of its kind, as a testimonial to the work he has done to the people of Gabon. UM believes it possible to arrange to supply and finance the entire educational and medical system for Gabon, using the same basic structure, on a very attractive low-cost, long-term basis."

The chairman asked for an opportunity to meet with President Mba during his "forthcoming visit to the United States," in order to discuss the "hospitals" (which, apparently, could just as easily be schools). He said a woman in America had "accepted the hospital in Dr. Schweitzer's name," and "has kindly consented to act as our agent to initiate negotiations with you."

So much for "the occasion of your eighty-seventh birthday." The real occasion for this gift was President Mba's visit to Washington. So much for "waiting anxiously" for Schweitzer's reply. Someone had accepted this hospital before the president of Union Metals even wrote Schweitzer. And so much for "In the interest of mankind."

Here it was, just a year after Gabon's independence: some early skirmishing by whites badgering an African nation to squander money on a "unique product of the 20th century" that was useless in tropical Africa. Union Metals was crafty—what better camouflage than le Grand Docteur?—but too quick off the mark. A decade later, they could have sold these glass boxes to President Bongo by the handful.

The more closely you examine what passes for philanthropy in Africa, whether practiced by capitalists, Socialists, or Communists, charities or corporations, the more it comes to resemble the charity of Union Metals, and the better Dr. Schweitzer looks. This was not always so. During the sixties, it was fashionable to criticize Schweitzer. Europeans and Africans imagined that by discrediting him, the best European in Africa, they could prove colonialism to be an evil of astonishing purity. So it was charged that his hospital was outdated and unhygienic; he was hostile to new technology; he treated his patients as though they were children; and he possessed an unseemly appetite for publicity. Every saint attracts debunkers, and le Grand Docteur was a tempting target. I can remember his picture on classroom walls, essays written on his life, his goodness forced on us like vegetables and cousins. And I remember being delighted by the attacks. He was just another lie from the older generation.

But if Schweitzer was really such a shameless seeker of publicity, why did he abandon a career as a theologian and musician that had already brought him considerable fame, and work at Lambarené for forty years, ignored until he won the Nobel Prize? His hospital was purposely ramshackle. By resembling an African village, it attracted patients who would avoid a forbidding European facility. There are no reports of the epidemics of staff infection that would have occurred if the hospital was as unsanitary as critics charged, and his preference for simple and economic procedures is now imitated by medical programs throughout rural Africa. Before Schweitzer, few cared about the health of rural Africans. Nowadays, even though communications and living conditions are far better, educated African doctors must be bribed or drafted to serve in the countryside, and Europeans usually come on short contracts and are generously compensated. To accuse Schweitzer of paternalism is to judge an early twentieth-century missionary by late twentieth-century morality, whereas, in fact, his attitudes were progressive for a man of his generation. "I expect I am not the only white man who feels himself put to shame by the natives," he wrote in 1922. "Who can describe the injustice and cruelties that in the course of centuries they have suffered at the hands of Europeans? . . . Anything we give them is not benevolence but atonement. . . . That is the foundation from which all deliberations about 'works of mercy' out there must begin." Measure this against the Union Metals style of humanitarianism, now widespread in Africa.

Le Grand Docteur's paper clip nagged at my conscience. In exchange, I decided to give José Maria's picture to the hospital. Perhaps it would cheer up the abandoned grandparents. Lambarené was within fifty miles of the equator, close enough to make an exception. Madame Suzanne insisted I present it to Maria Lagendijk, the only surviving member of Schweitzer's European staff. With her large, handsome features, she resembled Schweitzer as much as any woman could. Her rooms reflected his frugality and precision, and she managed the women sweeping her compound with an authoritative but kindly manner, perhaps patterned on his. She had decided to come here after reading his *On the Edge of the Primeval Forest*, and, like him, she had spent years preparing herself in Europe, training as a nurse and anesthesiologist. She promised to hang José Maria's picture in the leper colony. In exchange, I could have my pick from a dusty storeroom filled with curios made by the patients. There were blunt wooden knives, chipped turtle shells, and carved animals which, like the lepers, were uniquely deformed. I chose a crocodile with crippled legs.

I asked who would look after Schweitzer's house after she and Madame Suzanne died. "There are thousands here who are alive only because of le Grand Docteur," she said. "They will keep his memory and tend his house."

I complimented her tidy rooms, and she said, "Le Grand Docteur was a great organizer."

I said I had never been anywhere as uncomfortably hot as Lambarené, and she said, "Le Grand Docteur always told us you must have great spiritual activity to fight the heat." She named some of the Swiss, Dutch, and German nurses and doctors who, lacking such activity, had fled.

I asked how Schweitzer had chosen his European staff. "Le Grand Docteur did not demand diplomas. Instead he asked, 'Do you sleep well?' 'Do you have a sense of humor?' and 'What is your hobby?'" She gave me a penetrating stare, waiting for answers.

The European doctors from the new hospital still ate in the old dining hall, sitting like campers at long tables underneath a portrait of le Grand Docteur. For years following his death, a place was set for him and food heaped on his plate (another memorial he would have disliked). Afterwards, the food was fed to his pet antelopes, which lived in a pen near his grave.

A surgeon at my table praised Lambarené as "a great opportunity for us. I can perform operations I would not be allowed to do for years in Europe." Another agreed. He had enjoyed a year's experience in only a month. Later I read in an article, "A senior physician from Switzerland . . . is full of enthusiasm for the medical work one can do in Lambaréné. 'We see cases here that would make a European medical professor's mouth water,' he says."

The doctors had two-year contracts. After the first year they returned to Europe for a month's vacation, and, according to the ones I met at lunch, many never returned. There were no Gabonese doctors on staff. "They insist on Libreville," a Frenchman said bitterly. "For them, the rest of Gabon is punishment." But who could blame them for choosing Libreville's Atlantic breezes over Lambaréné's choking humidity? If educated Europeans would not stay more than two years in Lambaréné, how could they expect Gabonese with European educations to come for a lifetime? Perhaps only le Grand Docteur had the right to expect this.

I asked Schweitzer's questions. They said:

"None of us sleeps well here."

"Yes, of course the heat bothers us!"

"We are too busy for hobbies."

On their day off, they played cards and listened to tapes on Sony Walkmans. None had traveled to Samkita or Ndjolé. A Canadian dentist was amazed I was taking a train to Booué tomorrow. He had not known Gabon had a railway.

The mail arrived with dessert, bringing more cassettes. A woman draped herself over her French boyfriend, rumpling his hair. Maria Lagendijk looked uncomfortable. She scraped the young doctors' plates onto her own and went outside. I left her feeding their scraps to Schweitzer's antelopes.

No buses or bush taxis connected Lambaréné to the Ndjolé station. Everyone went in the other direction, west to Libreville. The taxi drivers refused to take me, claiming they lacked proper documents. Finally Rafion, owner of the least roadworthy vehicle in Lambaréné, agreed to go, because, he explained, "I enjoy a fast trip." The trip was eighty miles on dirt road. At the hotel I was advised to leave three hours, departing at 6:00 A.M. to catch the 9:40 train. Rafion disagreed. His record to Ndjolé was two hours, and he hoped to better it. I insisted we start at six. He picked me up at 7:15, in a stroke converting me to his preference for a fast trip.

The road was narrow and potholed, its shoulders sliding away to forested ravines. During the first half hour I counted the skeletons of seven cars. The wrecks were unsettling because the road was lightly traveled. We met our first truck, and I learned the rules. When two vehicles met, the larger moved into the center and accelerated. The smaller swerved onto the shoulder, if there was one. The most dangerous vehicles were the new yellow Japanese trucks belonging to the Ministry of Transport. Their drivers had converted them to bush taxis so that instead of fixing the roads, they chewed them up while speeding between villages with passengers and freight.

Villages stood in red moons of cleared forest. The houses were patched together from bamboo, mud, and kindling. Libreville had vacuumed up the men, leaving women, children, and grandparents to stagger around under heaps of firewood. Diet and commerce were simple. People grew and ate manioc and bananas. They sold their surplus for the one thing available everywhere — beer. Today was beer delivery day, so stacked crates of empties marked every village. You could estimate the wealth of a place by the ratio of crates to huts.

Rafion accelerated through these villages, took curves on the wrong side, and moved into the center on the hills.

"This is a dangerous road, Rafion," I said, after a truck almost elbowed us into a ditch.

"Only if you are unlucky."

"But suppose we meet a car on the curve —"

"It has never happened. It would be very unlucky."

"But it only takes one truck. Why not keep right?"

"If the road curves left, I drive on the left. It is faster."

Just as I concluded that Rafion and I were made of different clay, we came over a hill to see a fresh accident. One of the yellow trucks had plunged into a gully. Rafion slammed on the brakes and scrambled down. A branch had impaled the driver's window. Wet blood covered the windshield. A few minutes earlier, and we might have carried the driver's corpse to Ndjolé.

Rafion fell silent and shook his head when I mentioned the accident. He drove slowly now, taking every curve on the right. I thought, Good, this reckless bastard has learned his lesson. But then again, not so good, since at this speed I would miss the only train of the day. Outside Ndjolé we passed another of the yellow trucks. Rafion honked wildly and waved it down, to tell the driver about the accident, I thought. Instead they embraced, laughed, and exchanged cigarettes.

"My brother," Rafion said with a huge smile.

"But if you thought that was your brother's truck in the accident, why not speed to Ndjolé?" I asked. "He might have been alive in the hospital." This sudden caution made no sense.

"We might both have been cursed with bad luck, so I had to be careful." He accelerated, driving again in the old style.

The train was arriving two hours late from Libreville. Again the Parisian chimes tinkled, and men urinated against the door of a bolted toilet. I met a Belgian engineer who was building the next leg of track. He said the railway was costing five million dollars a mile, money lent by France and the European Economic Community after the World Bank had rejected the project as unnecessary. He described bulldozers sinking into lakes of mud, trees smashing steam shovels, and mountains blasted into pebbles. I heard about crates of luxuries hauled from the coast to pamper the 400 expatriate workers. I heard about heroic Pakistani bulldozer drivers, and about European foremen lying in their jungle-hugged trailers, spinning dreams of the homes and businesses they would buy with their salaries.

The Belgian had the pink face and thick glasses of the kind of schoolboy who tinkers with radios. He said, "When they started this service, the trains were perfect, running to the minute, like *les trains suisses*." Pressing thumb and forefinger together, he gave a little kiss of perfection. "But now the service is a horror. No maintenance, no one cares. Like the trains in . . ."

"The United States?"

"I hope they are not this bad, and certainly not for the same reason." To celebrate the inaugural run, President Bongo had presented the conductors and stationmasters with wristwatches. His picture, of course, was on the dial. "*Alors*, they check the time, and what do they see? The president staring at them. Genius! But the watches were cheap, so they broke. Some were sold. Now that the president is not watching them, the railroad employees become lazy. *Voilà!* The reason the Transgabonaise deteriorates."

It sounded like another of the cruel apocryphal stories about Africa that Europeans are always inventing or embroidering. I said I doubted that this explained today's delayed train to Booué. He gave me a pitying look. "Of course, you are American."

For eighty miles between Ndjolé and Booué the Transgabonaise hugs the south bank of the Ogooué. The equator is five miles across the river, running through the foothills of the Cristal mountains. Nowhere else does a road or train parallel the equator so closely for even this brief distance, and as much as you can "follow" the equator anywhere, it is along this stretch of the Transgabonaise.

The Ogooué was a different river here: no pirogues, mission stations, or villages, only logging camps and rapids. Lumbering had given the land the checkerboard look of farmland planted in different crops. Some hills were fire-blackened; others smoked; still others were ash-gray, angry red, or the delicate green of a new lawn. But they were never the midnight green of primary forest that I saw in French Guiana.

At Bissouma, a delegation of workmen in white overalls met a European who had carried a small tool kit from Libreville. They followed him in procession down the tracks, watching while he unlocked a shed and set to work repairing a generator.

At Lopé, a boy sold dead monkeys. He had slit their tails in half, tying both ends around their necks to make handles so he could swing them like briefcases. He fluffed their fur and made slicing motions, suggesting how they might be turned into steaks. We had just entered the Lopé-Okanda nature reserve.

Stacks of beer crates and butchered okoume trees marked every station. The okoume grows upward of a hundred and thirty feet, and its wood is prized for plywood paneling, bureau drawers, picture frames, and cigar boxes. The logs were gigantic. Each raw end was painted with black numbers.

When we arrived in Booué, the Belgian engineer coarsened his language and deepened his scowl. He was met by a barrel-shaped Frenchman named Paul, more the kind of roustabout I expected to find building the Transgabonaise. Nicotine had yellowed his fingers and teeth, and someone had carved a scar shaped like an exclamation mark into his forehead. For some reason he was anxious I like this colonial relic of a town. He drove slowly down a dusty road shaded by mangoes, pointing out that their trunks had been whitewashed in the manner of plane trees along a French highway. He stopped opposite peeling government buildings and then a parade ground facing a dilapidated barracks. "The vestiges of France," he said without irony.

We ended the tour at Booué's beauty spot, a restaurant overlooking the river and the railway. The French patron wore a Bjorn Borg tennis outfit, complete to the sweatbands. Without asking, he brought us a tray of Oranginas. They were as popular with the two-year-contract colonialists of Booué as with the teen-age Legionnaires of St. Georges. Paul and the Belgian drank one after another, all the time cursing their *ordinateurs* — "computers." They were a *connerie*.

Paul repeated the gossip of the Booué railway encampment. It revolved around men drinking, gambling, and running up debts while their wives fled their trailer homes. The Belgian mentioned a name, and Paul said, *"Sa femme est partie"* — "His wife has left."

"Connerie!" The Belgian said another name.

"Oui, his wife too, gone to Libreville."

"Connerie!" Another name.

"His wife flew to France, and his . . ." And so on.

"Connerie! Connerie!" the Belgian shouted. "How about him?"

"A crook. He left us with debts."

"Quelle connerie!"

"Connerie!"

"Connerie!"

They smoked, fell silent, smoked, stared at the river and unfinished railway, drummed their fingers, drank another Orangina, and built pyramids of empty cans. The pauses between their profanity lengthened. I looked at them: two men with nothing in common but Booué, already bored by one another.

From here I had a panoramic view of my dilemma. To my right, the unfinished railway forked sharply south; to my left, the road turned north. Straight ahead was the equator and unbroken rain forest. Paul and the Belgian insisted there was no road to the Congo. The *patron* said the journey by truck to Mekambo, the last village in Gabon, might take two weeks, and he doubted a European could enter the Congo there. The Gabonese in the bar had never heard of anyone going that way. They said there was nothing to see but forest, nothing to eat but manioc. I decided to double back to Libreville. I had already spent nearly two weeks in Gabon, and I could not gamble another two. I would have to fly to Brazzaville, cross the Zaïre River to Kinshasa, and travel by river to Mbandaka and the equator. But first I could have dinner with Patrice.

Halfway back, the train uncoupled. I woke with a jolt to see the second-class carriages rolling backward down a steep incline, their windows dimly lit by emergency generators. They gathered speed and vanished like a sinking liner. The foreign engineers offered me a beer, and I heard again the story of President Bongo's wristwatches.

I asked if these incidents were frequent on the Trans-gabonaise. This was only my third trip, but each had been plagued by problems.

"Yes, already this train is fucked," one man said. "No maintenance; no one cares."

But these men had spent months, even years, in a hellish climate, laying tracks through difficult terrain. Did they not find it depressing, even humiliating, to have their train break in two while they were riding it?

"No, we find it amusing," one said.

"Anyway, we didn't work on this sector," another said. "That was someone else."

"I say 'Good!' This means more work for us. When we finish Booué to Franceville, we can rebuild Owendo to Ndjolé."

"Then it will be time to rebuild Booué to Franceville. There is work here for generations of engineers."

As we inched backward, one man said, "My friend, I don't care what they do with this railroad. I do my work; I get paid. Finished. Afterwards I'm never coming back. For all I care they can eat this fucking train."

We moved a hundred yards and uncoupled again. The Europeans laughed themselves sick.

On my way to Patrice's apartment, I decided it was not impossible that France had sent someone to spy on Americans in Gabon. The colonial French have always distrusted the Anglo-Saxons. During the Second World War, the Allies and Vichy France fought in North Africa, the Middle East, Dakar, and Madagascar. I can remember hitchhiking across southern France in the late sixties with recently exiled French Algerians who blamed their misfortunes first on De Gaulle, then on President Kennedy. When I was a Peace Corps trainee, in Tunisia, the director insisted our mission was to replace the French language with English and "drive that bastard Couve de Murville into the sea." Now the French in Gabon were touchy because just after their oil companies abandoned the offshore concessions, American companies discovered rich fields. The man from the embassy who identified Patrice as a spy had also accused the French of persuading the Gabonese media to omit any mention of the bombing of the French military installation in Beirut, so only the clumsy American Marines appeared to have been victimized by terrorist bombs.

Patrice's apartment had the look of a spy's den, a stark, modern flat bordering the ocean, with a terrace lit by moonlight and rooms echoing with a gentle surf. But inside was her bourgeois granny, here to recover from the death of a husband and bustling through the living room emptying ashtrays, bringing out snack foods, and clanging pots as she concocted soup for herself and a sickly young Frenchman from next door. This was not how I had pictured my evening with France's woman in Libreville.

But then Patrice suggested we speak English, "so my grandmother won't understand us," and began asking about the conference and the other delegates. I felt a thrill. Surely these were the questions of a spy.

Her granny and the sick French boy slurped soup in a dining alcove, and I changed my mind.

She said the Peace Corps volunteers were marvelous. They lived in the countryside and really knew Gabon. They were a fantastic source of information about the country. Had I met any yet?

My suspicions clicked like a metronome. She was not a spy. She was. She spied for the French, for President Bongo, for both, for none. I asked about her American husband, and she described an unhappy marriage to a New York intellectual whose family belittled her because she was not an artist or writer. She had returned to Paris where her parents had connections in the government, explaining her job as an adviser to President Bongo. She had come to the tropics to recover from a bad marriage. It was that simple.

Or was it? I mentioned the American delegates priming

themselves with double martinis for a presidential banquet they expected to be dry, and she quickly said, "But that is hilarious! I will tell the president tomorrow. Do you remember which delegates believed there would be no drinks?"

I could not remember.

"But how amusing if it was those congressmen."

We ate on the terrace of a restaurant catering to young French and Gabonese. Patrice was beginning to disappoint. Her favorite subjects were her American marriage and Bwiti, the local voodoo rite. She had a photograph of a metal culvert on the Transgabonaise. It had been wrenched out of the ground and split open, as if struck by lightning. Two smiling Africans stood alongside, like hunters with a trophy. She said it was the work of Bwiti magicians unhappy with the railway's route.

She described a Bwiti ceremony. You ate the bark of a tree — presumably a hallucinogen — and had the pleasure of meeting your ancestors. A European friend had met his this way. From a Gabonese I might have taken this more seriously, but the idea of Europeans dabbling in Bwiti to meet their relatives struck me as absurd, not to mention cruel to the ancestors summoned up. How did a nineteenth-century Frenchman feel about suddenly finding himself in Gabon?

She sensed my skepticism. "Listen, there is a man at the palace, an educated man, who consults his dead father. He takes notes of his father's advice. And the president, he is so scared of Bwiti he has outlawed it."

"Do you believe in it?"

"Yes." Her eyes were burning. "On his deathbed, President Mba swore he'd get his wife for being unfaithful. Afterwards she had a car accident. The car was scarcely dented. The chauffeur was unscratched. She was killed and her sexual organs destroyed. Now do you see?"

I asked Patrice if she was Christian. No, she did not believe any longer. And the resurrection? No again. The willingness of lapsed Christians to accept the fantastic miracles of other religions is intriguing. Here were men consulting dead fathers and Old Testament vengeance from the grave, all believed more likely than a single resurrection. She shrugged. "Well, maybe that happened too."

Over coffee I mentioned the Franco-American rivalry I had noticed in Libreville.

"Who do you mean?" she asked—too quickly, I thought.

"One American diplomat thinks that after the bombing of the French and American military camps in Lebanon, the French persuaded the Gabonese to remove all mention of France from official broadcasts, so it sounded as if only the American Marines had been humiliated."

"Who told you that?" She was suddenly alert.

"Someone at the embassy. I can't remember who."

"Oh, but try to remember. It would be . . . it would be so amusing to know."

Now I was almost certain the American diplomat was right, Patrice was a spy. "Why would it be amusing?"

"Because it is so sick. No, it is incredible . . . it is . . ." She burst into hysterics. "It is too funny for words." She caught her breath. "That happened because those were the weeks the president was mad at the French over that unflattering book. He banned the word 'France' from the news. That's why France was omitted from the Beirut dispatches."

She laughed so hard she got the hiccups. "What a comedy, what a farce they are, these intrigues . . . this Gabon."

7

THE ARRIVAL FORMALITIES AT BRAZZAVILLE'S MAYA-MAYA AIR-port resemble those of a popular New York discotheque. This is not surprising, since both cater to elites. At Maya-Maya, the "fixers" stand on tiptoe, checking passengers and identifying their clients to the immigration officers. This elite is waved to the front and hurried through to the curtained booths where travelers to the People's Republic of the Congo first confront its bureaucracy. Since every foreign embassy, organization, or corporation employs airport fixers, any visitor of consequence is met. All others come under suspicion. I was asked, "What is your business here?" I had none. "The purpose of your trip?" Travel. "Where is your ticket to leave the Congo?" I said I was taking the ferry to Kinshasa. "Are you married?" Yes. "But where is your family? If you are a tourist, why haven't you brought them?" I said I had come to visit my friend the American ambassador. (A lie.) "Then why hasn't he sent someone to meet you?" "My visit is a surprise." Until recently, it would have been impossible to enter the Congo by claiming friendship with the American ambassador. During the 1960s, Maoist militia groups harassed American diplomats, and diplomatic relations were broken. Now the Congo had changed from being an ideological Marxist state — "the Albania of Africa" — to a pragmatic one welcoming capitalist enterprise. American oil companies were in Point Noir, the embassy had reopened, and the policeman at the airport, not wishing to risk my being a personal friend of the ambassador, pulled open the curtain and welcomed me.

Even at night, I could see that Brazzaville was one of Africa's prettiest capitals. Mature trees and flowering hedges bordered its boulevards, and arcades shaded shops and government ministries constructed in the thick-walled, white-stucco, French colonial style. Our headlights picked out billboards. They said, in French: STOP THE SABOTEURS OF OUR ECONOMY! WORK IS THE FUNDAMENTAL CONDITION OF HUMAN NATURE! STOP ABSENTEEISM AND THE SLOW PACE OF WORK! Slightly rewritten, they could have hectored workers on any capitalist assembly line. As slogans go, they were more inspirational than PRESIDENT BONGO IS THE NATION'S FUTURE!

Giant portraits of Marx, Lenin, Arafat, Assad, the Congolese leader Colonel Denis Sassou-Nguesso, and other "progressives" decorated Brazzaville. All were done in the same primitive style, perhaps by the same Congolese Grandma Moses. Everyone, even the usually starved Lenin, had chipmunk cheeks, bowling-ball heads, Levantine lips, and crazy eyes. Everyone's skin was yellow: butterscotch for Marx and Lenin, marigold for Assad and Arafat. Colonel Denis was the dead yellow of an autumn leaf, fairer than his European heroes. A slogan under one portrait said, Truth Is His ——. His what? His tool? His shield and defender? His favorite thing? Was the artist waiting for a ruling from the politburo?

I never learned what Colonel Denis believed the truth to be, because while I slept Brazzaville's slogans were covered with red paint, liquidated. The next morning, pedestrians stared at blank signs. No one could explain it, only that it sometimes happened and that the billboards might remain empty for days. Once there had been signs saying DOWN WITH CAPITALIST BLOODSUCKERS! These had vanished the same way. I was told these empty billboards made people uneasy. Perhaps that was the point.

The Congolese were no strangers to political ferment. They had crammed two centuries' worth of Balkan paranoia, xenophobia, murders, poisonings, and coups into their first twenty-five years. They had tried a parliamentary system, free enterprise, "scientific socialism," a Marxist military regime, and now a "pragmatic Marxism" that was more capitalist than the Mobutuism of "anti-communist" Zaïre, across the river. There was a people's palace to which the government seldom admitted the people, a revered leader murdered under mysterious circumstances, and an archbishop—the last man to see the leader alive—murdered under circumstances even more mysterious. The twitchy soldiers guarding the palace had last year killed a British engineer on a motorbike, and last month they had, inexplicably, machine-gunned a municipal bus, wounding forty-four passengers. The clandestine FROLIBABA, le Front de Libération des Batékés et des Bagangoulous, had set off bombs in downtown Brazzaville, and commandos had staged raids from across the river, one ending with the leader's corpse being exhibited on Brazzaville television with dollar bills stuffed in his mouth. But oil revenues had recently brought increased prosperity. Literacy was high, crime low, and the civil servants relatively honest, and every university graduate could count on a job, resulting in a shortage of desks.

From Brazzaville's riverbank, Kinshasa was all spires and glass towers, shimmering by day, sparkling by night. It looked a busy port with its piers, ships, and cranes, but the river between the two cities was flat and empty as a frozen pond. There was an hourly ferry service, and I had imagined taking it whenever I tired of Brazzaville. I was wrong. To cross between these cities, where the same tribal people spoke the same European and African languages, I needed a *laissez-passer* from the Zaïre embassy, in addition to my Zaïre visa. I would have to pay a fee, surrender my passport, and, "If you're lucky," said the hotel clerk, "you'll have a *laissez-passer* in a week—or less, if you are sponsored by your embassy."

Even this *laissez-passer* did not guarantee a quick crossing. Relations between these neighbors were poor. Each leader imagined the other conspiring against him, sometimes with reason, and retaliated by suspending the ferry service. This usually happened before and after national holidays, international conferences, and state visits, presumably to foil the *franc-tireurs* each imagined the other sending across to spoil the festivities.

I did not fancy a week of staring at Kinshasa's skyline, unable to travel elsewhere in the Congo because my passport was on the desk of a Zaïrian diplomat, so I went to the American embassy. Before leaving, I had told the United States Information Agency (USIA) that I would lecture at African universities near the equator. These lectures would be informal, arranged at the last minute and at my convenience. While I would not accept fees or expenses, I was told the embassies might offer me "facilitative assistance" in return.

The USIA man in Brazzaville was on leave, so I was handed over to his Congolese assistant, a young man known to everyone as J.J., who was a graduate of the university's English department. He was soft-spoken and modest, and I had to dig out the fact that he had earned an honors degree and had once been named Best Student in Brazzaville. Now the "Best Student" in this Marxist country worked for the United States Information Agency. He scheduled a lecture for the following day, and promised to take my passport to the Zaïre embassy. I would have a *laissez-passer* in three days. His opposite number in Kinshasa would schedule a lecture there and meet me on the ferry dock — more facilitative assistance. At last I would be among the Men Who Are Met.

The equator crosses the Congo 300 miles north of Brazzaville, but I would have to skip it. I could not leave the city without a passport, and the Zaïrians would keep mine until they issued a *laissez-passer,* which I would have to use quickly before it expired. The single road leading to the equator was a cul-de-sac. The principal appeal of the swampy, sparsely populated equatorial zone was that it was the birthplace of Colonel Denis and his cabinet. J.J. volunteered to drive me thirty miles up this highway to see what I was missing.

It was a surprising landscape of rolling savanna, lightly cultivated and populated. We turned back at a lonely village where J.J. bought ears of corn, a treat for his children. He had visited France, the United States, and Japan, but he admitted that this was as far north as he had traveled in his own country. We stopped at a weedy yard, a tree nursery, where he bought saplings. "One is for my children to adorn next Christmas," he said. "I could never celebrate a holiday by killing a tree. In my home, no dead trees." He would plant the saplings around his new house to keep his family cool. He disapproved of air conditioning. "Become accustomed to modern conveniences and you are deranged when they vanish," he said.

After hearing more of these Oriental-sounding epigrams, I asked why he had visited Japan. "I went to dedicate our shrine," he said, explaining that he belonged to Malikali, a Japanese religious sect he described as "a round-up of all religious," making it sound perfect for the experimental Congolese. It had reached Brazzaville in 1981 and already claimed a thousand members.

Ahead of us a Land-Rover swerved across the highway. Stenciled white letters said Police. The men in back wore baggy black uniforms and carried rifles. J.J. tried to pass, but when we were abreast the driver swerved left. J.J. swore and braked. The policemen laughed, slapping their thighs. J.J. tried again and the driver slowed, waving us on. We pulled out, almost colliding with a truck. The police threw mock salutes.

I suggested we stop. "No! That would give them a victory." Gripping the wheel and pounding the horn, J.J. pulled close. The policemen shifted their rifles, pointing the barrels at our windshield. One man pretended to take aim. J.J.'s face was frozen in hatred. He pounded a fist against the dashboard. "If they only knew who I was, if they knew how much trouble I could cause, they would not be laughing." Here he was, the "best student in Brazzaville," the man in charge of the USIA, the man who had visited Japan, taunted by these thugs, and here was one reason many educated Africans live in Europe or America.

The taxi drivers of Brazzaville were good-natured and honest, and such good company I took to hanging around a taxi stand near my hotel. They thought I was a fool to go to Kinshasa. "Stay *chez nous*," one said. "There is no one there but thieves."

Another agreed.

"Be careful of their taxis. The drivers pretend to break down, and when their passengers push they steal their valises."

"Never carry a valise over your shoulder. You must hold it hugged to your chest like a precious infant."

"Monsieur, the truth is we Congolese do not like that city because the soldiers demand money and beat us on the dock." This turned out to be true.

Jacques, the driver who showed me Brazzaville, wrote out a list of sights he called "our schedule." "We taxi drivers hate the Russians," he said, beginning our schedule by tooting his horn and swerving toward some Soviet pedestrians. "We call them *les*

faux blancs ["the fake whites"] because they walk or ride motorbikes but never take taxis. They don't spend money like other
whites. We're glad you Americans have returned, and the French
too, although of course they never really left. *Regardez!*" Two
cinder-block-shaped *faux blancs* had crammed themselves onto a
motorbike. Jacques pulled close and blasted them. They wobbled
onto the shoulder. Jacques laughed. "Shall I take you to the Russian embassy?" Presumably a good place to hunt more *faux
blancs.* I said no, and he drove instead to the shuttered Cosmos
hotel, built by the Russians ten years before and already closed.
"Tombé en ruine," Jacques said. *"Beaucoup de rats."*

Because he thought it would please me, I saw Brazzaville's
capitalist landmarks: the Canada Dry bottling plant; the brewery;
the Agence Toyota ("Would you care to tour it?"); the Supermarket M'Pla ("Many American products for sale!"); and the ferry
terminal, where smugglers hawked contraband on the steps of the
Douane.

Jacques said Brazzaville's Ouzey market was notable for its
smoked monkeys, although "smoked," implying as it does a delicacy, is misleading. The monkeys in Ouzey were charcoaled, their
limbs brittle as overcooked chicken wings. Each was trussed with
a cord, like a man, or a baby, prepared for the electric chair. The
merchants had stacked them by size, and bouquets of flies buzzed
around their fists and mouths. Their deaths had not been
painless. Their faces were frozen in a grimace of bared teeth and
screaming mouth, as if they had been smoked alive.

Seeing them made Jacques hungry. He cruised the stalls
sniffing and pinching. Some were *"trop petit"*—"too small"; others
"trop vieux"—"too old." He settled on the clenched hand of an
already hacked-up monkey, all he could afford.

"But you have a large family. How can they all dine on this
little paw?" I asked.

"My wife is an excellent *cuisinier,*" he said. "She will make
monkey fricassee with shredded coconut and peppers. My favorite."

Even to buy this paw Jacques needed an advance, and for a
moment I considered treating him to an entire animal. It would
have pleased him, but I could not tip a man a charcoaled monkey.

The fetish market was hidden behind a wall of Chinese toilet
paper. It reminded me of a health-food store in my neigh-

borhood, The Health Nuts. It had the same musky smell of dried fruit, nuts, and pods, and its merchants, like the health-food clerks, believed in what they sold. They fussed over their stock, arranging squirrel skulls and turtle shells by size, wrapping rubber bands around feathers, and pushing heaps of pebbles around like croupiers. They were careful to separate ingredients, as if mixing snake skins and hawk talons would trigger an explosion. When a woman requested swatches of red cloth, two species of twigs, a tablespoon of yellow powder, and a leg of skeletal rat, the fetish merchant wrapped each individually and placed them gently in her plastic shopping bag, on top of her onions and tins of sardines.

The merchants were elderly, brittle as their snake skins. I was a window-shopper, but they were happy to discuss their trade. They did not sell fetishes or potions, only their ingredients. It was the fetisher who conducted the diagnostic interview, prescribing the articles needed for a cure. A patient bought these at the market, and the fetisher constructed the amulet or potion. "We are all disturbed by the developments in Nigeria," one merchant whispered. "There, fetishers sell the ingredients themselves, and we fear this will spread down the coast." They had hired a local fetish doctor to put a hex on this innovation.

The Ouzey fetish merchants were rumored to sell gorilla skulls. I asked to see one, and they shook their heads. These were highly prized and immediately sold, and not only to the patients of fetish doctors. Since Europe discovered the gorilla in the mid-nineteenth century, there has been a trophy trade in mounted gorilla heads. In Rwanda, where this market has nearly killed off the mountain gorilla, thirty heads were recently seized from a prominent European resident said to be engaged in smuggling them to "collectors."

"This is as powerful as gorilla," a merchant said, pointing to an elephant's trunk. It rested on a cardboard rectangle, pre-sliced like a strudel. The nostrils cost the most.

His neighbor lifted a handkerchief, revealing a gorilla's forearm. "*Voila!* A female!" Two fingers remained. They cost $1.12 each. Yesterday I could have purchased the whole hand for $3.50.

Jacques whistled. Even this butchered arm inspired awe. "This is very serious magic," he said. "Very grave."

The arm looked human. Perhaps gorillas are also a missing

link between animal and human sacrifice, a substitute for the greater magic of a human skull. The problem with killing an animal for religious purposes is that it can stimulate an appetite for human sacrifice. I have never heard it argued, even by vegetarians, that eating a chicken encourages cannibalism. Nor does it follow that if a small animal is tasty, then a larger one, like a dog, a gorilla, or a human being, is tastier still. But when animals are butchered for their magical properties, size and human attributes often become important. The larger and more human the animal, the more powerful the magic invoked by its bones and entrails. That morning's newspaper described the trial of four young men accused of abducting and killing female children. The victims were found identically mutilated. "The lack of apparent motive," reported this heavily censored government newspaper, "leads to the conclusion that the crimes were committed for the purpose of obtaining 'religious necessities.'"

Jacques insisted on eating lunch in the Jo-Burger, a fast-food restaurant recently opened by a Lebanese merchant named Jo. The Congolese staff wore baseball caps and red vests with JB patches. There was rock music, and the walls were decorated with pictures of cowboys and cartoon heroes. The plastic garbage cans resembled laughing clowns, and you threw garbage into their open mouths. Jacques could not lock his taxi, so he carried the monkey paw inside, laying it on one of the molded plastic chairs designed to discomfort a patron after twelve minutes. We ate our Big Big Jo-Burgers alone, the only customers. Jacques said the restaurant filled with students later, but a Lebanese at the cash register admitted business was slow. The people of Brazzaville were *"non-civilisés."*

I went to the Poto-Poto art school hoping to meet the artists responsible for the butterscotch-colored leaders. Instead, I found rooms of silent students applying paint to canvas with the concentration of diamond-cutters. Their work filled the rambling house: pink Cubist elephants stampeding out of jungles; Dali fetish priests brewing kettles of wriggling snakes; Le Douanier lions staring with glistening eyes; and pirogues gliding down a river of Seurat pastel dots. One Poto-Poto artist had gone through a "blue period," producing canvases of blue market women walking through blue jungles and villages. The paintings were vigorous adaptations, Africa as European artists might have depicted it. The best were signed "Dimi Joseph."

I turned to face a young man who had the distant manner of an aristocrat opening his ancestral estate to tourists. It was Dimi Joseph. I went into the next room and he followed like a shadow. I stopped before one of his, an elephant grinning like the Cheshire Cat, and he said, "I have experimented in all these styles. I wear many *chapeaux* to see what works. One must try everything."

"And what do you think works?"

"Still I am not certain." He considered the walls of paintings. "Every artist is influenced by others, yet adds his inspiration. Will you tell me your favorite?"

I picked the grinning elephant, making the mistake of asking its price. He tipped the canvas to check a number written on back. It was 180,000 CFA, almost $400. Before I could react to this extravagant price, he had proposed an equally extravagant discount, "a special price because we are friends."

"But we've just met."

"Then I'll make a special price because I'm here! You see, if the artist isn't here he cannot offer a reduction. OK, special price is twenty thousand CFA." Before, it was too expensive; now it was too cheap. I was embarrassed. He was too good to be so desperate. I would have bought it had the post office and customs regulations not been so complicated.

I wandered into a back room and he became flustered, saying, "No, the art here is not for you." The paintings were identical, red-and-green stickmen with blue Afros, dancing across a black background.

"The other artists make these in an instant, but I refuse," he said. "They are for the *faux blancs*."

"Why do they like them?"

"That is a mystery. At first we think it is because the *faux blancs* are cheap. But we raised the prices and still they buy. Is it possible they like them?" Dimi Joseph smiled like his elephant.

The longer I stayed in Brazzaville, the more I pitied the *faux blancs*. Here they were, these cinder-block Soviets, perspiring into thick suits, collecting hideous artwork, and ridden into the gutters by cursing taxi drivers in front of huge portraits of Marx and

Lenin, all because they could not spend like capitalists. They could not all be training the police in KGB interrogation techniques. There had to be an idealist here, upset by the welcome of his Congolese comrades.

The ground zero of Russian despair was the Rasputin, a restaurant run by a clique of Russian women who had married Congolese students in Moscow. In Brazzaville their marriages soured. Their in-laws persecuted them and their husbands took second wives. They were abandoned or ignored, and homesick for a place where they no longer wished to live. In the Rasputin they sat perched like crows on barstools, greeting one another with clumsy double-cheek kisses, drinking glasses of tea from a samovar, and fattening on borscht and meat pies. Their teeth were gold or black, and their white arms jiggled with fat. Every glass at my table had a faint smear of their gaudy lipsticks.

On my last afternoon in Brazzaville, I met with the Union of Congolese Writers, then with the minister of culture — more of J.J.'s facilitative assistance. The writers described paying editors to read their books, publishers to print them, and distributors to circulate them, and watching while all three battled to steal the royalties. They complained about the difficulty of obtaining visas to attend conferences in African countries. One writer had been expelled from Gabon "like a dog." It was easier to travel to Europe, so they did. Most had not been to Kinshasa in years, and they met Zaïrians only at foreign symposiums. One man said, "Remember, it was France and Belgium who turned our river into a frontier and started this *laissez-passer* business."

"But we've had twenty-five years to stop that nonsense," argued the man expelled from Gabon. "We should have a free-trade zone, the same airport and municipal services, even a bridge!" The others laughed at this hopeless visionary.

The minister of culture's coffee table overflowed with material for a forthcoming symposium of African historians. Scholars were coming to present papers commemorating the hundredth anniversary of the Berlin Conference, at which the colonial powers codified boundaries and divided unclaimed African territories into illogical parcels. As the minister described his conference, it became clear that the colonialists would receive a much-deserved roasting.

But he did not mention, or perhaps he did not know, that across the river the Zaïrian minister of culture had organized an identical symposium. The Congolese one was scheduled for the end of the month. The one in Zaïre began two weeks later. Each was the kind of event that sometimes prompted the other side to cancel the ferry. I was leaving just in time.

8

AS THE FERRY TO KINSHASA LEFT THE DOCK, TWO SMUGGLERS vaulted the barricades, dodged the gendarmes, and jumped. One missed, and we left him swimming along the shore, chased by furious soldiers. The other came aboard to cheers. Strapped to his back was a nylon bag containing his contraband: five Belgian soup-hens, frozen but thawing fast.

The smugglers—every passenger but me—formed stock-market huddles. This thirty-minute ride was their last chance to adjust loads and bargain. Boys darted across the deck, carrying cash and merchandise. Men filled hidden pockets with bricks of cash, and women stuffed bank notes down cleavages. A girl buried eggs in a bowl of rice, and a shoeshine boy slid a wax-paper package into his box. Two men removed their shirts and, exchanging amused looks, wrapped themselves like mummies in swathes of cloth. The smugglers flipped soap, cigarettes, and cologne like jugglers: hens for smokes for money for cloth for eggs. It seemed synchronized to the chugging engines. Some merchandise was available on both banks of the river, making their smuggling slightly mad. I heard several explanations. It was because tastes differed, and cloth scorned in Brazzaville could fetch a price in Kinshasa; because being smuggled gave products a cachet; or because here, on the deck of this ferry, was freedom.

We bounced against the pilings, and the smugglers ran for the exit. The dock was a stockyard of gates, fences, and chutes. The smugglers shouted and waved at officials corrupted in advance. Almost no luggage was inspected; everyone was met. Rather than halting smuggling, the Zaïrian *douaniers* facilitated it.

Someone pushed open the gate too soon, and smugglers coming from Brazzaville and those waiting to go collided like rival armies. Frozen hens flew, bowls tumbled from heads. Men grabbed bundles and ran. The soldiers struck out with whips. Their beatings were accepted indifferently. Being whipped at the ferry was expected.

The fixer sent by the embassy led me away by the wrist. For the elite there was an air-conditioned trailer, curtained against the pandemonium. The following morning I paid for this luxury by lecturing to the senior English class at the National Pedagogical Institute (IPN), the jewel in the crown of President Mobutu's educational system. I was driven there through "the district of the big shots," past high concrete walls that made the road as claustrophobic as a railway cutting. Through open gates, and there were few of these, I saw flashes of green lawn and the sun sparkling off the chrome of sizable cars. Beyond the bolted gates of a ministry, lines of women danced and sang the praises of a "politician." Their performance was witnessed by soldiers and filmed by a solitary cameraman. Then we passed the military base where President Mobutu, "guide" of his people and winner of his last election by 99.16 percent of the vote, dared shut his eyes and sleep.

The director of the IPN hurried me through a side door and into a deserted classroom. Through some mix-up, the senior English class had gathered elsewhere. As we searched for them, he was forced to show me his campus. We walked down corridors where every light fixture had been stolen, peering into classrooms of shattered windows and leaking walls. In a dusty courtyard we broad-jumped puddles of black water and skirted garbage fires. The best university in Zaïre smelled of ashes and urine.

The director was unflappable. "These are the first-year classrooms, the teachers' common room, the boarders' dormitory," he said, describing one smashed room and building after another. Someone, perhaps by mistake, splattered us with a bowl of water thrown from a high dormitory window. The director said, "A temporary problem with the plumbing," and offered a handkerchief. The "problem" was that his desperate students had ripped out faucets and pipes and sold them for scrap. With the proceeds, they bought books and bribed their teachers for admittance to class and grades.

My students had gathered in a room that was in better shape than most. They wore clean white shirts and sat perfectly straight. Their eyes never left me and they fought to ask questions, slapping down the hands of neighbors. There was not a stupid face or a stupid question among them. They had been reading Hemingway and Orwell and were interested in *Animal Farm*. "Who is Snowball? Who *really* is Napoleon?" one boy asked with a sly smile. Was Orwell thinking of a particular dictator—Stalin, for example—or a general type of dictator?

(President Mobutu, for example.)

Their teacher met my eyes and gently shook his head. I gave vague answers, but they persisted. "Is it a fable only about Communist dictators?" asked a girl. She was grinning.

I distracted them with covers from my books. One was about crime and Swiss banks. I explained "money laundering," and two boys exchanged looks and whispered. Mobutu had not fooled these sharp students. They knew what had happened to the money to fix their school, buy their textbooks, and pay a fair salary to their professors.

Someone asked, "Who hides their money in Swiss banks? Criminals?"

"Yes."

"Drug dealers?"

"Yes."

A pause. "Political leaders?"

Class dismissed. Several students followed me into the parking lot, thrusting forward underlined passages from favorite books and demanding explanations. A tall boy from Kivu handed me an essay. It was about *Nineteen Eighty-Four*, and he wanted me to read it.

"Here? Now?"

"Yes, you must! It's my only copy. I'm afraid to give it away."

It was too long: ten pages of single-spaced, spidery handwriting.

"If you can't read it now you must tell me your address." I gave him my New York address. "No, I must have your address in Kinshasa." I said I was leaving soon for Mbandaka. "Then I will travel into the city tomorrow. You *must* read my essay. I *must* know if it is correct."

We agreed on a time, but he never came. A Zaïrian familiar with the university said, "That boy probably could not find money for the jitney."

"But why did he insist so?" I asked.

"Because professors demand money to read essays and their students wonder: 'Did he praise me because I bribed him?' 'Did he dislike it because I paid too little?' That boy hoped you would tell him honestly."

The man who said this worked for a foreign development organization. When I met him, he was clutching a volume of Proust—"My project this year," he said. His dream was to teach literature at a university, but he could not afford to study for a doctorate. "In my heart, I cannot abandon my dream," he said. "I *must* be a professor. It pays nothing. I will starve or take money from my students, but I want it because it is something unfairly denied to me. I *should* be a professor. Inside I *feel* like a professor." He thumped his chest with *À La Recherche du Temps Perdu*.

A foreigner who had taught at the IPN in Lumbumbashi insisted I really had seen the best university in Zaïre. In Lumbumbashi, *every* window was shattered, and money allocated for building the toilets had been stolen. The students had filled a neighboring field with their feces.

I met John, a graduate of the IPN in Kisangani, who thought conditions at Zaïre's universities would become worse. The government was cutting financial assistance to boarders, he said, "so soon only the children of rich businessmen and functionaries will be able to attend. The students will protest, but that is probably what our 'Gros Légume'—the 'Big Vegetable'—wants."

"The Gros Légume?"

"Yes, we call him that, or 'the big shot.' Oh, for him we have many names. He is angry because the university students did not applaud when he visited their campus. Now he will punish all the students by withholding scholarships. I think he is afraid. He knows that for years after graduation, we students write to exchange our news, and this, more than anything, worries our Gros Légume."

John made Kisangani sound worst of all. "I built my own chair because someone had sold our benches. We paid our professors, but no one blamed them. No one. We knew otherwise their families would starve, and in a few years we ourselves might be teachers demanding bribes from our students. I took my teachers to dinner and watched them eat because I couldn't afford two dinners. I made photostatic copies of books and sold them to other students. I had British teachers who didn't charge, then Zaïrian teachers again, but still I succeeded. I was so smart they couldn't ignore me."

I liked John's smile. It was amused but distant, as if he were a disinterested spectator to this waste of his talents. It invited you to join him in thinking, Isn't it absurd, someone with my intelligence, my *comprend*, stuck in this clerk's job? His cynicism and optimism were in balance: He knew Zaïre was rotten, yet he was convinced he would succeed anyway. His friends in Kisangani had left school to trade in poached ivory. Some had become wealthy. He had stayed to graduate. "Not because I like elephants. I wanted to finish what I started. I am not in a hurry, because I believe if you have brains you will learn how to succeed and overcome any difficulty. Soon I will move up and become successful."

For a short time he had worked as a driver and expediter for an American company, even saving enough to buy an old automobile. But the Americans left when the metals boom collapsed. Now he worked in an office. The wage was too small to support his large family so he rented out his car for $125 a month. This money permitted him to view with amused detachment the corruption he might otherwise have joined.

The next morning he took me back to the ferry dock. As we leaned on a railing twenty yards down the bank, he commented on the action with the authority of a handicapper in a paddock.

"Here we have some of the wealthiest people in Kinshasa. Even the deckhands own beautiful cars. They pay huge bribes to win their jobs, but then they can smuggle soap ten times a day."

"Only soap?"

John flashed his trademark smile. "Sometimes there are diamonds in the soap."

I mentioned that the crowd was larger than when I arrived.

I saw the smile again. "Sunday is a busy day. The traffic police are off duty, so the smugglers can avoid paying bribes on their way to the dock. Those police are the wealthiest police in Kinshasa. The functionaries who sign the *laissez-passers* are next. It is supposed to take several days to secure a *laissez-passer*, but without a bribe it may take a month. If you pay thirty cents, it takes two days; for fifty cents, you wait thirty minutes; for two dollars, it is immediate.

"The next wealthiest men are the soldiers at the dock. They must first bribe their officers to be assigned here. To earn this money they sell shares in themselves to relatives."

"How do you know all this?"

He looked amazed. "Here, everyone knows this."

But I thought that for someone promising to succeed on his brainpower, he knew rather too much about this dock. A mob of smugglers disembarked, and he said, "Watch how everyone — even the poorest man — has his own soldier. No one comes off that boat unmet except some stupid Europeans. See that soldier making a note? He estimates how much his client is smuggling and writes how much to charge later. Trusted clients pay by the week."

A dozen cripples in motorized wheelchairs waited among the passengers waiting to board. They were sleek, well-fed, and serene, the calm eye in this hurricane of smuggling. They drank soda pop through straws and barked orders to the perspiring retainers whose job it was to fan them, fetch food, and maneuver the bulky chairs. Bored with waiting, they gunned their chairs, slamming into the arriving smugglers like a panzer division.

"Why are so many cripples going to Brazzaville?" I asked.

When John had stopped laughing, he said, "Whoo-ee! They're the richest smugglers in Kinshasa. Because of their handicap, the government permits them to cross twice a week without paying or being searched."

I was impressed. Instead of burdening the state, these cripples had become successful entrepreneurs, retailing their smuggling potential to investment syndicates. They honeycombed their
chairs with gorilla parts, currency, gold, and diamonds in such
quantity that the Congo, with no mines of its own, had become a
major exporter. From Kinshasa to Brazzaville, they draped their
shriveled legs over ivory; from Brazzaville, they brought back ammunition for Zaïrian poachers. A round trip knocked off a herd of
elephants.

A smuggler jackknifed off the upper deck and swam for
shore. "I think he stole some dried fish," John said. "Yes, a man is
yelling about fish."

Two women shook their fists. "Aha! They are screaming
about money. He pretended to steal fish because he stole their
money."

The soldiers abandoned the gate, crowding the bank. "They
suspect he is smuggling something so valuable he does not wish
to pay them. They are promising to beat him, so naturally he stays
in the water."

The soldiers waved bank notes, trying to lure him ashore
with — what else? — a bribe. The smuggler trod water, crooning a
mad song and spitting fountains of filthy water. "He is acting
crazy to scare the soldiers. No! He's been paid to distract the soldiers. See for yourself." Dozens of smugglers poured through the
unguarded gate. Cartons of cigarettes sailed through the air. A
ragged woman threw herself at the soldiers, clutching at their
legs, wailing and ripping her garments. "His sister. She is upset
or, more likely, she worries the soldiers tire of the performance
and will return to their posts. But you know, Thurston, everything
could be true. He has stolen from the other smugglers, and he is
smuggling something valuable, and the smugglers have paid him
to create a disturbance. Here, you must take every chance to
make money or—"

"You starve."

The smile again. "We say that, but in truth no one starves in
Kinshasa. There is too much garbage."

"Whoo-ee!" John whistled. "Here come the big shots."
Two limousines discharged a party of dignitaries and their wives.
The Zaïrians had Nehru jackets, prescribed by the Gros Légume
as the uniform of revolutionaries. The other Africans wore tailored

suits. Chauffeurs and security men followed the wives, carrying
vanity cases and full shopping bags. They had visited the Galeries
Présidentielles, a mall of boutiques under the patronage of
Madame Mobutu. As they kissed and shook hands, I saw the traditional color of the African big shot: gold. There were gold bracelets, cuff links, and wristwatches on the men; gold necklaces and
earrings on the women; sunglasses rimmed in gold; and gold ini-
tials stamped on the soft leather cases that sometimes carry gold
across borders.

"Are they taking the ferry?" I asked.

John shook his head. I was a slow pupil. "The big shots never
take that boat. For them there is a *vedette* ["speedboat"]. It costs a
hundred dollars, but that is nonsense because they never pay."

To reach the *vedette,* the big shots had to detour around the
wailing sister, the amphibious smuggler, and soldiers whipping
back inquisitive children. None of them broke stride, turned
heads, or interrupted the flow of pleasantries. It all glanced off
their eyeballs as easily as the sun off their mirrored sunglasses.

Over the weekend, while I waited to buy a boat ticket to
Mbandaka, I found myself becoming interested in Kinshasa's corruption because, like the snakes in French Guiana, it was everywhere. People had the knack of turning the most casual exchange
into a commercial transaction, and I soon fell into the habit of
rewarding the most trivial kindness. I would not have been surprised had someone tried to sell me a smile. Corruption explained
why market women had the darting, lateral eyes of a hunted species; why soldiers walked with the loose-jointed stride of mug-
gers; why bank notes were so pungent — because people stuffed
them deep into the folds of their perspiring bodies; and why
geysers of water spouted from sidewalk holes, and brief showers
left roads flooded — because pipes could be sold for scrap, and
storm drains were prized as barbecue grills.

Those who could not extort or smuggle, stole. Employers expected theft just as restaurant patrons expect to tip. Chauffeurs
sold gasoline back to black-market fuel dealers known as
"Qadaffis," who re-sold it from roadside oil drums. Corruption
had corrupted language. A "friend" was someone bribed on a
steady basis. And the question "Can I have confidence in you?"

meant "Pay me so I can trust you." Corruption had a geography. People followed circuitous routes to avoid passing army barracks and intersections favored by the police. Corruption had rules. The military police were the cavalry, roaming the city in flying squads and sometimes arresting the rapacious soldiers and gendarmes. Irregular identity papers were the usual pretext for a "fine," but if a victim presented a driver's license, registration, and identity card, stamped to prove he or she had "voted" in the last election, then a soldier might ask, "But, *citoyen,* where is your baptismal certificate?" So *citoyens* soon began carrying these, forcing soldiers to ask, "But, *citoyen,* where is your copy of the president's five-year plan?"—an unaccountably heavy document—"What? No copy of that?" They tsk-tsked and shook their heads. "That is grave, *citoyen,* very grave. *Comprend?"*

This *comprend*—"understand"—was the password. It meant, "*Comprend* that I must feed my family, so I have stopped you and I will make trouble unless you pay. *Comprend?* Yes, others are walking past, but that's bad luck for you. *Comprend?"* And people did *comprend.* I watched the faces of market women pulling tattered bank notes from knotted handkerchiefs, and I saw not hate but resignation, and flashes of good humor.

To understand that soldiers stole more from desperation than greed you had only to see their barracks, places of broken windows stuffed with rags and children defecating on littered parade grounds. If the Gros Légume was punishing the students, then he was punishing his soldiers even more. A report smuggled from Zaïre by dissident officers said, "While the high-ranking military leaders deprive themselves of nothing, their common subordinates and their families starve. . . . While high-ranking leaders keep on building houses, already starving, extorted, reduced to scrounging, the garrisoned Zaïrian soldiers and their families live in unacceptable circumstances which are incompatible with any morality."

Seeing these army barracks made you wonder: If this was how soldiers lived in the capital, how much worse could conditions be in the countryside? And if the army suffered like this, then how bad were the jails? If soldiers stole to eat, what chance did their prisoners have?

Large portraits of the man responsible for this misery decorated Kinshasa. They had been erected for an election held eight months earlier. Removing them might be construed as disloyalty, so they remained, peeling in the rain and collapsing into parks, so bleached by sunlight that the face became whiter and more featureless by the week, a scrubbed potato wearing glasses.

The electoral farces staged by despots are windows on their souls. In Zaïre, elections only confirmed Mobutu as president of the Popular Movement of the Revolution (MPR). But under the constitution, written by Mobutu, the MPR was the only political party, so its leader automatically became the president of Zaïre. Furthermore, the constitution of the MPR stated its official doctrine as Mobutuism, and there was a law requiring each and every citizen of Zaïre to become a member of the MPR at birth! The Gros Légume wanted it all: all the votes and everyone belonging to his party, Mobutuists from the day they were born.

The slogans underneath his portraits nicely summarized Mobutuism. They said Long Live Mobutu! and Good Health and Success to the Guide! This was Mobutuism: success, long life, and wealth — for Mobutu. After twenty years he was the richest man in Africa (or perhaps the second richest, after Qadaffi), while his country was among the poorest. It had considerable mineral resources — diamonds, cobalt, copper, and magnesium — but its per capita income was falling. It had a tenth of the world's hydroelectric potential, yet blackouts plagued its cities. It had fertile volcanic soil in the east, yet food had to be imported, and a quarter of its children died of protein deficiencies by the age of five. Its factories worked at a quarter of capacity, its roads and bridges were crumbling, its foreign debt was staggering. There was desperate unemployment in the cities and a return to subsistence agriculture in the countryside, but through it all Mobutu, his family, and his associates — the "barons" of the regime — had become fabulously wealthy.

There was nothing elegant about the Gros Légume's thievery. He embezzled from the Bank of Zaïre by ordering foreign funds transferred to his personal account. The national mining company sold copper, and the proceeds went to Mobutu. Air Zaïre smuggled cobalt and diamonds to Europe, and the money landed in Mobutu's Swiss accounts. Just as Mobutu "owned" his people by insisting they become members of his party, he owned

Zaïre, and he stole from it in the same crude, unapologetic fashion as King Leopold had when it was his.

If Mobutuism had an ideology, it was capitalist consumption without capitalist production, and theft on a grand scale by Mobutu, and on a petty scale by everyone else as they battled for whatever scraps he missed. What made Mobutuism even more tragic was that the Zaïrians are an exceptionally quick-witted, intelligent, and humorous people, good company in spite of — because of? — everything. Nowhere in Africa did I enjoy as many impromptu conversations and encounters; nowhere did I sense such a wasting of talent and energy.

John surprised me by refusing to join in ridiculing the Gros Légume's billboards. "That Gros Légume is necessary for us," he said.

"Necessary! Why?"

"Without him we would have terrible fighting and killing." This was the same justification — that Mobutu was the only alternative to the tribal wars and anarchy of the 1960s — that you sometimes heard from the official representatives of his foreign allies, such as the United States. I wondered if John was afraid of being reported, but he said, "If you knew my story, you would understand." During the civil wars, his family had fled into the forest outside Kisangani, living on rats and roots. His brother died. His father never recovered. "Better the Gros Légume than the forest," John said, and who could blame anyone who believed that was the choice?

Not everyone believed the Gros Légume's peace-keeping abilities worth the price. I lost a notebook in Zaïre, so I cannot remember precisely why or where I was being taken by the middle-aged Zaïrian in the American embassy mini-van, although it was somehow part of my facilitative assistance. But I do remember him detouring through what I hope is Kinshasa's most desperate slum. We were alone in the car, but still he dropped his voice to an urgent whisper, all the time laughing and smiling, as if we were spies exchanging secrets in public.

"Look, Clarke, what do you see? Ha! Ha! Ha! Miserable people."

I saw streets stuffed with children and families living under cardboard roofs held down by rocks. He slowed to the speed of a pedestrian. "The children, Clarke. Look at them; think about them."

I recognized their ragged clothes. They wore T-shirts advertising American athletic teams, restaurants, and jogging contests. American charities sold them to brokers who shipped them to the tropics in bales.

"Ask yourself: 'How long can this continue?'"

A long time, I thought. Regimes crueler than this had endured because of Africans' capacity to absorb suffering, their kindness toward relatives, and their willingness to carve food and living space into microscopic portions.

"We are not a stupid people. We know this is a rich country, but we have nothing. Ask yourself: 'How can people have less of nothing every year and survive?' He stopped at an appalling street of coffin-sized houses. "Disgusting how they live." He whispered, still holding his expansive smile. "Disgusting that he has so much. But it won't last forever, or even much longer."

But for twenty years he had been crushing secession movements, imprisoning the plotters and driving his opponents into exile.

"Oh, Clarke, things change very fast in this country. No one thought the Belgians would leave and then, click, they were gone in six months." The "click" he made with his tongue sounded like a pistol being cocked. "The same thing could happen again, even faster. Click click click click, click!"

He turned onto a paved highway and accelerated. The wretched back alleys flickered past like a silent movie. "Fast with the Belgians, and so fast with him he may not escape. All those houses in Europe, and we'd have him here!" For the first time he laughed genuinely. "Believe me, it will happen, and I'll live to see it. Comprend?"

If you wanted, you could avoid these streets. Kinshasa had been built to the specifications of the Belgian "big vegetables," and its geography encouraged myopia in big vegetables of any race. Like most colonial capitals it was two cities: an imitation European one, with a commercial center and garden suburbs; and the native quarter, identified on Belgian maps as the Cité Indigène, now known simply as the Cité. The native city was inland; the European city hogged the riverfront, a knot of banks, ministries, embassies, docks, and trading companies gathered where the Zaïre River widened into the Pool Malebo. This city had flourished during two economic booms: the Belgian one, lasting from the end of the war until independence, in 1960; and the copper boom of the early seventies. These booms had left behind guidebooks that could have been written by the same fabulist. The Belgian one described "thousands of cyclists [who] ride along the tarred avenues of the Native City, reminding one of Copenhagen [!]," and "a new city, a young city, full of vitality which causes factories to arise, houses to spring up, and which is gradually giving birth to a civilization of boundless energy which enthusiasts are spreading without restraint." Twenty years later, the Gros Légume's guidebook likened the Boulevard of June 30th, "this handsome artery," to the Champs Élysées, and said that for the visitor Kinshasa provided "an inexhaustible supply of landscapes, thrills and memories." It was a "pilot city . . . which purports to be an accurate reflection of the unshakable will of a people aware of its destiny and eager to assume this destiny to the hilt."

Kinshasa's "destiny" was now apparent. Like pack ice in the spring, the European city was breaking into islets of prosperity, all walled and guarded. There were the foreign embassies, the compounds of the wealthy, the Intercontinental Hotel, and Madame Mobutu's Galeries Présidentielles, where, the Gros Légume's guidebook boasted, "well-dressed women with well-lined purses . . . fling their money around . . . [and] . . . the parade of chauffeured Mercedes in front of its escalators is evidence of the high level of transactions that take place here."

The most sinister islet of prosperity was the pink Sozacom skyscraper. Its every architectural detail spoke menace. A black hat of magnesium capped it, and cement canopies shaded its balconies like hooded eyes ready to blink their steel shutters. The terraces were crenellated, the entrance reached by a ramp arching over an imaginary moat. It was the castle of a science fiction villain, cold, remote, and promising a sinister future. It was a convenient headquarters for Sozacom, the government-controlled minerals-trading society. The men who stole Zaïre's natural wealth could live in apartments on upper floors and juggle the books in the offices below. On the ground floor was the ticket office of Swissair.

Between these islets of prosperity, European Kinshasa was a wasteland of flooded streets and cracked sidewalks, smoldering garbage and bars catering to whores and lonely white men. There was an end-of-civilization atmosphere, with survivors finding shelter in the rubble. This disturbed me — because, I suppose, the civilization ending was mine. Everywhere squatters lived among twisted iron and crumbling cinder blocks on the top floors of the unfinished buildings that represented the high-water mark of the copper boom. In the former Belgian neighborhood of Limité, huge families occupied houses modeled after a Brussels suburb. Half were maintained; the rest were overgrown and blackened by indoor cooking fires, their owners inundated by relatives escaping the interior.

The stark, futuristic outline of a radio tower dominated the eastern horizon. When construction began, in 1965, it was the Lumumba Monument. When the Gros Légume changed his politics, it became the Monument to the Martyrs of Independence. From a distace it resembled a world's-fair space needle — and perhaps its Tunisian architect had this in mind — but the funds to complete it had disappeared, leaving an iron skeleton balanced on cracked pillars. Underneath a television mast was the frame of an observation deck and the inevitable revolving restaurant. The base was circled by an expressway to accommodate motorcades, and an elevated highway shot out from the pedestal, ending in midair. Here the big vegetables must have pictured themselves marching in official processions, laying wreaths and giving orations before an eternal flame. Now squatters lived underneath the archways, huddling around oil-drum fires. The concrete ramps had become a makeshift playground. Screaming children whooshed down them on flattened cardboard boxes, casting prehistoric, firelit shadows.

I first visited the Cité at night, with an American couple who preferred it to the dreary European town. We ate on a terrace facing a square blazing with light and echoing with pop music. All around was the gorging-on-fun crowd of a state fair, the good-natured crowd you hope to find in Times Square or Piccadilly Circus, but never do. Since independence, the Cité's population has increased from three hundred thousand to three million. People came to escape civil wars, find work, educate children, and, they hoped, cure illnesses. But you had only to see the bars of the Cité — the courtyard bars strung with lights, the throbbing, windowless bars that opened at midnight, the curbside bars with men huddled around centerpieces of green beer bottles — to see that people had also come to Kinshasa for fun. And some of them, the men anyway, had found it.

The next morning, the Cité was a seedy nightclub with the bright lights turned on after closing, an illusion shattered. The buildings were black and greasy, as if the ramshackle trucks had changed their oil in everyone's front yard. Trickles of sewage ran down back-street tributaries, emptying into canals in perpetual flood. On foot, I searched for the streets I had seen the night before. It was impossible. There were no rivers, hills, or valleys, none of the natural features that can distinguish a slum and define its limits. I drank a warm beer in an outdoor bar and was surrounded by men sprawled in chairs. Their wives trudged past us piled with babies, firewood, and the hairy manioc roots that require hours of preparation. Their children lugged water, ran errands, and swept yards. The men paid little attention to this struggling procession. Like the big shots boarding the *vedette*, their eyeballs were well trained.

On Sunday night I went out without a flashlight and stepped into one of the storm drains that had surrendered its cover for a barbecue grill. I fell in up to my waist, but I had a lucky landing, only gashing one thigh and suffering a slight sprain. I washed in antiseptic and woke the next morning with a limp, feverish and eager to leave. I had postponed until Monday buying a boat ticket to Mbandaka, thinking that reaching the equator from Kinshasa would be easy. The Zaïre is the only large river the equator intersects twice. When the dry season in the northern hemisphere shrivels its northern tributaries, the wet season in the southern hemisphere fills its southern ones, and vice versa, guaranteeing year-round navigation among Kinshasa, Mbandaka, and Kisangani. I heard that service on the river had deteriorated. There were fewer boats, channels had silted, and markers disappeared, but a river journey was still possible, and there was a weekly boat.

It was raining as I limped through Kinshasa to buy a ticket. Several hundred men had gathered outside ONATRA, the government agency running cargo and passenger boats on the river. They lay under dripping palms or sat on the curb, heads in hands. One said, "We are the stevedores, and we are striking for more pay." They earned twenty-five dollars a month, a subsistence wage turned into a starvation one by a recent devaluation. Their trousers were loose at the waist and they wore plastic sandals. It could not be much fun, lifting and loading, being a stevedore in plastic sandals.

"We are angry," one man said in a flat voice.

"Yes, very angry," another said, a hollow echo. "And tomorrow we may throw stones at the ONATRA building."

They did not seem angry to me, only wet and extraordinarily quiet. John confirmed what they told me, that during the strike no ONATRA boat would leave Kinshasa. It might be weeks before regular service resumed. There were no trains or roads to Mbandaka, and flying was difficult. Last year the government airline, Air Zaïre, promised a daily flight. Now a more realistic timetable showed two a week, but these might be canceled or delayed for days. The planes were often cannibalized for parts or requisitioned for the Gros Légume's errands. There were rumors of crashes, hushed up, and some embassies and organizations had ordered personnel not to fly Air Zaïre. They chartered planes instead. The only reliable way to fly to Mbandaka, Zaïre's fifth largest city, was a small private airline owned by SCIBE, the country's largest coffee exporter. It had the suitable name of Air Lift and operated a limited schedule to eastern Zaïre.

No sooner had I found a way to get to Mbandaka than I was surrounded by people claiming I was a fool to bother. John had been stranded there three days when a ferry broke down. "Whoo-ee! There is nothing there. Nothing!" he said. I would be staying a week, longer if the strike ended and I waited for boats to start running to Kisangani. I had always planned a long visit to Mbandaka. With a population of a quarter million, it is the largest city in the world on the equator. Stanley had founded it, naming it Equatorville, and according to my Belgian guidebook it was filled with equatorial attractions. There was a marker in the garden of the regional commissioner showing the equator's path.

There was a Museum of the Equator and the Eala Botanical Garden, described as the "third best" tropical garden in the world. The Gros Légume's guidebook praised the city as "one of Zaïre's handsomest. . . . Its broad thoroughfares rank among the finest and best kept. . . . Its Avenue Bolenge, a splendid corniche drive along the river, . . . [holds] endless enticements for sightseers. Planted with rows of white-trunked royal palms, brightly lighted at night, they are a favorite haunt of local denizens." And Equateur Province, of which Mbandaka was the capital, was the birthplace of the Gros Légume and many of his generals and ministers. Mbandaka was the site of his boyhood school, which received "a steady stream of delegations from the Popular Revolutionary Movement bent on pilgrimages."

Kate Newman, who had spent a year in Mbandaka as regional director of the Peace Corps, was a Mbandaka fan. She thought it a swell place and hoped to return for a holiday. She worried my visit was too short. "Only a week! But you'll need several to see it all." She filled a page with suggestions, making Mbandaka seem as packed with attractions as Rome. She introduced me to Aaron Zee, her successor, who was in Kinshasa on business. He was a friendly bear of a man who offered me the use of his house and Land Rover and promised to radio Mbandaka, the only reliable way to communicate with the city, and tell his driver to meet my Air Lift.

When I asked John to join me on my last evening in Kinshasa, I imagined us drinking in the outdoor bars and clubs of the Cité. But he surprised me by arriving in his car, a dented old Ford Cortina he had repossessed after his "friend" fell behind in the payments and smashed the doors. John had insurance, but filing a claim meant bribing the adjuster, insurance agent, and garage. Suing his friend for the overdue rent meant a bribe to the judge. It was cheaper to accept the loss. But having the car was no advantage, since buying gas to drive to work cost more than he earned in a day. "And if I rent it to a stranger," he said, "it will surely be stolen."

Instead of the Cité, John insisted on the Intercontinental Hotel. He had bought enough fuel to drive there, but not to the Cité. He refused my offer to buy more. This was his parting gift. The doorman and the waitress in the patio bar greeted him warmly, and he confessed to coming here to acquire black-market diamonds for his former employers, the American businessmen. "I like this place," he admitted, his eyes shuttling like a typewriter carriage, devouring the luxury and tranquility.

"Whooo-eee!" He whistled. "Many big shots here today." The sky turned pink. A breeze stirred the palms. He stared into his beer and spoke in a dreamy voice, repeating his thoughts. "I have my brains . . . Yes . . . I'll survive . . . But in my job, even if I advance, even if I succeed, still . . ."

A waitress brought more beers. Colored lights clicked on in the garden. A European woman splashed in the pool with her daughters. "You know, Thurston, I must help my family more . . . much more," he said. "Everyone who wants to provide for their family must steal or smuggle or find extra business. *Comprend?*" His hand snaked across the table, slithering between salary and bribery, labor and theft.

"But you're surviving," I said. "And you don't—"

"Because of the car. But that's finished. That man, I thought he was a friend, a real friend. And now I've lost a month's rent. That is grave for my family." He swallowed his beer in quick gulps. "But you know, I could earn five thousand Zaïres, more than a month's salary, as much as I charged for that car. I could make all that money easily."

"How?"

He leaned across the table. "One tusk."

"Smuggle ivory?" I felt betrayed. I had bought this believing-in-my-brains business.

He flashed the smile. "Only the big shots get legal permits."

I love elephants. They are the reason to go to a zoo or a circus.

He gripped my forearm. "My savings and car—all worthless. In Zaïre one thing is certain: elephants."

In a low, urgent voice he explained his plan. He would not kill the elephant himself but be in the middle of a chain of middlemen. He would travel to Kisangani and buy his tusk from a middleman who had bought it from the poacher. He would be the internal smuggler, bringing it to Kinshasa on the boat and selling it to another middleman who would pass it to the external smuggler. "But first I need capital." He held my eyes. I could volunteer, but he was too proud to ask.

"Capital?"

"Money for a ticket to Kisangani, for buying the first tusk, and for feeding my family while I'm gone."

I shook my head. Nothing could convince me to back this enterprise.

"Listen . . . to . . . me," he said. "Just one tusk to start. I'll work hard, reinvesting my profits so the next time I can buy two. Then four. Then hire someone else to go to Kisangani. I have brains so I'm certain to succeed, but to start I must have this capital." He squeezed my arm, hard. *"Comprend?"*

9

A FRENZY OF PARTYING AND DEAL-MAKING ON THE SPRAWLING veranda of Mbandaka's air terminal absorbed the Air Lift passengers from Kinshasa. Families embraced. Local big shots presented bouquets to arriving ones. Everyone joined the beer parties in progress at the outdoor tables. Fixers bobbed and weaved, waving baggage stubs and identity cards. Although this was an internal flight, these formalities gave the authorities a pretext for their larcenies. A boy shined my shoes without permission. A woman measured out rubbery peanuts with a shot glass. A girl followed her, shelling them for a tip. Soldiers wandered in threes, holding hands by one finger like paper dolls. Somewhere a Belgian waffle iron still performed: From the same tray, a man sold waffles and pink caterpillars, packed in plastic sandwich bags with a comforting mulch of dirt and moss. He dropped a bag on a table and soldiers wagered peanuts on which way the caterpillars would crawl.

I met "Charlie Hall," the son of missionaries. He spoke several African languages and lived in Mbandaka, but he had the square-jawed face and the deliberate walk and nonchalant manner of a cowboy hero. "Better relax and have another beer," he said. "Be at least an hour before that tractor pulls the luggage into customs. Let me handle the police. The game here is physical control of the passport." And sure enough, he had to cajole a policeman into sliding my passport across a counter. With a treacherous smile, the officer said, *"Bienvenue à* Mbandaka." Charlie laughed. "He'll get you on the way out, when you're afraid of missing the plane. Come over to the brewery. We'll all be playing basketball, and it's near your equator."

Aaron Zee's driver, Mouila, drove carefully, not because traffic was dangerous but because there was so little that people walked or rode bicycles down the middle of Mbandaka's avenues, and he feared hitting them. The lonely cars bouncing over wide, dusty streets reminded me of Macapá and Calçoene, except here the jungle frontier was contracting instead of expanding.

The praise lavished on Mbandaka by the Gros Légume's guidebook was not inaccurate. Its "broad thoroughfares" probably do rank among "the finest and best-kept of Zaïre's cities," if only because there are so few vehicles churning them into canyons. The old Belgian villas, post office, palace of justice, and other official buildings were still "gracious," and still "imposing hulks." But at slower speeds they were peeling, sagging, and collapsing. I kept staring at these relics, believing that if I stared long enough I might see a plank tumble, a tile fall, or a porch slide into the weeds.

Mbandaka had its islet of prosperity. It sat on a hill west of the commercial district, ringed by fences. Sprinklers watered golf-course lawns and gardeners fussed over flowering hedges. Zaïrian and European professionals strode across parking lots and gravel paths, clutching clipboards and holding purposeful conversations. Workers wore gauze masks and rubber gloves. Machinery sparkled. Everything was antiseptic. No, this was not the Hôpital Mama Mobutu Sese Soukou, a place so appalling Mouila shook his head furiously as we passed it. It was the Primus brewery, built and managed by Heineken.

I followed the sound of tennis balls to the Brewery Club, where Europeans and educated Zaïrians played tennis and basketball or sat in garden furniture gossiping and drinking. Despite the Zaïrian members, there were echoes here of the colonial club and of the social distinctions of colonial society. The Belgian and American volunteer teachers and development workers were permitted to play tennis and basketball, but not to swim in a pool reserved for the brewery executives. The Dutch manager had the status of a governor-general, and the younger men treated him with an exaggerated deference, offering chairs, bringing drinks, and amusing his wife. And I heard echoes of the colonial club in the languid conversations that, with the change of a word or two, could easily have filled the humid, late-afternoon air of an earlier time.

"Measles are raging in the Cité."

"An epidemic."

"No one trusts the hospital."

"They are sending their children into the bush, to live with the grandparents."

"How many have died?"

"Who knows? They expire in the bush."

"The vice-governor arrived today."

"The new governor comes next week, and they are declaring a school holiday so the children can welcome him."

"And the workers too, they are being ordered to greet him."

The Primus beer was delicious, cold and fresh and better than an ordinary Heineken. A European brewer said it was Mbandaka's best product and principal pleasure. The brewery had its own generator; elsewhere, people went weeks without electricity. The brewery drew water from its own spring; elswhere, water trickled from taps. The brewery had its own teletypewriter and shortwave, because calling long distance took hours, and telegrams took a week from Kinshasa. Last year Mbandaka had gone six weeks without mail, although boats docked and planes landed. Then gasoline became so scarce the governor requisitioned even the "Qaddaffis"'s black-market barrels. "Is there really a riverboat strike?" someone asked. "We hadn't noticed."

No one had heard of the Museum of the Equator or visited the Eala gardens, but a Zaïrian schoolteacher said, "Be careful there. They hit dogs with a pipe and feed them to that crocodile." (But why should *I* be careful?)

No one could agree on the equator's location. The bartender said it crossed the road to Wangata a mile from the brewery and was marked by a monument.

"Nah, that's only Stanley's equator," Charlie said, coming off the tennis court.

The teacher nodded. "That rock is the equator for the whites, the colonialist equator."

"But your governor held the ceremonies there last year," said a Dutch brewer. The ceremonies had marked the hundredth anniversary of the founding of Equatorville, later to become Coquilhatville and, still later, Mbandaka.

"He was celebrating the town," Charlie said, "not the equator."

"But didn't Stanley found Equatorville *on* the equator?" I asked, rooting for the colonialist equator, hoping it did not run unmarked through nearby rain forest.

"Perhaps Stanley was wrong," the teacher said. "We knew about the equator before Stanley. We did not need a European to give it to us."

"Then where's the African equator?"

"At the rock," insisted the bartender, holding out for the colonialist line.

"Nope," said Charlie. "A few years ago some American oil drillers surveyed. They said the real equator is south of that rock."

The teacher laughed. "Maybe they found it by luck, but the real equator is our secret."

The following day, Mouila drove me down a dirt track to Wangata and the white man's equator. It was marked by a boulder on a concrete pedestal. Since it was a Belgian relic, the plaque had disappeared during the Gros Légume's revolution. More recently, the equatorial rock had returned to favor, and the government had permitted the American drillers to erect an ambiguous sign saying EQUATOR. HERE WAS FOUNDED THE FIRST EQUATOR TOWN IN 1883. And, in smaller letters, Near the Geographical Equator 0 2'.

In 1983, the government had built a small outdoor bar here to celebrate the centenary of Equatorville. Since then, its thatched roof had disappeared, and its bathrooms and refrigerator cannibalized. Left untouched was a portrait of the Gros Légume in a white uniform. Mouila spoke a rudimentary French, so we communicated in nouns and sign language. It took me ten minutes to learn that this bar had been popular. People sat under its strings of colored lights. They liked to drink Primus. They had fun. Then, months after the ceremony, thieves stole the chairs, the lights, and the refrigerator's motor.

A Zaïrian colonel and a barrel-shaped Portuguese couple I recognized from the plane climbed from a black sedan. The colonel gestured toward the bar and the equatorial rock, as if presenting the Grand Canyon. He smiled at me, glad of another tourist to prove this a significant attraction.

The couple had a video camera, and the man posed the colonel and his wife in front of the sign announcing that this might or might not be the equator. Then the colonel filmed the couple leaning against the vandalized bar. The camera had a microphone and I heard him say, "You are now standing exactly on the equator."

"Are you sure this is the equator?" I asked. "The sign says it's further south."

"No! *Here* our governor celebrated the anniversary."

In the Gros Légume's guidebook I had read, "A marker in the garden of the Regional Commissioner's residence symbolizes the line of the equator that passes through the city." I asked the colonel for directions to this residence.

"There is no such place." He eyed my equatorial expedition button. "Who are you?"

"Only a tourist."

Charlie lived nearby, on the southern bank of the Zaïre and near where the equator must cross it — that is, if the equator is marked by the boulder. His parents were visiting when I arrived. According to Mrs. Hall, the dispute was not between an African or a colonialist equator but between a Belgian or an American one: the Belgian rock versus the unmarked site of the American oil drillers. The Belgian consul in Mbandaka had protested the American sign, insisting the Belgian equator was the true one, but since then he had been expelled for refusing to name the members of an underground group. She thought the regional commissioner's residence was "that old mansion next door." During the fifties, it had belonged to the president of the Belgian palm-oil company. He had never invited them over. Nor had the Zaïrian governor, who inherited it at independence. Then Mobutu took it for his Mbandaka estate but never spent a night there. Now it stood abandoned.

As we walked to it along an overgrown path, we were joined by Charlie's dog and a chimpanzee adopted by visiting zoologists. A tree had fallen into a guardhouse, and fence posts had taken root and sprouted. The house was vaguely Venetian. So was the river. Islands had reduced it to an intimate width, and fishermen poled pirogues like gondoliers. The light was blurred and milky. The dog and the chimp chased each other up a stone staircase, their barking and chattering echoing off vaulted ceilings. The chimp trampolined on a bed, grabbed wires dangling from vandalized fixtures, and swung around a statue decorating a cracked fountain. The dog pissed in corners and lapped puddles. Rain had fallen through holes in the roof, and water gushed from broken pipes. In Mobutu's ruined mansion, the water pressure was still strong.

The chimp led me by the hand to a winter garden. It faced the river, but vines grew through shattered windows and foliage would soon block the view. But why had the terrace been glassed rather than screened? Then I shivered, feeling goose bumps for the first time in Africa, and understood: This was a cold spot, supernatural in its chill. There were natural explanations. The house faced north, built to catch wind off the river, and it was shaded by mangoes and swaddled in forest. But that would account for it being cool, not cold.

"I can't believe that's still here," Charlie said, staring at an abandoned toilet. "They cost a fortune on the black market." Mbandaka's legacy of European toilets was shrinking faster than the number of people accustomed to them. Seats and cisterns cracked, and there were no replacements. Those unused to squatting in a field or an outhouse became desperate, and thieves stole from occupied houses. Victims of the toilet bandits visited neighbors and found themselves using familiar porcelain.

"What a waste," Mrs. Hall said, rubbing the chill from her arms. "Yes, I declare, what a terrible shame." But for whom? Perhaps for Europeans who had devoted a lifetime to Mbandaka, but not for the squatters who slept on these stained mattresses, cooked over fires made from doors and windows, drank clean water, bathed in a tub dragged into the ballroom, and filled that cracked toilet with their feces. It *was* a shame — if you thought, Here is a splendid house going to waste. But a splendid house for whom? The Belgian palm-oil kings and governors-general were gone. Even Mobutu and his big vegetables had no use for bogus

Mediterranean villas. They had decimated cities like Mbandaka in order to buy the real thing.

The forest had reclaimed the ornamental garden, swallowing a gazebo and breaching a stone wall. A single bougainvillaea flowered in a sunny corner. I beat back weeds and underbrush with a branch, searching for an equatorial marker. It was hopeless. I could have slashed for days and still missed it. But a marker here would have lined up perfectly with the boulder on the Wangata road. If you believed the Belgians, then this was the regional commissioner's house, where the equator crossed the Zaïre River.

As we left, a squatter living on the foundations of the guardhouse jumped up and ran after us, shouting, *"Patron! Patron! Stop!"* We stopped. "How would you like"—he caught his breath—"to buy a toilet?"

Back at Charlie's house, a slight young Indian with liquid eyes stood in front of a white Mercedes, wiping specks of mud from his white loafers with a handkerchief. His driver polished the car. "Meet Mr. Patel," Charlie said, describing him as the most important businessman and landowner in Mbandaka. Mr. Patel was embarrassed, but he did not challenge the description.

"Mr. Patel was born in Mbandaka."

"Yes, born and raised here." Mr. Patel began his sentences with "Yes," then echoed whatever had been said, a habit he had presumably acquired while performing whatever delicate ballet allowed him to stay in Mbandaka.

"If anyone can tell you about the equator," Charlie said, "it's Patel."

"Yes, about the equator. I have important documents to that effect. You must come to my office tomorrow morning."

His office was off the Avenue Bolenge, behind an arcade of empty stores crowned with huge letters spelling P A T E L. A gate under the T led to a courtyard filled with blossoms and caged birds. Mr. Patel was working in a cavernous office, reading *Fundamentals of Small Business Management* and doing sums on a pocket calculator. A servant brought us warm sodas. Mr. Patel apologized. He would like to have offered me a chilled drink, but the electricity had failed and . . . A light flickered and the overhead fan revolved.

Underneath a dust cover, an adding machine hummed. "Aha! An hour late," Patel said. "But better late than—"

Everything stopped. "Good! Better you should see this. Now you understand why our city is going backwards. Without reliable current there is no industry. Without industry, no salaries. Without salaries, no clients for the shops. No shops, and no one is renting my properties. All Patel stores on side streets are empty because remaining clients only wish to shop on Broadway [Mr. Patel's name for the Avenue Bolenge]."

I mentioned the Patel Pharmacy. It was not on "Broadway," yet it had customers.

"Yes, not on Broadway, but people trust it more than the hospital. No one dies in Patel's pharmacy. It will be the last to close."

He walked me down the arcade of empty stores outside his office. "This was Bata Shoes. That was a boutique selling best-quality radios from Japan. This was the Ciné Eros, my brother's idea." Behind double glass doors I saw a poster advertising a kung fu movie. "Once there were rivers of money here. Rivers. Now no one can afford a high-class cinema."

Mr. Patel had rented a store to himself. It sold only coffee. When they saw us, two clerks shoveled beans from a sack into a scale, making a show of weighing them. They poured them back as we left. "See!" Mr. Patel said. "No clients." He was curiously satisfied.

Then why keep his stores in such good repair? They had new windows, varnished shelves, and fresh paint.

"Yes. Why I keep them this way . . . because I am always hoping for the big boom!" He flashed a hopeless smile.

"Surely you'd have some warning of that."

Mr. Patel lowered his voice. "OK. I tell you why. I do it for my father."

"Does he live in Mbandaka?"

"Dead since 1967. But he would be displeased to see his stores tumbling into ruin. He owned fifty, now down to thirty but I'm fixing them up, *every one*! And when there's electricity I turn it on. They shine with lights. See that?" He pointed to the P A T E L. "These stores honor my father's name. If there are no merchants to rent them, no clients to buy, no money, no goods, nothing, still I will fix them up just so the name Patel doesn't go poof in the wind." He took a deep breath and his eyes teared. "Ah, my father, a real moving man. He traded in Java and Sumatra, then India, Kenya, and Uganda, then Goma and Kisangani. In 1927 he came to Mbandaka and said, 'No more moving, here I stay.'"

"Why did he stay?" I asked when we returned to Patel's office.

"Yes. Why here?" He stared at the broiling courtyard, searching for what had pleased his father. "Because he was the first Indian to come here and . . . and because he liked Mbandaka!"

The first explanation was more likely. In the twenties, Mbandaka must have been an El Dorado for the first Indian trader. Most of the rubber and palm oil from the Congo basin passed through its wharves.

"He liked Mbandaka so much he sent for his relatives from East Africa. Other Indian families came, and at independence there were hundreds of us. During the difficulties many fled, but he remained, and look! this was his fate." Patel waved a green file. Water rings stained its front, proving it was always close at hand. He pulled out a blurred carbon of a letter written by his father in 1964 to the governor, passing it to me on his palms as though it were a treasure. It said: "For thirty years I have invested my life in Mbandaka and never taken a thing away from the city." (I wondered if this was entirely true.) He claimed to have reinvested his profits, and that "the benefits are still visible." He listed the buildings financed by Patels and reminded the governor he had demonstrated his faith in Mbandaka by raising eight children there. Other traders fled, but the Patels had stayed. Now he wished to transfer ten thousand pounds to Bombay to build a retirement home. The rest of his money, his enterprises, and his sons would remain in Mbandaka. This was all couched in painfully obsequious prose. The governor's "goodness and wisdom" were "known and applauded far and wide." He believed his request would "receive the full benefit of his excellency's honesty and fairness." Of course the governor refused, and soon afterwards Patel Senior died, in Mbandaka.

Had the governor found this letter as pleasurable as Patel found it painful? Perhaps his family had rented property from Patels. Certainly they had shopped in Patel stores, all the while feeling the eyes of vigilant Patels. Patel Senior mentioned "benefits [to Mbandaka] that are still visible." But were there also invisible scars? A residual resentment against penniless Indians who could float down that river and make a fortune? And did the governor, or his sons, also keep the original of this letter equally close at hand? (And would Ruurd's children preserve his suitcase of "problems"? And why are third-world minorities such fanatics for documenting these ancient wrongs?)

I asked Patel about his equatorial documents.

"Yes, about the equator," he echoed, putting down his Fanta can and adding one more ring to the green file.

"Do you think it's at the rock, or down the road where—"

"If the governor celebrated the equator at the rock, then who can dispute? And I have documentary proof he believes the equator is there."

He showed me his letters from the governor. The first described a celebration being organized to mark the centenary of Mbandaka's founding. Donations were needed to erect a memorial where the equator crossed the Wangata road. When Mr. Patel did not respond, he received a reminder that ended ominously, "You will want to give."

Mr. Patel gave. "All the merchants did," he said. "And money was raised from the workers and civil servants. With it they built that pavilion." He was referring to the Bar of the Equator, the governor's "memorial."

"But how much could that have cost?"

Patel eyed my notebook and fell silent. I assumed the civil servants had embezzled the funds. Why else such a hullabaloo over the founding of a trading post by an American mercenary in the pay of a Belgian king who had so cruelly exploited the Congo? Why else would a government that forbade European clothes or names celebrate this colonialist event, unless as a pretext for graft? What better proof that Mobutuism was simply theft than the alacrity with which it was abandoned when it interfered with theft?

At the end, Patel said, "Perhaps as a writer you, sir, can do me a great service and intervene on my behalf with the Book-of-the-Month Club. This club is my link to America and modernity, but many books never arrive. I think they are stolen in Kinshasa. I pay anyway because I wish to remain member in good standing." He showed me a club bulletin. He had circled *When Bad Things*

Happen to Good People. "I am very eager to receive this. Eighteen months I am waiting." It was described as "a book about courage and faith in the face of adversity. If God is all-Good and all-Powerful, why do innocent and virtuous people suffer?"

He had also ordered *The Hite Report on Male Sexuality.* "Most certainly stolen in Kinshasa, but soon I will be living there myself and receiving these books."

I was stunned. I wanted to say, What? You too, Patel! Leaving Mbandaka after so many years? Who will light your empty stores and pay to dust their shelves? And the pharamacy, what will become of that?

He read my shock and asked, "How would you like to spend the young years of your life alone, in Mbandaka? Before dying, my father divided the family, giving my brothers enterprises in Matadi and Kinshasa, where we have branch offices. But someone had to stay at headquarters. I was taken from school to run our business. I gave my chance to the others. I have sisters married and living in the States, and a brother in San Jose. People don't always have the same chance in life. Some must sacrifice themselves. Now it's my turn to move to Kinshasa and find a wife."

And if you can manage it, I thought, join those sisters in California.

"But do not think I'm abandoning Mbandaka. I will return often to be sure our property is maintained, that our name does not go poof in the wind. You can be sure of that." He sounded very unsure. The lights flickered again. "You know it is because of electricity this town does not progress. Why, with good energy we would have a different aspect here. When that problem is solved, people will invest. There will be demand for Patel shops, and I will return to live with my wife. I promise you that." He raised his voice, so loud Patel Senior might hear, if his spirit were lodged in this dusty tomb.

The building that once housed the Museum of the Equator was a baroque jewel box of arches and ornaments. It was painted in faded pastels and faced Mbandaka's moribund wharves. The museum might have explained how such a building came to be constructed here, but it had become the Regional Division of Culture and Arts. The director's office reminded me of others in Mbandaka I had visited to inquire about the equator: barren places stripped of valuables and left with rickety chairs, scarred tables, and a typewriter—the minimum. At Culture and Arts, a chair shortage forced employees to sit on tables. The director was absent the three times I went there. His private secretary said he had "many responsibilities."

"Where is the museum?" I asked. Were its exhibits in that locked office next door? One book described them as "a lavish collection of ancient objects" that "delight the eye." There were weapons, masks, drums, and perhaps the plaque wrenched off that equatorial rock. It might indicate whether the Belgian surveyors had considered it to be the actual equator or merely the original site of Equatorville.

"Next door is the municipal library," the private secretary said. "The Museum of the Equator has been moved to the National Museum, in Kinshasa. We are expanding Culture and Arts and need space for our offices."

Was there anything in Mbandaka not going to Kinshasa? The city had lost its traders, its museum, even its equator. "So if I returned to Kinshasa I could see the exhibits?" I asked.

The clerks exchanged looks. The private secretary stared out a window. "That would not be possible. Unfortunately, the exhibits are . . . well, they are in storage. Not ready for public display."

"Was everything sent? Even the plaque marking the equator?"

"Everything. But you may ask our librarian about the plaque. Perhaps he copied the inscription."

The next-door office was now open. A librarian was bent over stacks of file cards. "I am re-cataloguing our collection," he said. "A long task, but very necessary." I glanced at the cards. His handwriting was illegible. Had he copied the equatorial inscription I could not have deciphered it.

As I pulled books from the shelves, their bindings fell off in my hands. Signatures cracked, spilling pages. Paper crumbled, showering the floor with yellow confetti. To browse the Mbandaka library was to destroy it. I read the titles off volumes still having backs. They were mysteries, romances, and biographies of Belgian heroes. If anything had been acquired after 1960 I did not see it. "How many are on loan?" I asked.

"At present, none of our books is being read by a client."

I was suspicious of this word "client." "How does a client borrow a book?"

"He must fill out a card and pay in advance."

"Pay? How much must he pay?"

The librarian paused, a long time. "Fifteen Zaïres for three books, but for that he may keep them ten days. [In Mbandaka, a large loaf of bread cost only five Zaïres.] If you are here less than ten days I could reduce the price. Look on that shelf and you will find mysteries in English. And I have American magazines." He had two 1958 editions of *Argosy*.

Still, the library was sure to outlast the other Belgian relics. There was no black market for books, and at these prices no one could afford to borrow them. They were valuable only to the librarian. He knew if his volumes circulated they would quickly disintegrate, finishing his job. Other Zaïrians filling European positions showed a similar caution. They understood that when their buildings collapsed, or the last typewriter was sold, their salaries would stop. So their offices became museums in their own right, with their European relics maintained, without enthusiasm or affection, but to a bare minimum. The Museum of the Equator might have moved to Kinshasa, but Mbandaka itself had become an equatorial museum.

There was the exhibit of the abandoned gas stations with their cannibalized pumps and rust-spotted signs. The "Qaddaffis" squatted in front next to drums of black-market fuel, sucking like vampires on siphon hoses. They wrapped themselves in oily rags and cooked over fires set too close to their merchandise. They sickened from swallowing gasoline and breathing fumes. Their careers were brief.

There were the emporiums of the last Indian traders, hot and dark because of power failures and stocked with identical goods at identical prices. The clerks sat in shadowy corners, reading comic books and flicking their eyes, like Wimbledon spectators, between comic and African, comic and African, comic and African.

There was the butcher shop patronized by the last Belgians. The sharp-jawed nuns came on foot or bicycle. The old men, shrunk to pygmy size by heat and sickness, arrived in farting sedans. Their hair, after years of marinating in perspiration under wide-brimmed hats, was exhausted. Their sun-peeled faces were white and cracked, like a crocodile's belly. They bought sausages, fillets, and cans of soda. European social life in Mbandaka had shrunk to this: clutching a blood-stained parcel on the steps of the butcher's while exchanging news over cans of lukewarm cola.

There was the Hotel d'Afrique, the *"bijou* d'Afrique," according to a sign warning in large letters to beware the thieves. From the outside it resembled a motel on a bypassed highway, but its waiters, whose red jackets had been patched and bleached to the last thread, heroically ignored its dilapidation. At every meal my waiter presented the same ambitious carte du jour, although the "jour" typed next to the chef's signature was always September 28, 1984. While apologizing that everything on it was unavailable, he arranged empty salt and pepper shakers to cover holes in the tablecloth. He opened an empty mustard jar, polishing a spoon with his cloth and laying it alongside. Scabs of dried mustard had been dug from even the threads in the screw cap. When the food arrived, he warned that the cold plate was "very hot," and, with an expression defying laughter, wished me *"bon appétit."*

Aaron Zee's house could also have been an exhibit in Mbandaka's museum of European relics. For a week I was the white bachelor *patron,* overseeing the kind of household staff that has soothed generations of Europeans in Africa. The house was a simple bungalow, built for a junior Belgian official. It was simply furnished, and its staff of four was modest for Africa really the minimum, given Aaron Zee's responsibilities. Aside from Mouila, there was a day guard, a dreamy maid named Mary Louise, and a night guard who walked the compound on cat's feet, coughing under my window. I felt like the mayor of a small village. Mary Louise brought her children, and the day guard had visitors. A sharp student named Yonda arrived from an outlying village. He had finished his examinations and walked all day to come to Mbandaka for "a vacation." He said Aaron Zee allowed him to stay here, and I believed him.

The night guard usually came early and sat whittling his arrows to needle sharpness. The cats and dogs fought, Mary Louise swept, and her children crawled through the dust. Someone was always hugging, rocking, stroking, or talking to these children. Instead of owning toys, they were the toys of the adults. My responsibilities as temporary *patron* revolved around keys, another colonial echo. I was supposed to take the car keys back from

Mouila every evening and lock myself in the house at night, un-
bolting the kitchen door when I woke. Mouila was not trusted
with the key to the gas tank. It was hidden on a hook behind a
tennis racket, something Aaron Zee had forgotten to mention,
although he had luckily entrusted this information to Yonda. In a
country where integrity is more likely to be penalized than prized,
and hard work seldom rewarded, Yonda was a marvel. His idea of
a vacation was to study from first light until last power failure.
"Luxury" was working under an electric lamp. "My dream in life,"
he said, looking up from a textbook, "is to attend the National
Pedagogical Institute in Kinshasa." And a few years later, I
thought, you'll dream of a tusk.

While Yonda studied, I discovered that at night Mbandaka
became the pleasant city promised by its boosters. It was cooler,
darkness hid the decay, and I saw only what was white or lighted:
the white paint on the trunks of the royal palms, the lamplit faces of
the boy merchants asleep on their cigarettes and gum, and people
sitting in witches' circles around the fires of outdoor restaurants in
Revolution Park. Everywhere I smelled laundry soap — on other
pedestrians, near the stalls where it was sold in unwrapped blocks,
in alleyways hung with drying clothes. If you gave the citizens of
Mbandaka a handicap based on the price of soap and the erratic
water supply, they might rank with the Dutch in cleanliness.

The patrons of the outdoor restaurants looked convivial, yet
they made me uneasy. It was not because I worried about
hygiene — I have eaten often from street stalls without sickness —
but because their cooking fires reminded me of the bonfires described by Sartre in his introduction to Franz Fanon's *Wretched of
the Earth,* a book few college students of the sixties could escape.
Sartre wrote: "Europeans, you must open this book and enter into
it. After a few steps in the darkness you will see strangers gathered around a fire; come close, and listen, for they are talking of
the destiny they will mete out to your trading centers and to the
hired soldiers who defend them. . . . A fire warms them and
sheds light around them, and you have not lit it. Now, at a respectful distance, it is you who will feel furtive, nightbound and
perished with cold."

When this was written, in 1960, men did huddle around fires
in Algeria, Zaïre, and elsewhere, plotting the fate of Europeans.
But now there were so few Europeans left in Zaïre's "trading cen-

ters" that I sometimes heard the complaint that "in Gabon and the Congo the French have stayed to help, but our whites, the Belgians, have abandoned us." In parts of Zaïre, Europeans had become a court of last resort, providing medicine, education, and work without favoring a relative or demanding a bribe. When I finally made myself eat in Mbandaka's outdoor restaurants, I learned that Europeans here were closely watched. People knew I was staying in the Peace Corps house and asking about the equator. They insisted I eat this or that cut of meat; soft voices whispered *"bon soir"*; a man laid his hand over mine, showing me how to move bottle caps across a game board drawn in the dirt; and I felt the opposite of "nightbound and cold." Now the conspiracies hatched around these fires were more likely to involve stealing a European's toilet seat than slitting his throat.

The reason Mbandaka has become a museum of European relics is revealed by these figures: At independence, in 1960, it was a city of 1,200 Europeans and 30,000 Africans, none trained to fill European positions, while a quarter of a century later it was a city of 50 Europeans and 250,000 Africans. There are few places in Africa where the European legacy collapsed so quickly or so completely, a debacle best explained by Zaïre's history: five centuries of contact with Europe that amount to a long, brutal period followed by a short, paternalistic one. For three centuries the slave trade depopulated the interior and spread epidemics. Then, in 1880, the Belgian monarch Leopold II hired Henry Stanley to build eight trading stations on the Congo [now the Zaïre] River, among them Equatorville. Two years later, at the Berlin Conference, the European powers recognized Leopold's personal claim to the curiously named Congo Free State [later known as the Belgian Congo, to distinguish it from the French Congo across the river], and the rich center of Africa became his personal property, to do with as he pleased. He instituted a trading monopoly and required Africans to harvest a quota of tropical products which could be sold only to his agents. Those who failed were brutally punished by his private army. The entire country was one man's slave plantation.

The exposure of Leopold's atrocities forced the Belgian government to annex the Congo in 1908. For the next half century, Belgium pursued a program of paternalism that brought economic progress and built an impressive European infrastructure, but that

at the same time utterly failed to prepare the Congolese to operate it. Instead of creating a Europeanized elite, Belgian colonial
theory called for slowly raising all the Congolese to a European
living standard. In comparison to other African colonies, Congolese workers were supplied with exemplary housing and health
care, but they were not allowed to rise in the civil service above
the rank of clerk. Half of all Congolese children attended primary
school—more than in other African colonies—but few continued
on to secondary school. The first students did not graduate from
the first Congolese university until 1956.

The Belgians allowed this because as late as 1958 they believed they would rule the Congo into the twenty-first century.
Instead, independence in neighboring countries led to riots in
Leopoldville, and, unprepared for a costly colonial war, Belgium
capitulated. In 1960 the Belgian Congo became an independent
nation without trained army officers, businessmen, civil servants,
teachers, or politicians. The fact that politicians in the first election
campaign promised the repayment of all taxes assessed during the
colonial period, and the resurrection of dead relatives, reflects
more on the Belgians than on the Congolese. A week after independence, the army mutinied, and forty thousand Belgians fled in
panic. During the next five years secessionist wars plagued the
country, severely damaging the economic machine constructed by
Belgium. The metals boom of the early seventies was a last chance
to repair it. Instead, revenues were stolen or mismanaged, and the
country's debt increased. Now, in Zaïre [the name was changed
by Mobutu], roads are disappearing, and the Belgian infrastructure has decayed beyond the point of no return. Twenty-five years
ago, few African colonies were richer than Zaïre; now, few African
nations are poorer. And every year it becomes, according to the
statistics, 2 percent more impoverished.

The junction of the Zaïre and Ruki rivers at Mbandaka cre-
ates a triangle of land. The Zaïre River is the western boundary,
the Ruki the eastern one, the commercial center of Mbandaka is
at the apex, inside the northern hemisphere, and the equator is
the base line. If you choose to believe in the Belgian equator, then
this base line crosses the Zaïre at the ruined mansion and disappears into the forest for about ten miles before reemerging to intersect the Ruki River at the Eala Botanical Garden. If you believe

in the American equator, then the Mbandaka triangle is slightly larger, and the equator crosses the Zaïre several miles south of the mansion and hits the Ruki below Eala, at the Catholic mission of Bamanya. My Michelin map voted for the Belgians, and its equator cut through the words "Jardin Botanique." My guidebook to tropical plants placed Eala on a list of recommended botanic gardens and parks in the tropics (a recommendation somewhat tarnished by its location being identified as "near Coquilhatville," as Mbandaka was once known), and Gé had remembered his visit there as one of the high points of his childhood in Africa. Which all goes to explain why, when Mouila stopped in a place of no distinction and said, "Here, *patron,*" I said, "Here? Impossible." Here, on this narrow forest track, near the subsistence villages and the women selling bundles of twigs? "No, this can't be Eala."

For the first time, Mouila lost his smile. A cloudburst had flooded the dips and holes, and he had wrestled the wheel of the Land Rover like a captain in a typhoon. "Yes, here! . . . *patron* [an afterthought]." He pointed to a sign lying face up in a ditch. I read INSTITUT DE JARDINS ZOOLOGIQUE & BOTANIQUES OUEST DE ZAÏRE. A half mile later another sign said Founded 3.2.1900 so that everyone can learn about the riches of Central African vegetation and agricultural possibilities . . . Rust had erased the rest.

The road widened into a parkway divided by a mall and shaded by palms and mangoes. Lawns stretched up a gentle hill. At the top, a sign welcomed visitors to the only botanical garden on the equator. Gravel paths led into gardens. The forest had swallowed some of the 3,200 edible, medicinal, industrial, and ornamental species; weeds had choked others. Gardeners performed the horticultural equivalent of cataloguing the Mbandaka library.

I found the director in a brick bungalow, sitting with his staff in a room thick with cigarette smoke. "What do you want from us?" he asked testily. "You are interrupting our meeting."

I wanted to purchase a map of Eala.

"We are awaiting new maps from Kinshasa. Meanwhile, you may copy information from the map in the hallway." I had already seen that one, dated 1917 and saying nothing about the equator. "Why do you need a map?"

"I want to know where the equator is."

"Ah, that is easy," someone said, "it runs through the zoo-logical exhibits."

"Near the crocodile," another man added without conviction. They wanted to get rid of me.

The crocodile pool smelled of sewage. Mouila insisted that underneath these clumps of excrement and algae lived the croco-dile that ate dogs. I pressed a handkerchief to my nose and waited. At last the water broke, and I stared into the yellow, mad-man's eyes of what must be the man-hatingest crocodile in the world. There was more to this zoo. Two monkeys were locked in solitary cages. One rolled lethargically in a paste of excrement while the other bared his teeth and jiggled like St. Vitus. A man sweeping leaves from a path said, "It's closed." I thought he meant the zoo, which should have been, but pointing to a large brick building he said, "The museum. It's always closed."

A bronze plaque said it had been built in 1904 in memory of the botanist Emile Laurant. Through its dusty windows I saw a Mr. Masse collection of jarred fetuses and stuffed animals. A young man came running, waving his arms and broad-jumping the puddles. He was handsome and athletic, a sleek greyhound. He wore a gold wristwatch and moccasins polished to a high shine. Polished with what? It could not be easy, maintaining this elegant pose in Eala.

He introduced himself as Zombo, winked, and said, sotto voce, "But you may call me Jean-Paul." I liked this. He had a sense of humor, and the confidence of a bright young man. He was the curator of the museum, which, he admitted, was closed, but only temporarily. "Soon, when the money comes from Kinshasa, everything will be repaired and polished. However, since you are a friend of the director, he has instructed me to make an exception and give you a special tour, provided you re-member that in a matter of months it will be entirely new."

I was suspicious. Nothing in our brief meeting had indicated that the director counted me among his friends. We pushed our way through a wall of cobwebs while Jean-Paul groped for light switches on the wrong walls. There was a hole in the roof, and dead leaves littered the floor. Stuffed monkeys had shed fur, and birds had lost feathers. Their naked bodies had exploded, littering the room with gray fluff balls, the remains of the taxidermist's stuffing. The formaldehyde had leaked from some jars, leaving the fetuses shriveled and white. Other jars had shattered in the heat. I stepped on a bat embryo that went crunch.

Jean-Paul soccer-kicked some shards under a table and pouted. "For a year Kinshasa has promised funds. Once they come the museum will be, as I said, like new." He smiled bleakly. We both knew his museum was, like Mbandaka, beyond repair.

"Even better — much better — would be a visit from the president. When he came ten years ago, park benches were constructed along the river." Here it was again, Africa's cargo cult: people believing, and with good cause, that only the leader in person could improve things. They prayed for his plane and sometimes it landed, bringing gifts.

"Do you come to the museum often?" I asked this gently, because I liked Jean-Paul.

"You must understand, I'm not the official curator, only a replacement until a new one is hired. My responsibilities lie elsewhere. Frankly, this position is not equal to my training."

"Which is. . . ?"

"A doctor of veterinary medicine. I was trained in Kinshasa. Here I'm in charge of the zoological exhibits." To prove it, he pulled a filthy hypodermic from his jacket. "I've been too occupied with the zoo to attend to the museum. The new governor is arriving next week, and he will wish to come here."

"Then you'd say the zoo is at its best for him?"

"Yes. Although with more funds — "

This was too much. I started back to the car. Jean-Paul ran behind, begging a ride to Mbandaka. I was happy when he splashed those polished shoes through a puddle. "There is no transport here, monsieur," he whined. "We are prisoners. At the mercy of traders who charge a fortune."

I shook my head. He was not a likely candidate for a favor.

"My daughter is ill. All day I have searched for transportation to the hospital. You must help." He blocked my way. "I didn't have permission to show you the museum. I took the risk so you'd drive her to the hospital."

We looked for his wife and daughter among lines of brick bungalows built by the Belgians for one African family. They were now crowded compounds, each supporting several lean-tos, cooking sheds, and families. Relatives had traveled hundreds of miles to live off a single wage earner: Africa's fatal generosity.

Jean-Paul's bungalow was no better than the rest. Quickly a crowd formed, begging rides to Mbandaka. Someone said Jean-Paul's wife had started on foot. We found her a mile down the road, clutching the child in her arms, running barefoot and stumbling. The child had a croupy cough. As we drove, Jean-Paul repeatedly counted his currency, undoubtedly hoping he had enough to bribe the staff and save her life. His tapered shirt was stained with sweat, his shoes splattered with mud. I felt like a bastard. Behind the smooth facade of the African functionary there is often this hysteria and desperation, the result of a huge, impoverishing family. Not to apply European morality to people with European educations is to risk being patronizing, but do it and you are proved a fool, or worse. But then again, when Mouila and I drove to Bamanya the next morning, there, rolling around the floor of the car, was that filthy hypodermic.

The Catholic mission of Bamanya is ten miles from Mbandaka, at the end of an hour of bad road. With its heavy cows, tidy stables, and lush meadows, and its air thick with insects and moisture, it could be a southern plantation in late June. Two elderly Flemish fathers sat rocking on the porch of a solid brick house. They wore suspenders and Panama hats. The Père Procureur had the heavy cheeks of a butcher. He was drinking lemonade and, so help me, reading a thick biography of King Leopold. Père Gustaaf was a fragile man in his eighties who had lived sixty years in Bamanya. His face was a Brazil nut decorated by a white goatee, and his eyes were Oriental. He was a dead ringer for Ho Chi Minh.

"You are wondering, monsieur *écrivain*," he said, "what is their secret? I will tell so you can write it in the notebook you would like to pull from that bag. Go on, take it out, and write: The secret of the Bamanya mission is that they have their Dutch cows for fresh milk, their vegetable gardens and fruit trees, a primary and secondary school, a seminary to train priests, a maternity ward with twelve beds, two nursing sisters, and a dentistry and dispensary. They are self-sufficient."

I described the veterinarian's sick daughter and he said, "But you should have brought that poor child to us. We have many patients from Mbandaka. Here they pay no bribes and heal, there they sicken. Here we have medicines, there the staff sells them on the black market. Did you know, monsieur *écrivain*, that many *functionnaires* come to our hospital? They are fortunate to have the means of transportation. The governor himself is our patient. Now tell me, monsieur *écrivain*," he said smiling faintly, "what do you think of that?"

I thought it was outrageous. After presiding over the mismanagement of the public facilities, the big vegetables had themselves driven to the Bamanya dispensary. On the other hand, how could any parent with a sick child be faulted for choosing Bamanya?

Père Gustaaf laughed. "No, monsieur *écrivain*, better not write what you think, or you'll be expelled."

A dragonfly landed on my arm. He raised it by one wing, releasing it into the air. "There is one thing in which Bamanya is not self-sufficient: people. Those we cannot grow." They had ten European sisters, all elderly, and four European priests, but only Father Hugo was young, the only young priest to come from Europe in years. At the moment he was off recruiting seminarians. "We can no longer expect missionaries from Europe. When we die, the Zaïrian priests must manage Bamanya. But we worry because they don't wish to cultivate or make bricks. They prefer cities and offices. We cannot offer that, so many depart, and the people left behind suffer. Up the Ruki and its tributaries, villages empty and missions dry like puddles. When people lose their schools and dispensaries, those wanting such things come to us before continuing to Mbandaka or Kinshasa. Last year the American Protestants abandoned their mission, and now we see their people. We worry what will happen when we die, and we pray for the Zaïrian priests. We know they are not exemplars — we understand it is difficult for them to be celibate — but we have faith."

"What do you expect to happen when —"

"Ask God that, monsieur *écrivain*. Bamanya is in his hands. I can only say that we shrink. Five years before there was a daily bus to Mbandaka; now there is none. Before, a hundred people attended our Sunday masses; now ten. Before, they came on bicycles; now the road is treacherous and their wheels twist in the holes. We have lost our old Bamanya families. We prayed they would stay, but their young insist on the cities. Tell me this, monsieur *écrivain*, who do you see in our villages?"

"Children, grandparents, and mothers."

"Then you have seen it all. The young men go to Mbandaka, sending for their wives, sometimes. The grandparents raise the children. But the people of Mbandaka do not ignore us. They walk down our road to harvest firewood. Every year they walk further. Soon they will be back here, where they started. The trees that border our roads, villages, and rivers are cut to feed their fires. Cut to heat the irons that press my shirts so nicely." He plucked at his starched tunic. "Here is our paradox: Fewer people live in our villages, but every year the land is more exhausted. Why is that, monsieur *écrivain*? I will tell you. Since there is no transportation, the forest one day's walk from Mbandaka is scoured for wood, while less accessible land, good land that was once cultivated, becomes forest.

"Here on your equator we have a simple equation. Once the forest is cut, thicker and uglier forest replaces it. This forest breeds more tsetse and mosquitoes. To escape it, more people go to Mbandaka, so we have more people journeying out from there, walking further into our forests to cut trees, and bringing us more sickness. How simple it is, this equation." He moved his hands up and down, scales out of balance.

"I have measured the temperature and it has become hotter, meaning fewer fish in our river. Dealers buy the remaining fish at prices beyond the reach of our people. They are smoked and sent to Kinshasa. People say, 'If we want to eat good fish we must go to Kinshasa.' So they go.

"I have measured the manioc roots. They are a quarter of their diameter of ten years past. There is no famine, only malnutrition. But only children die of that. Write this down, monsieur *écrivain*, and you'll be expelled for sure." He rocked back and forth. "Actually, if you write this down it won't make the slightest difference."

I asked if he thought the equator ran through Eala or Bamanya.

"Our municipality has anticipated your question. To settle this and other disputes they commissioned a scholar to make a study of the city's history."

"Do you have a copy?"

"No one has a copy, monsieur *écrivain.* Shall I tell you why? Because the 'scholar' took our money and vanished. But I will show you, for free, the equator."

He led me inside. On the wall was a 1951 aerial photograph of Mbandaka. He drew a finger east from the Gros Légume's ruined mansion. "Here is where Stanley believed the equator was, but he was wrong. It touches the road further south of that rock and goes through our backyard, a hundred yards from here. You are wondering, How does he know this? Because when they built a satellite-tracking station on the Bolenge road I befriended the Greek engineer, and we passed many pleasant evenings in this room. He told me he built the northern perimeter of the fence surrounding his radar so it corresponded exactly to the path of the equator."

I did not like this solution. The equator had so far touched uncannily accurate symbols: the projected soccer field in Brazil, the champagne bottles and railway in Gabon. In Mbandaka it should have intersected the ruined mansion and the tormented crocodile, not a radar station and this tidy mission.

"Are you certain the Greek was right?"

Père Gustaaf was. He said I might learn more next door in the Bibliothèque Aequatoria — the "Equatorial Library." Books and periodicals filled its rooms. Shelves stretched to the ceilings and boxes cluttered the aisles. A Belgian father was entering books in a catalogue that listed seven thousand volumes about the history, languages, and flora and fauna of central Africa, with emphasis on Equateur Province. A leaflet explained that Le Centre Aequatoria — the "Equatorial Center" — had started as the private collection of Father Gustaaf Hulstaert, who had "built a vast network of relations with African scholars of every country," interesting foreign scholars and universities in the culture of the Mongo people. He had launched *Annales Aequatoria,* a scholarly journal published by the center. A recent edition offered "The Names of Twins in Equateur Province," "Special Marriage Rites in the Harem of the King of Kuba," and "The Sorcery of the Mongo People," written by Father Gustaaf, who was, in short, the world's premier authority on Equateur Province.

The leaflet was a fund-raiser. It warned that the archives of the Equatorial Center were threatened, and that their disappearance would be "a considerable loss for the culture of Zaïre and the Equateur Province in particular." To guarantee their survival, the Bamanya fathers sought funds for an Aequatorial Foundation. Its first project would be "to construct a building in the center of Mbandaka and to transfer to it the Equatorial Library of Bamanya." In other words, even the Equatorial Center was moving off the equator, following Bamanya's "old families" to Mbandaka, where it might have a better chance. Not quite everything, as Père Gustaaf said, was being left "in God's hands." He was fighting to save his life's work.

I returned to find him in his garden, stroking his orchids under their chins and sniffing vanilla blossoms. He pointed to where a swampy field met the Ruki River and said, "Over there, monsieur écrivain, running across our land, is your equator. When you follow it to Kiribati, you must give my regards to my confrères."

"Where?"

"Kiribati. In the Pacific. Our order has a mission."

I had not recognized it because he had pronounced it correctly: "Kiribas." Sure enough, when I arrived there, I found a Sacred Heart Mission on the island of Abemama, just thirty miles from the equator and about as near to it as you can get in the Pacific, proving that Père Gustaaf was a man who knew his equator.

I ate my last dinner in Mbandaka with Protestant missionaries and an elderly European nurse with nervous eyes and itchy hands. "So what do you think of our city?" she asked. Before I could answer she said, "Do you know children are dying of measles by the hundreds? There is no vaccine. Not even on the black market."

I described Jean-Paul's daughter. Perhaps she was suffering from measles.

"So he is the man who feeds dogs to the crocodile."

"But he was trained at the university. He can't be the one who actually—"

"People have witnessed it. That crocodile eats dog, freshly clubbed."

"Perhaps it's all they have. If the president came—"

"He never comes. For years he's been promising. Don't you understand? Everyone has abandoned these people. Did you know that there is no eye doctor in all of Equateur? Haven't you heard about our Dr. Moanda? A brilliant man, educated by our church and trained in Europe. He wants to return, but the government has not purchased the mobile eye clinic he was promised, so he stays in Europe. Who can blame him? I will tell you how the people of Mbandaka get eyeglasses. When I was home, I persuaded my optician to save the old glasses that people trade for stronger prescriptions. Church groups send us used glasses, packed in barrels. Our patients grope through them, trying on pairs until they find one that helps."

I mentioned Mr. Patel and his move to Kinshasa. Everyone fell silent, eyes down, like criminals receiving a harsh sentence. A missionary said, "His pharmacy is bound to close. It's the only reliable source of drugs in Mbandaka."

"In all of Equateur," someone added.

"That's it, then," the nurse said softly. "His family has been here . . . forever. It's the end of an era."

And what era was that?

"The era of living in the remains of the Belgians, which is what we are doing, we and the Africans. Soon these remains will be finished. We will leave and they will be on their own again. After the vandals sacked Rome, it took the Romans five hundred years to recover. The Africans have sacked what the Belgians left, and why shouldn't it take them as long to rebuild that, if they want to? But do you, does anyone, honestly think they want to?"

It was also Yonda's last night. I lit a mosquito coil and he wished me "sweat dreams." Dreams in Mbandaka were certainly that, but it was still a strange wish. I had him repeat it several times before understanding he was wishing me "sweet dreams." But I had a restless night, dozing fitfully and lying awake for hours with dreams more sweaty than sweet. It was inaccurate to characterize Mbandaka as "sacked," I decided. Instead, the city was unraveling slowly, like a movie running backward, in slow motion. I saw the library books crumbling into yellow snowdrifts; the road to Bamanya turning into a footpath, then nothing; the ten people at the Bamanya Sunday services becoming five, and none; villages once accessible only on foot becoming that way again; riverboats running aground for the last time, channels silting, and Mbandaka becoming a forest-hemmed island infested with tsetse flies that, with a sinister whizzing, attacked the survivors.

I saw the cars of the pygmy Belgians turning to rust and their toilets cracking, the "Qaddaffis" sucking their black-market drums dry, the P A T E L sign becoming P   T E L, then P   T   L, then nothing. I saw fans revolving and lights flickering once a week, once a month, never. I saw the last functionaries selling the last desks and moving their families into their offices. I saw the soldiers going home after a last spasm of looting, and squatters moving into Revolution Park, turning it into an African village.

I woke to Yonda brushing his teeth and leaving in darkness, then woke again to thunder, battlefield flashes, and the coughs of the night guard. He was silhouetted against lightning, frozen in a hunter's crouch with an arrow threaded in his bow.

This backward movie was already in its final frames. Again Zaïre was owned by a despot who turned its resources into European bank balances, and again it was as difficult for travelers as in Stanley's time. At least he knew to bring his own supplies and did not expect roads, ferries, or hospitals. Now, in the last hours of Europe in Equateur Province, European institutions mocked themselves. The police were highwaymen, the public library discouraged borrowing, the army terrorized citizens, and in the hospital, a simple stitch might kill you.

And when these institutions collapsed, what would remain of Europe's interregnum? I turned on a flashlight and made a list:

- Soap, cigarettes, flashlights and batteries, sardines and chewing gum. (But weren't they the equivalent of the trinkets and beads that reached the interior centuries before European rule?)

- Hyacinths. A Belgian missionary had dropped one into the river, where it rapidly multiplied, becoming a navigational hazard. The Belgians reduced them but they were back, drifting in purple flotillas past the governor's ruined mansion.

- Beer. The Primus brewery would float in Mbandaka like a space station. Chartered planes could import parts, ingredients, and luxuries for the Dutch brewers. (But was beer really a European vestige? For centuries Africans had been making it from maize, millet, and bananas. Perhaps the brewery would survive because this was something Africans had liked, before.)

- Medicine. After Patel's pharmacy closed, people would buy pills randomly, trying them out to see what worked, like the nearsighted groping through those barrels of spectacles.

Judging by this list, colonialism had been a bad bargain for Equateur. Cigarettes, water hyacinths, medicine, and beer in bottles is not much reward for slavery, epidemics, and Leopold's atrocities. But perhaps this is all, except for the hyacinths, that the people of Equateur really wanted from Europe. There is a point of view, that of traditional Africa, from which this rejection of Europe can be considered progress.

Imagining another future for Mbandaka is difficult. It was built by Europeans to administer Equateur Province and extract tropical products that have since become less valuable. It is inconceivable that Europeans would invest lives and capital here again, or that a government in Kinshasa would rebuild a European trading city on the equator. In another quarter century, the only Europeans to see Mbandaka will probably arrive by chartered plane, if the airfield is maintained. Otherwise, they may come on river expeditions resembling Stanley's in their supplies and preparations, And after that, a new Stanley may discover Equatorville all over again.

The ONATRA strike continued. There were no boats in either direction, so I had to fly, via Kinshasa, to Goma, in eastern Zaïre, then travel overland to Kigali, in Rwanda. Here, if the Kampala computers had decided I was not an enemy of the Ugandan people, I could collect a Ugandan visa and rejoin the equator. The new governor of Equateur Province arrived on the plane I was taking out. A holiday had been declared so his people could welcome him. Students weeded traffic circles and wove palm fronds into a victory arch with the enthusiasm of a chain gang. Women and children walked along the shoulder, dragging placards. Truckloads of soldiers and functionaries sped past, stirring up dust. The men of Mbandaka belonged to outfits meriting a ride to the airport.

The airport was again a lively market. Passengers under the

weight allowance sold their excess, and customs officers shook parcels as if they were Christmas presents addressed to them. The Hotel d'Afrique had the restaurant concession, and its proud waiters were here in their threadbare jackets, serving beer and waffles. I saw the pygmy Belgians, the raw-faced missionaries, and an Indian family seeing off a son with suspiciously large suitcases.

The plane landed, a band played anthems, dancers in feather headdresses stamped the tarmac, and a tribe of functionary wives rushed forward with flowers. As children waved palm branches, the governor delivered an inaudible speech and the crowd, sullen extras, gave a flat cheer. The governor must have seen *Gandhi* on his video-cassette recorder, because as he entered the air-conditioned VIP lounge he turned to the crowd, slapped his palms together, and offered a humble bow. He had come to be their servant. The soldiers applauded and, not wishing to be seen the unenthusiastic white man, I joined them. My cowardice went unrewarded. A porter tapped my shoulder. The police wished to see me. A matter of urgency.

The plainclothes policeman closed the door and, holding my passport out of reach, said, "Monsieur Clarke, this is grave, very grave. You do not have a *carte de séjour*?"

"What is that?"

"A visitor to Mbandaka must obtain a *carte de séjour* upon arrival."

"But you stamped my passport when I arrived. Why didn't you tell me then?"

"Ah, Monsieur Clarke, it is the responsibility of the visitor to demand a *carte de séjour*. You should have asked me." He smiled. "Without a *carte de séjour*, you cannot leave Mbandaka."

"Fine, then give me one and I'll leave." We both looked at our watches. The plane departed in ten minutes.

"It is against regulations to issue a *carte de séjour* at the airport. But tomorrow you may present yourself at my office in town. That is where *cartes de séjour* are issued."

"But [goddammit] my *séjour* is over! My luggage is on the plane." (A mistake to admit this.)

"Perhaps I can assist you. I can issue a temporary *carte de séjour* here. Then you can stay in Mbandaka legally until the normal *carte de séjour* is prepared. After that, you may leave on the next plane." He slipped my passport into his briefcase. "This is a serious offense, Monsieur Clarke. Normally there is a fine."

At last. I would pay a "fine" and leave. I checked my watch. Seven minutes. He had showed his hand too soon. I have never bribed a public official in Africa, a record I wanted to preserve. I said I was a famous American professor who had delivered a series of lectures at the university in Kinshasa. There was no reaction. I was returning to give another lecture tomorrow. Still none. And to receive a *baccalauréat honoraire.* The rector of the university would hold him responsible.

"Then where are your credentials? Your letter of invitation from the university?"

I had won. Before leaving Kinshasa, I had obtained a letter from the embassy saying I had given a lecture at the IPN. The policeman read it with the functionary's reflex respect for printed stationery. "All right, I will accept this as your *carte de séjour,*" he said, slamming it angrily with his immigration stamp. I grabbed my passport and ran.

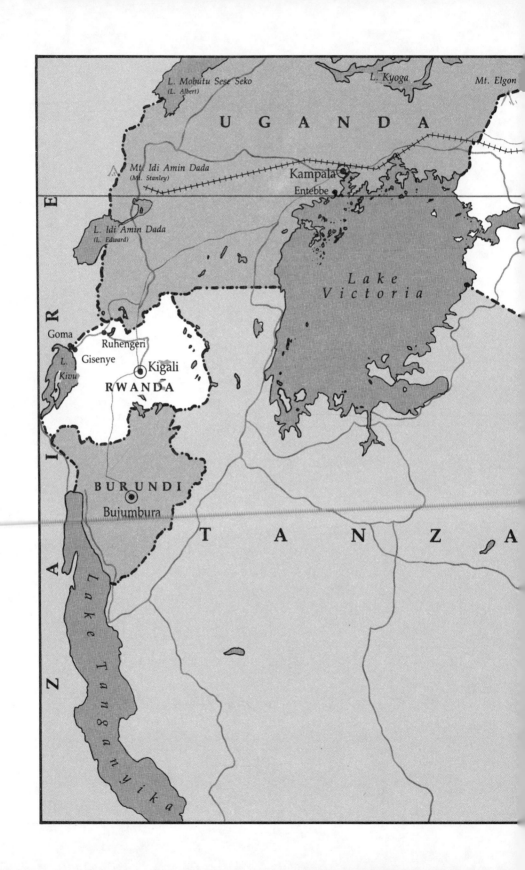

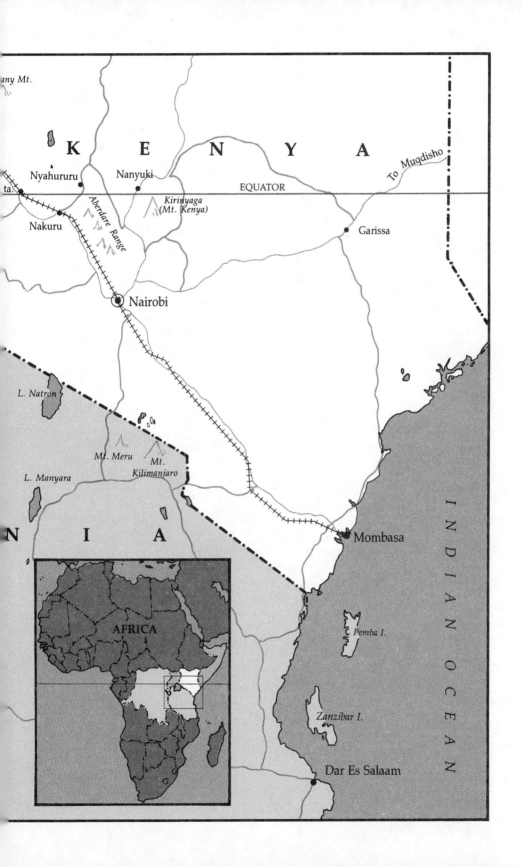

10

GOMA WAS SURROUNDED BY SPIKY MOUNTAINS AND MIST, A Chinese watercolor landscape. The sun swept nearby terraced green hills like a spotlight. The air was fresh and cool, the earth black. Not "rich," "dark," or "fertile," but a midnight, volcanic blackness.

The men who owned the only taxi at the airport were eager to drive me across the border to Gisenye, in Rwanda. There was gasoline there, and to cross the frontier they needed a passenger. Their names sounded like Goodheart and Mobile, pronounced like the city in Alabama. Goodheart was a compact Hutu who could barely see over the wheel. Mobile was a rangy Tusi who had to bend his neck like a swan to fit into the tiny car. He held a broken door shut with one hand and tapped the fuel gauge with the other, hoping to coax the needle into rising above the empty mark. As we coasted over rutted streets, their heads bobbed like pistons.

I saw the usual crumbling schools and barracks, dismembered trucks and splashing urchins, all looking more cruel and unnecessary in this spring climate and among these fertile hills. I had Zaïres I wanted to change before the border, so we stopped at the Friendship Bar, described by Goodheart as the bar of the money changers. The *patron* brought beers, collected my money, and admitted that the money changers had gone elsewhere. Goodheart and Mobile drove me to a deserted lot, where Mobile said, "Give us all your Zaïres." They planned to rob me. I was sure of it. They would take my passport and my luggage and I would be stranded in Goma, like the Pakistanis on the Oiapoque, forever.

Mobile giggled. "Don't worry. We'll hide your money and return it after the frontier."

"That's right. They never search us," Goodheart said. "You have nothing to fear. We are honest men."

But now I feared they might gyp me, so instead of thanking them I asked how much they would charge. Mobile looked hurt. "Free. We do it for friendship since you bought us a beer." He slid my Zaïres into a tear in the upholstery and I felt ashamed of myself.

Mobile cut the engine and we coasted down a road bordering Lake Kivu to the Zaïrian customs post. Goodheart asked my profession and, remembering my letter from the embassy, I said professor. "That is good, very good," he said. "There will be no problems. In Goma we have great respect for professors." I had heard this frontier was difficult. He shook his head. "With us, you'll be finished in an instant."

As we approached the police post, Goodheart shouted, "Here comes the professor! Make way for Professor Thurston!" Mobile dropped my bag at the customs inspector's feet. "The professor's luggage." A chair appeared. The immigration officer shook my hand and scolded my companions for bringing the professor's luggage inside. Even to unload it was an insult. Of course no inspection was necessary. But at the barrier, Mobile had to bribe a corporal thirty Zaïres to raise the striped post, a perfect exit from Zaïre. The soldier snapped his purchased salute and Goodheart said, "Don't worry, his bribe is included in your fare."

The money changers of Gisenye pulled bricks of cash from flight bags and ran at us. The two quickest wrenched open the back doors, throwing themselves into the taxi. I tried to make sense of their competing deals with pencil and paper. One wrote a figure the other refused to match. The loser climbed out, and immediately the winner raised his rate. I did not care. I was happy to exchange my filthy Zaïres — they all carried the Gros Légume's portrait — for Rwandan francs bearing pictures of a zebra, a woman gazing at a volcano, or a cheerful gorilla cradling her child.

Gisenye was a smuggler's town of money changers, lakeside villas, and well-stocked stores, a parasite sucking on huge, thrashing Zaïre. But smuggling alone could not explain a contrast that was as stark as that between East and West Berlin. The statistics said Rwanda was poorer than Zaïre, without minerals or industry, and the most densely populated nation in Africa. Then how to account for the brick school with its unshattered windows, the smooth, paved roads, smart soldiers guarding a spotless barracks, and the antiseptic hospital facing a courtyard ringed with whitewashed boulders? How to account for Gisenye's spooky prosperity?

A national holiday had filled a lakeside hotel with Europeans and *évolués* from the capital. Leggy French and Tusi teen-agers rode windsurfers, Indian families on the terrace devoured plates of French fries smothered, Belgian style, in mayonnaise, and two British teachers from neighboring Burundi loudly described a colleague's failings: "She actually believes her students must read and understand Beowulf, but that doesn't wash, not in Burundi." Hutu and Tusi women greeted each other in an exaggerated French style — two pantomime kisses on each cheek. The Tusi dipped like giraffes at a water hole to reach the squat Hutu. Kiss, kiss; kiss, kiss.

I had not expected this. By tradition, the Tusi were feudal aristocrats who owned herds of lyre-horned cattle, and the Hutu were serfs who milked Tusi cows, farmed their fields, and paid tribute. Hutu and Tusi physiques matched their status. The Tusi had stork legs, bony fingers, and fine-featured faces, and looked dangerously brittle, as if hard work would snap them like a twig. The Hutu were squashed, like medieval peasants. First German and then Belgian colonialists had left this relationship largely undisturbed. But in 1959, three years before independence, the Hutu in Rwanda massacred a hundred thousand Tusi. Many Tusi survivors fled into neighboring Burundi. Bertrand Russell described the killings as "the most horrible and systematic human massacre we have had occasion to witness since the extermination of the Jews by the Nazis." The Tusi rulers of Burundi took their revenge in 1972, slaughtering two hundred thousand Hutu in three months. During my stay, I was told several times that one explanation for Rwanda's stability and prosperity was that the massacres had "settled" the tribal rivalries plaguing other African nations. So, now that the Tusi comprised under 10 percent of the population in Rwanda and the Hutu were in power, Hutu and Tusi kissed on hotel terraces.

I swam in Lake Kivu, compared by its German discoverer to Lake Lugano, although its water was clearer and the mountains surrounding it steeper and closer. I drank coffee on the terrace of the Swiss Grill and watched the graceful Tusi glide past as if on roller skates. I walked lakeside paths, admiring the Technicolor birds. I peered through hedges at the villas and the putting-green lawns of politicians and coffee smugglers. And yet, despite the Mediterranean terraces, windsurfers, and Cinzano umbrellas, there was about Gisenye an inescapable, sunlit menace.

It may have been the low canopy of black clouds that all day slid nervously back and forth, watering the nearest hills while the lakefront remained dry, retreating, charging forward, and over-running the sun, pushing shadows over Lake Kivu and causing pedal boats to make for shore, girls to grab sweaters, and mothers to hug shivering children. It may have been knowing these clouds hid the volcanoes and permanent glaciers of the Ruwenzori mountains with their science fiction landscape of snowbound pinnacles glistening under moonlight, leafless shrubs and everlasting white flowers, groundsel shaped like huge artichokes, phallus-like purple lobelias, trees dripping with moss, and bamboo forests hiding the last mountain gorillas on earth. It may have been the shadow of massacres I saw in the Tusi social kisses, or the knowledge that this clear lake was safe for swimming only because methane gas at the bottom kills the snails that carry schistosomiasis. Or it may have been knowing that Gisenye bordered Zaïre, and wondering when *that* ominous cloud would sweep a few miles east. All of this I may have imagined, but it was not my imagination that even on this national holiday the smugglers' villas were shuttered, the driveways empty and the porch furniture stacked, and their silence broken only by growling dogs. Nor did I imagine the wild storm that came after sunset, when the fast-cooling volcanoes finally pushed their black clouds over Gisenye, the wind stirred up whitecaps, and lightning illuminated the silhouette of Goma, blacked out by a power shortage and looking dead as the lake.

I bought a seat in a van with a sign saying KIGALI EXPRESS. We left with seven passengers jammed onto benches built for three across, a human brick. My memories of African bush taxis are of generosity, shared food, and quick friendships, but in the Kigali Express, cassette players from the Orient had eliminated all that. Speeding down the curvy highway to Ruhengeri, I heard a French rock group singing, in English, "I want to marry an American, I want to live in Hollywood," and "Man, that chain gang, she tough!" while through the windshield I saw a rural city, busy as a factory at full tilt. It was a spectacle of overpopulation so dramatic that Planned Parenthood could have mounted a camera on the Kigali Express and filmed a documentary needing no sound track. Rwandan women are as fertile as the black soil clinging to their bare feet—each has an average of eight children— and so every hill was cleared up to its rounded peaks and down to its marshy valleys, circled by terracing and crisscrossed by paths busy as Wall Street sidewalks. Women carried babies, gourds, and baskets stuffed with cabbages, and no one—well, no woman—walked empty-handed. Brides were the exception, the occasion of her marriage being one of few times in her life a Rwandan woman can put one foot in front of the other without carrying something. It was the weekend, and every mile we passed another wedding procession. The brides wore orange scarfs that fluttered like pennants and walked to their ceremonies past unfinished schools and skeletal children, proof this rural city was already dangerously overcrowded.

The government had a program requiring everyone to spend one day a week working on community projects. In most villages, labor gangs poured foundations for schools and dispensaries, patched roads, and dug trenches. Everywhere a house was being roofed, bricks baked, or pylons erected. There was a certain heroism in this struggle to match population growth with these necessities and a beauty to this geography of overpopulation, to the hills with curving terraces, checkerboard crops, and earth so black it challenged farmers to exhaust it. It was only when you compared the shivering boys to the enormous cabbages they sold at roadside, or the little girls with knee socks of dried mud and war-orphan eyes to the healthy cattle they herded, that you realized this humming rural factory was tragic. Rich soil, hard work, a gentle climate, and a well-intentioned government were simply not enough to support Rwanda's three million inhabitants. Already marginal lands had been cultivated and farms subdivided into minuscule plots, yet by the turn of the century the population would double to six million.

Rwanda may be poor, but everyone had the fare for the Kigali Express. When they saw us, women grabbed bundles and ran into the road, flapping their palms. We dropped a passenger and they charged like bulls. New passengers sent ripples through the van. I traded the man who shook my side with coughs for a Hutu smothered in a greatcoat, then for a boy carrying five bricks—just five. The farmers brought the odors of mildew and onions; the herders, milk and manure. The women were sweat and soiled baby. The tantalizing smell of agricultural prosperity— peat and wet earth—hung over everyone.

Kigali was a leafy, low-slung little city, the perfect capital for Rwanda. Its center was a grid of asphalt roads atop a flattened hill, lined with embassies, government ministries, and villas built by the Germans. It was a city of country bumpkins who crossed its streets erratically, wary as deer or oblivious as tortoises. Farmers carried shovels and hoes down the Rue de la Révolution, and herders drove cattle around the Place de l'Indépendence. In the center of the city was an encouraging building, the president's palace, a structure so modest its roof was scarcely visible over low brick walls. The occupant, Major-General Juvenal Habyarimana, seized power in a coup, and his "elections" give him the traditional 99 percent, but he has not taken a name such as "The Guide," made himself emperor, or plastered his nation's currency, newspapers, and public places with his portrait. He is not afraid to sleep in his own palace, nor is he ringed by thugs with machine guns. He has only one Mercedes and is in the habit of piling his family into it and driving them to the beach. By all accounts he is a modest and sensible man, but even so, he alone is not enough to explain Rwanda's perplexing appearance of prosperity.

I saw another explanation while standing next to the traffic circle in the Place de la Constitution. Half the vehicles passing me belonged to foreign relief and development agencies. There was CARE and AFRICARE, and the EEC; the assistance programs of the French, American, Canadian, and German governments;

Protestant and Catholic organizations; United Nations agencies; and a bus stenciled Japan-Rwanda Cooperation. Even the Swiss had embraced Rwanda, building an embassy larger than the American or Russian ones. Perhaps this was because early travelers had called Rwanda the Switzerland of Africa, and it was still an apt comparison. In addition to its mountain landscape and clean little capital, Rwanda followed an economic policy positively Swiss in its stability and restraint. The national debt was low, and the treasury kept eight months of foreign exchange in reserve.

So many people wanted to help tiny Rwanda that the government ministries were overwhelmed, and there was a considerable backlog of charitable ventures awaiting approval. The foreign donors intrigued, competing like farmers for Rwanda's scarce land. At the moment, the World Bank wanted to finance a sugarcane plantation on the same land where the United Nations hoped to graze cattle. Whenever I met these donor representatives, I asked, "Why are you all here? Why is the world showering Rwanda with gifts?"

The said: "Because the government is serious about development and the functionaries are in their offices all day." "The people work hard — perhaps it is the cool climate." "There is no longer a tribal problem here." "It's so small we can visit our projects in a day." "Compared to the rest of Africa, there is no corruption."

"Look at this country's neighbors if you want to see why we're here," an American suggested. I did, concluding Rwanda really was like Switzerland, but Switzerland during the Second World War, when it was a peaceful refuge encircled by chaos.

At the Ugandan embassy, I was astonished to learn that the Kampala computers had approved my visa application — astonished and, to be honest, not as pleased as I had imagined I would be. Six years after Idi Amin, Uganda was still plagued by civil war, banditry, or insurgency, depending on who was describing it, and the American government had just denounced Ugandan president Milton Obote for presiding over, if not orchestrating, the murder of 100,000 Ugandans, even more than Amin had killed. Some European nations disputed the American figures. It was debated whether Obote's army had killed 50,000, or 70,000, or 200,000 people, but everyone agreed the killers wore Ugandan army uniforms, although President Obote claimed they were brigands in disguise. The Obote atrocities were terrifying for their randomness: a nun here, a priest and his Sunday congregation there; a family here, a village there; a wedding party here, an outing of schoolchildren there.

Before coming to Africa, I had not paid much attention to these massacres. In the newspapers they were column fillers or "News in Brief." There had been so much brutality in Uganda that people had come to accept it as part of the landscape. And I had not paid much attention because the equator appeared to be exempt from the worst massacres. They were confined to the so-called Luwero triangle, stretching northeast of Kampala, which anchored its lower corner. The equator ran well to the south of this zone, entering from Zaïre at Kasindi and traveling through lightly populated savanna until it crossed the Kigali-Kampala highway fifty miles south of Kampala and disappeared into Lake Victoria. On some maps it hit land next in Kenya, while on others it resurfaced briefly to touch the runway of the Entebbe airport.

A day after arriving in Kigali, I was at an expatriate party where a French diplomat looked at me over the top of his glasses and said, "It is OK, the Uganda, if you do not go on *le weekend* or after dark."

"Why is that?" I asked. How could anywhere be "OK" with those cautions attached?

"Because then the soldiers are drunk and their roadblocks are dangerous. That is what we tell our French citizens." He turned away, thinking, incredibly, that someone going to Uganda would not want to know more. I followed him, asking "Well, when do you send your French citizens to Uganda?"

"We tell them always, always, travel only in the early morning when the soldiers are sober."

"But isn't it too long a trip to Kampala, what with customs and everything, to be made entirely in the early morning?"

"*Précisément!* Which is why we, the official French, fly to Kampala—if we must go there."

The frontier was only fifty miles from Kigali, but I could find no one except the long-distance truck drivers who had recently crossed it. In the last month, the insurgents had broken out of the Luwero triangle. There was fighting in Fort Portal, and all of western Uganda was dangerous. But dangerous for whom? Surely not for these secular missionaries with FAO, UNICEF, OXFAM,

AID, and UNDP stenciled on the doors of their overland vehicles. I tried, delicately, to express these thoughts, but right away everyone knew what I meant, since my assumptions mirrored what theirs had been, until last year.

"But didn't you hear about those Swedes?" someone asked.

"Or the Soviet diplomat?"

"The Swiss engineers?"

"And there was a British accountant."

And so it went, with everyone recalling the nationalities and professions — but not the names — of Europeans recently killed or wounded in Uganda. The Soviet diplomat had been hit in downtown Kampala. The relief workers were shot in the north; it was thought they were Swedes and only lightly wounded, but no one was sure. Soldiers had pulled the Swiss engineers ("Swiss! Just imagine, Swiss!") from their car, murdering them in daylight by the side of a busy highway. The government blamed rebels disguised as soldiers, but not a single expatriate in Kigali believed this.

I decided to fly to Entebbe, land on the equator and travel by road to Kampala. From there I could work back to the Zaïre border or continue to Kenya. But an Englishman at my hotel said, "It's not the countryside that's dangerous, mate, it's that bloody road from Entebbe to Kampala." The murders of the Swiss engineers and the British accountant had not occurred, as I had assumed, at some remote rural crossroads, but on the busiest highway in Uganda. The victims had been returning from the Entebbe Yacht Club, and their killers, it was thought, were soldiers notorious for their brutality and whiskey consumption. They controlled the first roadblock after the airport.

One of Kigali's principal attractions was the photographs displayed in glass cases in front of the embassies along the Avenue de l'Indépendence. In some capitals this propaganda is treated with amused contempt, but the Rwandans stared open-mouthed at pictures of French nuclear reactors and American rockets. In front of a photograph of Soviet surgeons gathered around an open chest, I met a Twa Pygmy named Viateur, who said, "I bet you're going to see the gorillas."

It was a good bet that any new European in Kigali would want to visit the mountain gorillas in the Parc National des Vol-

cans. There are only two hundred and forty of these gorillas left—
none has survived captivity—and all live on the slopes of the Vir-
unga volcanoes. There are a few in Zaïre and Uganda, but most
are in Rwanda, where they have become the leading tourist attraction. Park rangers lead groups into the bamboo forests every
day to visit several troops that have been "habituated" to humans.
There are only twenty-four places on these treks, so the gorillas
are sometimes booked up for months. I had been lucky to find a
cancellation.

"I know about the gorillas because I worked at the Office of
Tourism," Viateur said, hopping from foot to foot and puffing up
his tiny chest. "But now I am employed by a commercial bank.
Can I write to you?" I gave him my address. "Good. I will bring a
present to your hotel."

"But we've just met. Why should you give me a present?"

"Because I like you."

"How do you know?"

"Because I like all whites." He showed me a notebook
filled with Europeans' addresses. I had read a book describing
the Twa as "potters and parasites," but "good dancers." They
entertained the Tusi noblemen much as dwarfs did the czars.
Since they are less than 1 percent of Rwanda's population, perhaps Viateur felt for Europeans the kinship of one minority for
another.

I asked about the gorilla group I was visiting, number thirteen.

He giggled. "Oh, I never paid attention to the numbers."

"Which group did you see?"

He doubled up with laughter. "Oh, no, no, no, I never went.
We are not very interested in the gorillas."

"Do any Africans visit them?"

"Only the highest functionaries, and they only go once. They
have to go once. But the gorillas"—he held out his little palms,
offering a gift—"they are for you, *les blancs.*"

Before visiting gorilla group thirteen, I met Bill Weber, an
American zoologist who helped habituate the group to human
visits. He had tracked gorillas through nettles and bamboo,
scratching like them, imitating their grunts of contentment, pretending to eat bamboo, and walking on hands and knees, so that

finally the gorillas thought . . . well, just what *did* they think of these little white-skinned gorillas pretending to be them?

Weber made group thirteen sound human. In 1979 a poacher had killed its male leader. There was fear this would split the family, but a young gorilla named Mirthi had assumed command, undergoing the hormonal change that gives a silver stripe to the leader's fur. Now Weber worried that the group was becoming too friendly, walking on visitors' chests and grabbing their feet. "The biggest problem with habituated gorillas," he said, "is that they will become like the bears in Yellowstone."

The four habituated gorilla groups earned two million dollars a year, making them Rwanda's fourth most important source of foreign exchange, and Weber used their hard-currency–earning abilities to argue for their protection. He said they attracted naturalists, zoologists, and film makers to Rwanda. Because of them, the Parc des Volcans was the only national park in Africa supported by gate receipts, with every visitor paying fifty dollars in park and guide fees, and most spending considerably more before leaving the country. During the summer, the twenty-four daily viewing slots were sold out to European tour operators, so the easiest way to see a gorilla was to come on an expensive package tour.

Habituation to tourists was only part of the conservationists' campaign. There were anti-poacher patrols and an educational program to persuade farmers that the slopes of the Ruwenzori were a vital watershed, soaking up rainwater and releasing it like a sponge to fields below. In 1969 the government had cleared 40 percent of the Parc des Volcans for the cultivation of pyrethrum, a daisy-like flower that is a natural pesticide. It has since become a less valuable export, and, Weber said with satisfaction, "Now the gorillas earn more foreign exchange than pyrethrum." There had been talk of turning more park land into pasture, but the conservationists had successfully argued that gorillas were more valuable than cattle, and that even if the entire park were cleared it would provide land for only thirty-five thousand farm families, less than a single year's increase in population.

The more Weber described the gorillas' tremendous earning power, the distances Europeans would travel to see them, and the lengths conservationists had gone to save them, the more I won-

dered why. Was it only because there were no mountain gorillas
in captivity? Every sizable zoo has a collection of lowland gorillas,
which are smaller but similar in appearance. If you contrasted the
brief time visitors spent with the gorillas to their considerable investment of money and time, and figured that only six thousand
people a year could see a gorilla, then this had to be among the
most expensive and elitist wildlife experiences in the world. No
wonder the gorillas were only for *les blancs.*

I drove to the Parc des Volcans with three American development experts from Kenya who also had tickets for group thirteen.
We spent the night before our trek in a small, colonial-era hotel
in Ruhengeri that resembled a threadbare club with dying membership. Europeans and elderly Rwandans slumped in its leather
armchairs, waiters played endless Ping-Pong on the patio, and
the bartender slept standing up. I had come to Ruhengeri to
watch gorillas, yet from the moment I arrived I was the one
watched. I took a beer onto the terrace and pedestrians slowed to
rubberneck. I went walking and a gang of boys followed. I was
not begged from or whistled at, just followed, and watched. At
sunset, clouds slid away from the volcanoes and a blizzard of
white birds filled the sky. I took a photograph and a crowd
formed, but at a safe distance, as if I were a fire not fully extinguished. Even the women hunched in distant fields, sensing
the presence of a strange European, swiveled their heads. A man
lay on his back in a courtyard, holding a laughing child in both
hands, twisting it and admiring it from every angle as you would
a diamond, and only he ignored me.

Boys selling model planes and cars built from garbage waited
for me at the hotel's entrance. *"Je suis un artiste,"* one said, thrusting forward a coat-hanger cowboy riding a milk-carton motorcycle. He spun the propeller of a plane. Its fuselage was a soap box,
its wings said Kiwi Shoe Polish, and its tires were broken rubber
bands. A wooden pilot sat in the cockpit. Each model was unique,
built from different refuse. The French anthropologist Claude
Lévi-Strauss has written, "The first thing we see as we travel
round the world is our own filth, thrown into the face of mankind." I wonder what he would think of these Ruhengeri teen-
agers. They had turned our filth into art and were selling it back
to us.

I asked the boy why he didn't build a gorilla, a more suitable souvenir for the gorilla watchers. He said he had seen airplanes land at the nearby strip, seen motorbikes and cowboys in movies, but had never seen a gorilla. What did one look like?

"But certainly you've seen photographs?" There was a poster of a gorilla mother on the wall of the bar.

"Yes, of the face, but never the whole animal."

"Why not?"

He laughed. He was trying to be polite, but my questions were simply too stupid. "It is too expensive for us to visit the gorillas. They are for you, *les blancs.*"

The next morning, we drove a half hour to the park refuge where gorilla watchers registered. As we neared it, the land became even more populated and cultivated. The refuge was a sprawling brick villa that was once in a forest clearing but now found itself circled by pyrethrum daisies and corn.

A party of Italians greeted us with cries of *"Gorilla malato! Gorilla malato!"* A woman explained that one of the four gorilla groups was ill and could not be visited for weeks. Half the Italians had booked an overnight trek to a remote group that was healthy; the others had flown three thousand miles and stayed five days in Rwanda, only to be told their friends and relatives would be seeing a gorilla but they would not. "They are not an airline, these gorillas," she said. "When one is broken they cannot bring us another." She had a ticket to see the healthy gorillas.

It was a good analogy. The refuge resembled a small airport, filled with long-stranded passengers competing for seats on the only flight of the day. Three Canadians with bloodshot eyes and matted hair had slept three nights in their overland van, hoping for a cancellation. They had exhausted their food and currency, and unless they scrounged a ticket today they would have to leave. There were parties of British and French standbys, all enemies now. The French had attempted to bribe a park ranger. The British were indignant, although one offered me a hundred dollars for my place.

Some Rwandan farmers stood on a bluff, watching us prepare to watch the gorillas. They leaned on hoes, cleaned their teeth with green twigs, and whispered behind their hands, briefing friends who had arrived midway into the entertainment. They moved their heads back and forth in unison as the Europeans struck tents, threw tantrums, and ran between refuge and privy.

The Italians were the star attraction. They pulled a parade of beautifully designed gadgets from pink rucksacks. They tested thumbnail-sized flashlights that could illuminate parking lots, traded packets of freeze-dried food, and from velvet pouches shook out miniature stoves that unfolded like flowers.

We of gorilla group thirteen drove in convoy with a French couple to a farm village at the edge of the park. There we met two Rwandan guides whose names sounded like George and Machete. They said group thirteen had ten gorillas, which they usually found within three hours. We were not to point at the gorillas, shake the vegetation, or take photographs if a male charged. We walked on worn paths, zigzagging along sweet-potato, banana, and pyrethrum fields that before 1969 had been thick forest and gorillas. The children were habituated to the six Europeans who crossed their land every morning. They threw down tools and dashed through the waist-high daisies, wailing like ambulances. They braked a foot away, flipped up palms, and in hoarse adult voices said, *"Cadeau!"*—"Gift!"

I asked Machete if they had seen a gorilla. He looked startled. The idea was fantastic. "No, never! They would have to pay, and for them it is too much money." Their fathers had planted to the edge of the park. The boundary was dramatic: on one side, conical huts, laboring women, and densely populated farmland; on the other, a Tarzan forest of vines and mossy trees and a population density of zero. Over there were gorillas who every day received delegations of Europeans, and here, less than a mile away, were Africans who had never seen a gorilla. When Bill Weber had surveyed these farmers, only half could name even a single gorilla physical characteristic.

Gorilla troops usually wander less than a quarter of a mile from where they nested the night before, so tracking the same troop every day is not difficult. If Machete and George are typical, it involves sniffing the air for an odor of zoo, following notches they cut into trees the day before, and sifting dung. It took us an hour to find group thirteen. We walked between clearings where they had stripped the bamboo of leaves, and found droppings electric with flies. Machete said, "They have been here . . " George caressed their dung and whispered, "Yesterday." Afterwards, I asked what he looked for. He said flies. The more they swarmed, the fresher the dung. He felt for consistency and checked for eggs. It was a science of sorts.

Machete pointed to the matted vegetation in another clearing and said, "They have eaten here . . ."

George plunged his fingers into more dung. "Last night!"

We followed broken bamboo to another dung pile. George straightened up with a wet hand and triumphant smile. "Today!"

We heard grunts that Machete and George answered with the phlegm-clearing growls of old smokers. Suddenly gorillas were everywhere. A mother climbed a tree, pulled off shoots, and threw them to a son who ate the leaves one by one, like grapes. A male held an infant high in his hands, turning her in the sunlight like the father in Ruhengeri. The gorillas were easy to spot. Their black fur was sharp against the green, and they would have been a cinch to shoot.

We followed Mirthi, the silver-back male, to a water hole where a mother and two children had formed a gorilla daisy chain: A young gorilla nibbled insects off the coat of another, who picked ticks off the next, who scratched the first. Their fur was silky and healthy, without the bald patches and clumps of feces you see in a zoo. We squatted around them like gypsies at a fire, close enough to pick their lice. The French never stopped taking pictures of the gorillas. The woman used a telephoto lens, getting close-ups of their tunnel noses, wrinkled fingers, and marble eyes. I know I examined each feature, comparing it to my own. They moved their fingers and I wiggled mine. They yawned, I yawned. I contrasted the size of our forearms and remembered the severed arm in the Ouzey market. I studied them with the same determination I brought to ignoring whatever features I shared with the child beggars a mile away.

The more intently we stared at these gorillas, the more they ignored us. They looked into the French cameras without blinking, their eyes bored. If they sensed these visits were protecting them from the poachers' pangas, they did not show it. Were we registering on their gorilla retinas? I doubted it. I felt invisible, and strangely hurt at being so easily ignored. But perhaps gorilla group thirteen had noticed us, because, as we backed away on hands and knees like supplicants leaving the court of an Oriental potentate, a mother turned and farted in our faces.

An hour later we were back among fields of corn and sweet potatoes, hearing the whoops of running children. I examined them more carefully. They flashed twisted grins, but there was contempt in their dull eyes. They knew we cared more for the gorillas. The French couple persuaded a brother and sister to pose in front of their mud hut. Hoping to please, or because they knew of no other way to face a white, they thrust out palms. Just as the French persuaded them to drop this pose, a man blocked their camera. It was their father, demanding a fee. He would have accepted a sou, but the French, who had just paid so handsomely to photograph the gorillas, refused. It was the principle of the thing. The French stamped back to their van, indignant, but turning once, out of spite, to snap with their telephoto lens a long-distance picture of the enraged family.

Afterwards I found myself thinking less about the gorillas than the phenomenon of their conservation. They owed their survival to the late Dian Fossey, an American naturalist who had devoted her life to studying them, pleading for their conservation and starting her own controversial anti-poaching patrols. And she owed much of her success to Rwanda's political stability. Poachers have decimated gorilla troops in Zaïre and Uganda, and if similar anarchy ever spreads to Rwanda, the gorillas of the Parc des Volcans will suffer the same fate, particularly since the habituation to human visits has robbed them of their only defense, fear of man. Fossey foresaw this danger and habituated only the gorillas she studied to European visitors. But what may be practical for wildlife conservation is impractical in an independent African nation. Hence native guides like Machete and George, and behind them the danger that if Rwanda becomes another Uganda or Zaïre, poachers will make quick work of group thirteen.

Efforts to preserve African wildlife are heroic, yet successful African game parks often have the atmosphere of a European enclave. There are African politicians who understand the value of the parks, but they are usually European by education and temperament. There are dedicated African rangers and wildlife enthusiasts, but every colonial army had its loyal noncommissioned officers, ready to die for a foreign cause. Of course, if Africa had never been colonized and developed, its wildlife would not be endangered. But now, without the recolonization of African enclaves—the game parks—it cannot possibly be saved.

*   *   *

An invitation to visit the Nyagahanga Women's School of Agronomy gave me an excuse to postpone Uganda. The school was described as the most successful development program in Rwanda, and the only school of its kind in central Africa. It was supported by Dutch and American development agencies and managed by Belgian nuns. It had started with thirty students, and now it put two hundred through a five-year course in practical agriculture whose stated goals were "training women for rural agricultural development" and "lowering the agricultural workload by new and improved farming techniques." Its effect was something else.

I drove to Nyagahanga with the AID program officer for the school and Genevieve, who had just graduated with honors, winning a scholarship to study soils and fruit trees at the University of Maryland. She was returning to say good-bye to the nuns, rub this rabbit's-foot of a place one more time, and, judging from the intensity with which she stared out the window, take some memory pictures she could replay during what she imagined would be Maryland's arctic winters.

"How cold is Maryland?" she asked as we neared the school.

To encourage her I made it sound like Miami. She turned around in the front seat and stared. She had a pioneer face — long, sinewy, and hollow — and the habit of flicking her eyes to the horizon, as if searching for tornadoes. "That's not true," she said. "It snows in Maryland."

I was not the first man she had caught in a lie. "Well, I suppose it snows in Maryland, but not that much."

"If it snows, it must be cold there." She turned back to the panorama of women washing clothes, harvesting cabbages, and swishing sickles. I did not think Genevieve would be impressed with the kinds of excuses that can be mustered for the Rwandan men: Women's work is daily, while men perform seasonal and irregular tasks such as plowing, clearing fields, and building fences and houses; or, before first the Germans and then the Belgians had colonized Rwanda, men hunted wild game and defended villages, but the colonial powers introduced cash crops, destroying the habitat of game animals and imposing a peace that left African men with leisure and African women with chores. If you averaged the work done by men and women over several centuries, it might be in some kind of rough balance, cold comfort to a donkey-loaded Rwandan woman in the twentieth century.

A woman in rural Africa can be betrothed at birth, sent to live with the husband's family, enslaved to her mother-in-law, and made to bear rivers of children until her sons marry and she can persecute her own daughters-in-law, singing at their weddings joyful songs such as "I shall no longer go to fetch wood! And to fetch water! I shall no longer pound the grain!" And the women of Rwanda and Burundi sounded worse off than even this low average. In an account of their lives by a French anthropologist who was unable to conceal her disgust, I had read:

> The herders sometimes argue about the relative superiority of women and cows; both sources of milk appear to have their partisans.

> It is believed that women are better suited by nature than men for manual labor. They work longer and better in the fields than men.

> It is nonetheless believed that the male role is more important than that of the female in procreation. Woman, says the proverb, is only the passive earth; it is man who provides the seed.

> If a husband finds his wife in bed with another man, he is morally obligated to beat his wife and to quarrel a little with the man.

> Beauty does not count very heavily, but a man is not displeased if people notice that his wife is attractive and well-fleshed, has a long and narrow nose, a light skin, and is somewhat like a cow.

> Regarding the sentiments of the husband towards the wife, or of men in general towards women, it is enough to mention that in the rich oral literature of Burundi, there is not one poem or song of love.

The Nyagahanga Women's School of Agronomy was a green salad in the bottom of a brown bowl of eroded hills. The director, a Belgian nun with the large features of a Flemish portrait, recited for me a litany of Nyagahanga progress: a new infirmary and classrooms, goats and pigs added to the curriculum, and the first coffee harvest. "Our students have made a nice profit on their sweet potatoes, and they have planted five hundred eucalyptus. Imagine, five hundred!" she said, all the time staring at Genevieve, a parent devouring a favorite child. "And soon the girls will cultivate the marsh across the road and we will be self-sufficient. Imagine, self-sufficient!"

Genevieve led me through the school fields, practicing for Maryland by speaking English. "Cabbage, rhubarb, and spinach," she said, pointing to rows of sprouting vegetables. There were potatoes under tin roofs, corn, sorghum, sugar cane, beets and papaya saplings, fishponds, and rabbits sniffing clean cages. Like the Hmong, the Nyagahanga girls cultivated a little of everything. "What do they grow in Maryland?" she asked, defiant.

I had no idea, but I said corn, carrots, cabbage, and yes, leeks too.

"And endive?"

"I don't think so, but perhaps you can introduce it." I liked the idea of Genevieve bringing Belgian endive to Baltimore.

When I thought we were finished, she led me through a hedge to see strawberries, eggplants, and embryonic pineapples. She pointed to banana trees, saying "They are *not* for beer."

I asked how students had time to attend classes and cultivate these fields.

"We are disciplined. We start at dawn. We divide into teams, competing to grow the best crops. Sometimes we grow so much we need help with the harvest. Then we hire local farmers, the men." I saw a sly smile.

I wondered about the white plastic purse she clutched in one hand, and the high-heeled sandals, so unsuited to tramping through Nyagahanga. I asked if she would be returning to Rwanda after Maryland. She said, "Of course!" but so quickly and emphatically I thought I had found her out.

While she visited a favorite teacher I wandered through spotless dormitories and classrooms, overhearing a lecture devoted as much to women's consciousness-raising as practical agriculture. A bulletin board in the dining room showed that these students had fabulous names: Epiphanie, Cancilde, Célerine, Consolée, and Spéciose. I could match these with Nyagahanga's girls, but not with the stick-figure women laboring outside its gates.

A girl pounded a huge drum, announcing lunch. The students came in tan skirts and white shirts, walking erect and swinging arms like plebes at a military academy. A Rwandan teacher said they hoped to place a Nyagahanga graduate in each of the country's 141 communes, where they would "instruct" the other women. In more than agriculture, I thought. These women, better educated than their brothers and husbands, were certain to stir up their villages. This school was far more subversive than any of the Marxist mumbo-jumbo or "authenticity" that passes for revolution in Africa. It held out the hope of changing the order of things more surely than any camp of embittered partisans.

11

I DISEMBARKED AT THE ENTEBBE AIRPORT WITH FOUR ANGLICAN priests, old men with turkey necks rattling in clerical collars. They had come for a conference and a VIP van collected them, leaving me alone. The crew and transit passengers stayed in the plane. There were no brisk women with clipboards meeting us, only a bored policeman, a sharp wind off Lake Victoria, and an empty runway intersected somewhere by the equator. I felt like a rabbit in a winter field, twitchy and ready to dart back into that comfortable hole of the plane and continue to Nairobi. Then I saw my bag being wheeled toward the terminal.

The arrivals hall was a concrete cavern with wet floors and a scattering of broken machinery. It appeared empty, but echoed with shouts and clanging doors. It had been built by Idi Amin, financed by Colonel Qaddaffi, and, for all I knew, designed by them as well: the architecture of horror. But when I complained to a young man in a Uganda Airways blazer that my bag had not arrived, instead of shrugging it off he said, "Follow me!" and we sprinted outside to find two luggage handlers crouched over it like vultures. Our shouts sent them flapping. My padlock had held, but they had ripped open the zipper.

The health officer wore a surgeon's smock flecked with blood. In a pocket he carried a hypodermic, needle up. "Your vaccination certificate is not in order," he said, smiling, his arms folded in the posture of a television doctor. "You must come to my surgery." The year on my yellow-fever certificate was smudged, and he could not decide if it was 1981 or 1982 — no matter that either way the shot was still effective. He shut the door and said, "I will have to re-vaccinate you." He plucked a gray cotton ball from a used ashtray and fingered the needle. It was beginning to be rumored that AIDS was widespread in Uganda. (Since my journey, AIDS has been found to be present in tragic proportions in Uganda and several other African nations.) As I reached for my wallet, the door banged open. It was the Uganda Airways agent, announcing that he had fixed the zipper and that my bag was at customs. His eyes met the health officer's. Finally the health officer said, "I suppose you could be re-vaccinated by your embassy." Afterwards the agent refused my five dollars. "It is our job at Uganda Airways to serve passengers," he said. I looked closely. He was a teen-ager.

"The Kingdom of Uganda is a fairy tale," wrote Winston Churchill in 1908. "You climb up a railway instead of a beanstalk and at the end there is a wonderful new world." Only when we drove from the terminal into the sunlight did I realize I would be seeing this "fairy tale" through a spider web of cracks running from a bullet hole in the taxi's windshield, on the passenger side. I saw the abandoned terminal where Israeli commandos had rescued the Entebbe hostages; the empty Lake Victoria, where my pharmacist's son had contracted schistosomiasis; and an airport roadblock manned by giggly policemen with machine guns who asked, "Where you come from?" Kigali. "Tee-hee-hee, how's the weather there?" Rainy. "Tee-hee-hee, it's better here. Everything's — tee-hee-hee — better in Uganda."

Convoys of dignitaries sped to the airport down the center of a winding, crumbling highway. They came at us fast around corners, appearing suddenly over hills, headlights blinking and sirens wailing. First a jeep, then Land Rovers and trucks bristling like porcupines with soldiers' rifles, then the great man himself in a black sedan. With each convoy my driver swerved to the side. In its haste to clear the road, a panel truck tumbled into a ditch.

Five miles beyond the airport we stopped at the first army roadblock, the one where the Swiss and the Briton had been murdered. Soldiers in camouflage fatigues were living in a grove of trees. They cooked, slept, and played cards while one man checked cars. He waved his machine gun and my driver skidded to a stop, cut the engine, and hunched over the wheel, taking himself out of the line of fire. Another soldier struggled to his feet and staggered toward us. How the hell had this happened? An hour before I was eating *assiette anglaise* on Sabena. Now I was in a bullet-scarred taxi, about to be questioned by one of the drunken, teen-age soldiers of the most murderous, least disciplined army on earth.

He tapped his gun against the door. His cap was balanced on a halo of uncut hair, his eyes blanker than the gorillas'. "Where you going?" It was almost a shout.

"Kampala."

There was a pause. His eyes came alive and darted around the taxi, taking inventory. "Coming from?"

"Kigali."

He banged the door in time to his words. "What . . . do . . . you . . . have . . . for . . . *me!*"

"Have for you?" I repeated stupidly.

"Yes, you must have something in your bags for me."

"Well, I don't know. What do you like?" I was handling this poorly, but what was the etiquette? Did I give him a shirt? The whole bag? If I offered cash, would he arrest me for bribery in hope of extorting more?

"I like cigarettes. Give me all your cigarettes."

"I don't smoke."

"What?"

I cleared my throat. "I don't smoke." The driver, in despair, laid his head on the steering wheel. He had not looked around once. No matter what, he would stare straight ahead, driving away without a backward glance at the body.

Two other soldiers picked up rifles and weaved forward. The teen-ager slammed his rifle butt against the door. "Why . . . don't . . . you . . . smoke?"

"I don't know."

"You *must* have something for me!"

I plunged a hand into my bag, searching for Ugandan shillings. I came up with a handful of the official buttons of the Great Equatorial Expedition. Except in Ndjolé, these had been a flop. But he grabbed them all, demanding more for his family. The others wanted some too, and I left them pinning them on and throwing mock salutes. They really were drunk.

My driver stopped at a store and said, "I insist you buy cigarettes for the soldiers." I passed them out at the other roadblocks. One soldier thanked me with a salute that echoed a British parade ground. There was an echo of Britain too in their uniforms. This was a shock. I expected thuggish soldiers to speak Arabic or Spanish or French, and to wear uniforms matching these languages. I had never been in an English-speaking nightmare country. This army was not an entirely homegrown evil. The British, by recruiting northern Moslems into it to pacify the southern Buganda, had encouraged the regional and tribal divisions that bedevil Uganda. When the country became independent, it was the Israelis who, hoping to promote instability in southern Sudan, transformed a sleepy battalion of a thousand into a modern force and later welcomed Idi Amin's coup. So there was a certain rough justice in plainclothes British army commandos being stationed in Kampala to protect British diplomats, and in Israeli commandos at Entebbe battling an army they had trained. Still, it is easier to savor these little historical ironies sitting in New York than while driving to Kampala.

I arrived an hour before sunset, a time when you first noticed people ordering their lives to a curfew all the more sinister for being unofficial, yet so faithfully observed. The sun neared the horizon, and pedestrians moved with the skittish walk of silent movies. Guards dragging old rifles appeared in the Speke Hotel to protect guests from "uniformed bandits." Traffic quickened, then shrank to a diplomatic sedan, a police car, and soldiers standing jammed in the rear of trucks, their red berets swaying like windblown poppies.

The sun disappeared and shutters banged shut, shoeshine men vanished, and Kampala's Stonehenge of unfinished skyscrapers stood sharp against the sky. By eight there was a midnight stillness. From the terrace of the Speke I could see the only creatures who braved the curfew: whores and marabou storks. The storks shoved their beaks into garbage and flapped into Independence Park. Double a vulture, put it on stilts, and you have a marabou stork. They have bald red heads, fleshy pink necks, and wings that fold to an oval, like the morning coats of bridegrooms or undertakers. My *Field Guide to the National Parks of East Africa* says, "Generally silent except for bill rattling and short grunting sounds. . . . Mainly a scavenger which associates with vultures at carrion; also occurs near open water where it feeds on frogs." I hoped this was why they were flapping into the park, to devour the screaming frogs.

Whores sat on both sides of me, scissoring their legs and kissing the air. "I will give a *very* nice back rub," one said, pulling up a chair and demanding a beer. She had transitional sentences that brought every conversation back to my room number, which I refused to reveal, and a back rub, which I did not want. I had a beer delivered to a distant table on condition she drink it there. The waiter said, "You were wise to send her off, sir. She is a very sick lady. Everyone here knows that, so she offers herself to visitors."

A moon-faced girl wandered into my pool of light, selling *Munnasi*, a mimeographed newspaper published by the opposition to the Obote government. Among its articles:

EIGHT VILLAGERS MURDERED IN COLD BLOOD. The murderers had hacked children into unrecognizable pieces. The article termed these killings political, since currency was found scattered on the corpses.

MAKERE MEDICAL DEGREE DENIED RECOGNITION. The General Medical Council of Great Britain had done this, the result of so many key African and European professors fleeing Uganda.

NEW TORTURE CHAMBERS ESTABLISHED IN MITYANA. The mutilated bodies of twenty-seven people had been found in a eucalyptus forest. Three days later, soldiers in the same town, for no apparent reason, had fired into a wedding, killing twelve celebrants.

There was also U.C.B. [Uganda Commercial Bank] RUNS OUT OF CASH, UGANDA AIRWAYS IN TROUBLE, FOREIGN MINISTRY STAFF MISS THEIR SALARIES, and INSECURITY ENGULFS KAMPALA AT NIGHT. This article said, "Quite a number of pedestrians during the last few weeks have been assaulted and robbed and even stripped naked by armed, uniformed thugs in the poorly lit streets of Kampala. . . . Last Friday a group of armed thugs attacked late travellers at South Street and robbed them. . . . Two days earlier, just a few meters away from the Mini-Bata shop, three uniformed men snatched from a porter and ran away with a vessel of cooked food. 'It is as if these soldiers are starved,' remarked one lady, 'otherwise how can they steal cooked food.'"

I was surprised to see this seditious paper. Few other African nations would have tolerated it. I had discounted Uganda's claim to being a democracy. After all, what democracy encourages the security forces to murder its citizens at will? My surprise lasted until I learned that two weeks earlier, soldiers had rampaged through *Munnasi*'s editorial offices, smashing presses and arresting the staff, explaining why it was now crudely mimeographed and sold by illiterate girls who could plead ignorance of its contents.

I had a restless night, brushing roaches off my face and waking to gunfire or backfiring trucks. The next morning I sat on the terrace drinking coffee and watching the usual collection of donor trucks and Land Rovers — OXFAM, Gift of the People of Sweden, CARE, etc. — stirring up the dust of Kampala's crumbling streets. In nightmare countries like Ethiopia and Uganda, the international donors face a moral dilemma, they tell you. There is no question that food and development aid protect a government from the righteous anger of its citizens. So how to weigh the alleviation of suffering against this unavoidable side effect? Should the donors abandon a country, hoping their action will accelerate change in the long run? Or should they stay despite the atrocities and embezzlement, since, after all, there is no long run for those who starve in the meantime? But in Uganda, I thought, this justification was thin. In private, the donors would agree that Obote's government was not simply exploiting or mistreating or torturing or killing a few dozen or a few hundred Ugandans, but murdering them on an industrial scale. So what, in God's name, were all these idealistic Europeans doing zipping around Kampala in their Land Rovers and trucks?

"That's easy," said the representative of a major relief organization, not missing a beat. "We're fattening them up to be bigger targets."

I should not have been surprised that in the twilight of this shuttered room, inside a gloomy walled house in the capital of the most terrifying country on a continent with many contenders, I had found the most bitter and disillusioned Good Samaritan in Africa, my Kurtz. He was a large-featured, soft-spoken man whom I will call Bob, because anyone this honest needs protection. He had worked for relief and development organizations in Africa for twenty years, and every year and every country seemed worse than the one before. He did not dispute the American figure of a hundred thousand murdered by Obote. Each week brought massacres in the countryside and murders in Kampala. Army officers hired out their men as assassins, keeping most of their wages. Cabinet ministers contracted with military units to terrorize opponents. Parties to personal feuds paid soldiers to murder their enemies. Several months before, Bob had heard gunfire every night, and frequently he saw bodies swept into gutters like dead cats. He had discovered the corpse of his neighbor's night watchman, and an army truck had tried to run him off the road. "Amazingly, these soldiers love Bibles," he said. "The missionaries say they can't keep enough in stock."

"Why don't the donors leave?" I asked.

"Leave? Ha! We're begging to be allowed back, to expand our programs."

"Why?"

He gave me a suspicious glance. "You really don't know?" I shook my head. "Because there's money to be made here, lots of it."

"But you're all nonprofit."

He looked at me wide-eyed. "Of course our organizations are nonprofit, but like any bureaucracy they want to survive and grow. And the people who work for them, they certainly profit. In most countries we live in pleasant houses with plenty of servants, leading interesting lives. And we enjoy a clean conscience, because we're only in the game to help people, to save lives!

"And don't forget there's good money in famine and economic development for the consultants, and grants for the universities. Development aid and emergency relief are big business. We sell hope to poor countries, clean consciences to the rich, and our corporate logo, our clever marketing tool, is 'the starving child'!"

"Are you saying 'Let them starve'?"

"See what I mean? See what an effective sales tool they are? What would we do without them? You're right. How can you say no to a starving child? You can't! In the war between economic facts and starving children, the children win every time. But remember that twenty years from now these malnourished children will be malnourished adults, clearing marginal lands, promoting erosion, placing more burdens on their primitive economies, and raising their own huge families of malnourished children. By ensuring they all survive, we're guaranteeing more starvation and suffering. If you want to see the future of Africa, go to Haiti, because that's what this continent is going to become: an overpopulated, eroded wasteland filled with malnourished, terrorized people. And much of the blame will be ours.

"Ask yourself this: If we Europeans decide we have a responsibility to save this particular generation of African children, don't we also have a responsibility to face the consequences of our charity and support the same entirely too large generation throughout its miserable, suffering life? Already the cost is incredible, and we spend too much of the money battling host governments, trying to outwit people living in the capitals who couldn't care less if people starve in the countryside. Thanks to them, it costs a fortune to deliver charity a few hundred miles. And there's no chance the situation will improve. By every economic measurement most African countries are becoming poorer. Every year their factories are less productive and they lose arable land. Their foreign debt is already incredible, and no one seriously believes it can be repaid.

"Eventually the burden of keeping the maximum number of Africans alive at the edge of starvation will become too much. Fifteen or twenty years from now, that Dutch couple who have one child because they can't afford more or because they believe in zero population growth will wonder why they're being taxed to support Rwandan or Ugandan families with ten. And when the rich countries at last rebel against this endless, limitless, destructive charity, then there will be suffering and starvation of incredible magnitude."

I interrupted, asking if other expatriate donors agreed with him.

"Oh, publicly we're all very optimistic that if there's enough food or money or projects, we can save Africa from itself. Blah, blah, blah! But in private, we're pessimistic. We understand that Africa has ensnared us in a moral dilemma: Feeding a generation of Africans is too great a burden to bear forever, yet too terrible in its immediate consequences to lay down."

I argued for economic development. Some Asian countries

had made great progress. Why couldn't African countries match this?

"They can't because substantial economic growth is organic, but our projects of intervention pick out five or ten variables, concentrate on enhancing these, and then something always goes wrong because there are really a hundred variables. We put our fingers in five holes in the dike and leaks spring elsewhere. Economic development assumes you can artificially accelerate growth, but in most African countries there is no growth to accelerate because their economies are decelerating, going backwards. In Uganda a fifth of the farmers have sold their tools, even their pangas. They're planting and harvesting with their hands. Another third use hand hoes because they've eaten their oxen. Tell me how you 'accelerate' their growth?"

For Bob, the fundamental question was: Would Africa ever compete in the world economy with Asia, Europe, and the Americas? And despite all his black humor and pessimism, he was still a Samaritan, and, like every Samaritan in Africa, he had a plan. When Kampala was at its most dangerous, and increasing the size of the soldiers' targets must have seemed particularly pointless, he had written a paper analyzing the problems of African development and proposing a solution. He had composed it in this shuttered house, to a background of night gunfire. "I did it for myself," he said. "To let off steam." I borrowed a copy and read it at sunset on the terrace of the Speke Hotel, as truckloads of soldiers were setting forth for their night's work and donors were hurrying home to their compounds.

He described the problem of African economies as "the question of human achievement in Africa," or "the apparent incapacity of Africans to maintain or expand the colonial infrastructure . . . to run the machinery of modern society." (I wondered, though, if it was something the Africans really wanted to maintain, expand, or run.) He thought their incapacity [or lack of interest?] was understandable given the brevity of the colonial period. It would have been more surprising if the Ugandans, for example, had laid aside the cultural practices of thousands of years to become Europeanized in a century.

He thought aid from Europe consisted largely of "reconstituting the western edifice from the rubble of successive cave-ins." The technical experts in the capital, and the European volunteers and missionaries in the countryside, made the difference between a quick collapse and the current state of gradual regression. This was not promoting development but "reinforcing failure." In the capitals, African civil servants became bystanders, wondering why they should work when European advisers were putting in eight-hour days. Instead, they spent their time on personal business, making "addled" economic decisions based on family and tribe and fulfilling the public expectation that they would steal. From the point of view of an African official, an African nation was a rather efficient mechanism for accumulating wealth and power on a personal level. They dominated the public life of a nation while women and children performed the agricultural labor. They operated according to a value system celebrating potency, strength, cunning, and the ability to accumulate power and prerogatives, one suitable to pre-colonial chiefs, hunters, and warriors. Lacking was a belief in compromise and a tolerance of dissent, values necessary in a democracy, and ones found in Africa more among women than men.

Bob believed that to compete in the world economy, Africa would have to develop its human capital. This meant acquiring the intellectual skills that made people profit-makers and led to wealth creation. It meant the "feminization" of African political life so democracies could survive. It meant indexing aid from the West to decreases in population. This aid would go to mothercraft and early-education programs. If African children were to compete with the West, young boys would have to be weaned from their little-chief syndrome and taught a toleration for feminine values. The most promising students would attend elite academies and be trained to manage competitive industries. In short, Bob wanted hundreds of Nyagahanga Schools—but for the boys.

I have not done his program full justice. It was more sophisticated than it appears in this synopsis. But it was essentially one more grand European scheme for Africa. In its early stages it would be financed and administered by Europeans, and if recent African history teaches anything, it is that grandiose European interventions fail, whereas smaller ones like the Nyagahanga School succeed. If this revolution was what Africans wanted, they would have to come to it themselves.

After Bob, I met only Pollyannas in Kampala. Their gaiety

and fanatical optimism made a certain sense, since, unlike Bob, they would be in Uganda for what one bright student at Makere University described as "my one and only precious life."

There was "Jenny," a bird-like Indian with a face perpetually hidden in shadows. Idi Amin had expelled the Asians, but some had returned to reclaim their dismembered enterprises. When the car we were sharing stopped before a huge hole and I said I had never seen roads in such poor repair, she replied, "Actually, our highways are much better than last year. The government has a program and, well, we have our hopes . . ."

We bumped along Queens Road and Lumumba Road, and past the unfinished East African Telecommunications skyscraper with its stained cement and paralyzed cranes. Jenny said, "Soon we will be finishing that building."

I asked about Makere University. "Before, it was closed, but now it is open!"

I asked about the medical school. "True, it has lost its accreditation, but it is sure to regain it!"

I asked about the forlorn shops on Commercial Row. "That one was closed, but now it is in business again. And he is soon to reopen. It was once — well, honestly, it was once our Harrod's. You know, we do have our hopes that it could be that way again, honestly we do . . ." I did not share these hopes. As in Mbandaka, it seemed unlikely anyone would ever invest the capital or energy to rebuild this European infrastructure.

There was Mr. David B'ouma, moderator of the "Writer's Club" program on Radio Uganda, who opened his show with, "Hello, literature lovers of Uganda!" Listening to Mr. B'ouma's enthusiastic recommendations, it was impossible to believe they were not available at every Kampala bookstore. But at what he called "our number-one book shop," I found only religious tracts, crossword puzzles, comics, and romance novels about nurses and air hostesses. I bought a copy of the only Ugandan literary journal on sale, an oppressively optimistic mimeographed paper called, inexplicably, Come Gazette — Bulletin For Pleasure Reading. Its table of contents offered "Child with Baboon's Heart," "What About Your Face," "Christmas — Why All the Bother?" and "Proud to Be Ugandan." Mr. Pampilio Amatium had written an editorial advising that "To make the best out of life should be everyone's prime concern. There is no need to settle down at your minimals and wait for some other good times. This is the time. Yesterday is gone forever and tomorrow is still far away. Be happy now and work hard to make yourself a paradise on earth. It is possible. Enjoy everything that you can lay your hands on. Make beautiful days and let nothing discouraging beset you. Reach out to the hope and opportunity before you and stand up in joyous victory." It was enough to make you cry.

There was the dean of the arts faculty at Makere University. A sign on his door distinguished among Hours for Regular Business, Serious Inquiries, and Emergencies. He was a shy man with patched clothes, a chewed pipe, and the mannerisms of a British don. He led me through his office to an unmarked door. "This is my 'cave,'" he said with a wink, "where I escape the students and relax with my favorite books." I made the mistake of swinging my eyes too obviously around his cave, with its exploding armchair, shattered windowpanes, and shelf half-full of paperbacks. He gave an embarrassed smile. "There is no spare glass for windows in my country. I suppose there is no foreign exchange to import it from Kenya or wherever. I've been waiting a year for these repairs, but perhaps soon . . ." As we left his cave, the doorknob came off in his hand, forcing him to laugh and make a brittle joke. His students had been reading cast-off paperback thrillers, the only modern literature readily available in Kampala, and they analyzed Jack Higgins and Alistair MacLean with as much intelligence as can be brought to them. "We will never be students again," one said afterwards, "so we must treasure this valuable time. We must try to enjoy our one and only precious lives."

One boy gave me an out-of-date copy of the student humor magazine, *The Betlet*, described on the cover as a collection of "Crushing, Potent, Living, Curtain-Raising *Fun.*" But its contents had a mocking, chilly tone set by the editorial: "I, you, and the rest need fun. It helps cool off the high-tension states and cement otherwise threatened relationships. . . . Fun can relieve the distressed depressed down-trodden from the individual cocoons of sorrow. In time of isolation, written fun is a great company. . . . The Struggle continues. Wishing you a laugh. Otim-Bele, Information Minister/Lumumba Hall." The poems in this "humor magazine" had titles like "You Gotta Believe Scandals By Men," "Alcoholism The Root Of All Misery," "The Struggle," and "Uganda's Epitaph" ("Oh Lord! Ugandans have / EMACIATED

too much. Please, / EMANCIPATE US"). Mr. Otim-Bele had contributed a poem, too long to repeat in its entirety, but here are
some lines, examples of what passes for "written fun" in Uganda:
"Man is the dirtiest, the filthiest and darkest of heart of all beings
/ Man being what he is, adores any emptiness as far as it satisfies
his primitive part of the mind / Man being dirty as he is knows
and enjoys the shit he dwells in."

The university inspiring this humor had been among the
finest in the Commonwealth, with departments on a par with
London and Edinburgh. It had attracted students from across Africa, but now its handsome classrooms and dormitories were bullet-scarred, its students came mostly from Uganda, and there was
no money for books, supplies, or even a pane of glass. Peasants
fleeing rural pogroms had built squatter villages on nearby hills.
At night they stole onto the grounds with flashlights, tending the
bananas and manioc they had planted on the once-landscaped
grounds. I saw a sign saying REMOVE CULTIVATION TEN DAYS FROM
TODAY, and then a long-ago date. The university police carried out
threats to burn these illegal crops, but the squatters returned.
Their new bananas grew fast on the burned-over soil, and they
used the signs for firewood.

After I left, conditions in Uganda became, although this is
hard to believe, much worse. Obote was overthrown by a general
who was, in turn, put to flight by the rebel army of young boys,
many of them former boy scouts. This description appeared in *The
New York Times:* "They [foreign evacuees] said they witnessed
army patrols shooting at soldiers who were engaging in widespread looting, enlisted men and civilians plundering the dwellings of poor Ugandans as well as the shops of Asian merchants
and young children wielding long knives to rob the looters of
their booty. According to these accounts, part of Kampala, the
capital, had been reduced to a jumble of trash, smoldering buildings and broken glass."

I read this and wondered what had happened to the editors
of *The Betlet* and the *Come Gazette,* to the optimistic Jenny, to Mr.
B'ouma and his booklovers, to the dean and his plucky students. I
wondered if their good humor and determination to wring some
pleasure from their "one and only precious lives" had survived
the events described in these clippings my wife collected while I
followed the equator across the Pacific:

61 BODIES ARE FOUND NEAR UGANDA'S CAPITAL. A truck believed to belong to the Ugandan army had taken people to a secluded spot near Kibutu, a village forty miles west of Kampala, where they were "hacked, bayoneted or shot" to death.

GUNMEN SHOOT JUDGE IN UGANDA COURT. "Gunmen shot one of Uganda's top judges today and hurled a grenade in the courtroom where he was opening the murder trial of a Government soldier who is accused of atrocities against rebels, witnesses said. . . . The gunman and the murder suspect escaped."

REMAINS OF 2,000 UGANDANS REPORTEDLY FOUND ON RANCH. "A Ugandan newspaper said today that it had discovered the skeletons of more than 2,000 people believed to have been killed by the army. . . . The reporter said . . . 'The ranch resembles a field covered with snow as it is thickly covered with the white skulls and skeletons.'"

12

AFTER KINSHASA AND KAMPALA, I WAS SICK OF VENAL SOLDIERS and crumbling towns. I flew to Nairobi without incident, rented a car with a driver, and doubled back to where the equator first crosses the Kampala-to-Nairobi highway. The car was expensive, but the equator touches so many roads and villages in Kenya that it was the best way to see them.

YOU ARE NOW CROSSING THE EQUATOR, a yellow sign said, depicting it as a white band bisecting a black continent. But here, at nine thousand feet in the former "White Highlands," with cows, pine forests, thin air, puffy clouds, sharp light, and perfect shadows, I thought of the high-altitude ranches of New Mexico or Colorado. As I photographed the equatorial sign, a shepherd ran from the forest, chasing a cow into the northern hemisphere. He wore a Don Quixote costume: rubber boots, a cloak, and a broad-brimmed plastic rain hat. He was toothless, and his earlobes, once stretched by ornamental tokens, hung like rubber bands without snap. He took an equatorial button and said his name was Kipkeyitanyi Arap Kikui and that he was a Nandi. The farm to the east, intersected by the equator, had belonged to "Europes," but the government had expropriated it for Nandi farmers. To the west, the equator ran through government forest, and every month he paid a shilling to graze his forty cows there.

My driver, Kibet, whistled. "Forty cows! He is a rich man to have so many."

"Do you often graze your cows on the equator?" I asked.

Kipkeyitanyi's eyes darted from equatorial button to equatorial sign, and, surmising I was a partisan of the equator, he nodded so emphatically his earlobes slapped against his cheeks. "Yes! Always he brings his cows to the equator," Kibet translated, "They love the grass here. They become fat on the equator . . ." On he went, so fanatical and unstoppable I suspected Kibet of exaggerating his answers.

"Such a nice man," Kibet said as we left. "We were lucky to find him. If he was a Kikuyu, he would have charged shillings for talking to you." He laughed, admitting to being prejudiced because he was a Kipsigis, a small tribe of farmers and herders allied with the Nandi. Kibet was also "a nice man," and I was lucky to have found him. He had a long, Talmudic face and the runner's physique common among his people. When we stopped at Lake Nakuru, it was he who stared longest through binoculars at the flamingos and said, "This is a pretty place," and he who pointed out an eagle in a thorn tree, saying with disapproval that it preyed on flamingos and scattered thousands with a flap of its wings. When we stopped at a bookstore in Nakuru, he paid several days' wages for a book, *The Mystery of Flamingos*. In free moments he gazed at the photographs, moving one finger along the text, all the while smiling.

Three miles east of the equator sign, we stopped at a town named Equator, a line of wooden stores along a plank sidewalk. There was an Equator Pharmacy, an Equator Store, and an Equator School, where boys kicked soccer balls while girls windmilled their arms and kept warm playing leapfrog. It was noon, and sunny, but at this altitude they had to wear sweaters.

A line of whitewashed bricks ran across the dirt platform of the Equator railway station, stopping at a globe mounted on a pedestal bearing a sign: EQUATOR. ALTITUDE 8,617 FEET. After so many countries where you could only take pictures with a "photography permit," I celebrated being in liberal Kenya by snapping dozens. The Equator station was a sepia-toned Victorian dollhouse. A dog snoozed under a tree. A boy and a stationmaster in a white uniform stood on the platform, staring blankly, like forgotten relatives in antique photographs. There was not a passenger, train, or box of freight in sight. A hundred yards into the northern hemisphere, the track fell over a hill like a roller coaster. I walked toward the station slowly, wondering if, when my photographs were developed, the will-o'-the-wisp stationmaster and boy would have vanished like ghosts.

The stationmaster was disappointed. "I had hoped you were a passenger," he said. People had deserted Kenya's trains for the speedier buses and bush taxis. This jewel of a station had been built for European settlers, but its Kenyan stationmasters had done a good embalming job. Like Schweitzer's bungalow, it was perfect. Antique pendulum clocks ticked, brass shone, and the cabinets smelled of polish. An old switch box glistened with oil, and plaques announced that Equator Station had won "Best Kept Station Prize" in 1961, 1962, and 1963. Kenya had become independent at the end of 1963 and, according to the stationmaster, the prize was temporarily discontinued. "When it is resumed we will win it," he said.

I complimented him on his station, and he scowled. "Yes, all you Europeans like it, but you never use it." He gestured to the distant cows, the simple-faced boy, and the tracks disappearing as if they were at the top of the world, and said, "This place is lonely for me."

"But he is really lonely," Kibet said afterwards, "because he is the wrong tribe for this place."

We drove ten miles into the southern hemisphere, then turned north onto an unpaved road to Eldama Ravine. We climbed through pine forests, crossing full streams and meeting the equator again near a village of woodcutters' cabins. We stayed above it for twenty miles, then veered south, losing several thousand feet of altitude before crossing it again in a desert of thorn trees, cacti, and cracked riverbeds. There was another You are Now Crossing the Equator sign, with a white line shooting across a black continent. A man strode along wearing a blue suit and swinging a briefcase. I walked a hundred yards with him, handing over a button as he crossed the line. He pinned it on without stopping. He would not tell me where he was going in this deserted landscape. Kibet said, "He would not talk because he is Kikuyu."

We turned north at Nakuru, heading back to the equator through farmland as populated as Rwanda's. When I drove through this countryside in 1970, there were eleven million Kenyans. Now there are twenty million, and at the end of the century there will be forty. Kenya's rate of population growth, the highest in the world, defies the theory that as a country prospers its birthrate falls. Throughout Kenya's economic expansion in the late seventies, its population grew faster than ever. The explanations offered for this phenomenon were that no tribe wished to be the first to have a decreasing birthrate, that women needed written permission from doctors to use family-planning services, and that with their men working in the cities, women wanted as many children as possible to share farming chores. Now Kenya's economic growth rate has fallen to about zero, while its population grows at 6 percent, and population pressure is at the heart of its problems: a crime wave, an attempted coup, the subdivision of its farms into uneconomic parcels, demonstrations by university students, political repression, and the twitchiness of an elite rumored to be quietly sending its children and wealth to Europe and America.

I saw evidence of these additional nine million Kenyans in the corn planted on highway shoulders, the signs pointing to primary schools, the passengers clinging to bush taxis, and, finally, the mob of curio salesmen gathered around a sign marking the spot where the equator cuts across the main highway from Nakuru to Nyahururu. As we stopped, they raced for their stalls, scooping up armloads of miniature chess sets and soapstone animals, each hoping to be the first to show me a hippo with Equator Altitude, 7,747 Feet carved across its belly. They sold identical curios from identical stalls. To compete, they appealed to a customer's conscience. I heard: "You looked into my stall first!"

"But you walked into mine first!"

"No, you saw mine first. That is more important."

"My stall is the first in the row."

"But I'm the last so you must buy from me."

And, from a man close to tears, "But my stall is the *third*." I was the first European to stop in two days, he said, yet every month another man opened a stall.

Kibet bought a sugar bowl. He said, "They are nice men, so we mustn't disappoint them." (Later he admitted buying from "a

man from my tribe.") I bought carved animals from different merchants — probably paying too much, since the last man threw in a
free ashtray. In return, I offered him the Lambaréné crocodile,
making the mistake of identifying its provenance. He pushed it
back into my hands. "You must not give it away," he said. "It is
too valuable for us to take." Another said, "It is a gift to you, not
us. Put it back in your bag and accept a present from us." He
handed me a box with a frog perched on a sliding top. I pulled it
back and a cobra sprang out at the frog. With the best of intentions, we had offered one another terrifying gifts.

Kibet's friend Wilson owned a farm near the equator. His
wife, Ruth, met us at the gate, explaining that to earn money for
the children's education Wilson drove a truck in Nakuru, returning on weekends. It is common in rural Kenya for men to take
salaried jobs in the cities to support their huge families, although
many return "home" for only a week every year, taking second
wives in the city. Ruth was luckier than most Kenyan "widows."
She saw Wilson on weekends, and their separation was eased by
a miraculous possession, a telephone. She pulled away a cloth to
reveal it, and Kibet's eyes widened. "I did not know they had a
telephone," he whispered. "That Wilson must be a rich man."
Ruth said their number was 37, but I should not imagine there
were thirty-six other telephones in the village. Theirs was the only
one in this neighborhood. "My husband calls every week from
Nakuru. He does not want me to be lonely," she said, so defiantly
that she surely suspected him of philandering.

We sat for an hour making small talk in her parlor. Its dirt
floor smelled of sour milk, and calendars and magazine photographs decorated its walls, making me wish I still had José Maria's
Alpine picture to pass along. It would have gone well here. How
many of the other shanties I had passed contained these surprising consumer luxuries, a television or a telephone linking their
owners to the world? After all, Kenya has direct international di-
aling, so Ruth could have spun fourteen numbers and rung my
telephone in New York.

Her children stared and giggled. They had seen white men
on the road, but I was the first to come inside. She showed me a
photograph album, flipping fast through baby pictures, gradua-
tions, and first communions, but insisting I admire each wedding

picture. "Does your husband return every weekend?" I asked, before realizing it was a cruel question.

"He comes when he can," she said, turning sullen and leading me outside, where two mongrels bared teeth and went for my
ankles. The children beat them back with sticks. I escaped into the
car, and she said, "Many people would like to steal our things."

"Why is that?"

"Because we are all alone here."

Alone? Plowed fields and houses surrounded us.

"They are Kikuyu, we are Nandi." When the government
took this European farm and divided it into plots, her husband
had by chance received a Kikuyu-encircled farm. They were looking to exchange with a Kikuyu farmer surrounded by Nandi. Until
then, she would live here "alone," protected by her vicious dogs
and comforted by a telephone that rang once a week with a call
from a husband she did not entirely trust.

After Nyahururu, the road fell again toward the equator and
we exchanged farms for ranches, windmills, squashed bugs on the
windshield, and telephone poles running to the horizon. The irregular peaks of the Aberdares rose directly ahead, and to the east
Mount Kenya sat alone on a high plateau, like a volcanic island in
the doldrums. Again, curio vendors crowded the equator. When I
admitted having bought carvings from their competitors, a man
with a whiskey nose kicked up clouds of dust. "Ah, damn, man!
Damn, damn! You have made your purchases at that other
damned equator." He took my arm, walking me between hemispheres, past the forlorn curio stalls. Two boys had fallen asleep
underneath the equator sign. Its narrow shadow covered their
eyes. "We are in great difficulty here, and you, my dear sir, could
be the answer to our many prayers. I speak not for myself but for
all these hungry boys."

"I can't carry any more equatorial carvings."

"No, we accept you have made your purchases. Our difficulties cannot be solved so easily. It's those other sellers, at that
other damned equator. They bribe the tourist vans to stop, and
we cannot afford those payments. If you help us, you'll be helping
these very desperate boys."

"But what can I do?"

"You could help us with the authorities." The desperate boys gathered in a circle, perspiring and stamping like bulls. "Tell your friends to help us!" one shouted.

"What friends?" I asked.

"Your white friends. Tell the whites to visit our equator."

"And speak to the authorities."

"But I don't know any authorities here," I said. No one believed this. Europeans stopped at the equator, and Europeans had brought the idea of an equator. So why couldn't a European, if he wanted, make their equator as profitable as the other?

"Tell them to put an altitude on our sign."

"Yes!" the others chorused, "That other equator has an altitude. Whites don't stop because we don't have an altitude."

A man's eyes brimmed with tears. "We had the altitude, but those other boys painted it over, just to hurt us."

"And the government must raise our sign. The whites hit their heads and become angry."

They followed me to the car, shouting more complaints. Why didn't they paint any old damned altitude on their sign? Or raise the sign themselves? Was it because the equator, like the gorillas, was only for *les blancs*? I gave them equatorial buttons, exhausting the supply I had brought to Africa. They pinned them to caps and shirts, polishing them with handkerchiefs and shirttails, so pleased I did not have the heart to say I had already scattered these same lucky charms among their arch-rivals at that other damned equator.

I slept twenty-five miles south of the equator, in a lodge in the Aberdares where guests could stay up all night watching from an outdoor deck while animals licked salt from spotlit puddles. I went to this place because the equator did not intersect Kenya's more accessible game parks and, like many Europeans, I felt a trip to East Africa was incomplete unless I had seen at least one wild animal.

Getting to this lodge was not simple. Every morning, the guests gathered outside the park at a "country club" that was really a former colonial mansion. It was called a club, I was told, sotto voce, by a white Kenyan in the lobby, "so they can keep the wrong kind of African from the liquor." No matter that waiting at the bar for the bus to the lodge was a roster of what most clubs would consider the "wrong kind" of white: two drunk Brits in mesh T-shirts, a Frenchwoman wearing a bathing suit, and Americans wondering loudly how much a pornographic magazine would pay for a picture of elephants fucking. Everyone took pictures of everything—the peacocks on the lawn, the giant aloe, and each other. When a woman pointed her camera at me, I jumped behind a tree. I did not want to be the anonymous stranger in somebody's holiday scrapbook ("And who was *that*?" "Oh, no one, some tourist who got in the way"), and I began to understand why Africans ran, or charged a fee.

We were lucky, as the staff at the lodge reminded us endlessly, because no sooner had we arrived than a rhino came to have a lick at the salt. Then an elephant came, and then another, until there were fourteen. They held trunks like shy teen-agers or stuck them deep in the salt. Calves trotted underneath their mothers, and families huddled together. A young orphan broke from the bush, heading for the salt. The others trumpeted and charged, scaring her back. She lurked on the perimeter, watching mothers stroke their young, being charged and run off whenever she tried for the salt.

The lodge resembled an ocean liner: You climbed aboard and could not leave until the next morning. We slept in cabin-like rooms, sat outside on wooden decks, and ate large buffet meals at shared tables where we could fraternize with the "officers." I sat opposite a white Kenyan hostess named Richenda. She said she loved her job, perhaps accounting for the good humor with which she explained—and certainly not for the first time—that her name was the invention of a father hoping for a Richard. The guests loved Richenda. She was attractive in an outdoor way, and her childhood was out of the *National Geographic*. She had been raised on the edge of the Nairobi National Park and described giraffes browsing in her mother's garden and pythons wriggling across the lawn. Everyone was enthralled. Hot damn, they were thinking, this is the real thing, the old-time Kenya of plucky tomboys growing up with animals. She had probably fed orphaned gazelles with a bottle. The women said how much they envied Richenda, but then a Brit who had arrived to fill one of the two-year expatriate slots asked if her family had any "security problems" in that isolated suburb.

"No problems at all," she said, "since we put in the bombs."

The bombs? What was this? We looked up open-mouthed from our overfilled plates of cruise-liner food.

"Bombs?" an American woman repeated, thinking she had misunderstood.

"And jolly big bombs they are too. We have them front and back, tied to trip wires." Richenda spoke briskly. "And we have rifles and grenades, so now they leave us alone."

"They," she explained matter-of-factly, were Africans from the neighboring village. "It's very simple. The village grew from five to twenty thousand in five years, but the number of jobs stayed the same. That's why it happened."

The "it" was three robberies in two years. "The first time the police caught them, but their relatives bribed the jailers so they escaped and came back to steal again. The third time a panga gang broke in and slashed my mother's back." She explained a panga gang: fifteen to twenty thieves who suddenly attacked a suburban house, slashing with pangas (machetes) at whatever or whoever stood in their way.

Expressions around the table changed from horror to skepticism. Perhaps what we had here, instead of a *National Geographic* tomboy, was an embittered little colonial racist, exaggerating to turn us against the natives.

"Now we're terrified," she admitted in a flat, unterrified voice, making the terror all the more commonplace, and terrifying. "If they come back while we're there, they'll simply kill us."

"Surely you can call your neighbors or the police," said the wife of the new British expatriate.

"We're too far out for a telephone line, and our neighbors moved out. They were afraid. We're alone there."

"Why don't you move?"

"Like to. And we own land on the coast. But it's not bloody likely we could sell. Everyone knows our story. Our best hope is to sell to someone who's just arrived and likes the location and the idea of being near the animals, but doesn't know the rest."

The British couple exchanged looks, perhaps pondering their narrow escape.

Nanyuki is the last sizable town in Africa touched by the equator and home to "the world famous Equator Line Bar." This bar is one of two things people know about the equator. The other is watching water drain from sinks. In the Equator Bar, I was told, the equator is a white line painted down the middle of the room, so you can drink with a foot in each hemisphere. I arrived to find that the Equator Bar had burned down ten years earlier, leaving only a foundation and two chimneys.

The owner and manager of the New Silverbeck Hotel on the Equator was Mr. Jimmy Mwai, a bouncy country publican wearing a blazer and a club tie. He drew a line across the foundation with the tip of a polished shoe, indicating the equator. "The fire commenced in the kitchen, but we cannot allow ourselves to rule out sabotage," he said. "It is possible our competitors were jealous of the many tourists we attracted."

He led me across the parking lot to Jimmy's Premium Bar, a large room facing a garden scattered with tables. It was lunchtime, but there were no patrons. "After building this new bar, we found tourists will not stop for one that is near the equator. It must be on it. We hope to rebuild the Equator Bar. The only small thing stopping us is our cash problem." Meanwhile, Jimmy Mwai was counting on the cleanliness of his "twenty-six Old Kenya Colony Cottages." There were twenty-five vacancies but, he said, "we definitely have visitors from Europe, and they definitely love our cottages." They were little temples of hygiene, smelling sharply of disinfectant. Floors gleamed and taps sparkled. "Go on, look under the beds," Mr. Mwai urged, challenging me to find a fluff ball or a dead insect. "We are a big favorite with people from Switzerland." He raised his voice. "We may have lost our Equator Bar, but there is no cottage hotel beating us on cleanliness."

This was something of a theme in Nanyuki: cleanliness. The Nanyuki War Cemetery, which Kibet believed was touched by the equator, held soldiers killed during the campaign against Italian Somaliland and Ethiopia. It said a lot about life in colonial Kenya. Whites were buried at the top of the hill, with the best view of Mount Kenya. The Africans were further down, arranged in clumps that complemented the landscaping. The Jews had their section, the Muslims theirs. The gardener insisted I sign a visitor's book with space for comments. Most British visitors had mentioned "bravery," "the gallant fallen," and "heroic sacrifice." Appearing several times was "RIP, brave men."

But instead of a memorial to heroism, the Africans saw a

monument to European cleanliness. They wrote: "This place is well kept, as far as cleanliness is concerned. Keep up!"

"As a matter of fact I was impressed by the cleanliness."

"Good, clean and nice for snap-taking."

"Clean enough."

"The cleanliness is maintained to the maximum."

"A credit to cleanliness!"

Staring at the rows of white headstones and closely mowed lawn, the clipped shrubs and the flowering trees whose blossoms were instantly swept away by the gardener, I realized the Africans had noticed something I had always missed: Cemeteries are incredibly clean places — more clean, in fact, than heroic.

Several miles east of the cemetery, a sign on the lawn of the Mount Kenya Safari Club said LATITUDE: 00 00 (EQUATOR) / LONGITUDE: 37 7 E. / ALTITUDE: 2296 M 7000 FT / FOUNDED 1959 FOR MEMBERS AND GUESTS. As I sat on a terrace overlooking acres of lawns and gardens, a blanket of black clouds lifted to reveal Mount Kenya, so covered with snow and ice it seemed to light up the surrounding sky. The combination of symmetry and isolation is what makes this mountain so dramatic. There are no distracting foothills, no neighboring peaks with which to confuse it. It rises to a height exceeding any European Alp, and its ski-jump slopes and round snowcap make it a perfect mountain, a rival to Mount Fuji. It is not surprising that the Kikuyu face it while praying to a god believed to live among its glaciers, and that forty years earlier it so mesmerized three Italian prisoners-of-war that they escaped from a British POW camp in Nanyuki solely to scale it. They fashioned crampons and ice axes from metal in the camp rubbish dump. Their map was a picture of Mount Kenya found on a can of Kenylon meat-and-vegetable rations. After climbing the mountain and planting an Italian flag, they gave themselves up. Few other peaks could have inspired this lunacy.

One of the founders of the Mount Kenya Safari Club was the actor William Holden, perhaps explaining the California–country-club atmosphere. There were men in green uniforms hauling hoses over their shoulders, scrubbing the pool with long brushes, and crawling along garden borders, endlessly trimming. And there were artificial ponds, a golf course and a putting green, ranch-house condominiums overlooking the fairways, and a rambling clubhouse that was all picture windows and striped awnings. The club, however, is open to temporary members, meaning anyone with the price of a room. While I sat on the terrace, Land Rovers arrived, spilling out jet-lagged American package tourists. They stumbled across the huge lawns, looking stunned and disoriented among the peacocks and storks. Paunchy men in Bermuda shorts and black socks chewed cigars and toothpicks, and elderly ladies with handbags dangling from wrists insisted, like visitors to a stately home, on endless pictures of themselves standing in front of the clubhouse.

When this was really a private club, Lord Mountbatten and Bing Crosby, Winston Churchill and Conrad Hilton had been visitors. But its appeal to this clientele lessened when Kenya banned big-game hunting. Nanyuki is halfway around the world from Hollywood, and how many times can even a jet-setter fly that distance to take photographs? So now there was Muzak in the corridors, a video library offering *Friday the Thirteenth Part III,* tourists in sneakers who had to borrow a coat and tie, as I did, to satisfy a "Members must dress for dinner" rule, and, among the new "members" boasted by the club's magazine, "two members of the Saudi Arabian Royal Family, President Gafaar Numeiri of the Sudan, and His Excellency President El Hadj Omar Bongo of Gabon."

The most authentic "Kenya Colony" relic I saw was a party of elderly British ranchers who really had "dressed," in dinner jackets. They amused themselves by being rude to the tourists. "Do you mind, old chap?" a bald man asked, and before I could answer he had squashed out his cigar in my ashtray. With a "Would you mind terribly?" a woman stole my other chair, ignoring my protest that I was waiting for someone. Another scooped a hand into my bowl of cashews as she passed, saying, "You've got so many and we're out." I left before they drank my gin.

After the Safari Club, the equator crosses the northern slope of Mount Kenya, missing its glaciers and peaks by ten miles before running four hundred miles across Kenyan and Somali deserts to the Indian Ocean. There is a track across this desert, but when I returned to Nairobi I was told it had been washed out by unusually strong and early spring rains. I could take a bus to Garissa, a desert town just south of the equator, but afterwards I would still have to return to Nairobi and fly to Somalia.

Nairobi was as dull as I remembered, low skyscrapers

dumped on a featureless plateau, like those cities in the American West where you find office workers by day and, at night, corporate symbols winking neon over deserted streets. Many of the changes in the fifteen years since I last visited it were the result of population growth. Every year the 400,000 students graduating from Kenya's schools compete for 20,000 jobs, and most of the disappointed 380,000 end up in Nairobi's slums — among them, most likely, the thieves who had slashed Richenda's mother. This "security problem" has turned Nairobi's suburbs into places of barking dogs, high walls, and prominent signs declaring houses to be protected by Pinkerton, Force 4, or some other security outfit. The guards from these services dress in brown shirts, uniforms with red piping and gold braid, or black jump suits. They carry the weapons of medieval knights, ball-and-chain or studded clubs. They hold large shields to absorb panga slashes and small ones to blunt daggers. They wear chest pads and crash helmets, equipped with face guards and neck flaps, to prevent them being beheaded from the rear. One look tells you this is a city of desperate thieves.

Nairobi's newspapers carry daily stories of thieves executed by mobs or the hangman. "Robbery with violence" is punishable by death, and I read of a death sentence passed on four men "found guilty of robbing Jane Wanijku Sindiyo of sh300 [about $16], a radio car [presumably a toy], a camera and a torch on August 17, last year at Ngatu trading centre and using violence on her." The next day a man was executed for "using violence" while taking a box of detergent. There cannot be many places where a man would risk being hung by the government, stoned by a mob, or beaten by these terrifying private guards, simply to steal a box of soap.

I visited an American development expert I shall call Bill, hoping to discuss Kenya's economic problems. But he kept returning to the moral dilemma facing an expatriate who is mugged on a Nairobi street. "The problem is — well, the problem is that they beat thieves to death here." He spoke hesitantly. "I haven't seen a someone-beaten-to-death story for weeks but, honestly, it happens all the time. A smiling, laughing crowd chases them down like rabbits and kills them with sticks or fists, whatever's handy."

Bill's greatest fear was that he would shout "Thief!" and be responsible for someone, maybe the wrong someone, being murdered by the mobs that formed at this word.

"What about the police?"

He walked to the window. "Six weeks ago I looked down there and saw a man shot at point-blank range, on a public street at midday, and he was in police custody, begging for his life. It happened there, opposite the Hilton, and it unfolded like a play or an opera." His voice became dreamy and he stared at the busy corner, transfixed, as if seeing it again. "He had grabbed money from a teller in the Standard Bank. The guards chased him, trapping him between parked cars. They beat him with clubs. He slipped away and ran, but someone tripped him and the guards beat him again. He struggled up, staggering a few feet before a plainclothes policeman stepped from the crowd, drawing his revolver. The thief grabbed the barrel, trying to point it away. He was crying, screaming, begging for his life. Then another cop just walked up and shot him in the head. He died on the sidewalk. The police flipped open his coat and retrieved the money. I read it was nine thousand shillings [$480]. They left his body there, and for an hour people walked around it."

I described Richenda's parents, and he said, "We all live that way, but without the bombs. In the closer suburbs you can hire a good security service. Come to dinner tomorrow and see."

A sign on Bill's gate said his property was protected by Force 4. A guard opened the gate, and barking dogs lunged for my taxi. As we walked inside, Bill bragged that Force 4 was the best, promising uniformed men at a house within five minutes of an alarm. His front door had five locks and an iron gate secured by three bolts, each fastened by padlocks and wired to Force 4 alarms. His other doors and windows were also barred and wired, and when his wife ventured into the garden she carried a portable panic button. The guard on the gate also had a button. That was his job: to sound the alarm and then lock himself in the outside toilet, waiting for the Force 4 cavalry.

"My next project," Bill said with the enthusiasm of a weekend gardener showing off his vegetables, "is to put a sliding steel door across the foyer. Then, even if a panga gang bursts through the front door and the response team is delayed, we can still hold out." He had already installed a steel cage over the top of the staircase, shutting the bedrooms off from downstairs. There was a panic button over the bed and a short-wave radio on a nightstand, "because they've been known to cut the phones and electricity before attacking." He turned on the radio and called Force 4. A hard voice asked for his code number. He said, "Four-nine-three — only a test." There was a coiled rope ladder so he and his wife could escape through the window if their attackers set a fire, or if there was a normal fire and he could not find, on his ring of thirty keys, the ones to unlock his doors. He opened a bedroom closet, revealing another steel door. "Our safe haven. We could last twenty minutes before they hacked through the walls. Then I'd have to use this." He showed me a revolver.

The other dinner guests were American, French, and Dutch, all secular missionaries sent to help Kenya "develop," yet finding themselves imitating the British during the Mau Mau rebellion, locked into fortress houses at night, afraid of natives with pangas, depending on short-wave radios and home arsenals. They admitted to living like Bill, although they agreed he was rather a perfectionist. Their African neighbors took similar precautions. Since the gangs chose the least protected homes, a security innovation not copied from a neighbor might invite an attack, perhaps explaining why the topic of innovations in home security dominated the evening's conversation. After dinner, there was an extra mug on the coffee tray. Bill explained he made coffee for the night guard, to keep him alert. I saw one couple exchange looks and wondered if soon night guards across Nairobi might not be enjoying pots of coffee, brewed strong and black.

A friend had recommended that I meet Peter Muthemba (I have changed his name), who was described as a retired inspector in the Nairobi police department. I thought an ex-detective would be just the man to defend the police against charges of street-corner executions, and to confirm my suspicions that these expatriate fears of crime were exaggerated. I had walked around Nairobi without incident and it had struck me as less menacing than New York, and I had been entertained at two European homes lacking Bill's precautions, although one bordered a well-traveled thoroughfare and the other was in a densely settled neighborhood near the university.

I met Inspector Muthemba at the terrace bar of the Norfolk Hotel where, among the tourists, Sikhs, Kenyan big shots, and

Brits in khaki shorts, he gathered with his friends every Friday evening for an end-of-the-week beer-drinking session. Because of the "retired," I had not expected the wiry, scrappy man of about my age with a chipped front tooth that gave him a rakish smile. He had taken early retirement and started his own private-investigations agency, although he was "temporarily without an office." His friends hooted. Apparently Muthemba was always "temporarily without an office." He had been an air-force pilot, a policeman battling bandits on the northwest frontier, and then a Nairobi detective, and now he combined the boyish enthusiasm of a pilot with the cynicism of a cop. His informal drinking club included a banker with a pencil moustache, a fatherly insurance agent, and his cousin, a rogue with an open shirt and gold chains. There was something to like about each of them. They had only stopped for a quick beer on the way home, but we drank one liter after another. It was the kind of drinking I remembered from university, with every conversation ending in laughter and jokes, until I mentioned the panga gangs.

"Who told you that?" Muthemba demanded, jealous of his town's reputation.

I described Richenda and Bill.

"Why, my friends and I walk in Nairobi at night with no fear. It is much safer than New York."

"Everyone says their city is safer than New York."

"Aha! But I say it because the moment I arrived in New York I was robbed of sixty dollars, and by a taxi driver. He drove to a deserted place and pulled a gun."

I asked if Muthemba had been in New York on police business.

"I went to the U.S.A. for my commercial pilot's license. It was my dream—understand, my *dream*—to earn that license. Even when money was scarce I kept my commercial flight manual current at a cost of two hundred forty shillings a year. When I resigned from the police, I decided to pursue my dream. I saved hard for that trip, but after eleven days I was deported."

I asked him to explain, but he shook his head. "These boys have heard it too often. We can talk tomorrow during your program. Yes, we must fix a program for you. At eleven A.M. we have tea, then drinking beer, then driving through Nairobi seeing the sights, then lunch, then talking and drinking beer until six, then beer and more talking. There. That will be our program."

The next morning, Muthemba and Paul, his buck-toothed brother-in-law, collected me in Paul's jalopy. It had a wiggly wheel, springs shooting through the upholstery, and a bad muffler. "I have a Volkswagen," Muthemba said, "but for the present I cannot afford repairs. I am still recovering from that trip to the U.S.A., and my bill-paying program was interrupted by the Christmas rush. You know, if my debtors settled my bills as promptly as I work for them, why, I could rent an office and fix my automobile. Until that day I borrow cars from relatives. Sometimes I must take local transport." His expression showed this was a last resort. Who could respect a private detective who came into town on a mammy wagon? "What I need is a ten-thousand-shilling loan. I've tried the banks, but if you're not with the government or a big firm they do not lend to you."

Speeding through Nairobi in Paul's jalopy, I felt young and reckless, like a teen-ager setting out for a marathon of drinking, bullshitting, and hairy driving. Like teen-agers, we squealed around corners and passed blind on hills, pooled change to buy gas in small quantities, visited friends, pursued aimless errands, drank beer, and sauntered through a shopping mall. We had a flat tire and borrowed a jack to change it for the bald spare.

While Paul delivered an envelope, I told Muthemba I had read of another thief attacked by a crowd. Was that usual? "Robbery is a bad habit in Nairobi," he conceded. "But beating robbers to death is also a bad habit, particularly if it is the wrong man. So my advice to people visiting Nairobi is never run. Someone running is a robber." In his opinion, the people who beat robbers were "idlers" who did it for a thrill. The robbers were also "idlers," taking a risk because they too were bored, or desperate. There was not much difference, really, between vigilante and victim. He opposed the official solution to robbery. "Always, *always*, I have been opposed to hanging. Ever since they began that 'hanging for robbery with violence' business, there has been more robbery with violence."

I mentioned the police executions, and he stared at his feet. "That is why I retired from the force. It was after the attorney-general's order permitting policemen to shoot robbery suspects on sight. I cannot remember the exact words, but it was to that effect. I disagreed strongly with that policy."

He shook his head, as if his stubbornness still perplexed him. "I can't explain it. I just believed it was wrong, turning the police into executioners. Besides, if I'm against capital punishment, how can I 'convict' someone on the spot and kill them? And I know there are many trigger-happy boys on the force. Even worse was the chance some boys would hire themselves out. I decided not to allow that attorney-general to turn me into an executioner. One day he called in twenty-five of us to discuss this new order, and I was the only one to disagree. After that I didn't want to be a policeman. I resigned so fast I lost a month's salary."

Had others quit?

"I was alone, the only one. My friends thought I was crazy. Here in Kenya no one really chooses a job. You take what you get and keep it forever. My wife thought I was mad, although she came around. She works as a secretary in a government office, and her salary kept us going."

We ate lunch at Muthemba's home, the last unit in a well-maintained government project. A cloth covered the screen of an old television, and Muthemba said his children could only watch on weekends and holidays. On weekdays they read. To encourage them, he had bought hundreds of paperbacks. "My library is larger than this," he said. "But I keep buying books, and my friends, they keep pinching." He admitted to writing his autobiography. I anticipated a notebook. Instead, he dropped an eight-hundred-page handwritten manuscript in my lap.

His autobiography included a description of that disastrous American trip. He had decided on a flight school in Dallas because, even including the airfare, it was cheaper than paying bribes in Kenya. Friends, relatives, and his member of Parliament loaned him money for the ticket. Because he had left Nairobi in a rush to make the start of the course and planned staying in the States only two months, he made the mistake of securing a visitor's visa instead of a student one. When he arrived in New York, an immigration inspector discovered a letter from the school. But Muthemba had soon charmed the immigration authorities into agreeing he could stay if one of his American friends vouched for him. He called these friends, but it was the Fourth of July weekend, and he reached their answering machines, telling him to leave a message at the sound of the beep.

Still, the immigration inspectors took pity on Muthemba, allowing him to go to Washington, where his friends lived, and check in after the weekend. But after being robbed by a New York gypsy-cab driver, he disobeyed and flew to Dallas. Immigration officers tracked him down but gave him a final chance to contact his American friends. Again he heard their recorded voices. He was deported and lost his flight-school fees. At the London airport, officials saw the cancellation on his American visa, concluded he was an undesirable alien, and put him on the next plane to Nairobi, a full British Airways flight en route to Johannesburg. He was seated next to an Afrikaner who made loud protests about sitting near a kaffir. Inspector Muthemba's humiliation was complete.

The extraordinary thing about Muthemba's odyssey was how commonplace it has become. I had been approached countless times by Africans, some in rags, who wanted my address so they could call when they arrived. With his shelves of books, updated flight manual, and autobiography, Muthemba proved how education and ambition have so outstripped opportunity that many Africans can only imagine their dreams being fulfilled abroad.

After lunch, Muthemba and his brother-in-law drove me to Mathere Valley, Nairobi's largest shantytown. It was a ribbon of hovels crammed into a narrow valley. They regarded it as an awesome force of nature, like a tidal wave or a lava flow. Muthemba pointed out newly plowed lots, evidence of the continuous battles fought by the government to prevent squatters from climbing out of the valley and overwhelming the housing developments. As we drove along, he identified the historical boundaries. "Five years ago it was here . . . two years later it moved this far down the valley . . . that was last year's limit . . . last week it was here, and . . ." He slapped his head in amazement. "Why, already it has moved!" A hundred yards from the edge of the slum, pioneers were erecting new hovels.

We crossed it on a nameless dirt track. Rain had turned alleys into rivers running black with garbage and human waste. Butchers had draped their stalls with intestines, brains, and guts; expensive cuts went elsewhere. People walked barefoot through the mud. They wrapped themselves in rags and slept under card-board. The lucky ones cooked up gut stews over garbage fires. "Mother Theresa has just built a mission here," Muthemba said, strangely proud that Mathere had earned the status of world-class horror.

We drove up the opposite slope of the valley to his favorite bar. It sat on a leveled hill with a panoramic view of the slum. From here, Mathere seemed to be a city of chicken coops and outhouses. You could see how it lapped against the housing es-tates and fit perfectly into the contours of the snaking valley, and how easily you could bulldoze these eroded hills into it, filling it like a trench, or a grave.

The wind shifted, carrying smoke and stench from below and making me wonder about the appeal of this oddly situated bar. Men of Muthemba's age filled its tables, enjoying their weekend beers. Was it like a restaurant on top of a skyscraper, popular for its panorama? Or did these men come to be reminded of their good fortune, and of how easily they could slide down this slope into the valley? While we sat under a gray sky, drinking liters of beer and staring at Mathere, Muthemba described again, but this time in a slow, hypnotized voice, the astonishment of his friends at learning he had left the police. "Everyone said the same thing: 'In Nairobi, no one who has a job should dare leave it.' Going to the U.S.A. was my last chance. I'm too old now to become a commercial pilot, so I will never, never have my dream. But at least I had a chance." He turned from the view. "But there is always my autobiography. I simply must finish that and find a publisher." And so Inspector Muthemba moved briskly on to the next dream.

I begged off the rest of the program, and he dropped me at the Norfolk. While waiting for soda water and aspirin, I heard from the next table: "I had three half-hour sessions under a sun lamp before I came here."

"Why, you old cheat!"

"They've rented him an apartment next door, overlooking the pool."

"Who?"

"Don't be silly. Robert Redford." (He was in Kenya to film *Out of Africa*.)

". . . and they've promised he'll be there tonight for drinks."

"Who?"

"Robert Redford, of course!"

A broad-faced African boy slid into the empty chair opposite mine, interrupting my eavesdropping and saying, "I must go to computer school."

His name was Edward Ochieng. He was an only child and an orphan, raised by an impoverished uncle in a fishing village on Lake Victoria. He had left there because his uncle would not feed him. "He begs for old fishing nets and gets four shillings for his catch," Edward said, "and he has six children, with three in primary school, so there was no room for me."

He had come to Nairobi, where he was helped by a Catholic mission. Later, I read a To-whom-it-may-concern letter from a European priest: "This is to certify that Mr. Edward Ochieng is well known to us. Since he is an orphan and had nobody to support him, I had provided him board and lodging in Equator High School Thika. . . . Edward has appreciated this help, he worked hard in school and helped during his free time as janitor in Thika Youth Centre. He is trustworthy and deserves assistance."

Edward explained that the priest who sponsored him had left the country. "The other fathers told me I must find a job and make my own way. They are sympathetic to me, but they must help younger boys even less fortunate than I." For six months he had looked for work while sleeping on the floor of his cousin's house. "There are thousands like me," he said. "I have too much education to sweep an Indian's store. They only take uneducated boys. To have a good job you must bribe, or find a big man to help you. But since I am without brothers, sisters, parents, or grandparents, I have no big men." He held my eyes. "Let me tell you this: Someone without a big man has no hope in Nairobi."

Edward refused my offer of a drink, saying, "No cigarettes or beer for me. If I try those luxuries I fear I will need them; then if I don't have money there will be temptations . . ." He trailed off, but we both knew what these "temptations" were: stealing, perhaps from Europeans such as myself, perhaps from Africans, and perhaps being beaten to death.

Edward had fifteen shillings in his pocket and one set of clothes he washed every other night. If they had not dried by morning he sat in his underwear, waiting. He was running out of soap powder, and his cousin had ordered him to move. He had come to the Norfolk because there were Europeans here, and his only hope, he believed, was to find a new European sponsor. "I have no one to help me, no big man, no one!" He said, as if he still could not believe it, "Why, I could starve!"

Or join a panga gang. There are Edwards by the hundreds of thousands in Africa. I might have given him shillings and sent him off if he had not said that his cousin's house, where he slept on the floor, was in Mathere Valley; or if I had not liked the idea of an orphan from that place earning a living in computers; or if I had not just come from Inspector Muthemba and his shattered dreams; or if I had not seen that orphan elephant in the Aberdares; or if he had not been so handsome and earnest; or, perhaps, if he had not once attended Equator High School.

He had thought out computer school rather well. He had seen newspaper advertisements for computer programmers and reasoned that since he did not have a big man or bribe money, his best hope was to acquire a skill in demand, even one that did not interest him. "I'll tell you the truth." He lowered his voice. "It would be easy to lie and claim skill in mathematics, but I'm actually more of an arts-and-letters man."

I insisted he write a memorandum describing the school and proposing a budget. If I agreed, I would pay the registrar directly, with instructions the money be refunded to me if Edward quit. He took this to mean I would definitely help him. His legs jiggled with excitement, jarring the table and sloshing my beer. He said, "I will not fail because it will be my only chance!"

"But I haven't promised yet. I have to be sure—"

"I am a good man. When I had extra money, I gave it to beggars. If I have money again, I promise to help orphans and widows, anyone! God help me. Anyone! No racial discrimination. Whites even!"

He leaned across the table, whispering "Do you mind if I tell you a secret? Someday I will study liberal arts in the U.S.A. This computer work will be to earn money for that."

Where do they get these dreams? These extravagant, incredible, impossible dreams? From school? From the television sets mounted in bars? Where?

When we met the next day, I was glad to see him wearing the same clothes, still damp from last night's washing. I wanted to believe Edward, and here was evidence he had told the truth, or

that he was cunning. He had brought the computer-school catalogue and a letter titled "Re: Confirm Further Information About
the College."

"I have done a research about the important of computer
programming course and I came to realize that the course is so
nice and more marketable in Kenya but it depend on how you
know people who works in big Companies or Banks . . .

"My cousin agreed to help me with food but only supper not
lunch even now I always spend lunch outside or pass the day in
town everyday so there's no problem about lunch. . . . I found its
not possible to get someone in Nairobi to help me because with
African people even if you find a rich man they doesn't bother
helping their brothers who are really suffering on the streets. African people have dark jealousy and selfishness." (This comment
makes sense from Edward's standpoint, for while most Africans
are incredibly generous, it is usually toward their own relatives.)

He concluded that the three-month course, "including lunch
transportation and books and soap is 3,400 shillings [about $225]
without any extra enjoyments."

It was not the cost but the following paragraph that made me
question his plan: "Well to get a job in Kenya nowadays is very
hard unless you have some proper connection with big bosses
who works as directors, personnels and super viziers [sic]. Otherwise it's very very impossible to work in a good company in
Kenya."

"Then how will you find a computer job without bribing
someone?" I asked.

"That will not happen because computers are modern." To
Edward, "modern" meant uncorrupted. Last month he had
missed a job in the post office because he lacked bribe money. His
cousin Phillip knew an assistant manager, but since Edward was
not a relative, the man had demanded two thousand shillings.

The computer school was on one floor of a downtown office
building. It had glossy brochures and a room of terminals. The
family of Indians running it described employers fighting over
their graduates. Edward would be no exception, particularly if he
took the more expensive four-month course. But I still wondered
what chance a dreamy orphan who admitted preferring "the arts"
would have of finding a computer job after attending this school. I

wondered if I could have found a computer job in Nairobi after attending this school.

"Is that position in the post office still open?" I asked him.

"There are always jobs there if you have the money."

"I would rather bribe the post office than pay tuition to that school. Then you'll have a job for certain." (And I could leave Nairobi in good conscience.) Since I was paying, he was easily persuaded. I suggested he save his salary, taking the computer course later, but we both knew this was nonsense.

He insisted on walking me back to the hotel, "so nothing happens to you." Several times he prevented me crossing a street until the lights were in my favor. He was not really much fun, this non–beer-drinking, safe-street-crossing, earnest, and, to be honest, none-too-bright orphan. And I was tiring of hearing how God had brought me as a miracle. I was ready to stuff him into the post office and be done with it.

I had imagined handing my bribe to a minor functionary and saying, "So this is how an orphan boy gets a crummy job at your post office: He finds someone to pay you two thousand shillings." But Edward said this would not do. The functionary belonged to his cousin Phillip's informal beer-drinking club, so Phillip would have to present the money.

Phillip sold meat in the New Quarry market. As we drove there, I asked Edward why this cousin, who after all owned his own business, could not help him. "It is because he is paying school fees for his brother, and he has four children by his first wife in the country, and he is now taking a second wife in Nairobi. He needs all his money for that second wife."

Well, this was just great. I had met Edward the day before yesterday, but I was paying a socking big bribe so he could sort letters while his only relative in Nairobi saved to buy a second wife. Bob in Uganda would have enjoyed this, I was like his zero-population-growth Dutch couple. But instead of protesting to Edward—and what good would that have done?—I asked how Phillip's first wife was reacting to this news. He said, "Oh, here it doesn't matter what the women want. We men decide everything."

Phillip's "butcher shop" was a room facing the market's busiest alley. It was more than a stall and less than a store, but it had a glass window, several employees, and a sideline in fish. Phillip was a thin, dapper man, and instead of a bloody smock he wore a brown sports jacket that I liked better than any of mine. We went to a noisy truckers' bar where, without being asked, he told me why he could not help Edward more. During the two years he had spent searching for work, his children had nearly starved. He had roasted ears of corn on the street and saved, finally renting this store. He was in debt, and so on. But none of it really explained why someone who could afford a second wife could not buy Edward a packet of detergent or a second pair of trousers. (He was damp again.)

I grew tired of this. "How much will Edward make at the post office?" I asked. "Do you have confidence in this man? Tell me what will happen on Monday."

The manager, according to Phillip, was "an honest man" who would deliver the job. "First, we will meet in his office and have a conversation about Edward. Then, in a private place, I will give him the envelope. He will not count the money because he trusts me." To give Phillip credit, he seemed embarrassed by this. He stared at his polished shoes and said, "I'm sorry, but that's the way it is in Kenya."

Several times I thought of telling him to postpone that second wife and pay the bribe himself. But then I noticed Edward moving his head back and forth between these two men who were debating and planning his future, his eyes filled with love and with amazement that such a thing could be happening.

Phillip slipped my money into a breast pocket protected by a zipper against pickpockets. So there with a zip went my record of never paying an African bribe. I had fought to keep a few pennies, and now I was surrendering over a hundred dollars. As I feared, this was not the end of Edward. Months later, in New York, my telephone rang, and over a crackling line I heard his voice, recounting a sad story and struggling to explain how an orphan from Mathere Valley could afford to bounce his begging off one of those communication satellites that hover over the equator.

13

THE EQUATOR DISAPPEARS INTO THE INDIAN OCEAN NEAR
Kismayu, in southern Somalia. This territory was once British,
known as the Trans-Juba, but Britain gave it to Italy after the First
World War, and soon Mussolini had marked his equator with a
large obelisk, which was dynamited by the British when they captured Somalia during the Second World War. I had already spent
two months in Africa, all I could afford in time and money, and I
had no strong urge to gaze on the rubble of the Kismayu obelisk
or to see the functional sign the British had erected in its place, if
it was still there. Anyway, the heavy rains had taken this decision
out of my hands. Still, I was reluctant to stop in Nairobi, 400 miles
short of the edge of the continent. On maps, the coast of Somalia
looks undistinguished, a smooth line with few rivers or ports. I
told myself one place on it would be pretty much like the next:
desert meeting ocean. There was a twice-weekly flight to Muqdisho. I could stop there several days and perhaps see the same
thing I would have seen further south on the equator — an empty
beach.

Muqdisho, however, was a city impossible to confuse with
any other, the only Italianate, Muslim, nomadic, desert, coastal

city in East Africa. Being both coastal and desert, its steady wind was gritty with sand and sticky with salt, and everywhere I heard a chorus of dry mouths coughing and spitting. Being Muslim, it had crenellated walls, thick-walled houses with peephole windows, purdah screens rattling in the wind, a dark-skinned and traditionally abused slave caste, strings of colored lights, and nasal songs booming from its radios. Having been Italian, it had twin campaniles on a small cathedral, a triumphal arch dedicated to King Umberto, and houses stuccoed in faded pastels. Italian and Islamic architectural styles are complementary, so the European and traditional cities melted together. It was the most attractive capital I have seen in Africa, and also the most exotic, a place where narcotic-chewing nomads in skirts mumbled "*Ciao*" and "*Buona sera*," while squatting underneath a sign saying, HA DHUMIL XAQAAGA EE DOORD, an exhortation to vote. There was a mad, tick-tocking market where men wandered with rows of wristwatches on their forearms, while holding clocks on strings. There were too many taxis and too little fuel. The taxis formed long lines at petrol stations, with their bored drivers endlessly wiping away salt and sand. The KGB, of all things, was responsible for this glut. When the Soviets were in favor, the KGB had trained a cumbersome Somali security service, giving its new undercover officers taxis, presumably so they could report on conversations held in their back seats. But when the Soviets supported the Ethiopians during the 1970 war, this same Somali government expelled the Soviets and embraced the United States, which would be in favor as long as it supplied weapons that could be turned against the detested Ethiopians.

As it has been for centuries, Muqdisho was gripped by a religious war. The Somalis are Muslim, the Ethiopians Christian, and it is the latter who hold the Ogaden, a wedge of land pushing deep into Somalia. One of the city's most widely traveled and educated men told me, in his high-pitched nomad voice, "We hate the Russians because they have trampled on what we hold most dear: our pride, and our hatred of the Ethiopians." Recruiting foreign powers was an old trick. The Ethiopians had enlisted the Portuguese in the sixteenth century. The British and Italians had been brought in during the twentieth. Any suggestion that the Somalis care about Marxism or capitalism is absurd. They want the Ogaden, and to kill Ethiopians wholesale.

Muqdisho is also probably the only third-world capital where you could see a party of Japanese businessmen whipped across the kneecaps at the airport. I witnessed this when I arrived. There were four of them, wearing dark suits and carrying briefcases and plastic bags of duty-free whiskey. After the hour-long immigration, health, and currency formalities, our luggage was placed behind a white line. Then, for some reason, we were ordered to point out our bags to a soldier who carried them two feet across this line, placing them at our feet. The Japanese were impatient. Disregarding the shouted warnings of expatriate residents, they reached for their own bags, and Whack! whack! whack! A little sergeant smacked them smartly across the knees with a swagger stick. The Japanese dropped their duty-free sacks and screamed, more in surprise than pain. This was not the welcome they had expected from a third-world country eager for their yen. But I thought, Good for the plucky Somalis. At least no one could be under any illusion as to who ran this country: a people sufficiently proud and self-confident to welcome a Japanese trade delegation with a crack across the kneecaps.

There cannot be many cities with Muqdisho's thriving trade in Nazi memorabilia, even though the only Germans were advisers to the routed Italians. Several street salesmen offered me Iron Crosses, badges, and other insignia. The most persistent man lived on the curb in front of the hotel. He had metallic eyes and the twisted smile of a camel thief, and he caught my attention by hissing like a snake, then whispering, "Hitler . . . Hitler." When I stopped to see why a Somali was whispering "Hitler", he grabbed my sleeve. He had silver bracelets running up both arms, chains around his neck, and the Nazi stuff in a leather pouch. He opened a hand to reveal a swastika medal dated 1939, a fitting souvenir from a city dotted with Mussolini monuments. I asked where he found it. "In the desert," he lied. But this idle question convinced him I would buy it, if only we could settle the price. Whenever I appeared in the hotel lobby, he pressed it against a windowpane and shouted, "Hitler!" Whenever I returned from a walk he followed me to the doorway, crying, "Nazi good! Nazi good!" I began approaching the hotel from across the street, waiting until he was distracted, then running for the door.

The Croce del Sud was the most romantic and least expensive hotel I found anywhere. It sat in the Italian city center like a

Foreign Legion post, a hulking, thick-walled white fortress with gates front and rear and two floors of rooms surrounding a courtyard. The Italian woman who owned it had the high cheekbones, exaggerated mannerisms, and weary smile of an aging film star. Once a week, when an Alitalia flight crew stayed at the hotel, she wore a long dress and jewelry. After changing my dollars for wads of greasy currency, she shook a bottle of alcohol over her hands, wiping them with a clean guest towel. I complimented her hotel, and she began her reply with the favorite word of Europeans in Africa: "Before . . .", although in her case "before" did not mean "before independence" but "before the Somali alliance with the Soviet Union."

"Before it was better, much better." She stared over my left shoulder, as if "before" were there. "Before the Russians came, this was an open town, an Italian town. We had barber shops open late, supplies in the stores, and we kept the hotel entrances open all day. We had sidewalk cafés, and one was in front of the hotel, but my husband had to close it because of thieves. They came at the same time as the Russians. Why? No one knows.

"The Russians built walls: around their villas, around their offices, everywhere. The Somali officials imitated them, and now we have walls in Muqdisho, and thieves. And there is simply no more style here. Before — why, before, this was the most marvelous, marvelous place." She lowered her gaze and stared hard, daring me to dispute that before the Russians, Muqdisho had indeed been the most marvelous place in the world.

The Croce del Sud still had style. Its restaurant had tile floors, starched tablecloths, red wicker chairs, and lazy fans throwing a shadow play against the walls. At night I drank fizzy mineral water from Umbria and ate stuffed peppers and fried squid in a courtyard illuminated by high yellow lamps that glowed like moons above the trees. Conversations from neighboring tables spiraled up like smoke, disappearing into a square of black sky. A palsied waiter shuffled across the flagstones, rattling plates like castanets, and a breeze shook the palms, sending down propeller-shaped leaves. I heard the bells of the Italian cathedral, then an amplified prayer from a mosque. In the kitchen, someone was whistling opera.

The Ethiopian wars had filled Muqdisho's suburbs with refugee camps and its center with idle men and cripples, so many that a small corner of the market catered to them, selling canes and crutches. After Zaïre and Uganda, I had become accustomed to the disfigured and dying dragging themselves through town, but not in such numbers. Lines of blind men crossed the streets, gripping shirts. Elephantiasis sufferers pulled swollen extremities in little carts. In a single block I saw lumps in necks, empty sleeves, twisted legs, and a twelve-year-old hunchback contorted with tics. Lepers who could not afford wheelchairs had strapped plastic sandals onto whatever was left and scuttled like water bugs, at ankle level. One evening I heard sandals slapping the pavement behind me. I spun around, seeing nothing until finally I looked down to find a voiceless leper wearing a Nehru cap, banging his sandals in frustration, perspiring, and begging for alms.

The idle men of Muqdisho lay sprawled against walls or sat evenly spaced on curbs, like ornamental bushes. They watched puddles of spit evaporate in the dust and fingered worry beads. Even in good times there was little work in Muqdisho. Government offices were open only in the morning, salaries were so low civil servants had second jobs, and the crime of choice was embezzlement. Even the shoeshine men had divided the work. One man washed laces, another applied polish, a third buffed, a fourth was cashier. This fitful economic activity was overseen by the customary portraits of the leader, Siad Barre. Although Barre's picture was everywhere, his appearance was indefinite, as chameleon-like as his politics. Each portrait was the work of a different propaganda artist, so he appeared fat-cheeked or gaunt, yellow- or brown-skinned, with sparkling Santa Claus eyes or hooded, sleepy ones, with a sharp chin or none at all, resembling Anwar Sadat or Charlie Chaplin in *The Great Dictator*. I resumed my quest, abandoned in Brazzaville, to meet the creators of this folk art.

At the National Museum, a nineteenth-century seaside fortress built by the sultan of Zanzibar, the curator's office was filled with portraits of the leader and his cabinet. They lay against walls, filled tables, or sat in chairs. "But they aren't part of our museum," the young curator said quickly. "They had an exhibit in the Al-Uruba Hotel of this . . . this political material, and afterwards the Ministry of Propaganda [its formal name was the Ministry of Information and National Guidance] dumped them on us.

I haven't a clue what to do with them." He gave a thin smile. "Obviously we can't throw them away."

He flipped through a stack fast, showing off the best. "We hope soon they'll be displayed in the new museum." This was a political museum being constructed by the Ministry of Propaganda. It would contain what the curator called "'relics' from 1969, the date of our revolution, to the present."

"How can they fill a museum with just twenty years of this 'political material'?"

"Oh, that will be no problem." He waved at piles of the leader's portrait. "It's easy to manufacture this stuff."

"And who does that?"

"There are dozens of artists, although I have never taken time to meet them."

Like many Somali men, the curator had a pianist's fine fingers, the rangy build of a swimmer, and the high-pitched voice of an adolescent. He also had the ironic smile I now recognized as the badge of the young educated African who has decided that since his talents are being wasted, he might as well squeeze some amusement from the spectacle. He was not very interested in his museum. He hurried me past the curved swords, cannons, spears, muskets, and daggers that testified to the favorite occupation of Somali men, and past the coins and silver that were the booty of these wars. We stopped before a replica of a grass hut. Scattered around were the bowls, blankets, and cooking pots of a typical nomadic family. "You know," he said, "I grew up in a hut exactly like that one." And now he was in charge of a museum displaying it as an attraction.

His English was curious, and he had the habit of inserting a strange word or phrase in the middle of his sentences. When I interrupted to ask what he meant, he looked shamefaced. "I'm afraid it's a Russian word. I become confused and mix Russian or German words into my English. You must excuse me. I had to learn those languages rapidly." When Somalia was Marxist, he had gone to the Soviet Union to study graphic design. When Russia sided with Ethiopia in the Ogaden war, the government transferred him to a university in West Germany. His fractured languages reflected his country's recent history. Not many Somalis went abroad to train as graphic designers, and as he completed his studies he wondered how his talents could be used in Muqdisho. The government promised him the job of designing a new catalogue for the National Museum. He was told the museum was being renovated, and that considerable sums had been allocated to improve the collection. It sounded like an honor.

"As soon as I returned," he said, "they said the money for the catalogue was being spent instead on the Museum of the Revolution. Then I was appointed acting curator of this museum. I have tried making improvements, but it is difficult with so much clutter." He gestured toward the leader's portraits. "But it doesn't matter. We really don't have proper materials for graphic designing here." I saw the ironic smile again. "So I couldn't have done that catalogue anyway."

I chose as my honorary equator Muqdisho's Lido, surely one of the cheapest and, as I soon learned, most dangerous seaside resorts anywhere. It is at the end of a road, a few miles north of the city, and, except for its long lines of KGB taxis, as lonely as a seaside village in the bleakest, windiest corner of Calabria. Chipped walls ringed its villas, and the wind had piled up little sand dunes behind the backs of guards asleep on mats. The last buildings were bordellos or restaurants. At one, I ate a lunch of spaghetti and papaya, watching from a terrace as children kicked balls and nomads stood, hands behind backs, staring into the Indian Ocean. The thin Somali boys struggled to walk against the wind, digging in their heels with each step. The wind curved their stick-men bodies, billowing their cloaks like spinnakers.

No one was swimming. Offshore, whitecaps dotted the ocean, but a reef broke the waves, leaving gentle breakers to roll into an endless beach. Dunes curved north to the horizon; more stretched inland. A mile away, a white fort crowned a sandy hill. I decided to walk there, imagine the equator running across a similar landscape to the south, then swim back along the beach.

Everyone tried to stop me. A man threw a basket of fish in my path, shouting, "Sold yesterday!"

"You mean 'caught.'"

"Yes, sold." He followed, shouting and throwing fish at my feet until I stepped over his basket.

A madman in a gold bathing suit grabbed my arm, shouting, "Can you help me? I must go to the United States and be a farmer like Michael Jackson." I corrected him and he threw a tantrum at my feet, shouting, "No, no, no, a *farmer*, like Michael Jackson. Give me your address. I will write so you can help me."

As I neared the fort, an old man jumped over a sand dune, snapping his hand around my wrist. He turned me around, leading me back toward the Lido and saying, *"Pericoloso, pericoloso, morte, morte"* —"danger," "death"—and then, "Thif, thif." In broken English he described the thieves who preyed on lone walkers. There had been incidents. He drew a finger across his throat, the international sign for cutthroats. Then he pointed to the water and turned his hand into a shark's fin. Now I understood why no one swam and why the boys darted in quickly to retrieve their ball. The Muqdisho Lido was infested with sharks. What I took for a fortress turned out to be a Soviet-built abattoir that every day discharged blood and offal into the surf, attracting sharks who glided down to the Lido for dessert. Their access to this feast had been improved by the EEC development organization that had opened a hole in the reef during a port improvement project. The Marxists had thrown out the bait, the capitalists had opened the door, and the sharks feasted on Somalis, or so went the stories I heard:

"The sharks come through the hole in the reef and glide along the beach on their sides, hiding their fins until they strike."

"All the time children are eaten at the Lido, maybe one a week, but no one knows the score because there are no newspapers here."

"In the breeding season, when they are vicious, no expatriates swim, and the Somalis play soccer above the dunes."

The old man left me in front of a seaside bordello where, in a courtyard, behind peeling walls and under colored lights, the two major Somali hang-ups, sex and drink, were being indifferently pursued. Cats dozed in every corner and two students lay drunk and snoring. A line of men sat on a bench, whispering and rocking, arms clasped around knees. A secret policeman—you knew from the suit and sunglasses—stopped writing in a notebook to ask my name. I slurred the words and, too proud to ask again, he marched back to his table, probably to transcribe it into one of those Somali words that are all *q*'s, *x*'s, and double vowels. The whores sat on the terrace wall, yawning and listening to tinny Egyptian music on a cassette player. They wore purple scarves and long white dresses. When a man approached, they stared at the horizon. When the men made them dance, they went slack, forcing the men to rub their bodies furiously, as if reviving the victims of frostbite. The wind muffled music and conversation. Everyone struggled against it, walking and dancing in slow motion. High walls on three sides had narrowed the view to empty beach and shark-filled sea and it was so silent, windy, and forlorn you could be brought here blindfolded, yet sense you were at the end of a road, on the edge of a continent.

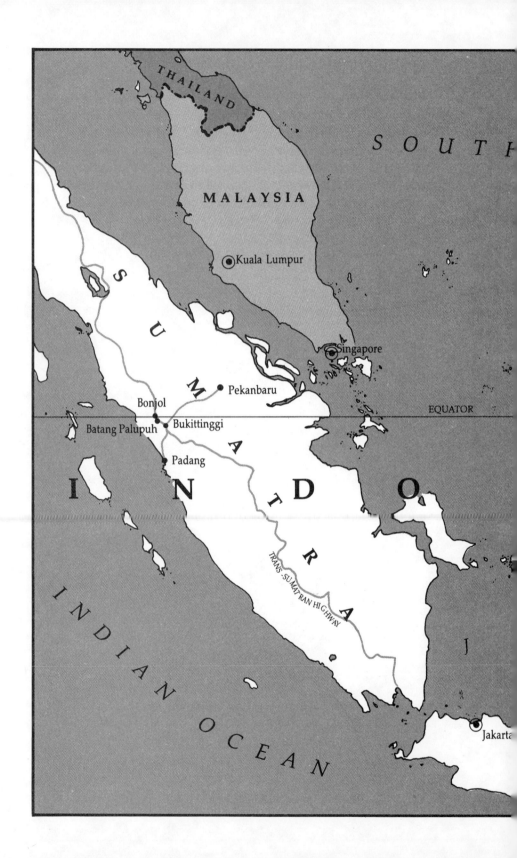

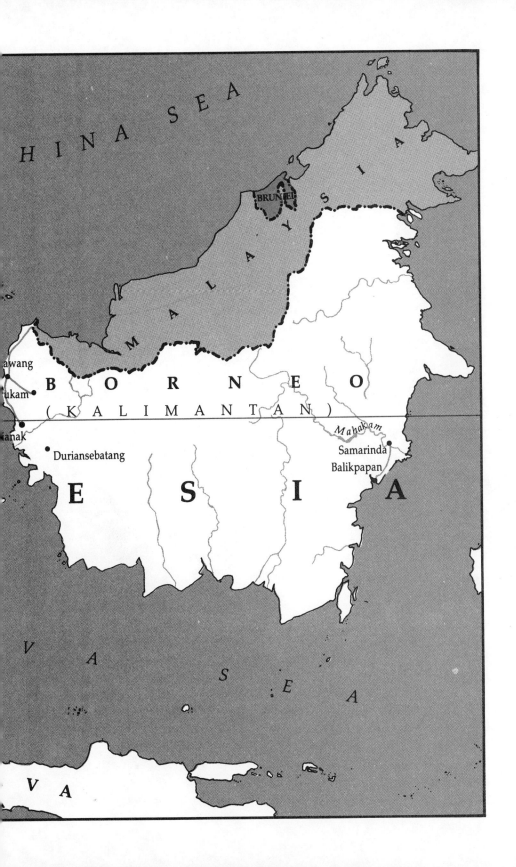

14

FROM AFRICA TO THE WEST COAST OF SUMATRA, THE EQUATOR crosses 3,500 miles of ocean without touching land. In the Indian Ocean it gives its name to an equatorial channel that separates the northern coral atolls of the Maldive Islands from the southern ones, and I considered visiting the channel until I read that the government of this conservative Islamic nation had set aside "tourist atolls" for package-tour Europeans, and discouraged foreigners from visiting the others. The Maldives' capital, Male, is 300 miles and a week-long sea journey north of the equatorial channel. After crossing the channel, I would have arrived at Addu Atoll to find the skeleton hangars and rocky playing fields of a former British air base. Here is how an otherwise optimistic government pamphlet describes Addu: "Today many houses and blocks of land stand vacant while their occupants reside in Male for their money and their means. . . . [But] accommodation is cheap and easy to find amongst the vacant two-story coral houses." But I almost changed my mind and stopped in the Maldives after reading in *Operation World,* a handbook describing the state of the world from the point of view of evangelical Christians, that *"There are no Maldivian Christians—*the only totally unevangelized nation in Asia. No Christian propaganda is permitted, for Christianity is abhorred by the people. Pray for these people in their sin and need—it would appear that their major hobby is immorality."

Instead, I continued to Singapore, sixty miles north of the equator, where the major hobby is shopping—at a pace some might consider immoral—and the principal religion is luxury-level Asian materialism. Singapore is competing with Hong Kong to be the Vatican of this religion, and it is a troubling place for someone who, like me, has been hard on equatorial Africa for its lack of entrepreneurial spirit and economic progress. In two decades, Singapore has become the second wealthiest county in Asia, and an examplar of success and progress other third-world countries are forever being encouraged to copy. Instead of squandering royalties from natural resources, it has created wealth from trade, shipping, banking, industry, and tourism. It is a miniature miracle of no litter, poverty, corruption or crime; a multiracial society without significant tension; a capitalist welfare state with subsidized hospitals, birth control, total literacy, and a television in nine of ten homes; and a place where the fanaticism that taints both its socialism and capitalism can be, depending on your mood, faintly ridiculous or faintly sinister.

I did not see the famous MALES WITH LONG HAIR WILL BE SERVED LAST signs or the wall posters exhorting smaller families or better manners. But I was driven through archways prohibiting vehicles without central-city traffic permits, and down expressways bounded by the ugly projects where, soon, four fifths of the population will live, all to the accompaniment of the musical chimes that by law must sound in every Singapore automobile exceeding the 80-kilometer speed limit. Meanwhile, trucks are outfitted with roof lights that wink at their speed limit of 60 kilometers, betraying their owners to the traffic police. So in Singapore, people in impressive numbers owned vehicles—but then again, some of these vehicles were police informers.

Singapore has an amusement-park skyline. Most colonial-era buildings have been razed and replaced with skyscraper hotels, office buildings and shopping malls topped with revolving bars, flying-saucer restaurants, ornamental pagodas, and health clubs under circus tents reached by space-capsule elevators. Underneath them you find the remnants of Chinatown, and here and there a decapitated arcade of shuttered nineteenth-century stores or a wooden bungalow, all awaiting an inevitable death, much like the old men who once lay crammed into cubicles on the famous Street of the Dead, which has itself become a bulldozed lot, awaiting construction.

I visited a relative working for a foreign company and found his family living in a former British officer's bungalow. There were ceiling fans, outside staircases, louvered windows, and, a hundred yards away, the concrete wall of the new hotel that would soon claim this property, even though Singapore's tourist industry was in a slump and its hotels, built on the graves of the exotica that once brought visitors to this city, were empty.

I tried walking along Orchard Road and was delayed at every block by lines of cars snaking into indoor parking garages beneath the office buildings and shopping malls where life is lived in Singapore. These indoor malls have become a principal tourist attraction. Their appeal is not in the type of merchandise. Virtually everything they offer can be purchased at a mall in suburban New Jersey. Nor is it based on atmosphere: Most are ugly concrete boxes, fluorescent-lit, poorly ventilated, and haunted by merchants with pallid, nighttime faces. Instead, you shop in Singapore hoping to buy Sony or Vuitton, Hermès or Toshiba, more cheaply than at home. This explained the frantic Japanese I saw three-deep at the Gucci counter, shoving and waving money because they were leaving tomorrow and the store closed in half an hour. And it explained the touts in dirty polo shirts lurking around the mall escalators whispering, "Psst, hey mistuh . . ."— and not "My sistuh?" or "Change money?" or "Dirty pictures?" but—"*Shopping*?" Their racket was to steer you to a store offering the best price. It was this simple: I hate shopping, so I hated Singapore.

I flew 200 miles east to Pekanbaru, an inland port 160 kilometers up the Siak River, on the Indonesian island of Sumatra, a former oil-boom town circled by swamps and punctuated by television aerials. Within ten minutes I had met Jimmy Siregar, the self-described most famous guide in Sumatra. In Indonesia I would need a Jimmy. Elsewhere the official languages had been English, French, or Portuguese, and I could handle these, but after a week with tapes and a phrase book, my Indonesian was limited to greetings, asking the price of a fruit or the way to the bus station or toilet, and saying "equator," which is *"katistiwa."* Yet, with the exception of this word, these were precisely the phrases I did not need, since the English vocabulary of the people I met was usually limited to greeting me — "Hello, mister!" — telling me the price of things, and pointing out bus stations and toilets. I had always suspected phrase books of being a waste of time, and now I knew why. (And just before leaving Indonesia I discovered my book had taught me a rather harsh way of demanding "How much?", which was perhaps why so many merchants struck me as rude, and a hilariously obsequious "Pleased to meet you," undoubtedly why so many people impressed me, according to one note, as "giggly.")

Jimmy was happy to see me. As part of government "Indonesianization," Caltex (an American oil company) had withdrawn most of its American employees, leaving him feeling almost as abandoned and betrayed as the faithful Vietnamese "Jimmys" who missed that last helicopter from Saigon. His special talent had been bribing clerks of the national airline to find last-minute seats for Caltex employees, because "You Americans — and excuse me, sir, for saying this — don't know how to bribe. You offer and it is refused, so you must hire Jimmy." He had adjusted to Indonesianization by becoming a guide and travel agent specializing in what he called hippies. His advertisements, placed in student hostels across Sumatra, said For Cheap Tickets See Jimmy in Pekan baru. They worked, luring travelers who, after noticing them everywhere, detoured to Pekanbaru just to meet the legendary Jimmy. He sold them seats on a creaky propeller plane that flew to an Indonesian island near Singapore, or tickets on a boat that ploughed across the Pekanbaru swamps, finally docking in Singapore ("You see nothing and everyone vomit — but cheap").

Jimmy offered me a tour, Pekanbaru by Night. It entailed seeing the sights from the back of his motorbike. I agreed, despite two reservations: First, Jimmy was shaped like a cannonball, so I could not picture us both fitting on any motorbike; and second, I had already seen Pekanbaru by day.

Its main street was a line of two-story concrete stores where oil workers turned their paychecks into appliances and motorbikes. I had already walked up this road with a cheerful swindler who, in exchange for taking me to a money changer, made a half-hearted attempt to charge 10 percent of the transaction. And I had already stepped over open sewers to admire the video-cassette rental stores, one boasting Pekanbaru's greatest sight: a robot that made cotton candy in its gut, then lurched forward to present it to squealing children. A hundred years before, a Dutch planter had taken shelter from a storm in a native hut illuminated by a torch covered by a wet black substance. Afterwards, villagers showed him a spring thick with petroleum. This led to Royal Dutch Shell, which led to oil discoveries in Sumatra, to Indonesia becoming a major oil producer, and to gadgets like this in Pekanbaru.

To put me in the mood for Pekanbaru by Night, Jimmy had oiled his moustache and adopted the swagger of a taller man. His gap-toothed smile promised debauchery, but his motorbike was a bust. We sputtered and wobbled like the *faux blancs* in Brazzaville, stopping so often to repair the engine or prevent me sliding off the rear that I suggested walking. Out of the question, he said. No one walked but children and poor people. Everyone else had joined the evening's slow-moving cavalcade of motorbikes. They waved, tooted horns, and stopped for gossip. Jimmy said this motorbike paseo was a major attraction of Pekanbaru by Night. We bumped over streets smelling of coconut and diesel where every shanty boasted an aerial and a motorbike. We putt-putted down a boulevard smelling of sewage and sugar so Jimmy could point out the store selling tropical fish (proof of the town's prosperity), the bored television salesmen playing video games on their merchandise, and the 200 motorbikes parked in front of a Sylvester Stallone movie.

Jimmy's tribe was the Batak, an agricultural people living on a volcanic plateau in north-central Sumatra. We had dinner in a restaurant popular with other expatriate Bataks, where stout men like Jimmy ate the specialty, Fried chicken American style, and dug with toothpicks at stringy bits left in their teeth. Until the early twentieth century, the Batak practiced ritual cannibalism, and a favorite, and memorable, Batak curse went, "I pick the flesh of your relatives from between my teeth." Sir Thomas Raffles visited the Batak in the early nineteenth century, reporting that "the flesh [of criminals] was sometimes eaten raw, or grilled and eaten with lime, salt, pepper, and a little rice. . . . Palms of the hands and the soles of the feet were delicacies of the epicures."

After dinner, the brakes of Jimmy's motorbike failed, forcing us to walk to the next attraction: a street lined with motorbike pimps. They had splayed themselves suggestively across their seats as an advertisement. They saw us and gunned their engines. "They are here," Jimmy said, ushering me forward like a head-waiter, "to take you to Telegau, our village of whores." This was the climax of Pekanbaru by Night, and had his brakes not failed Jimmy would have taken me himself. "You will like it," he said. "One fuck is only five thousand rupiahs." Jimmy smoothed down his moustache and smiled. He was hoping I would treat us both to rides, and whores too, explaining why the price of Pekanbaru by Night had seemed such a bargain.

"How much is the motorbike taxi?" I asked.

"Only twenty-five hundred, same as half a fuck."

I did not like the sound of a whorehouse, or, for that matter, a village of whores costing only twice the price of transportation to it. It sounded like one of Jimmy's boat trips where passengers saw nothing, vomited, and enjoyed the triumph of paying little. I was curious, but not that curious. I liked Jimmy, but not enough to pay for his whoring. I said no and felt like a heel.

Sumatra resembles a fat fish. Its mouth nibbles at Java and its tail wiggles at the Nicobar Islands. There is a narrow coastal plain on the west, a swamp squishy with oil running down the east coast, and volcanic mountains and fertile plateaus in the center. The equator cuts it at the broadest point, dividing it almost as perfectly as it does the earth. Because I had started in Singapore, I would have to backtrack, following the equator east to west. Pekanbaru is twenty miles north of the equator, Bukittinggi thirty-five miles south, and the road connecting them follows it roughly, crossing between hemispheres at the village of Kotoalam. Buses make the trip in six hours, but I chose a long-distance taxi, hoping to persuade the driver to stop in Kotoalam. Tomorrow was a national holiday, and the other passengers were students shuttling home. They were good company. Two brothers were ham-radio enthusiasts who had learned English from hams in Guam and Hawaii and the BBC. They wanted to talk about the royal family. Their father had a cassette of the royal wedding. Did I have one? No, I said, shocking them by admitting to not owning a VCR. They thought I was joking.

Outside Pekanbaru, immigrant farmers had cleared a mile-

wide corridor on either side of the road. Sumatra is the fifth largest island in the world but, with only twenty-five million people,
among the least populated, so I was surprised to see this landscape of charcoaled earth, scrub, and scorched trees. The radio
enthusiasts said many of the farmers came from Java. Its population density was forty times Sumatra's, and to relieve it the government encouraged interisland migration. We left the coast, and
the valleys became deep pockets, sprinkled with emerald paddies
and shadowed by sawtoothed mountains. Rickety villages clung
to hairpin turns or huddled in gorges. The road climbed monkey-
filled hills and threaded canyons weeping waterfalls and vines, a
good terrain for an ambush. The light was aquamarine, as if
Sumatra were an underwater movie.

Everything was sharp. There were jagged hills, pointed horns
on the buffaloes ploughing rice paddies, and pointed gables on
the saddle-roofed houses that echoed buffalo horns. These houses
sat on stilts and had palm-fiber roofs and walls covered in ornate
carvings. They sheltered several families headed by daughters of
the same mother or grandmother. The Minangkabau (or Minang)
people of West Sumatra are matrilineal, meaning property and
power are passed from mother to daughter. When a daughter
marries, her husband moves into her family home, adding another wing and a buffalo-horn roof. Large families appear to live
beneath a herd of buffaloes. It seemed fantastic that a people
known as the most advanced and educated in Indonesia would
build such traditional houses. I had imagined a few being preserved as museums or cultural centers, but here were dozens,
ringed by livestock, with a truck or car in front and laundry flapping in back, although some thatched roofs had been replaced by
tin ones of the same shape.

I was staring out the wrong side of the taxi when we sped
through Kotoalam into the southern hemisphere. The ham-radio
operators shouted, "The equator!" and I turned to see a huge
concrete ball, mounted on a pedestal and circled by a double red-
and-black line. By the time someone had translated my request to
stop, we were a mile away. The driver shook his head. "He won't
go back because he is hungry," the boy said. "And he prefers the
restaurants in the next place."

We stopped in Harau Canyon, the steepest and shadiest of the
gorges. A cool breeze blew through and passengers threw on

sweaters. Water dripped from rock walls, and songbirds perched in painted cages hung outside restaurants. It was a popular stopping place. Several long-distance taxis and a bus were here, their passengers already gorging. The restaurants of West Sumatra are perfect for travelers speaking no Indonesian. Cooked food sits in enamel bowls stacked in restaurant windows, so you can see at a glance what is available. You sit and a waiter automatically brings rice and small plates of food from each bowl. Afterwards, he counts empty plates, and you pay for what you have eaten. The only drawback is that your rejects are returned to the pot, allowing the same goose-pimply chicken wing to visit many tables in an afternoon. Minang food is famous for its heat and spice, and every buffalo, egg, beef, and chicken stew is red with chili or yellow with curry. I never found a restaurant I did not like, nor one that did not provoke waterfalls of perspiration. But it is not a cuisine suited to these curvy mountain roads, perhaps the reason why Sumatran buses supply passengers with pink vomit bags.

Bukittinggi is a miraculous little highland city, a university and market town with warm days, cool nights, and racing clouds. It has more urban pleasures than American cities ten times its size: public tennis courts; a "panoramic park" with cafés and children's rides; a clock tower capped with a bull's-horn roof (giving rise to the city's nickname, "the Big Ben town"); an aquarium you enter through the jaws of a concrete fish; a military museum with an exhibit celobrating a heroic carrier pigeon; a cultural museum displaying a stuffed, two-headed baby buffalo; a market with whole streets selling blue duck eggs, crispy snack foods, and goldfish (for eating); and a zoo where the sign over the sun-bear pit begs visitors to TAKE PITY ON THE ANIMALS, and they do.

It is a city splashed with reds and pinks. Frangipani and geraniums fill parks, and poinsettias decorate front yards. Pink African violets are sold in the market, children lick pink ice-cream cones, women favor red scarves, and red pompons bob on the heads of the sturdy ponies that pull carriages up streets lined with billboards of smiling teeth and pink gums, advertisements for dentists.

I climbed to the Dutch fort for a view of minarets and mosques mingled with the saddle roofs decorating public offices, a clock tower, the covered market, hotels, schools, and the buildings of distant villages. At sunset, the encircling jungle mountains changed from green to blue to black, volcanoes released fists of clouds, and the scent of cinammon filled the air. I heard calls to prayer from a loudspeaker mounted in a nearby mosque, and I thought it amazing that Islam could find such enthusiastic adherents in a land already resembling the Muslim heaven of babbling streams, green parks, and plenty.

There are no slums lining the approaches to Bukittinggi, no police roadblocks, and no beggars except the blind and the genuinely infirm. Instead of sewers, you smell coconut; instead of crones lugging water, you see schoolgirls with scrubbed faces and ribboned hair. The streets are washed and swept every night, cart horses jangle with silver ornaments, and when taxis reverse, their chimes warn pedestrians by playing "Turkey in the Straw" or "Rudolf the Red-Nosed Reindeer." Consumer goods at low prices fill stores and customers pack restaurants; women buy ornamental plants and men pursue a favorite Minangkabau pastime, flying kites.

I heard many explanations for these marvels: The volcanic ash was low in acidity, making the land exceptionally fertile; Sumatra was rich in resources; Indonesia had enjoyed twenty years of political stability; and the Minangkabau were famous merchants and travelers who sent remittances home and had a cultural tradition of democracy and practicality, proven by sayings such as "When the flood comes, the bathing place changes," and "There are no entanglements which can't be undone, no muddy waters which can't be made clear." There is truth to all this, but I decided the main reason for the Minang's success was that their traditional culture, or *adat,* made them natural businessmen, and, to a surprising degree, the Indonesian government had stayed out of their way.

Perhaps I liked Bukittinggi so much because I could not speak the language. If people were rude, I could not understand them. If they had complaints about the government, the weather, or the price of rice, I was oblivious. The horse-cart drivers were toothless men in flapping nightshirts, mutterers all, but I could not decipher their muttering. It was an easy way to travel, since everywhere I saw, without dissent, confirmation of what I already knew about the Minangkabau.

I knew they were devout Muslims, so I was not surprised to find traffic halted for a parade of boys graduating from the

Koranic school. They wore the cloaks of Arabian sheiks and marched behind a papier-mâché Koran tied to the back of a Japanese pickup. A band played, appropriately, "Never On a Sunday." When an old man asked, "You, Muslim?" I said no, and he unleashed a torrent of words spoken in a cadence and with facial expressions that could have signaled disapproval, curiosity, or an attempt at conversion.

I knew the Minang were famous travelers who have a tradition of *merentau,* which, roughly translated, means leaving the home village in search of wealth, knowledge, and fame. They emigrate not only because of population pressure or the attractions of a city, but because travel is believed to season a young man, and I like to think the Minang have come to dominate Indonesian literature and cinema because this travel has broadened them. Knowing about *merentau,* I was not surprised, after hiking across a canyon to a village at the foot of Mount Singgalang, to see only scratching brown dogs, women pushing wheelbarrows, and old men sucking cigarettes as they shuffled to a mosque. In a smoky café, a circle of young men with bloodshot eyes ate seeds while listening to rock tapes. It was the losers' café, a place of hung-over idlers too lazy or too timid to leave. There is a name for them, the *parewa.* In some villages they extort money from bus drivers for promising not to scatter nails on the road. But, not speaking Indonesian, I could not know for sure who these men were and why they were idle.

I knew that the Minangkabau are the largest and healthiest matrilineal society in the world, with men living as guests in their wives' familial homes, women proposing marriage, and children being raised by a maternal uncle and looking to him for discipline and advice. So perhaps it is no wonder Minang men take long trips, complain of being "ashes on the stump" for all the consideration they receive at home, or call their daughters *limapeh rumah nan godang*—the "iron butterflies."

There was a table of iron butterflies at my hotel, part of a large family outing that had reserved most of the rooms. During the day, they piled into vans to visit another lake or canyon. In the evening, the iron butterflies, wearing jewelry and silk dresses, occupied a long table in the center of the room while their husbands and sons, dressed in cheap sport shirts, filled side tables. It was a solar configuration: small, dim planets set around a glittering sun. I wanted to ask the men if they really allowed their wives' uncles to raise their sons. And had their wives asked them to marry? And how did they reconcile Islam with this matrilineal tradition? Instead, we could only exchange simple pleasantries.

There was a young clerk at the hotel, named Ranson, who spoke English but would entertain only one subject: Ronald Reagan. "Can you obtain for me a picture of my hero, Ronald Reagan?" he said, changing the subject from the Minang. "I have written several times to your embassy. They ignore me."

"Is President Reagan popular in Bukittinggi?"

"We all love him because he is tough with the Communists. Many of my friends have his photograph, usually the one on the horse. That is common and not so valuable." There cannot be many third-world cities where a photograph of Ronald Reagan is such a treasure. I put it down to the traditional conservatism of a mountain people, or the residue of the 1958 civil war, when western Sumatra was one of several regions to rebel against Sukarno's regime, accusing it of being too anti-Muslim and pro-Communist.

Ranson was not the only man in Bukittinggi to greet the news that I was American with a big smile and a "Ronald Reagan!" But he was certainly the president's most fanatical admirer. He was a pleasant young man, full of jokes and smiles, so Reagan probably would have liked him, but I grew tired of being asked if I had yet written to the embassy on his behalf (I had not), or if I would consider calling them (I would not). I asked questions about Bukittinggi, and Ranson said, "I hope for a picture of my hero and his lovely wife," or "Is there a photograph of his entire family, on horses? Would your embassy send me that?" When he said no one in Bukittinggi spoke better English than he, I was thrown into despair and onto the mercy of the expatriate community.

There were only two foreign families in the entire city. One, an Australian couple, had lived here two years while he reopened a Dutch gold mine known as the Aequator Concession. It was intersected by the equator, and the original lease had been held by the Mining Company of the Aequator. He gave me a sample, a white rock with gold speckles embedded in a black seam, and said there was a gold rush along the equator in Sumatra and Borneo, and Australian mining companies were competing for leases. When I asked them to recommend an English-speaking interpreter, she said, "In two years we really haven't made friends. Believe me, we've tried, but I can't recall being invited to anyone's house." He agreed. "The Minang are a hard, self-reliant people and not very interested in foreigners."

Bukittinggi's other expatriate was an anthropologist from South Carolina studying "emotional ethnography." He had followed the same Minang youngsters for four years, videotaping their expressions under different situations. Today was his last day in Bukittinggi. He had packed his video tapes and books, and we were interrupted by neighbors bargaining for his furniture. I was not surprised to hear him call the Minang the most intelligent and hardworking of all Indonesians. Most anthropologists root for their own. But I was surprised that even he was uncertain why these devout Muslims were so faithfully matrilineal. "Here are these rigorously Islamic people," he said, "a masculine faith that originally extolled the patriarch, warrior, orator, begetter, and provider of sons while making women inferior, following a traditional *adat* that gives the women everything. When the fundamentalist Wahabis invaded Sumatra, they cured the Minang of lesser heresies but failed totally to change the matrilineal system." He recommended an interpreter named Ar who, he said, was "all right for a few days, but not much longer."

Ar was slight and handsome, and, like many Minang men, he looked barely sixteen. His shirts were always pressed, his hair glistened, and he had enough sparkling teeth for two mouths. He lived by the expression Manners make the man, and he was forever offering drinks, sharing food, and observing a tense and punctilious etiquette. There was much to like in Ar, but I soon found exhausting his unceasing concern over whether I was enjoying myself, and his constant searching of my face — all the time with a pained expression on his — for bulletins as to my pleasure or discomfort. These were common characteristics, and the Minang men had acquired them, I imagine, while courting their fearsome iron butterflies.

While we hunted for a Rafflesia flower in the steep rain forests outside Batang Palupuh, Ar described his frustrating courtship of his girlfriend, Nevi. I had hired a car so she could accompany us to Batang Palupuh and on to Bonjol, where the equator intersects the grandiloquently named Trans-Sumatran Highway. Ar hoped to impress her with this excursion, but she stood us up, and after waiting half an hour he had suggested, with a pained, toothy smile, that we leave without her.

Sir Thomas Raffles, discoverer of the Rafflesia, described it as "perhaps the largest and most magnificent flower in the world." Its blossom measures a yard across and weighs fifteen pounds. It is native to the forests of Sumatra and Borneo, but it is rare and difficult to find because it needs eighteen months to bud and nine to flower, and its blossom wilts in four days. Somewhere on the equator there may be a Rafflesia blooming, but finding it can be a labor of years. Botanists tramp the western Sumatran highlands for weeks, seeing only buds or decayed flowers, described as having an odor of rotting flesh. It is this smell that promotes the Rafflesia's sex life, attracting the carrion flies that are its chief pollinators and leading to its nickname, "the corpse flower." Not surprisingly, visitors and locals are curious to see an enormous, rare, red blossom that achieves sexual climax by giving off the odor of a corpse, and so there is a Rafflesia nature reserve on the steep hills overlooking the village of Batang Palupuh. You have a better chance of finding a Rafflesia here because park rangers rub seeds on exposed vines and surround budding plants with chicken wire. Even so, Ar had seen only four blossoms in his lifetime.

Palupuh was a busy village where, like Cacao, everyone did a little of everything: raising chickens and ducks, drying coffee beans, cultivating rice, growing saffron and cinammon, and raising goldfish. We walked a mile along paths bordered by wildflowers and paddies. The ranger's house was closed, so we would have to find a Rafflesia ourselves. We rested in the shade of his roof, sucking orange candies and perspiring. Two red dragonflies motored back and forth at eye level, mating. Ar said, "I encouraged Nevi to come; I was sure she would. Perhaps she was shy to meet you. Her English is better than mine, but she is embarrassed to speak. Yes, that must be why she changed her mind."

I described what I knew about Minang women and he nodded. "Yes, yes, all that is true. They own the land, the houses, everything. But that means they have to look after them too." I saw a sly smile. "And it leaves us free to adventure, to voyage wherever we want."

But Ar was not enjoying this privilege. He was mooching

around Bukittinggi, hoping to marry Nevi. "And it's true that women ask the men to marry?" I asked.

"Yes, but the formal request must be made from her uncle to my uncle. But we are not ready yet," he added quickly.

"You're almost thirty."

He sighed. His eyes followed the dragonflies. "Well, maybe she is not ready."

As we climbed into the hills, he said, "I have been asking 'Do you think we are possibly, almost ready?' I am trying to let her know I would say yes, since a woman will not ask unless she is certain of being accepted, but still . . . oh, it is a very complicated business for us. I wonder if because we are university graduates she expects me to ask? And now her uncle is promoting a man from Medan. She claims to prefer me, but I am not sure. She might marry him to please her uncle, so perhaps I must ask first. And now I am wondering why she did not come today . . ."

For an hour we followed the jungle paths, using roots as handholds, sliding down muddy embankments, and walking through clearings glittering with butterflies. We found walnut-shaped buds growing from roots that Ar said were months from blooming. We came on one resembling a scorched basketball, and he said, "Maybe next month." We had given up when I almost stepped on a Rafflesia. It had blossomed only recently, but it was already a purplish cadaver, busy with flies and carrion beetles and emitting a faint odor of spoiled meat. I stared at this slimy puddle, trying to match it with the *National Geographic* photographs of a fiery diaphragm and vivid red petals splotched with white warts. "It's good Nevi didn't come," Ar said. "This would have disappointed her."

On a straight line, the Rafflesia reserve is only fifteen miles south of the equator, but the road to Bonjol twists through steep mountains for fifty. For three hours we drove through magnificent countryside. Villages lay tucked in secret hollows and buried under giant sunflowers and bamboo. Flowers dripped from the mouths of creamy cows, and lazy water buffaloes dragged plows through fields. Mosques squatted on distant paddies like frogs on lily pads. It was a rolling, storm-tossed landscape, one still being shaped.

Ar insisted on stopping at a roadside attraction, the site of "last year's most famous bus jumping." We had already just missed hitting several buses on this narrow road. They came careening around corners, wheels spitting gravel off the crumbling shoulders and destination signs promising cities two days away. They were chrome boxes, modern from a distance and promising "full air-con," but up close you saw that their smeared windows were open and their passengers crammed in, knees to chin. The most expensive had televisions showing Indian romances and kung fu adventures. Strings of colored lights lit their chassis so at night they resembled speeding Christmas trees.

"Here the driver fell asleep." Ar pointed to a swath of crushed trees and underbrush. "The bus rolled a hundred feet and people tried escaping, but the other trees broke from the weight, so it fell." The authorities had erected a hundred yards of guardrail, perhaps as a kind of memorial, since for miles the road was equally narrow and unstable, and the drop just as precipitous, as at this spot.

We lunched at a barn-like restaurant catering to long-distance buses. A manager welcomed passengers over a loudspeaker, directing them to baths and a small mosque. Ar looked up in surprise from our circle of curry dishes to see his friend Hendra, who was going to Medan to be married. The uncle of Hendra's fiancée had made the proposal three days before. Hendra had dropped everything and was hurrying north for the ceremony, treating himself to a bus with "full video." He planned to live in Medan, where his in-laws had promised to find him a job. "My life is settled," he said, sitting down to share our meal. He was also a fan of Ronald Reagan, and he lowered his voice to ask, "You are not, sir, by any chance a member of his staff?" Then his bus blasted its air horn and he was gone, leaving Ar dumbfounded. "But he is my best, my very best friend in Bukittinggi. I saw him only last week, and he made no mention . . . Why, if we had not stopped here by chance I might have never seen him again. He is right, his life is settled." Ar was close to tears.

At Bonjol, the mountains that had smothered the highway since Bukittinggi opened into a broad valley, as if to give the equator more room. Two hundred yards north of the market, a white line crossed the road, connecting an impressive double monument. On the western side of the road was a three-story-high white concrete obelisk crowned with a blue globe with EQUATOR lettered in red across a white band. The eastern side had a rectangular pillar with EQUATOR! written lengthwise down its broadest sides in red paint. It was dated June 1, 1973, and seemed the most recent monument, but no one in Bonjol could tell me why such different markers announced their equator or why the word had come to be written in English rather than Dutch, *Euenaar,* or Indonesian, *Katistiwa.* The site recalled Macapá, but instead of a soccer field, the equator divided a volleyball court and a wooden Minang pavilion used for cultural events. A cleared lot in the southern hemisphere was the future site of a museum celebrating Imam Bonjol, a nineteenth-century Sumatran hero. The government had already erected a statue of the imam, his sword raised to behead a few Dutchmen.

Two travelers, Sylvia and Dov, stood in the shade of the obelisk, trying to hitch a ride. They could afford buses, but taking them was such a miserable experience that they preferred begging rides from trucks. She was British, with blond hair cut short as an army recruit. He wore a beard and a beatific California smile and appeared oblivious to the crowd of children making an afternoon of touching his skin and exploring his knapsack. I asked where he had been and he listed, in chronological order, the dozens of Asian and European countries he had visited since leaving Los Angeles. "And today is my anniversary," he said in the smooth voice of an expensive California education, "the twenty-first month to the day I started traveling. I wanted to celebrate on the equator, but we're a bit disappointed."

Sylvia agreed. "That's right. It's not all we expected."

"Well, what did you expect from the equator?" I thought Bonjol had packed rather a lot onto its equator. Dov should be grateful he was not celebrating his twenty-first month at Entebbe.

"I dunno. More, I guess."

More? How could he expect more? There was more here than anywhere: a volleyball court and outdoor theater, two monuments, a line in the road, a statue, and soon a museum. Did he expect an amusement park? Souvenir stands? I wanted to say, Use your imagination! Think of picking up a hairy thick rope, shaking it, and seeing it ripple through these jungly hills to the coast, then across the Indian Ocean, over Mount Kenya, through the Bamanya mission, along the Transgabonaise, across São Tomé, and back to a cabin in Macapá!

Ar and I walked a hundred yards west along the equator,

crossing a hedge and a drainage ditch to emerge in a prosperous neighborhood of widely spaced homes surrounded by paddies. I estimated the equator ran through the living room of a wooden house that resembled a Swiss chalet. A sullen, bare-chested man sat in a gravel driveway repairing a fishing net. He muttered at us without looking up. Ar said, "His name is Irwin, the husband," and then ignored him.

We stood at the front door several minutes until a round-faced woman appeared and asked us inside. We sat in her parlor on brand-new chairs. There were house plants, curtains, and a large silver radio. Her name was Sus, and her parents had built this house as a wedding present. She had been married three months, and the unshaven man outside, whom I had taken for an underpaid family servant, was her husband. He drove a taxi van, but enough about him. She introduced her parents, who also lived in this honeymoon cottage. Her father was a toothless pixie who passed the time giving sweets to neighborhood children. Her mother had the bearing of the Queen Mother. After every sentence, Sus checked her mother's face for a reaction.

Sus said the biggest advantage to living on the equator was electricity. The authorities had run power lines from the main highway to their neighborhood, perhaps because they were building the Imam Bonjol Museum.

I asked why she had not constructed her house in the traditional style, with a sweeping saddle roof. Everyone had a good laugh at this. Those houses took too much time to build and were more expensive. "Now we like to live modern," she said, looking at her mother, who nodded approval.

I wondered if her fondness for modernity might extend to allowing Irwin to have a hand in raising their children. Apparently not. "My brother should do that, but he is too young," she said, "so it will have to be a man from our clan living nearby." Her mother smiled. The sullen Irwin was not even in the running. I could see him through the open door, still hunched over his carp nets. He looked ripe for a long *merentau*.

I gave Sus an elephant from the Kenyan curio carvers (I had given up trying to unload the Lambarené crocodile), and she agreed to assemble the family for a photograph. The "family" meaning everyone but Irwin, who kept at his nets while she changed clothes and her grandparents and all the neighborhood children lined up in front of the house. But when she had not appeared in twenty minutes, Ar made inquiries and reported, "She decided she could not make herself pretty enough, and she is too embarrassed to tell you." One of the children said Sus would like my address, so she could remind me to send her a copy of the photograph she had declined to join. I was in no mood to say yes, but Ar insisted it would be rude to refuse. Incredibly, our visit to this honeymoon cottage had not dampened his enthusiasm for his own iron butterfly. As we stepped around the still muttering Irwin, he said, "Tomorrow there is a bullfight near Bukittinggi, and I am hoping, I am doing my best, to persuade Nevi to join us."

The next afternoon we drove to a village perched in a saddle between two active volcanoes. Men arrived from every direction, walking down paths marked by pennants and past black fields exploding with vegetables. We paid thirty-five cents to enter a village soccer field, where four water buffaloes stood tied to stakes. They were stout animals with broad horns, thick at the base but sharply pointed. Men surrounded one bull in a circle defined by the length of the tether. Many spectators, including Ar and Nevi, stood behind a fence.

The woman who had kept Ar in a perpetual state of anxiety and longing was a tiny creature with silky hair and pretty features grouped closely in the middle of her face. Since Minang bullfights are a male activity, Nevi had never seen one and had dressed inappropriately, in high heels and a silk dress. Ar was frantic, first apologizing for being unable to leave Nevi, then joining me in inspecting the bulls. He bought her sweets. He walked her to the hedge that served as a toilet. He ran back to apologize to me again. He worried this event might not promote their romance. I sympathized. I had once made the mistake of taking a girl to the dog races, and despite the spectacular setting, there was a certain dog-race atmosphere to this field, to the crackling speaker announcing owners and past performances, the haze of cigarette smoke, and the men, unshaven and plagued by hacking coughs. They slouched, whispered tips, and exchanged money even as an announcer warned betting was illegal. Aside from girls selling peanuts and two German travelers with scabby legs, Nevi was the only woman.

Ar turned to me, announcing in a loud voice "I am very

much in love with her." His iron butterfly just giggled, refusing to return the pledge. His smile became more pained. "Would you mind if we left early?" he whispered.

I would. The word "Minangkabau" means "victorious buffalo," and the legend is that instead of going to war, the people of West Sumatra and Java settled a dispute by staging a battle between water buffaloes. I did not want to miss the contest that had given the Minang their name.

The handlers untethered two bulls, led them into the center of the field, and ran. The animals locked horns and, heads lowered, shoved up and down the field. Their hooves churned the earth, shooting divots into the air. Most spectators ran for the fence. The others formed a cautious, fluid circle. I joined this group. The danger was that if a bull was pushed back too fast, he might trample you. Whenever the bulls disengaged, there was a minor Pamplona of panicked men sprinting in every direction. The back-and-forth was exciting if you were following them, watching their horns draw blood and their snouts blow clouds of dust. After ten minutes one bull ran for the woods, almost trampling a little boy. This bull was the loser, the one pushed off the field. I was told this had been an excellent fight—which it was, compared to the next one. It lasted thirty seconds and nearly killed a peanut vendor. Like dog races, the Minang bull fights were far less interesting than the betting, scheming, and socializing surrounding them.

Ar and Nevi feigned interest by asking which bull had won, but they really did not care, because while these monsters were jousting, something had happened. Somehow, this grotesque battle had furthered their romance. "I love her!" Ar shouted, so loudly everyone turned around. They laughed and punched each other's arms. I thought his iron butterfly had finally proposed, but as we left he said, "We are closer. I am sure she will ask me, perhaps very soon!"

Before taking a van to Padang, on the coast, I made the mistake of visiting the Bukittinggi Military Museum with its display cases of weapons from the war of independence and its lighted diorama illustrating the Situjuh Batur affair, where Dutch troops had surrounded and massacred sixty-nine Sumatran guerrillas planning to seize Payakumbah. I read a tribute to Latan, the heroic carrier pigeon used to carry messages to the front during the war for independence, and saw gruesome photographs of the seven Indonesian generals murdered by Communist conspirators during the abortive Communist coup of 1965. Their deaths had been indisputably appalling. Members of a left-wing women's movement had beaten them with clubs and rifle butts, gouged their eyeballs out, and thrown their mutilated corpses down a well. More appalling was the slaughter that followed this atrocity, and the absence of any display commemorating this slaughter only served to remind me of everything I had been trying to forget as I enjoyed Bukittinggi.

Amok, as in "to run amok," comes from the Indonesian *amuk*. The word means "to run viciously, frenzied for blood," which is what many Indonesians did in reaction to the attempted Communist coup. During the last two months of 1965, a million Indonesians were massacred by other Indonesians, sometimes by their neighbors. According to one description, "Corpses packed the rivers like log-jams. The fishermen . . . threw away their catch because the fishes' stomachs were packed with human fingers, ears, and other hacked-off parts."

The victims were Communists, Socialists, Chinese and other unpopular minorities, hated families and hated villages, and merchants and creditors. Their executioners were also a cross section: anti-Communists, soldiers and policemen, religious Muslims, and even Balinese villagers, blaming the Communists for a volcanic eruption. The killings were accomplished with knives, machetes, and small arms. Disposing of a million people in this primitive way and at such speed requires many willing executioners. The worst of the massacres occurred on Bali and Java, but Sumatra was not spared. Many of the men my age I passed on the streets of Bukittinggi must have belonged to the murderous youth groups.

If you travel burdened by these morbid thoughts, you will not have a cheerful trip. Scores of racial, political and religious massacres have recently occurred in tropical countries. If visitors find them easy to ignore, it may be because, like the Hutu and Tusi in Rwanda and Burundi, they received little attention at the time, or because they have been erased from official memory. I have traveled in India without dwelling on the communal massacres of 1948 in which several million perished, but in Indonesia the killings were more recent, and seemingly more at odds with the character of the people. And so, after visiting this museum, I began to be haunted by these massacres, and to search the smiling faces of people my age, wondering if they had participated, and how.

15

ANYONE ATTEMPTING TO TRAVEL FROM SUMATRA TO INDONE-
sian Borneo quickly sympathizes with Sumatran complaints of
Jakartan centralism. It is only 600 miles from Bonjol to where the
equator first strikes the coast of Borneo (or Kalimantan, as the
Indonesians call it), at the port of Pontianak, and only 375 miles
of ocean separate Sumatra and Borneo, yet shipping and air
routes all detour through Jakarta, an overpopulated capital
smothered under a pink haze of exhaust, smoke, and dust. It is a
sprawling, senseless jumble, where stores selling caged birds
border a Toyota dealership that is next to a merchant's walled
villa, which adjoins a stinking fish market close by a cardboard
squatters' settlement, all overshadowed by bank skyscrapers overlooking traffic-clogged boulevards that pedestrians cross like runners at the start of a race, one foot off the curb, leaning forward,
faces tensed, waiting to sprint at the first opening. A foreigner
who had lived here twenty years told me that during the last five
years the population growth, construction, and traffic had made
everyone tense. "There used to be these marvelous lazy parties
where the political and cultural elites met to exchange ideas," he

313

said. "Now, after long commutes and brutal traffic, these same people stagger home, lock their doors, and turn on their VCRs."

The next day I was in Pontianak, Borneo, a small Chinese trading city on the equator whose streets are in a transitional stage: starting to be quickened with farting motorbikes and darting Japanese sedans, but balanced by an aging fleet of bicycle rickshaws. There is something unseemly, not to say dated, about a beefy European being hauled around by a frail Asian furiously pedaling a bicycle. The last trishaw I rode was in India, where the driver's seat was in front, and all the way to the Taj Mahal I watched his pigeon shoulder blades working, saw him shivering through a tattered shirt, and listened as he crooned encouragement to himself. In Pontianak, trishaws lined every crossroads, their drivers curled up asleep in the carriages, bare feet sticking out the sides. Like the horse carts of Bukittinggi, these carriages were lovingly tended — painted a glistening red, bobbing with plumes, and jingling with bells and lucky trinkets — yet empty. And, unlike the trishaws of India, the Pontianak drivers sat behind, sparing you the sight of their exertions. As I glided through the city at sunset, I could imagine I was propelled by a motor, and I could enjoy, unobstructed, the panorama of a city gripped by durian madness.

The durian is a spiky, football-sized green fruit, prized in Southeast Asia to a degree unexplained by its beauty, odor, or taste. Perhaps its popularity comes from its scarcity, or its reputation as an aphrodisiac, for, according to one Malay proverb, "When the durians come down the sarongs go up." It is scarce because the tree blossoms at night and can only be pollinated by fireflies and bats, because the destruction of mangrove forests on the Malay peninsula has disturbed the habitat of these durian bats, and because the fruit grows high off the ground, ripening and falling only during two short seasons. I arrived in Pontianak on the second night of the most fructuous of these. I had seen Cairo like this on the first night after Ramadan, with streets packed with crowds and stalls overflowing with rich foods. But in Pontianak, everybody wanted just one food: the custard-textured, stuffed-up-toilet- and garlic-smelling paste enclosing the phallus-shaped durian seed. I knew this much about a durian because the hawkers had slit one open, as a temptation.

The Boulevard Imam Bonjol, which runs parallel to the docks, warehouses, and estuary, was the center of durian activity. Canals enabled merchants to unload the fruit directly from their boats onto wooden-planked sidewalks, like a catch of fish. Shirtless boys sniffed, weighed, and sorted durians into piles, working fast to clear out this lot before the next arrived. "Where do they come from?" I asked a perspiring sorter in my execrable Indonesian. Pointing inland, he shouted, "Duriansebatang." I found it on my map, a town named to honor this fruit.

Everywhere durians were on the move, heaped in trucks, piled in cars, strapped to motorbikes, and dangling from bicycle handlebars. Boys hired trishaws, piled them with durians, and trotted alongside. A family of four sat on the back of a motorbike, a durian hanging from each wrist. Durian spikes are sharp, so merchants tied the fruit in pink plastic ribbon, with a loop for carrying. No one could believe I did not want one. They shouted, "Hey, mistuh, *durian!*" They pointed to already-opened fruit, begging "Try one! Eat one free!" They believed they were selling the heroin of fruits: one taste and I would be hooked for life. "Curiosity and not taste first prompts the settler to attempt the fruit," wrote a nineteenth-century British settler. But every time I stuck my nose into an opened durian, smell overwhelmed curiosity.

Bats appeared at sunset, drawn by the odor. They fluttered over durian piles, ready to pollinate but confused to find the smell without the blossoms. A sudden wind rattled awnings and shutters and lightning strikes circled the town, illuminating the Boulevard Iman Bonjol so it resembled that war-movie scene in which streams of refugees evacuate a city carrying their most valuable possessions. In Pontianak, these were durians.

The rain drove me onto a covered restaurant terrace where everyone was eating durians except a tiny whore who called me "grandfather" (a sign of respect I disliked) and tried to catch my attention with bird calls. At the next table, six Chinese businessmen from Singapore sucked the custard off durian seeds. They had come for a weekend of feasting, something they did twice a year, usually hitting the first night because they employed spies to report when the fruit had ripened in villages like Duriansebatang. The durians in Singapore were not as good, and so expensive that if they ate enough here they made back their airfare. But they looked too prosperous to worry about that, and I suspected they came for the same reason many men fish and hunt, more for the camaraderie than the pleasure of shooting a deer, or eating a durian.

As they ate more durians, their laughter turned loud and coarse. They waved their arms, shouted at the waiter, and insulted the whore. They were drunk on durians and, like many drunks, uncomfortable in the presence of a teetotaler. They held out the custard-covered seeds, begging me to give them a suck. The more they insisted, the more stubbornly I refused. I had read that durian and alcohol were a lethal combination, so I used that excuse.

"Finish your beer, then durian!" one shouted. He kept swiveling his head, checking the level in my glass.

"Oh, all right, give me a durian," I said.

"Your first durian?" he asked, presenting two large seeds.

"Yes [dammit], my first," I said, smiling. Conversation stopped. They turned to watch.

I scraped custard off the largest seed with my teeth. It tasted just the way it smelled: nauseating, a garlic pudding spiked with sewage. As I was forcing a smile, it delivered its famous aftertaste: the seductive sweetness of a liqueur. But which one? And was the pain of the foretaste worth this reward? I sucked another seed, but I could not place it. Sherry? Licorice? I ate two more. The contrast was everything. First sour, then sweet; the pain, the reward. As I was deciding the durian was not worth it—better to eat a dish of ice cream—the hiccups began, loud and violent. I reached for the nearest liquid, beer. The Chinese looked disgusted. One said, "You must never mix beer and durian." He was right. I was up all night, belching, feeling uncomfortably full, and discovering that durian leaves a putrid halitosis that, unlike most bad breath, you can smell on yourself.

I woke with a durian hangover and went to the post office to check for mail. So few travelers passed through Pontianak that the Chinese clerk could hold the entire poste restante in his fist. I had my own fistful of dog-eared letters that I had carried through South America and Africa. They included a letter from the bishop of Boga, Zaïre, giving directions to his church; an introduction to a diamond trader in central Africa; and a letter from my parish priest saying I was interested in the work of foreign missionaries. I pinned great hopes on a letter from a Mr. Frizzell, field services manager of the Mission Aviation Fellowship (MAF) of Redlands, California, suggesting the names of MAF pilots I might contact along the equator and concluding, "Each of these gentlemen . . . may possibly be able to provide some transportation as needed to areas that might be of interest for your research. If you fail to get a timely response from any of these gentlemen . . . please don't hesitate to write to me and I'll see what I can do for you."

I came to think of this letter as an airline ticket to the interior. The MAF is a fundamentalist Protestant organization whose main work is transporting personnel and supplies to and from remote mission stations. Its fleet of a hundred light aircraft and helicopters transports government officials, airlifts medical emergencies, and brings relief supplies to disaster zones. My letter named a pilot in Pontianak who, I hoped, would drop me at a mission station near the equator.

The MAF office was papered with maps and crackling with radio static. The pilot, John Hook, was a laconic young man who returned my precious letter without reading it, saying he would happily take me anywhere he was going provided I paid a modest "seat charge" to offset fuel costs. My eyes followed the equator across his map of Borneo, searching for nearby missions. "The only problem," he continued, "is we're out of fuel, and I haven't been anywhere in six days."

But Indonesia was swimming in petroleum. How could there be a shortage?

"The Avigas for our Cessnas is not refined here. It's the second time in three months this has happened, and we've had to cancel all our conferences and services, although I've saved some fuel for medical emergencies." Tomorrow he was returning a family who had been on leave and bringing out a sick missionary, but these flights were full in both directions. He was deciding whether to use some precious fuel to fly to the mission hospital at Serukam. The hospital's administrator, Grey Phillips, was coming from Jakarta tomorrow, bringing ice cream for a Fourth of July celebration. Missionaries and their families had gathered from across western Borneo, some traveling long distances, and they would be disappointed without their ice cream.

Serukam was in the interior, across the equator and sixty miles northeast from Pontianak. Hook himself was based at the hospital there and was in Pontianak only to replace a pilot who had returned to the United States for emergency leave. Usually he flew a helicopter, transporting medical emergencies from the interior to Serukam. But while he was on vacation, the other pilot had crashed it. "Helicopters are more my thing," he said, explaining he had piloted one in Vietnam. I should have asked, So tell me how a Vietnam helicopter pilot ends up flying helicopters a few hundred miles south of Saigon and over identical jungle landscape? But I feared that if I hurried this question I would only hear, "It was the Lord's will." I was about to ease into it when his radio exploded with staccato messages and he said, "Come to the airport at nine tomorrow and I'll take you to Serukam. I just can't disappoint all those kids waiting for ice cream."

The MAF hangar was a hundred yards beyond the small Pontianak terminal. While waiting for Grey Phillips and the ice cream to arrive from Jakarta, I asked Hook how long he had lived in Borneo. He said, "About eleven years [meaning he had come directly from Vietnam], and during that time this place has really changed — lots of land cleared for timber and paddies. You can see it from the air. The topsoil is washing out, turning the rivers chocolate. The weather has changed too — hotter everywhere, and the wet seasons are shrinking." They were almost the same words I had heard from Mike Corser, in South America, and Father Gustaaf, in Africa: an equatorial refrain. "But the biggest changes are in Pontianak itself," he said. "Ten years ago everyone traveled by foot or bicycle, and goods moved on the canals. In the entire city there were scarcely a dozen motorized vehicles, mostly old sedans left by the Dutch, and two places to buy electrical equipment. Now we have dozens of stores selling televisions, even computers."

The plane from Jakarta brought Grey Phillips, his ice cream, and a missionary couple with two teen-age daughters. The parents were returning to their remote station on the Kapuas; the girls were coming for a summer visit. Not knowing about the fuel shortage, they had brought crates of special food, books, and records, anything to make their daughters' long visit enjoyable — which, from the bored expression of the younger girl, a blonde, would be utterly impossible.

They were sturdy, handsome girls of beauty-queen quality. The brunette was helpful, joining her parents in weighing and sorting the luggage and deciding what to abandon in Pontianak. The blonde was in agony. She sat on a box of rejected provisions, legs crossed, her back arched like a *Playboy* model. She chewed gum listlessly, yanked the earphones of her Walkman down around her neck—even that bored her—and stared across the shimmering runway at a hedge of jungle. The damp heat had blurred it to a watercolor green. A drop of mascara ran down her cheek, perspiration or a tear. I asked two stupid questions; she answered with sighs. I left her alone and she pulled out a crumpled air letter. It had an American postmark and the cramped handwriting of a teen-age boy. She read slowly, bending over as if savoring the aroma of a nourishing soup.

Sensing her despair, her father announced he would stay in Pontianak, perhaps catching a flight on one of the single-engine planes of DAS, a local air service (although since they too were affected by the Avigas shortage, he might be stuck here several days). He weighed almost two hundred pounds, so they could carry more food in his place. He announced this while hovering over his daughter, waiting for her to protest or to show pleasure that now she could bring these records or that box of peanut butter. But she never looked up from her letter, or missed a chew of her gum.

Hook decided to take us to Serukam first, returning later for this family. His wife and small children crammed themselves into the plane with me. They were returning home after two weeks in Pontianak. "We almost didn't make it," she said. "Last night we ate ice cream in one of those new American-style parlors, and we've been throwing up ever since."

As we climbed over a traffic circle surrounding a park on the city's northern border, Hook dipped the plane like an amusement-park ride. "That's the equator," his wife said with a thin laugh. He turned around, smiling and pointing down. "Lots of people believe they're feeling the equator," she said. "They even take pictures. Last month we bumped it so hard the fellow threw up. But John can't resist. I dunno . . . guess that's how we have our fun out here."

It was an instructive flight. First I saw the city's lumber mills and rubber warehouses, then logging roads fanning into the jungle like a delta, bulging at river landings and exploding into Rorschach blots of cleared land. I picked out a pelican, a boomerang, a dove of peace, and a hula dancer, all brown because the ground was covered with the trunks of what loggers call garbage trees.

Thirty miles inland, peat and mangrove swamp changed to hilly jungle splotched with brown bald spots, like the coat of a diseased dog. The spots were cleared land belonging to new immigrants and Borneo tribesmen. There are 200 different tribes in Borneo, but their members share certain cultural and agricultural practices and a common appearance, most being light-skinned with slanted eyes and high cheekbones. Outsiders call them all Dayaks, a term they never use themselves. Their dry-rice farming requires cutting, burning, and planting land every seven to ten years. Recently their population has exploded, and this splotchy landscape is the result.

Scattered between the Dayak plots, in valleys and along rivers, were the more geometrical farms of pioneers from the overpopulated islands of Java and Bali. Actually, "pioneer" hardly describes people selected by a government agency and restricted to couples between twenty and forty years old who are given free tools, land, seed, and transportation to the frontier, all underwritten by the World Bank or another international organization. The newer settlements are what you might expect of a World Bank pioneer village: identical tin-roofed bungalows, perfectly spaced and laid out in suburban-development curves. The only resemblance to the pioneers who settled the American West is that, like a wagon train under attack, their green paddies were circled by the brown slash-and-burn farms of the Dayaks.

The Indonesian transmigration program is controversial. Its critics, mostly European, charge that the land rights of tribal peoples on Sumatra and Borneo are being abused; that tropical jungle is an unsuitable frontier; that the best land has already been cultivated by indigenous people; that new migrants clear marginal acreage that can never support them, leading to deforestation and erosion; that it is wasteful to spend eight thousand dollars to settle a family making only a few hundred; that the few millions of people shifted from the crowded inner islands to underpopulated outer islands is insignificant, not even a year's increase in population; and that the program is a pretext for "Javanizing" and "Islamacizing" all of Indonesia. In a report published in London by the *Ecologist* magazine, critics said that transmigration had become associated with "such a catalogue of human and environmental abuse that the continued support provided to the program by the Western nations seems almost incomprehensible."

I met several Europeans and Indonesians working in the transmigration program who endorsed these criticisms. A Mennonite couple who helped new migrants adjust believed the program's impetus was more political than demographic, an attempt to colonize strategic rivers and borders with Javanese loyal to Jakarta. Where they worked, in the Lake Posso region of Sulewesi, the program called for settling a hundred thousand families a year for the next five years. They admitted the effect on the land and local communities was mostly negative, but the new migrants were human, and they had needs. How could these be ignored? An Australian consultant with a map of transmigration settlements on his wall told me, "The good land is along the riverbanks. There the migrants are successful; elsewhere the land is eroded, logged out, terrible. Their crops fail or wild pigs trample them. The roads to market are poor, and eventually they leave for the coast." They sounded like the pioneers Mr. Stirn had sent to French Guiana, the ones who turned up owning boutiques in Cayenne.

Outside Pontianak, I visited the transmigration camp of Rasaujaya, where the first wave of transmigrants had cleared the tropical forest, quickly exhausting the soil. Now they commuted to work in Pontianak's sawmills. There were cafés and stores, a van service to the city, and a population of fifteen thousand. Rasaujaya had become a suburban village circled by eroded fields. One settler told me many became homesick for Java and left, but now the village was attracting transmigrants fleeing newer pioneer villages in the interior. "This town has grown up," he said. And it had, but not into what its planners had imagined.

Despite all this, I wondered if Europeans had any business criticizing Indonesia for its transmigration program. After all, it was the Dutch who started transmigration, under the slogan Colonisation of the Outer Islands. They admitted it was to provide labor for outer-island plantations and alleviate population pressure on Java. And Dutch colonial policy was responsible for Java being so desperately overpopulated, a place where 65 percent of Indonesia's population lives on 7 percent of its land. In the early nineteenth century they introduced the notorious "cultivation system," levying a tax on Javanese land that had to be paid in labor or use of a peasant's land, thus encouraging the cultivation of cash crops like coffee, tea, sugar, copra, and rubber. Java became an enormous Dutch plantation, with Javanese peasants working as virtual slaves. The cultivation system's demand for native labor and cash crops triggered an explosive growth in the island's population. So if Indonesians are touchy about European criticisms of transmigration, it may be because they see citizens of the former colonial powers criticizing them for continuing a colonial solution to a problem that was itself the creation of a cruel colonial policy.

The Serukam mission station sat in a hollow bordering a range of jagged mountains. A grass landing strip climbed the slope of a hill, its angle designed to slow a plane's momentum. We circled once and made an approach through a slot in the mountains. I had seen enough newsclips of Vietnam to have this landscape remind me of it. I complimented Hook on the tricky landing and he said, "Yeah, but I'm really more of a helicopter man."

Grey Phillips showed me the hospital, a series of wooden buildings cooled by fans and louvered windows. The simplicity and the sensible construction echoed Lambaréné. The director was an American doctor named Wendell Geary. He had come in 1964, finding a clinic run by an elderly Dutchman and decorated with jars of decayed teeth yanked from the mouths of suffering Dayaks. Now Serukam had X-ray machines, incubators for premature infants, a pharmacy, three operating theaters, a staff of ten doctors, and a school to train Indonesian nurses. I thought its most impressive sight was a room stuffed with pink files detailing the treatment of the hospital's previous patients. At last count there were 108,520 files, and Grey Phillips was proud that when Dayaks from remote villages revisited the hospital, the doctors knew their medical histories in an instant. The hospital's expansion and the new equipment had been made possible by American congregations, but patient fees paid the operating expenses. People were charged what they could pay. For Dayaks, a doctor's appointment might cost fifty cents, and a bed in a ward, a dollar a night. The wealthy Chinese who came from Pontianak and Jakarta paid more.

Young men with legs in traction filled the wards. "Aside from tuberculosis, this is our most common medical problem," Phillips said. "There's an epidemic of broken legs every durian season.

They get impatient waiting for the fruit to fall, so they climb the trees. The others break their legs in motorbike accidents. We figure anyone who can afford a motorbike can afford a dollar to lie in our ward and recover."

This common-sense approach to charity surprised me. Since Serukam was under the aegis of the Conservative Baptist Mission Society of Wheaton, Illinois, I had expected hourly prayer sessions and hymn singing in the wards, with patient care restricted to converts, and so on. This was ridiculous, but the prejudices held by traditional Christians against fundamentalist missionaries are often as deep as the faith of the missionaries themselves. I can remember arriving in Niger during the famine to be told of missionaries in the interior insisting that Muslim tribesmen sing hymns and pray before receiving rations of millet. The truth was that one eccentric man did this; the other missionaries gave food to whoever appeared and, when that ran out, opened their family larders and sold their possessions in local markets to buy grain. But still I studied Serukam with a critical eye, searching for aggressive proselytizing and "cultural imperialism."

Grey Phillips was an unlikely villain, the kind of large, enthusiastic man you find playing scoutmaster. I believed him when, during lunch in his bungalow, he said, "All we want is to give good care and train good Christian doctors. Already seven of our ten physicians are Indonesian, and we know the Indonesians will eventually replace us. That's fine with me. I don't want to stay here until I die." In the meantime, he was building a hydroelectric plant on a mountain river and erecting pylons to carry power directly to the hospital, enabling it to scrap the expensive generators. "When Indonesianization is completed," he said, "we'll leave behind a self-sufficient hospital." And I believed him when, anticipating the usual criticisms, he raised his voice, saying, "We're accused of ruining the Dayak culture, but we don't care if they live in longhouses [the traditional long Dayak dwellings that are home to several dozen families], short houses, or big houses. It's the government that's discouraging the longhouses because they're unhealthy and spread tuberculosis. From a physical standpoint, the main effect of us converting a village is that it gets cleaner."

Remembering that room stuffed with pink Dayak medical files, I asked if keeping so many Dayaks alive wasn't really the biggest physical change. "Sure it is! We've stopped the measles epidemics that wiped out whole villages. And as families get healthier, they get bigger and need more land, a lot more. The government tries to encourage them to cultivate paddies, but so far most Dayak won't be persuaded. They can't suddenly change to paddies. It's not a choice for them. Slash-and-burn cultivation is at the center of their culture, in their souls. They used to leave land fallow for seven to ten years, but nowadays they burn it sooner, so their yields are lower and the following year they need still more land. Around here they're pushing up the sides of mountains, spilling into new territory, and there's almost no virgin forest left.

"I've agonized over this, believe me I have. How can we refuse to cure a sick individual or vaccinate against epidemics? But how can we ignore the long-term ecological problems caused by our work? I don't know. I worry about our hydroelectric project too. It will supply nearby villages with cheap power, much cheaper than their kerosene stoves. But what are the long-term consequences? Is it the right thing to do? I wish I knew."

During the Fourth of July festivities — the softball game, the hot-dog cookout, and swimming in a shady pool — I asked the missionaries what changes they had noticed since arriving. A physician's wife remembered a Dayak woman saying, "We can say one thing about you people: Since you came, there sure are a lot more of us!" Others remarked on the hot seasons becoming longer and drier, the wet seasons less rainy, the breeze less refreshing. One woman said, "When we came, in 1971, it rained almost every afternoon at three o'clock. Right now it hasn't rained for two weeks." So there it was: These missionaries sat baking in a valley that was becoming drier and hotter because of their own good works. Their hospital had increased the number of people, who then cleared more land, raising the temperature. From the air, Serukam appeared to be in a lush jungle clearing, but when I landed I saw that branches were brittle and roads dusty. The afternoon heat was so oppressive it slowed time: Insects hung in the thick air, and the towheaded missionary children ran in slow motion. I checked my watch after what seemed like an hour to find only fifteen minutes had passed. I began to understand the despair of that blond missionary daughter. She really *was* going up the Kapuas for an eternity of a summer.

The missionaries regarded the heat as a challenge, schedul-
ing their Fourth of July race for mid-afternoon and setting the
finish line at the top of a mountain. They swore it was a short
course, only a mile and a half, but it felt like four times that, all up
a steep road with several hairpins. I did not win but they gave me
a prize anyway, a T-shirt saying Happy Trails, in Indonesian.

From the finish line I walked along a jungle path with Wendell Geary, who, like many fundamentalist missionaries, was as
good a man as he was uncomplicated. We climbed through thick-
ets of bamboo, rubber trees oozing latex, and wild-pig traps only
recently abandoned. "Most wildlife left this range four years ago,"
he said. "The monkeys have fled one more range inland, and
there are no more pigs to trap. It's supposed to be a preserve
here, and the government does its best, even putting up signs. But
the Dayaks say it's always been their land, so they tear them
down."

We stood in a clearing, admiring a corridor of jungle cleared
for the hydroelectric cables. Distant hills were a patchwork of
black, brown, and shades of green, showing Dayak rice cultivation
in its different stages. But not all the wildlife had left this ridge. As
we left, a large serpent slipped across the path, disappearing so
fast I had no time to be scared. Geary was amazed. In twenty
years this was the first snake he had seen in the wild. He thought
it was due to this land being so recently cleared. Sunnier, more
open secondary jungle attracts snakes.

I drove back to the coast with a missionary couple who, fearing they had said too much, afterwards made me promise not to
use their names. So I will call them David and Hazel. If I had
been alone in one of the communal taxi vans, with no one speaking English, I would have had a different trip, seeing an unre-
markable landscape of rice paddies and trading villages,
sharecropper shacks and women walking under banana-leaf par-
asols. I would have assumed that the white monument we passed
commemorated another heroic battle against the Dutch, and I
would never have dreamed that whether you carried a basket of
onions on your head or your back could be a matter of life and
death.

David and Hazel knew better. They explained that the village
of perfectly spaced bungalows we passed was a military retirement village for soldiers who had married local women; that the

school around the next bend was an elite Catholic academy training Dayaks for positions in the bureaucracy; that those hills hid an overgrown Dutch hill station; that the caged bear outside this army barracks symbolized the famous Black Bear Division; and that "this hill is a terrifying place, where the drive shaft fell off our jeep in 1967."

"I'll never forget that night." Hazel shuddered. "It was rainy and dark, and we were driving without headlights in the mission's jeep, towing a trailer filled with terrified Chinese. Everywhere gangs of Dayaks were murdering them, and we had just crept through a village and seen the bodies of Chinese traders."

"Then the drive shaft went and we had to stop," David said. "The Chinese were frantic to quiet their children, and the Chinese truck driver vomited from fear. If the Dayaks had found us, they would have massacred us all. We were afraid to turn on the headlights, so we fixed it by candlelight. The funny thing was that twenty miles later we pulled into Singkawang to see all the markets open, lights burning, and the streets full of Chinese. It's a Chinese city, so they were safe there, but ten miles inland the Dayaks were killing them by the hundreds."

Here was another tropical massacre I had missed. I follow foreign news and once took courses in Southeast Asian history, yet it came as a surprise that West Borneo had experienced communal massacres matching the ferocity, although not the numbers, of the more notorious ones of Indonesia in 1965 or post-independence India. When I returned home, I searched newspaper archives for mention of them, finding only a brief Reuters dispatch describing thirty thousand Chinese driven from their homes by Dayaks who were "scouring the jungle with long knives and home-made muzzle-loaders." It said, "Whipped to a fury by kidnappings and murders by Chinese guerrillas, primitive Dyak [sic] tribesmen have struck back with beheadings, cannibalism and plunder that has brought ruin to the Chinese population over a wide area. The killings are continuing."

Before this, Chinese traders and farmers had lived in peace among the Dayaks of West Borneo, escaping the attacks and the discrimination that have plagued Chinese minorities on other Indonesian islands. The Dayaks sold the Chinese rice and rubber, and the Chinese sold the Dayaks food to carry them between harvests. This relationship was disturbed by two European political ideologies, nationalism and communism. In the early sixties, the government of President Sukarno had trained Chinese guerrilla units here, encouraging them in a border war against Malaysian Borneo. After the 1965 coup, the left-wing Sukarno was replaced by the rightist, anti-Communist Suharto government, which made peace with Malaysia. How many of Sukarno's Chinese guerrillas were Communist, or simply pro-Sukarno and anti-Malaysia, can be disputed. But after 1965 they were men without a country, hunted on both sides of the border. By 1967, a thousand survivors had become bandits, preying on nearby Dayaks. When the government press agency announced that forty armed Chinese had landed by sea to assist these remnants of Sukarno's guerrilla army, Dayak bands set out to hunt down the invaders. They were soon killing the rural Chinese and seizing their land and possessions. In the end, according to Hazel and David, the massacres left the Dayaks bewildered and sad. One Dayak brought the severed head of his Chinese neighbor to the hospital at Serukam, demanding the murderer be brought to justice, then breaking down and admitting having done it himself. Dayaks killed Chinese neighbors for their sewing machines, then burst into tears of remorse. "The Dayaks could not explain why they did it," Hazel said. "And for several years they had guilty consciences. 'Oh, how we miss our Chinese neighbors,' they said."

One does not think of massacres having ecological consequences, but this one did. Rats ravaged the abandoned Chinese paddies, and locusts attacked the Dayaks' plots. The killings changed the appearance of West Borneo. There were fewer rice paddies in the valleys, and the jungle mountains behind the hospital soon turned into a Dayak patchwork of light green and brown. A few Chinese returned, settling near the road, their emergency exit to Singkawang, and becoming spectators to conflicts between the Dayaks and the Madurese.

If I were a Dayak, I would treat the Madurese with care. They are a short, swarthy people from an overpopulated, infertile limestone island, and they are known to be hot-tempered, land-hungry, and skillful with sharp knives. Their wars with the Dayaks involved land. The Madurese grow wet rice, the Dayaks dry, and Madurese immigrants cultivated land that the Dayak, like most tribal peoples, owned through custom rather than law. If I had not traveled with the missionaries, I would not have noticed two peoples sharing this region. But David and Hazel knew each settlement. "That's a Dayak village, this is Madurese," they said, recounting the atrocities occurring in each during the past fifteen years. The government had built a roadside monument to commemorate what was hoped would be a permanent truce. It had white columns and a bronze freize depicting Madurese and Dayaks holding hands. Since its dedication, there had been two uprisings marked by torture and cannibalism.

But, outside their home villages, how did these people tell one another apart? They looked identical: stocky and dark, although the Dayaks have a steeper slant to their eyes and cheeks. Did they have the same infallible eye as the Lebanese or the Irish, knowing at a glance whom to murder? "They know because of the baskets," Hazel said. "The Dayaks women strap baskets to their backs; the Madurese carry them on their heads."

Singkawang was a sepia-toned Chinese town of bicycles, shuttered arcades, and red temples puffing smoke like dragons. It resembled photographs of Singapore or Hong Kong before the war. It was Sunday, and only the gold merchants were open, so I decided to continue by van down the coast to Pontianak, crossing back into the southern hemisphere and seeing the equator I had flown across with John Hook.

The equator came after sunset, surprising me. From the air, it appeared to be at the northern edge of Pontianak, and I had been watching the mileposts, not expecting to see it for one or two kilometers. Instead, at eleven kilometers we sped past a thin pillar crowned by a gyroscope globe. But then, ten kilometers later, came an even more elaborate equator, the one I had seen from the plane, a spotlighted globe balanced on a tall pedestal and surrounded by a traffic circle. There were benches and strolling families. Men sold grilled meats and candy. The setting was like Macapá, but the conflict was Mbandaka all over again: two equators.

During my absence, Pontianak's durian fever had slackened and its first supermarket had opened. It sold sugared breakfast foods, fruit tarts you cooked in a toaster, and other American junk food. Boys packed a video arcade nearby, and in an empty lot facing a river busy with sampans a merchant sold satellite dishes. His sign said, Space Tech TV Satellites. Other English signs advertised language schools: Regents English Course and Oxford Language Schools. I went to one hoping to hire a translator to accompany me back to the two equators. The schools were empty, but outside one I ran into young Gunwan. He was hugging a cannister of the imitation potato chips that are sold in a vacuum tube. He said they cost three dollars. He had just bought his first motor scooter, and his father was a banker. I offered him a job as interpreter. "Sure, why not?" he said, stuffing more imitation potato chips in his mouth. But the next morning he failed to appear, forcing me to call on Mr. Mustam.

After Mr. Mandoukou, I had been avoiding functionaries, but in Jakarta, a friend of a friend offered Mr. Mustam's address, describing him as speaking English and working for a government agency that provided social services to the transmigrants. He was a Dayak—and probably a bright one, to have made it to this government office—but I cannot say for sure, because his English was mostly short declarative sentences followed by apologetic smiles. He was my age, and for all I knew he had put away his share of Chinese and Madurese, but like everyone speaking a foreign language poorly, he compensated by being excessively smiley and eager to please. This was probably how I had come across in Brazil, with my nursery-school Portuguese.

"I am Dayak," he said. "Five thousand Dayaks in Pontianak." That was not many in a city of a quarter-million inhabitants.

"I like to study." This was Mr. Mustam's explanation for how he came to be a functionary instead of a slash-and-burn rice farmer. There was an interesting story here, but I was not going to learn it.

"I like Egypt!" Mr. Mustam had misunderstood one of my questions, but I asked him why anyway. "Because it stands up to Israel." Mr. Mustam's studying had ended in the mid-seventies.

"I like to go New York." He searched my face for more than polite interest, perhaps sponsorship of a visa application. I was now handling this line of questioning by saying that I myself was thinking of moving to Kenya, or Uganda, or Indonesia.

Unsettled by this response, or what he understood of it, he said, "I like Pontianak."

"Why, Mr. Mustam?" I asked.

"Because it is peaceful!"

Peaceful? With the farting vans, chugging boats, and music blaring from electronics stores? It had been peaceful in Serukam and along the road to Singkawang; it looked peaceful in the Dayak villages. "Mr. Mustam, are you sure you mean peaceful?"

"Peaceful!"

Maybe I was confusing quiet and peace. After all, in Pontianak, there were no Dayak-Chinese wars, no Madurese feuds, so from Mr. Mustam's perspective it was indeed peaceful.

We hired a taxi and drove across the new estuary bridge to what he insisted was Pontianak's only equator. It was the second and larger of the two. Two black columns supported a gyroscope globe made from two metal rings, one perforated with EUENAAR, Dutch for "equator." The Dutch had erected this Art Deco equator in 1936, and the municipality had just completed a program of improvements to honor its fiftieth anniversary. Four new marble blocks surrounded the base, each holding a spotlight that illuminated the equator at night, and an iron fence kept visitors at a distance, as if Pontianak's equator were an over-touristed attraction.

"OK. Let's go to that other equator," I said. Mr. Mustam and the taxi driver swore there was only one equator in Pontianak, but I insisted there were two. We drove north, with the driver calling out every milestone and turning around with raised eyebrows. The second equator appeared at eleven kilometers. It was taller than its competitor, a single concrete pillar topped by a replica of the gyroscope, but made of an inferior metal that had already rusted. Carved into the concrete base were the names of its builders and its date of completion, nineteen days before the improvements to the other monument. Across the street was the type of village I had seen by the hundreds, a line of wooden stores roofed in tin, with scuffed paths fanning out to shanties buried in foliage. In one store I met Mr. Idress, a member of the committee that had erected the second monument.

"That garden gives our equator a fine quality, don't you agree?" he asked. I agreed. There were thatched umbrellas for shade, benches, and a garden, and, unlike the other equator, it was open to the public.

"All built by our community," he said. "Everyone worked, even schoolchildren and university students. We merchants paid the money."

"But, Mr. Idress, down the road is that other *katistiwa*."

"That is certainly true," he said, smiling but offering no explanation.

"But there can't be two *katistiwas* . . ."

"If the government says the other is the true *katistiwa*, then it must be so." Mr. Idress sensed that Mr. Mustam was a functionary.

"But you have built your own equator here."

"Yes, that too is true . . ."

"Do some people think this the real equator?"

He nodded emphatically, and Mr. Mustam translated. "Yes, yes, there certainly are such people. Although we did not build our equator to compete, but to honor the other equator."

"But you finished yours first, beating the other by three weeks."

Mr. Idress laughed. "We worked very hard, and very fast. We are proud of living on the equator."

I almost said, But, Mr. Idress, you don't. And then I remembered that this really was a village that can be found by the tens of thousands — except for its equator.

Aside from that open drain in Kinshasa, I had been healthy, but in Indonesia my luck ran out. I had assumed that a spicy taco or a Bombay curry had prepared me for Minang cuisine. It had not. At a restaurant in Bukittinggi, each of the seven plates contained a dish more fiery than the one before. If chilies can burn the stomach, then this is what happened to me, and afterwards almost everything I ate, except eggs and toast, was rejected, one way or the other. Next, I developed a heat rash on my groin and arms, then a heavy cold and fever. I might have managed two of these ailments, but three at the same time defeated me. I stayed in a hotel room for two days and came out feeling worse. The sun was too bright and my dark glasses never dark enough. My throat became sore, I avoided conversation, and my notebooks suffered.

Borneo has 600 miles of equator, all within the Indonesian portion of the island. Except for river settlements, the interior is virtually empty, and crossing it from east to west is the work of several months. I had no choice but to fly southeast to Balikpapan and take the coastal road north to the equator. An earlier petroleum boom had tripled Balikpapan's population in fifteen years, briefly giving its people an income three times the national average and leaving it with stores selling cowboy boots, a Kentucky Fried Chicken outlet, dust devils swirling through abandoned construction sites, and small glass buildings like the ones Union Metals hoped to push on Gabon. Empty plastic water bottles floated in flooded ditches and sewers like dead fish, white and belly up, proof that Balikpapan's growth had outpaced its municipal services. People had converted their sudden prosperity into the two things that most quickly transform any city or culture: television and motorized transport. They wanted these pleasures fast, before clinics, sidewalks, and clean water, before improving their homes or public spaces. One hears that education and helping relatives are a priority for the newly wealthy in these countries, but my eyes tell me that easy entertainment and fast transportation usually come first.

I left Balikpapan after a few hours, taking a small bus north to Samarinda. For most of the way the road ran inland, through land scorched by forest fires. In 1983, the largest and longest-burning fire in recorded history destroyed 13,500 square miles of rain forest in an area of eastern Borneo stretching from the coastal swamps west to the inland rain forests and north to the equator. Peat bog and layers of dead leaves kept the fires burning for five months. Species as yet undiscovered became extinct, and countless mammals, birds, insects, trees, and plants perished. Indonesia lost billions in marketable timber, and villages lay under a pall of smoke for months. Fire lines licked at Balikpapan, and plumes of smoke closed its airport and drifted north to interrupt service at Singapore. Rain extinguished the blazes, but four years later seams of coal were still smoking along the road to Samarinda. But I was so feverish and sick I slept most of the way, missing this natural wonder.

Samarinda is a filthy old river port forty miles south of the equator. Its principal business is lumber, and all day rafts of logs float past its mills and warehouses, down a river becoming browner every year with soil runoff from new timber concessions. It is a stagnant place, with canals of fetid water and houses built on stilts over swamps. Even had I been healthier, I would not have liked it much, but I might have had the energy to escape by traveling further up the Markham River toward the equator. As it was, I found a hotel with air conditioning, where I only became more sick and restless. I took a motorbike taxi to the dock to inquire about riverboats, and for half an hour I bumped over Samarinda's bad roads, hugging the damp shirt of my "chauffeur" while trucks puffed exhaust in my face.

I tracked down an Australian expatriate who had lived through the fires. "Upriver, in my village, we lived under a cloud of smoke for three months," he said. "Soot covered our clothes, and people wet down the grasslands surrounding their houses so they wouldn't catch fire." The government had reacted slowly. There was no plan, equipment, or trained men, and, embarrassed by this, officials were now minimizing the destruction. Foreign consultants had written a damage report, but its conclusions were so gloomy it had disappeared from circulation.

In my hotel bar I met a trio of Australian prospectors out of a British comedy. "Peter" had a rugby player's square face, and "Rex" was a polished, gap-toothed man who wore a blazer with a military patch and resembled Terry-Thomas. "Alec" was a bald vulture leaving middle age. He talked nonstop and had a tricky smile, like Alastair Sim. "There are tremendous resources here, tremendous!" he said, his eyes narrowing and glittering yellow like a cat's.

The three of them had hurriedly cobbled together a mining consortium. Rex and Peter, who had been working for Australian mining companies, had joined forces and flown to Indonesia suddenly, on impulse. Friends introduced them to Alec, whose specialty was mining coal in Samarinda and lobbying functionaries in Jakarta. He spent most of the year here, returning to Australia only to visit his teen-age children. "Other than that, I make it a rule never to stray more than one point seven five degrees from the equator," he said. He had rich stories about tidal waves, Balinese rituals, and volcanic eruptions sure to bury priceless Javanese palaces. But as I was deciding into which Conrad novel to place him, he launched into a description of his health-food regime, the one followed by his teen-age children, his jogging habits, their jogging habits, and how fortunate it was that they had not, he thought, experimented with drugs.

They spoke guardedly of "resources" and "mining rights."

"Gold-mining rights?" I asked.

The word "gold" set them winking, raising eyebrows, and looking around the deserted bar. "You can bet we didn't get up at three o'clock this morning and go tramping around looking for coal, old chap," Rex said.

"The Indonesians could be out-producing South Africa by the turn of the century," Alec added. "There's a new geological technique for extracting epithermal gold. Every Australian mining company is trying to get a concession. It's our next gold rush."

"Our economy has been fucked by the buggering Socialists," Peter said, describing the newest Australian welfare scandal. Surfers were cashing in their welfare checks for cheap package holidays to Bali. One boy had enraged people like Peter by telling a reporter he was taking a holiday from surfing in Australia by surfing in Bali. "There's no opportunity in Australia any more," Peter said, "and no frontier left. This is our frontier now."

I had read in a Jakarta newspaper that sixty Australian consortia had applied for mining concessions, so many the government needed months to process them. New applications were no longer being accepted. I asked if this wouldn't pose a problem.

"Not for us it won't," Alec said. "Not if you know the right people, and how to deal with them. That's my job, smoothing things over in Jakarta." He made a planing motion with his hand.

"We're lucky to have Alec," Rex said. "You know, right now we Australians are not too popular here." Recent articles in the Australian press had accused the government of corruption on a Ferdinand Marcos scale.

"Irresponsible journalism! Monstrously unfair!" Alec boomed, ignoring the fact that if there were no corruption in Jakarta, Peter and Rex would not have needed his services. The more they talked, the more it seemed modern gold prospecting had come down to two businessmen finding an Alec to push their application to the top of the pile, although tomorrow they were setting off to inspect a promising site. The epic forest fire had, according to Alec, "made our work a hell of a lot easier. It wiped out the wildlife, but it also did in the leeches. Bloody marvelous, walking around without any leeches."

After several days in Samarinda, I was still too sick to travel north to where the equator intersected the Markham River. During the trip back to Balikpapan, I stayed awake and saw the forest-fire landscape, a First World War battlefield of churned earth, stagnant ponds, and shattered trunks. In the distance the land smoked, either from smoldering coal seams or the fires of cultivators. In places a green dusting of scrub and vine covered the ground, the start of new secondary forest that would be hotter, paler, and filled with different, more sun-loving species. Had I not known about the fire, I could easily have mistaken this for land cleared in the normal course of events. It was virtually indistinguishable from what I had seen outside Calçoene, along the Ogooué, near the immigration camp at Pontianak, and surrounding the road from Pekanbaru.

The unprecedented nine-month drought of 1982 had led to these fires. Instead of receiving over a hundred inches of rain a year, the jungles of East Borneo got almost none. Temperatures rose five degrees above normal and trees shed dry leaves, carpeting the ground with the equivalent of a layer of gasoline. The Dayak slash-and-burn fires had probably been the match, igniting blazes in several places.

The drought was the result of an unusually strong El Niño, Spanish for "the Child." This is an abnormal weather system occurring every two to seven years. Its effects are first felt off the coasts of Peru and Ecuador, around Christmas, and it causes a reversal of the patterns of winds, currents, and ocean temperatures in the Pacific. In normal years, winds blow east to west across the equatorial Pacific, from a high-pressure zone near South America to one of low pressure off Asia. Updrafts of wind near Asia cause high levels of rainfall in Indonesia. These same winds also push currents of warm water westward along the equator, causing warm water to build in the western Pacific and off the coast of the Indonesian islands. At the same time, below the ocean surface, an equatorial countercurrent brings cool water back to the coast of South America.

According to a widely held theory, El Niño is triggered by a dramatic accumulation of warm water along the equator in the central Pacific. At a certain thickness, this belt of warm water becomes so unstable that its direction can be influenced by minor and sudden wind shifts. In an El Niño year, the easterly winds falter, sometimes changing direction entirely. Influenced by these winds, the equatorial surface current also changes, now flowing west to east, from Asia to Ecuador, and a surge of warm water moves along the equator toward South America.

The weather too is reversed. Instead of monsoon rains in Asia, there is drought. Meanwhile, abnormally heavy rains fall on the coral atolls of the central Pacific and the coast of South America, bringing floods and mudslides and reducing plankton, fish, and seabird colonies. The side effects of this weather shift can include dry conditions in the Amazon, drought in Africa, and wet weather in North America, but it is across the equatorial Pacific that its effects are most severe.

So far, I had found that geography and economics caused most of the important tropical trains and highways to run north and south. To travel horizontally, parallel to the equator, was often impossible without long detours into either hemisphere. But this equatorial current was itself a kind of highway connecting Southeast Asia, the central Pacific, and South America, an equatorial highway ridden by El Niño, plankton, and the seeds of Indonesian flora that washed ashore to germinate on isolated atolls — and by the ancestors of the Micronesian people who, a thousand years before, had floated down it from Indonesia to the remote islands of the central Pacific.

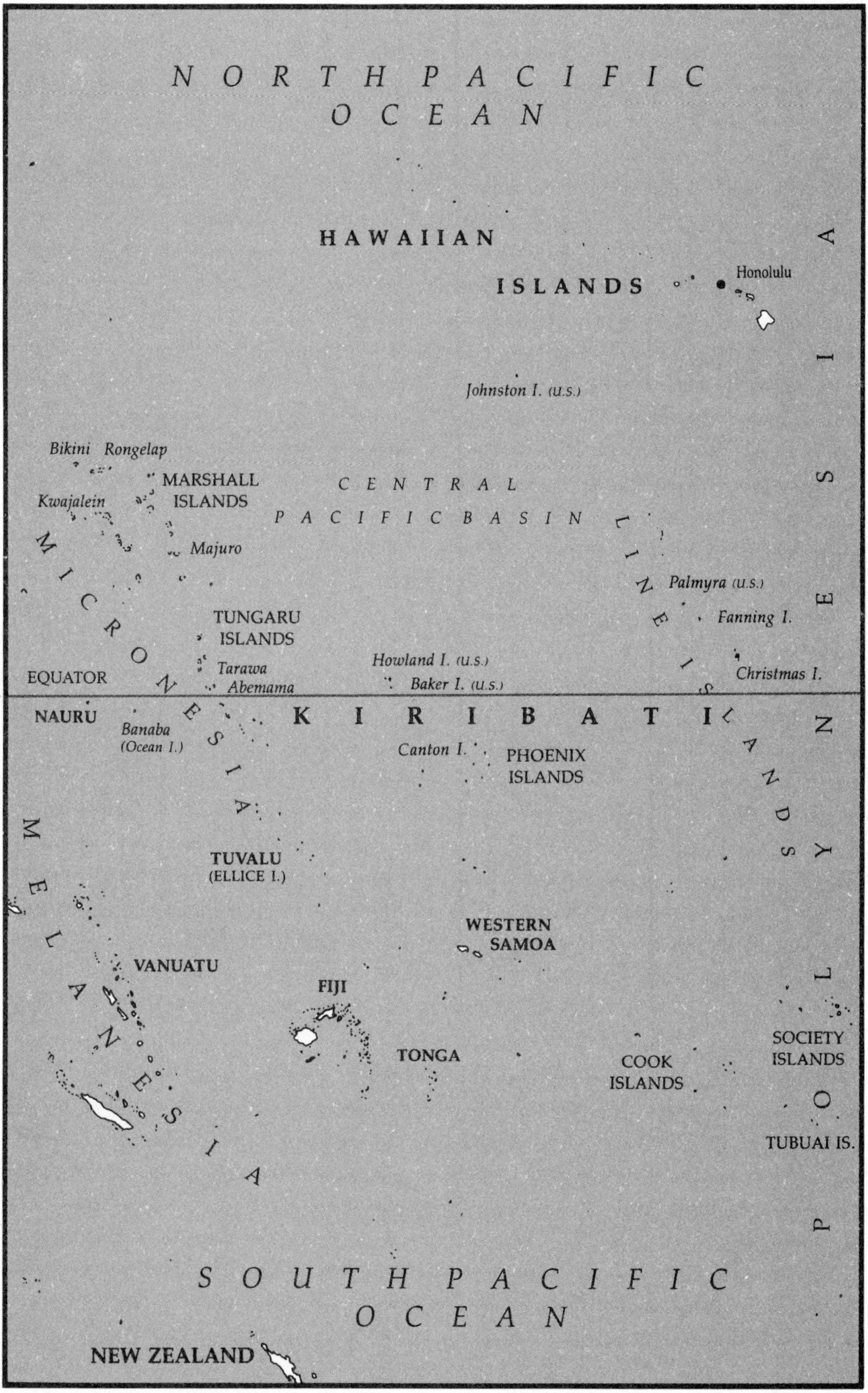
NORTH PACIFIC OCEAN
HAWAIIAN ISLANDS
Honolulu
Johnston I. (U.S.)
Bikini
Rongelap
MARSHALL ISLANDS
Kwajalein
Majuro
CENTRAL PACIFIC BASIN
MICRONESIA
LINE ISLANDS
Palmyra (U.S.)
Fanning I.
TUNGARU ISLANDS
Tarawa
Abemama
Howland I. (U.S.)
Baker I. (U.S.)
Christmas I.
EQUATOR
NAURU
KIRIBATI
Banaba (Ocean I.)
Canton I.
PHOENIX ISLANDS
POLYNESIA
TUVALU (ELLICE I.)
MELANESIA
WESTERN SAMOA
VANUATU
FIJI
TONGA
COOK ISLANDS
SOCIETY ISLANDS
TUBUAI IS.
SOUTH PACIFIC OCEAN
NEW ZEALAND

16

THERE ARE PACIFIC ATOLLS CLOSE TO THE EQUATOR, SOME uninhabited and accessible only by private yacht, others lightly populated but still difficult to reach. None is precisely on the line, so I chose two that it almost touches during its ten-thousand-mile journey from Borneo to Ecuador. I chose Christmas Island because it is one of the Line Islands, so called because the archipelago is intersected by the equator, and I chose Abemama, because it was there Robert Louis Stevenson had founded his Equator Town. He described it as a "splendid nightmare of light and heat," enjoying "a superb ocean climate, days of blinding sun and bracing wind, nights of a heavenly brightness." Its air was "like a bath of milk." Its sand sparkled at night "as with the dust of diamonds." I also liked its name, Abemama, "land of moonlight."

The journey to Abemama requires hopping down a string of islands, from Honolulu to Johnston to Majuro to Tarawa to Abemama, on increasingly smaller planes. It is a trip not unlike that inland from a tropical coast, with each river station or roadside settlement having more precarious communications and fewer amenities until finally, near the center of a continent, you reach the last town. But in this case, Honolulu was the civilized coastal port and Abemama was the last town, sitting not at the center of a continent but on the middle of the earth. Because of infrequent flights and poor connections, this journey can take a week. From Honolulu to Majuro, an atoll in the Marshall Islands, there is a jet that stops briefly on Johnston Island, where, according to an announcement as we landed, "passengers are forbidden to take pictures or leave the plane." Since Johnston is the ugliest and most lethal island on earth, these are easy rules to obey. It is mostly paved runway bordered by barracks and bunkers packed with nerve gas and chemical weapons too dangerous to be stored on any continent. There are no palms and no beach, and its "citizens" are military personnel without their families.

The four soldiers disembarking here had dressed for paradise, in shorts and Hawaiian shirts. Since Honolulu, they had been laughing and slapping palms at their good fortune, ordering Bloody Marys and jiggling to the music from their headsets. "Hey, what's that?" one shouted as we banked over Johnston. When a stewardess told them, they dropped their heads in their hands. I heard: "Oh shit, it can't be!"

"Not even one fucking palm tree."

"Sixty days, sixty fucking days. I can't believe it."

"This is not funny. This is not what they promised us in Texas."

After landing in Majuro, I had a similar reaction, although my sentence was five days rather than sixty. From the air it was gorgeous, an oval lagoon surrounded by ribbon-shaped islands thick with palms, still Stevenson's "Pearl of the Pacific." From the ground, it resembled Appalachia.

Men in baseball hats drove battered pickup trucks, listened to country music, and ate ham-and-egg meals at diners with names like The Runway and The De-light. Barefoot children walked through roadside puddles, drinking cans of Mountain Dew, and the pye-dogs were mean and followed by swarms of insects. The best houses were prefabricated boxes, the worst tar-paper-and-plywood shacks. All were jammed with large extended families clinging to a single wage-earner. The laundry hanging on their lines was gray and tattered, mostly children's sizes. People cooked, ate, and lived in their yards, defecating on the ocean reef or in outhouses built over the lagoon. They liked canned or boxed food that was packed with sugar and purchased with food stamps. Adults were obese, with a high rate of diabetes; their children looked malnourished and sickly. Tin cans, engine parts, and used diapers littered beaches and roadsides. Walls were smeared with graffiti — "hip-hop" — copied from break-dancing movies.

In Appalachia, at least some towns are ringed by green hills, and you can still find unpolluted hollows and creeks. The environment of a Pacific atoll is more fragile, and its space more limited. The soil is poor, the only useful flora are the pandanus, the breadfruit, and the coconut palm, and the only indigenous fauna, aside from the birds, is the Polynesian rat. The narrow islets enclosing a lagoon rarely rise more than twelve feet above sea level and once they are scarred by roads, covered with shanties, and divided and subdivided among families, there is simply no room for more people, more children, or more crap. There are no tropical forests, floodplains, or national parks to be cleared and settled, and once a plastic bag, a can, or a panel of tin arrives, it never leaves. There is profit in shipping crates of Australian beer or a Japanese truck to Majuro, but none in hauling tin cans or rusted trucks out again.

The main island on Majuro atoll, where you find the greatest American influence, is called, appropriately, DUD, an abbreviation for its three villages of Darrit, Uliga, and Delap (also known as Rita). It is three miles long and only a few hundred yards wide, but it has a population of twelve thousand. One hour on DUD should be enough to make any American a cautious critic of the colonial experiments of other nations. The Spanish claimed the Marshall Islands in 1886, but they made no attempt to colonize or exploit them and sold them to Germany thirteen years later. The Japanese captured them during the First World War; the United States took them from the Japanese during the second and has administered them ever since under a United Nations trusteeship. During this trusteeship, some atolls have been the sites for American nuclear tests that have poisoned their residents and left them uninhabitable. What is happening on DUD will surely have the same result, although it is taking longer to unfold.

The American trusteeship of the Marshall and other Micronesian islands has been a disaster in which liberals and conservatives, the military, and social activists, can all share the blame. Since the war, American military policy has been to ensure strategic interests in the region by keeping the Micronesians "happy," meaning well supplied with goods. It may not have been a conscious policy to make them dependent, but it has been the result. Both the Kennedy and Johnson administrations promoted a rapid expansion in government funds for Micronesia, and social-welfare programs were made available as if Micronesians lived in the South Bronx, or Appalachia. By the standards of American liberals of the sixties, people who lived in thatched huts without running water or electricity and ate fish, coconuts, taro root, and pandanus fruit were poor, and so the entire population of the Marshall Islands became eligible for free commodities that were soon arriving by the shipload. American conservatives and the military did not oppose these programs, since a population dependent on American charity was unlikely to protest American bases and missile tests. American liberals were pleased to have extended "basic human rights" to a people denied them—never mind the havoc American charity might cause to the Marshallese environment, culture, and health. There was money to ship the sugared cereals that could be purchased with food stamps, but little for curing the diabetes these foods aggravated. Of all the American priorities on the Marshalls—including keeping rights to the Kwajalein missile-testing base, keeping out Soviet influence, and keeping the Marshallese happy—the lowest seems to have been keeping the Marshallese alive.

My hotel, the Eastern Gateway, was typical of the disfigurement being visited on Micronesia. It was a half-built disaster of cracked foundations, sagging scaffolding, and rusting iron. When I arrived, only a Filipino workman pushing a wheelbarrow and a distant banging sound indicated that it was not abandoned. In the rear, I found a second Filipino hitting a hammer against a cement mixer, imitating the sound of work. Here also were the still-occupied remnants of the original hotel, a line of motel rooms and bungalows facing mounds of garbage and the lagoon. A boy in the office said he was the manager and that the hotel was full. When he found my reservation, he said the real manager was a Mr. Boogie Cool (I believe the last name was German, spelled "Kuhl"), who was off celebrating his fiftieth birthday. He was Nauruan, and this hotel was the property of the Nauru government.

I had read enough about Nauru to recognize this as bad news. It is an island nation west of Majuro whose six thousand people have the highest per capita income in the world, the result of royalties paid to mine guano. With its money, Nauru has launched an airline and a shipping company and bought foreign commercial enterprises notorious for their mismanagement. Among these is the Eastern Gateway Hotel. The boy called around and, upon learning the other hotels were full, admitted to having a spare bungalow, although it was "not suitable" for guests since it lacked an air conditioner. I told him to buy one, reasoning that for a Nauruan enterprise money would be no object. He said "Sure," and I returned an hour later to see six Filipinos hoisting an air conditioner into the wall.

I met Becky at a beach near the hotel. She had an Edvard Munch face hidden in the shadows of a huge bonnet. I asked where the best beach in DUD was, and in a thin voice she said, "I'm afraid this is it. The problem is the lagoon. It looks nice, but it's horribly polluted." Near where her sons paddled, a little girl was defecating into the water. "There's nothing for them to do but swim, so I let them, but they catch sore throats, the throw-ups, whatever . . ." She sighed. "At least they haven't gotten hepatitis yet. It's endemic here. I had it last year and I'm still recovering. My husband and I were in the Peace Corps in Africa, and even there we never saw such health problems. We'd never visited the Pacific, so when the chance came to work for Legal Services in Majuro we were excited. We imagined something . . . well, something different. No one told us the truth; no one prepared us for this . . . this *incredibly ugly island!*" As she spoke, the sky turned red and clouds rose like castles. The lagoon became a blue mirror. It was beautiful — if you stood with your back to DUD.

The people too were beautiful. The women are short and tending to fat, but their eyes are lively, their hair glistens, and

they have what teen-agers call "good personality." The men
are either Buddhas or leathery little iguanas who like wearing
tattoos and earrings and have a reputation for seamanship and
treachery, but if you look closely their earrings are often tiny
crucifixes. In 1820, the German explorer Otto von Kotzebue
wrote of his visit to the Marshall Islands, "From the first meeting it was to be concluded that we had to deal with a very
kind-hearted people." A hundred and fifty years later this was
still true.

During the four days I waited in DUD for the plane to Tarawa, I became a connoisseur of its bars. There was the Lanai,
where American functionaries perspired through games of clumsy
pool and where, at the bar one evening, a teacher said, "It's either
dengue fever or hepatitis" and fainted into a plate of canned carrots. There was the Smuggler's Cove disco, with its Christmas
lights and tinfoil walls, whores drinking beer from paper cups,
and elderly American sailors flapping their arms like chickens,
pretending to dance. There was Charlie's Club, with its 1940s,
New York–nightclub atmosphere of red banquettes, curving
leather bar, and ceiling pasted with silver stars. It was owned
by the minister of foreign affairs and offered free sashimi, a
back room of one-armed bandits, and the chance to meet DUD's
elite.

It was at Charlie's I learned that the 1979 tidal wave brought
more misery than earlier ones because of the innovation of tin
roofs. Before, people survived by lashing themselves to thatched
roofs, which floated like rafts. But the tin ones flew away like
kites.

It was there I learned that Laura village was named after
Lauren Bacall and Rita after Rita Hayworth, or Laura was for left
and Rita for right, or they were the names of wives of the wartime
American naval commanders.

I learned that the Eastern Gateway Hotel extension had been
under construction for three years, but that the Filipino laborers
were crafty rather than lazy. Knowing the hotel's completion
meant their deportation, they built just enough in which to hide,
play cards, and sleep. They took turns banging pipes and pushing
empty wheelbarrows, while working at night, under floodlights,
for local contractors at time-and-a-half. The Nauruans were too

rich to care, and the Eastern Gateway would probably be under construction forever.

I learned that Majuro was booming. Environmental and labor laws were minimal, and the local government put few restrictions on investment. The Koreans had built a dock, the British had financed a power plant, and the Taiwanese were constructing an underground communications cable. The United States and the Marshall Islands had negotiated a Compact Of Free Association, which awaited the approval of Congress. It ended the trusteeship and made the islands independent but guaranteed American military interests. It contained a fabulous tax loophole. Marshallese residing less than six months in the United States were assessed the low Marshallese tax rate of 9 percent on all American earnings, and Americans living more than six months in the Marshalls paid only 9 percent on U.S. earnings. Offshore banks were opening, and wealthy Americans were planning houses in which to park their ill and senile relatives, who could just as easily lie comatose in DUD and have their dividends taxed at only 9 percent. (A year later, the compact was ratified by Congress, but without the tax loophole.)

The Yacht Club was Majuro's best bar. It faced a sea channel at the end of Rita, beyond the roadside groceries selling Spam and Hershey's Kisses and beyond the Bahai temple, the Jehovah's Witnesses hall, and the Seventh-Day Adventist church. It had no yachts and was not a club, just a bar and restaurant overlooking the channel. There was a pool table, a jukebox with songs celebrating American truck drivers, a menu featuring pepperoni pizza, and, the first time I went there, a solitary drunk named Billy, who immediately joined me. "I have a great mystery," he said, straining to assemble his rubbery face into a serious expression. "I ask myself: Why? Why should they choose me for this great honor? Why should they make me an 'official visitor'? That is my mystery."

"For what great honor?"

"And I am only a schoolteacher, yet they are giving me a free trip to Japan. I will be at the ceremonies, a guest of honor."

Billy was a lonely, every-night drinker, and the other patrons avoided us. After much repetition and many slurred sentences, I learned he had been a schoolteacher on Rongelap in 1954, when

it was contaminated by radiation from a hydrogen-bomb test at
Bikini atoll. The American government argued that fallout from
this "Bravo" test was an accident, caused by unpredictable winds,
and immediately afterwards evacuated the islanders. Some critics
charge that the winds were easily predicted, and that the Defense
Nuclear Agency either was criminally careless or wanted guinea
pigs on whom to observe the effects of radiation poisoning. Since
1954, the Rongelap Islanders have suffered a high rate of miscar-
riages, stillbirths, and leukemia. In 1957 the U.S. government mistakenly permitted them to return home, and to gather coconuts
and pandanus fruit from the contaminated northern islands of
their chain. For decades, the Rongelap victims received neither
proper compensation nor medical attention, and the decision to
relocate them on another atoll was not made until 1985. Whatever
the original intentions or mistakes of the American officials, the
treatment of the islanders afterwards was surely an atrocity, one
made all the worse for having unfolded not in the heat of a battle,
but slowly and with deliberation. The villains, moreover, were not
terrified young soldiers but scientists, physicians, bureaucrats,
military officers, and politicians. And now I had in front of me
a witness to this horror, but one who was too drunk to make
sense.

I asked Billy if the discolorations on his face came from radiation burns. He hiccuped. I asked, "What do you remember?
Where were you during the blast?" He spoke gibberish. But, by
chance, I was skimming through a month-old local newspaper
the next morning and saw BRAVO MEMORIES RECALLED 30 YEARS
LATER. The article was an excerpt from Billy's diary. Here is
some of it, what I imagine he would have told me had he been
sober.

It was between 5:00 and 6:00 A.M. when the first flash
was noted. The lightning and its illumination did not last
long. As the lightning incident slightly faded out, a huge and
fiery sun-like object rose up in the western part of the
lagoon.

It was a sun because it was round, but it was much bigger than our sun. It was a sun for it was giving off heat, yet

its heat was far greater and much brighter, which left every islander aghast. As the terrible fireball rose above the western horizon, its upper portion erupted and a combination of particles spurted out and upward. . . . The whole atmosphere turned bloody colored. And the heat! it stung and burned our exposed skins . . .

The explosion . . . accompanied by a tornado-powered wind swept through our land, twisting coconut trees, uprooting bushes, smashing windows, and over-turned one house. My ten-year-old boy was knocked down . . .

The atmosphere engulfing the atoll had become heavily foggy. . . . At 11:30 the classes were dismissed and the students and I went out and were greeted by the powder-like particles as it [sic] began to fall on the land. It did not alarm the islanders . . . even the children were playing with it. They ran through it and they tried to catch it as if to see who could collect the most . . .

The snow-like object was continuously falling . . . [and] took effect on the islanders in a sudden and most suffering incident. An unusually irritating itching punished the islanders to a most agonizing situation . . . the kids were violently crying, scratching and more scratching; kicking, twisting and rolling . . .

The following day greeted us in a more calm and pleasant manner. The powder-like particles had been piled up about an inch or so thick. Surprisingly, it had also settled in our houses, in our water catchments, and it could be seen almost everywhere but in the lagoon. . . . I had nausea . . . and after a while the very food and water I had tried to consume were bitter. . . . Eventually all the islanders were affected with the same sickness . . .

It was near sunset when a seaplane flew over and landed in the ever calm blue lagoon of the main village . . . and within seconds three strange-looking beings jumped down. . . . [They] were clad with bright orange-colored overalls, exposing only their faces to the open air. Two of the

alien-like strangers grabbed a small machine . . . and quickly
ran up to me standing on the beach. The one with the machine asked me kindly to show them the water catchment, so
I led them to it. . . . I could only hear a series of clicking
sounds, while the other stranger was writing something in
his book as if he was taking notes in a lecture. . . . [Then]
they ran out to their boat and quickly shoved off. . . . Most of
the islanders had been gathered at the place expecting news
from the government about the situation we were in, but
without anything else . . . the plane left.

Very early in the morning of March 3rd an American
warship made its way into Rongelap's lagoon. . . . We were
told that we were moving out from our home as immediately
as possible. And we were ordered not to take anything at all
besides our body and, of course, the clothes on. Like a military invasion, the evacuation was conducted in a most dramatic and forceful nature . . .

After two days on Kwajalein, a group of military doctors
began their studying on the victims. Nausea, skin-burns, diarrhea, headaches, eye pain, hair fall-out, numbness, skin
discoloration were among common complaints . . . the children were more critical. My 10-year-old adopted son had severe burns in his body, feet, head, neck and ears I could not
help remembering those sleepless nights we had to hold him
down onto his bed as he would have jumped up and down,
scratching, rolling as though insane.

Billy's great "mystery" was that the Japanese had given him a
free trip to Hiroshima to be a guest of honor at their annual com-
memoration of the dropping of the atomic bomb in 1945. Why
they had asked him was really no mystery at all. They wanted to
connect America's wartime bombing of Hiroshima with the radiation poisoning of the Rongelap Islanders. The islanders were the
victims of a monstrous crime or a mistake, depending on whom
you believed. The Japanese were neither, but they hoped to claim
this status by joining their quite different tragedy to that of
Rongelap.

I began seeing Billy everywhere: at Charlie's Club, where he was too intoxicated to stand but had ordered three cans of beer because they were cheaper before seven; in the street, jumping from a taxi and blubbering about the nuclear explosion and his VIP trip to Japan; in the aisles of Gibson's supermarket, pushing an empty cart and dropping cans; and slumped over the Yacht Club bar, saying, "I must explain," then falling silent, his eyes filling with tears. He was as ever-present and unsettling as Death in an art film.

During my first evening at the Yacht Club, I also met Stewart, Kip, and Frank. They all worked for the Nauru shipping line, and they were all drunk. "You see before you," Stewart said in a slightly amused public-schoolboy voice, "three victims of the Idi Amin of the Pacific [he referred to the president of Nauru], and of his representative on Majuro, that bastard Boogie Cool." Stewart was the captain of the *CinPac II*, the Nauru Line freighter that had just arrived to unload copra at the processing plant. He was a boyish, curly-haired man who had signed on for one voyage while awaiting the results of his nautical pilot's examination in Sydney. Frank was the captain of the *Enna K.*, the other Nauru ship in port. He had a long poker face and wore a toupee, which must have worked because his girlfriend, Judy, was a pretty Taiwanese half his age who owned the best Chinese restaurant on DUD. Kip was third mate on the *CinPac II*, a sunblasted gnome who never stopped drinking, dancing, or changing his mind. One moment he was ready for Charlie's Club, the next he had ordered a triple Scotch and persuaded the waitress to caress his bald head. He capered, snapping his fingers like a flamenco dancer and shouting, "Let's twist, let's go to a disco, let's have double gins." He was about sixty-five.

"These Nauruans have no morals," Stewart said, laughing as if it were an endearing trait. "They have millions, but they never pay a bill. Every time the *CinPac* arrives in Melbourne, she's arrested for unpaid port fees. A sheriff comes aboard, hauls up a black flag, and sits on board until the fines are paid. Here in Majuro we can't get any fresh water because that bloody Boogie Cool owes thousands on his water bill. We can't get the stevedores to unload our copra because they haven't been paid for the last lot. And we can't get our laundry done because Boogie won't give me any money. So here we are, filthy and stranded, with a hold filled with rotting copra and—"

"And getting good and pissed every night," Kip added.

We were all stuck in Majuro, and all at the mercy of Boogie Cool. (My room, now that it was air conditioned, was suddenly needed for another guest.) This was enough for a drinking friendship. The next morning I remembered to go to Stewart's ship for lunch only because I found a crumpled paper in my pocket scribbled with "Lunch *CinPac II.*" The crew quarters resembled a women's dormitory, with Marshallese girls cooking, combing out their hair, and stringing wet underwear between bunks. I found Stewart, Kip, and Frank in the officers' lounge, already on their third beer. The clock struck twelve and Stewart said, "Well, we're supposed to be leaving now." He popped open another beer and laughed. "I saw that bloody man this morning and he ordered me to push off at noon. Said he wouldn't pay the stevedores so we could just bugger off to Tarawa. Naturally we're staying. I've been collecting quarters. We'll wash our sheets in the laundromat and wait him out. We could be here three or four days, three or four weeks, I couldn't care less. Look at old Frank. He's been here three months."

"And we haven't been paid yet either," Frank said. I asked where he had been before Majuro. "Nowhere," he said, looking surprised at the question. "Didn't you know? The *Enna K.* hasn't been out of the lagoon in two years. The crew changes every six months, but no one takes her out. We're all waiting until the president of Nauru's mother-in-law, or mother, or whoever the bloody *Enna K.* is named after, dies. Then we can scuttle her." He explained that two years before, the ship's insurance had expired while it was in Majuro. It was such a wreck no agency would renew the policy, but the Nauruans refused to scrap a vessel named for a relative of the president, at least while she was alive. So this eight-thousand-ton passenger-freighter sat in Majuro's lagoon, its lights blazing, its crew drinking, fighting, and whoring, waiting for an old woman in Nauru to expire.

We settled into a routine: drinks at Charlie's Club at five, then the Lanai, the Yacht Club, Judy's restaurant for dinner, back to the Yacht Club, and then to the Smuggler's Cove, where Kip liked to end the evening with a fight. We were often joined by

Kurt, a burly Portuguese-Hawaiian contractor who was employing the moonlighting Filipinos to build a new bank. He sometimes performed at the Yacht Club as "The Portuguese-Hawaiian Singing Cowboy."

In the locally published *Marshall Islands Guidebook,* I had read that Arno atoll, the nearest one to Majuro, was home to "the internationally famous 'love school' at Longar where young women were traditionally taught the arts of pleasing." Another book said, "The locals on Arno, still back in the macho era, have a school at Longar village to teach young Marshallese women how to be good wives. One technique involves a girl's lying in the bottom of a canoe to feel the motion of the sea—useful in lovemaking. Naturally, the graduates are in high demand." I read these passages out loud to Stewart and Kip, hoping to interest them in hiring a boat to visit the place.

Kip leered. "Perhaps they need some men to practice on."

"I certainly wouldn't mind taking a look," Stewart said.

I thought I had my charter and a way to escape Majuro for a day, but Kurt just laughed. "Everyone who comes here makes that mistake. You all imagine whole dormitories of those girls, marching to classes and raising a flag. Ha! It's just an island known for its good women. There's no school, nothing to see."

"Well, bugger that," Kip said.

"But they do learn sexual calisthenics," Kurt said, reviving interest.

"What kind of calisthenics?" Kip asked quickly. But the momentum was lost, and instead of the love island I spent the next morning with Dr. Todd Gullick, who was responsible for the health of the twenty thousand people living on the twenty-eight outer atolls that are spread over more than half-a-million square miles of ocean.

His greeting was, "Welcome to one of the unhealthiest places on earth." He was a young man, but he had already practiced medicine in Saudi Arabia, Southeast Asia, and Africa. Of all these, he believed the Marshall Islands, a trusteeship of the United States, was the most vulnerable to a serious epidemic. He worked in the Majuro hospital, in a windowless office lit mostly by the green glow of a computer screen on which he called up statistics explaining why these atolls were so lethal.

"I have children dying of gastroenteritis," he said. "But unlike other third-world countries, they die *after* they're weaned, when they're suddenly exposed to contaminated food and water. And I have typhoid." He swiveled back to his computer and his numbers. "Fifteen cases in the six months I've been here, which on a population basis is like the United States having thirty-four thousand cases, a major epidemic. But the biggest problem is diabetes. Forty percent of the people over seventeen have it, compared to"—he punched his computer—"only one percent in the United States. Eighty percent of the people in this hospital are here for complications arising out of diabetes." The reason was simple: They had embraced the sugar-packed diet introduced by the United States government.

"Then there's hepatitis. Blood tests in a sample group show that by the time they turn twenty-one, ninety-one percent of the population has contracted hep. Too many people defecate in the lagoon, and the water table is so near the surface it's polluted by fecal matter from outhouses. Water-sealed latrines for all of DUD and a good immunization program would make a bigger difference than a new hospital.

"One reason there's so much crowding on Majuro is that people move here from outer islands hoping for better medical attention, imagining that because this is an American dependency they'll find an American standard of care. Wanting your relatives, your children, the people you love to live better is a basic human emotion, and families suffer incredible hardships to be here, cramming themselves into a single plywood shack because they hope that on Majuro they will have a better chance. I know educated men with good government jobs living in houses with forty relatives camped outside. The tragic part is that by crowding onto DUD they increase the chances of an epidemic that could kill their children. And the immunization of children is a scandal. There's been no effective program for ten years. Already eight percent of the children catch whooping cough or diphtheria, and it could get worse. In Saudi Arabia I saw diphtheria take a whole generation of children in regions without immunization. That could easily happen here."

Dr. Gullick lit up his screen with more statistics. "In a cholera epidemic on the outer islands, forty percent of the under-fives would perish. If we were lucky and detected it before they started dying in big numbers, maybe we'd lose only twenty percent, or twelve hundred of the six thousand outer-island kids.

"The problem is money. There's a four-point-six-million-dollar budget for health care in the Marshalls, but most of it goes on the hospital and costly evacuations. They spend thirty-four thousand dollars to send a single stretcher case to Honolulu, yet often there's no penicillin available, and it might prevent the evacuation in the first place. They're spending twelve thousand dollars for color-coordinated trays for the new hospital, but my budget for the whole year is only fifty thousand dollars. In the United States—and don't forget this is still an American possession—two thousand dollars per capita is spent each year on medical care. On my outer islands it breaks down to five dollars and sixty-eight cents, and some of the pills I need cost a dollar apiece. When I agreed to come here, I never imagined I'd be stuck in this room, staring into this computer and presiding over a lot of deaths.

"You know, that's really all I do. I learned to fly so I could get to the outer islands fast, but there's no money for a plane. I have a boat, but gas is expensive, and if I make field trips I'm out of touch with the other atolls. Instead, I sit here diagnosing and prescribing over the radio. There are seventy clinics on the outer islands, staffed by nurses with six months' training. They just about know how to give injections, but in their communities they're presumed to be doctors. They have to treat their friends and members of their families, and watch them die. There's tremendous pressure for them to call for evacuation aircraft. There's no room for that in my budget, so I have to beg money from elsewhere. But evacuation is fairly worthless, because if they're really sick enough to be evacuated, they're usually dead or dying by the time we get them out, and if they survive the evacuation, then they probably didn't need it.

"Making a medically sound decision about an evacuation or treatment is almost impossible, because I only have six radios scattered among the clinics. I call up one of these six clinics and they contact the more remote islands over a CB. The symptoms have to be translated from Marshallese and relayed, sometimes several times, before I hear them. Last month I received a twice-relayed message about twins on a remote atoll. It said, 'Babies won't eat.' I asked for vital signs, but the second person in the radio chain didn't speak English and was no good with technical terms, so all I got back was, 'Babies won't eat.' And even to get this took a day. At the same time, another child on an atoll with better communications appeared to be seriously ill. I was sending a plane out for him, so I told the pilot to swing by and pick up the twins who wouldn't eat; otherwise, I would have left them there. It turned out the child we were evacuating was fine, but the twins were so dehydrated from dysentery their eyes had shrunk into their faces. When you pinched their skin it left a crease. One lived, but the other died immediately.

"See what I mean?" he said with a crooked smile. "About sitting here presiding over a whole lot of deaths?"

On my last day in Majuro, everyone had jammed into Boogie Cool's office. I was begging, as I did each morning, not to be thrown out of my room, an engineer from Frank's marooned *Enna K.* was screaming at the imperturbable Boogie because he had just received six months' wages in less-valuable Australian dollars instead of the American dollars promised, and Stewart was arguing for a small advance to pay the Chinese lady at the laundromat who for two days had been washing the ship's linen. Boogie listened, smiled, and answered in such a soft voice that everyone leaned forward to hear him say "No." He walked to his car, waved, tooted the horn, and drove off fast, leaving us grabbing at door handles and trotting behind, like fans following a rock star.

Stewart kicked the driveway. "Bloody man! Says he won't discuss work or money today. Seems it's his fiftieth birthday, and he's off to celebrate. I suppose it's an excuse of sorts."

I rented a car and drove to Laura, the furthest village accessible by road. It was said to be the least spoiled, with the best views and cleanest swimming. Many of the original inhabitants of DUD had moved here, fearing another tidal wave and appalled by the crowding and litter brought by immigrants from other atolls. It was a preview of what I hoped to find on Abemama. There were white picket fences, thatched cottages, and a whitewashed church. Handsome children wearing flowers in their hair sat in a circle on the church lawn, singing hymns. A hundred yards in one direction, breakers pounded a reef; on the other side, the lagoon was impossibly blue and fringed with palms and pink sand. But then I put on mask and fins, dove into the channel, and watched brilliant tropical fish weave through a tangle of beer cans, diaper boxes, and tires.

17

I FLEW SOUTH TO TARAWA ATOLL, THE CAPITAL OF KIRIBATI, ON the weekly propeller plane from Majuro. I waited to board this plane surrounded by the children of British expatriates, the youngest and most recent victims of the empire's casual acquisition of these inconvenient islands. They had flown without rest from London to San Francisco to Honolulu to Majuro, where, still clutching their heavy wool blazers with Latin mottoes, they fell asleep on one another's shoulders. The oldest girl woke to tell me, "It's rather hard, you know, coming so far for a holiday." In Tarawa, their parents met them with handshakes and reserved kisses, instead of the bear hugs they deserved.

The other passengers were missionaries, including two blond Mormon boys, an Anabaptist couple from Indiana, and Nazrullah, a young Iranian Bahai whose beautiful tropical clothes were soaked with perspiration. "I can't go home, ever," he said, glancing around nervously, as if assassins had infiltrated the Majuro airport. "The ayatollah, he kills us in bunches."

The Anabaptists planned on showing the I-Kiribati ("people of Kiribati") how to grow vegetables. He had red suspenders and Santa Claus cheeks and wanted it understood he was coming to teach, not convert. When I said growing vegetables in this sandy soil sounded ambitious, he shook his head furiously, as if doubt might rot his seed. "No! I promise you I'll have these people growing the most beautiful vegetables."

Bill had traveled from California to give free haircuts. He called himself a missionary hairdresser for a Protestant fundamentalist group, the Apostolic Church. He described it as "a church that doesn't push itself on people," then whispered that most missionaries in Tarawa stole each other's converts. "The people are so kind they join one group after another because they don't want to make anyone unhappy by saying no. That's not our way. We just hold out a helping hand, and if someone takes it, well, that's fine!" Bill's hand held a pair of scissors. "I start just giving shag cuts to church members, but the word gets around and soon everyone wants one. That gives me a chance to talk about our religion."

Kiribati's territory runs from Ocean Island to Christmas Island, and because it claims an exclusive economic zone of two hundred miles offshore, it appears on its own political maps as an irregular rectangle, floating across the center of the Pacific and containing 2,200 miles of equator, more than any nation on earth. There are three atoll groups: the Tungaru (formerly the Gilbert), the Phoenix, and the Line islands. Most of Kiribati's sixty thousand people live in the Tungaru group, with a third of them jammed onto Tarawa atoll.

The atolls of the Marshall Islands and Kiribati are geographically identical, all of them lagoons enclosed by reefs and narrow islands, and their inhabitants come from similar Micronesian stock and have been exposed to the same damaging procession of European whalers, slavers, traders, and soldiers. They were kidnapped and enslaved in South American mines, their copra and phosphates were exported at bargain prices, and their islands were turned into battlefields and nuclear-test zones. Colonialism was a far worse bargain for them than for most Asians or Africans, yet there are few places where a traveler finds more hospitality and trust.

Like Majuro, Tarawa suffers from overcrowding and pollution, yet it is vastly different in appearance and atmosphere. Despite local complaints over materialism and loss of traditional values, it is by comparison a paradise of thatched roofs and palm trees. This may be because the nineteenth-century Gilbertese were more ferocious, often murdering Europeans who landed on their atolls, or because Tarawa is more isolated, five hundred miles closer to the equator and further removed from main air and sea routes. Or it may simply be that rather than being a strategic link in the American and Japanese empires, Kiribati was always a distant outpost of the British one, and instead of giving its natives too much Britain gave them almost nothing, leaving them with little infrastructure and their only natural resource, the phosphate deposits on Ocean Island, "coincidentally" exhausted just one year after independence.

I arrived in Tarawa in the late afternoon to find everyone lying on mats or stretched out on log platforms in open-sided huts, heads in arms, round bodies rhythmically rising and falling in sleep, seemingly in the grip of a communal hangover. At the hotel, the desk clerk had curled up behind the counter, and in the bar a waiter dozed. It turned out everyone really was recovering from a binge. Yesterday had been Independence Day, an occasion for considerable beer- and sour-toddy drinking.

My first sunset in Tarawa was a classic equatorial one, with the sun hesitating an instant, as if taking a deep breath, before jumping into the sea. The wind dropped, clouds froze, and the sails of a native canoe sagged. The sun fell and the lagoon turned silver. Then a generator whumped, bulbs glowed, the taillights of motorbikes flickered between palm trees, and I wandered from the lagoon to the ocean through the village of Bikenibeu. It was as thickly settled as Majuro, with people packing one-room houses like guests at a cocktail party, but its coral paths were free of litter, and instead of rattletrap trucks and country music I heard choral singing from radios and men humming as they cultivated taro pits by lantern.

The Tarawans are more like desert nomads than hillbillies. The similarity lies not only in their dark complexions, their traditions of hospitality and murderous feuds, their delight in storytelling, their obsession with virgin brides, or their skillful survival in a barren, sandy landscape, but also their habits of sitting cross-legged and keeping clothing rolled in mats and valuables padlocked in tin suitcases. I suppose the theory is that no one would be so cruel as to steal a whole suitcase, although they might "borrow" a single item. This custom gives everyone the appearance of being able to break camp at a moment's notice. Never have I seen a people more prepared to make a hurried departure from a place where this was so obviously impossible.

During that first evening stroll I saw evidence of the three favorite Kiribati pastimes: card games, gossip, and taro cultivation. The New England whalers brought playing cards, and it is almost impossible to walk a coral lane without seeing someone dealing out a hand or playing patience. Kiribati's recreational gossip ranges from leisurely hobby to bitter war, with people defamed by rumors launching poisonous counterattacks. The rumors progress like soap operas, as characters are introduced and dropped. The people are real, relatives and neighbors, but the plots are so embroidered they quickly became fiction. During the four days I waited for my plane to Abemama, I heard about a mysterious virus that had struck down the airline pilots, forcing the cancellation of all flights; then it became an illness affecting only bus drivers; then everyone in Betio; and so on. I heard myself described as a missionary, an actor, and a spy investigating the fishing pact with the Soviet Union. Someone was always insisting everything I had just been told about a village or a custom was an utter lie, then substituting their own tall story. There was nothing malicious in this. On islands with so little, knowledge is a valuable commodity.

No knowledge is more jealously guarded than the techniques for cultivating mammoth taro plants, or babai, as they are known in Kiribati. These plants with broad leaves shaped like enormous elephant ears are grown in pits, dug as deep as six feet to reach the water table. Their roots were once a dietary staple, but their preparation is so time-consuming that people now prefer the convenience of canned foods, reducing the babai to a luxury or ceremonial food and their cultivation to a competitive venture. The unofficial winners grow the largest, most handsome leaves, and neighbors are forever peering into one another's pits, hands behind backs like judges at a flower show. The secret to a prize babai is in the combining of salt bush, heliotrope, and rotting coconut trunk into a compost, in the manner of packing humus baskets around plants, in weeding and watering, and in the recitation of magical verses over young shoots. These skills are kept within families and, like toddy-cutting, fishing, and canoe-building, are only revealed piecemeal from an old man to a chosen heir, with the last secret, the missing ingredient, whispered on a deathbed to whoever has been the most diligent nurse in the final hours. If an expert fisherman or babai cultivator dies before orchestrating this delicate transfer, then his secrets are lost forever.

This struck me as curious: that a people who so generously share sleeping space and land, whose architecture of open-sided buildings discourages privacy, who adopt the children of distant relatives and friends simply to bind families closer together, who enjoy the harmonies of large choral singing groups and can truthfully say, "We are plenty rich because when we want something we just club together and buy it," should be such misers with their technical skills. Perhaps these skills are hoarded because they are all, in this rigorously communal society, that a man can call his own, the only things custom does not force him to share.

Back at the hotel, a diplomatic reception was hogging the terrace. The New Zealand high commissioner and his wife had come from Fiji for Independence Day and were throwing this party for Kiribati notables and New Zealand expatriates. Since Nazrullah, the Iranian, was among the drinkers, and we had arrived together only hours earlier, I saw no reason not to crash. The Kiribati guests passed through a receiving line, had pictures taken with the high commissioner, and vanished, leaving behind a small band of New Zealand expatriates to drink warm gin and nibble at cabin crackers topped with hard-boiled egg. They were a weedy and weary bunch, like convalescents who had just struggled out of their bathrobes.

Nazrullah was huddled with the high commissioner's wife and two New Zealand punk rockers with dyed hair, knocked-out teeth, and several sizes of earrings. They had dressed for this diplomatic reception in sleeveless T-shirts. The high commissioner's wife introduced them as Boyd and Mike, "two of our most popular singers."

"Yeah, I had a big record once," Boyd said, flexing an arm and rippling a spider-web tattoo.

"But that's history," Mike said. "Now we're turning people on to the Bab." He described his conversion to the Bahai faith, summarizing in punk jargon the religion for which, back in Iran, Nazrullah's coreligionists were being slaughtered "in bunches."

Nazrullah, who had changed into a linen Nehru jacket, was silent with embarrassment. Throwing an arm around him, Boyd said, "We'll all be living together in the Bahai center for the next sixty days."

"Well, actually only fifty-seven," Nazrullah corrected.

"Have you made many converts?" I asked.

"Yeah, we done all right," Mike said. "There's a lotta groups here—Mormons, Adventists, Krishnas—but we've got a big advantage over them, one thing that really brings them to the Bab."

"And what's that?"

He laughed, nudging Nazrullah in the ribs. "We tell 'em, man, that with us it's *'No donations.'*"

South Tarawa is two islands: a narrow one, stretching eleven miles from the airport and hotel at Bikenibeu to the government offices at Bairiki; and Betio island, containing the commercial center, port, and Second World War battlefield. To reach Betio, I took a bus to Bairiki and then a ferry. The road was narrow and shaded by a tunnel of palms. The trees grew haphazardly, bent by vagaries of wind and sunlight, making it difficult to see more than a few yards, a scary terrain for a battle. On the ocean side of the Bairiki causeway, men raced miniature outrigger canoes, a traditional sport. The boats were hand-carved scale models of the fishing canoes I had seen in Bikenibeu. Their owners ran across mud flats, hurling them downwind so they skimmed like windsurfers across the shallows. On some Kiribati canoes, small outboard engines have replaced cloth sails, and on the fastest of these scale models, cloth sails had been replaced by plastic sheeting.

When the U.S. Marines landed at Betio, in November 1943, it was the most heavily garrisoned and fortified half-square-mile in a world with many contenders for that title. The Japanese had surrounded its priceless airfield with 500 pillboxes and 4,500 elite troops. They had mined the reef and constructed coconut-log barricades to funnel landing craft into a killing field of machine-gun fire. Concertinas of barbed wire crossed the sand, and palm trees sagged with snipers. The last major amphibious assault on a heavily fortified beach, at Gallipoli, in 1915, had resulted in the slow slaughter and final defeat of its British attackers. At Betio, the Marines won a victory, but at the cost of a quick slaughter.

Tarawa was so remote and unknown that the U.S. Navy relied on maps drawn by the naval expedition of Lieutenant Charles Wilkes. He had visited the Gilberts in 1841, and his charts bore

notations such as "This chart should be used with circumspec-
tion—the surveys are incomplete." Although Britain had administered the Gilberts for half a century, Admiralty charts showed
Betio incorrectly oriented. But local British and Kiribati residents
did know, and they warned the U.S. Navy about the extreme
neap tides that occur in the lagoon every autumn. During this
period, high tides are so low that the reef is either exposed or
covered by water too shallow to be traversed by large landing
craft. American naval commanders were in a hurry to capture
Betio's airfield, the first central Pacific stepping-stone to Tokyo
and the key to the Marshall Islands campaign. They were reluctant to delay another month and prepared to gamble that the
tides might be just high enough. An optimistic quartermaster
corps had even loaded one transport with a victory treat for the
Marines, 1,600 half-pints of ice cream.

When they attacked, the high tide turned out to be abnormally low, even for autumn, and the Marines slogged across
hundreds of yards of exposed reef and shallows, carrying
eighty-four-pound packs and wearing jungle fatigues, ideal targets against a dazzling blue lagoon and sky. It was the kind of
sunlit, sweltering, slow-motion, over-the-top walk into a wall
of machine-gun fire that fills battle nightmares. The Marines
took three days to cross 300 yards, all the while burning out
and dynamiting Betio's defenders, and surviving the first sui-
cidal banzai charge of the war, although it might be argued that
the first banzai charge was the American assault itself.

In thirty-six hours a thousand Americans died, half before
reaching land. All but nineteen of the Japanese defenders were
killed, and buried offshore or on Betio. To be more accurate, they
were bulldozed into shell holes by Seabees repairing the airfield,
meaning that twenty years later, when charter planes of Japanese
began arriving to honor their dead, they landed on the bones of
their sons and husbands. A quarter of the American dead are
listed as "Burial place unknown," so they too are scattered across
Betio. Imagine burying three thousand people in a plot half the
size of Central Park, and you quickly realize that Betio is a vast
cemetery, with a skeleton for every two inhabitants.

Since the war, Betio's inhabitants have dug babai pits and
excavated foundations, only to uncover leg bones, jaws, and el-
bows. The smaller bones, presumably Japanese, are thrown into

the lagoon, while the bigger American ones were for a long time
sent to a U.S. Army pathology laboratory in, of all places, Tokyo.
Until the late 1960s, the discovery of a bone or sometimes a whole
skeleton was a weekly occurrence; now it happens every few
months. When bones are no longer unearthed, it will not be because everyone has been found, but simply because the remains
have finally become indistinguishable from fragments of coral.

The battle that was once described as producing the war's
greatest concentration of death and destruction still marks Betio,
but in surprising ways. The new coconut palms are all roughly the
same height, and they produce nuts and toddy in prodigious
quantities. The babai are spectacular, huge green fans exploding
from deep pits. Agronomists studying the miracle of Betio's recov-
ery have concluded that "it may be attributed to the 3,000 bodies
buried on this islet and also to the sanitary habits of the Japanese
during the occupation, which may have added as much as 40 kg
of excreta per month per man for 20 months. There may also have
been some benefit gained from the indirect action of nitro-
explosives, abandoned scrap iron, etc. Whatever the reason, the
fertility of some areas of Betio is probably the best in the archipelago."

My ferry from Bairiki docked near the junction of Red Beach
2 and Red Beach 3, where the Marines suffered heavy casualties.
Even at high tide I could see rusty iron posts, a blackened tractor,
and the wheel of an artillery piece poking from the water. Men
stood in the shallows tossing out nets, careful not to snag them
on jagged metal as they harvested fish that swam in large schools
through blasted landing craft. On shore, the Japanese block-
houses had become urinals, lovers' lanes, graffiti billboards, and,
in one case, the Betio Squash Club. Pigs snuffled in pens fashioned from beach defenses, and children ran barefoot through
fields of rusted scrap, now a minefield of tetanus. Betio's people
accepted this as part of their landscape, seeing nothing odd in
living amidst the garbage of a half-century-old battle that had not
involved them. I know this because I asked people riding the
ferry, a woman giving haircuts in the shade of a Japanese bunker,
and the merchant marine cadets I met in a tin warehouse calling
itself Betio's Top Nite Spot!

By afternoon the tide had ebbed, revealing rusting military
garbage stretching hundreds of yards into the lagoon and ocean.

A man with a good memory could return here and locate the burned-out hull of the amphibious tractor in which he almost drowned, the shore battery he attacked, or the bunker his friends died capturing. You had to wonder why this wreckage has remained so long, cluttering up the backyards and beaches of these noncombatants. A token few of Normandy's bunkers and guns are preserved in a memorial park; Berlin has been rebuilt; and at Pearl Harbor the wreck of the *Arizona* is a shrine. The United States has spent millions reconstructing the shattered cities and economies of its former enemies, but it feels no responsibility to cart away this rubbish. Instead, it has built a modest memorial to its Marines and refuses to pay royalties for tuna fished from Kiribati waters. Meanwhile, Britain, which governed Tarawa for twenty-four years after the war, did not try, or failed, to persuade either its wartime ally or its defeated enemy to clean up Betio. British army ordnance experts did spend a year on the island detonating live shells and ammunition, but this was not until 1965. And Japan, which invaded the islands and erected these shattered defenses, has given Kiribati some surplus rice and built a warehouse at the end of a pier, situated so it overshadows the American memorial.

Of course it is costly to haul scrap from the central Pacific, and Kiribati is powerless and remote — although not that remote, since Japanese relatives have returned to dedicate a peace park, and Japanese delegations have come to cremate Japanese remains. And on the twentieth, twenty-fifth, and fortieth anniversaries of the battle, American dignitaries have delivered speeches and dedicated a memorial with a good view of America's military garbage. Still, it has apparently occurred to no one in Washington or Tokyo that they have a responsibility to do what children are taught at an early age: pick up their own mess.

I returned to Betio the next day to reserve a bed at Abemama's only hotel, the Robert Louis Stevenson, although "hotel" may be too grand a term for a half-dozen thatched huts facing a channel. It was necessary to reserve, not because the hotel might be full but so its manager could meet me at the airstrip in one of the island's only trucks. The only communication between Tarawa and Abemama is by radio, and the only radio in Tarawa making a nightly call to the hotel belongs to its owner, Brian Orme, an Irish trader who has lived here thirty years, fathering or adopting twenty-nine children by wives so numerous he had difficulty producing an exact figure. He says he bought the hotel on Abemama, which he calls his "pub," because one night its owner refused to serve him a can of beer, or "cold piss."

"Want some cold piss?" he demanded the moment I arrived, smiling and becoming more friendly when I accepted.

He was a red Irishman, a stringy six-foot bantam-weight with a hula dancer on one arm and other faded tattoos half covered by his polo shirt. He liked to talk while standing, twisting the ends of his red handlebar moustache and strutting. "You'll be the only bloody guest," he said. "The plane service is terrible, and I'm going broke because I can't get anyone there. I bought it because I was drunk, which I always am; and I was broke, which I always am; and that shifty prick Shutz wouldn't serve me. His pub had the only icebox on the island and I was so thirsty I could have killed for a can of cold piss, but that bugger refused, so I threatened him. He pulled a .22, squeezed the bloody trigger too, but the thing didn't fire, so I said 'Bugger you,' radioed Tarawa, and bought the pub out from under him. The next day I had all the cold piss I wanted. But once I owned the bloody place I had to do something with it, so I built some cottages and turned it into a hotel. I called it the Robert Louis Stevenson because it's on his Equator Town."

He drained his first beer and started another. "Well, maybe it's a hundred yards from Equator Town . . . maybe two or three hundred. [It turned out to be about half a mile.] And my first wife's grandfather was Stevenson's translator when he lived on Abemama, which is the truth. When I was a boy I read his books and wanted to be a South Seas trader, and now, by God, I am! Not many can say they've done what they wanted, can they? You're fucking right they can't!"

As a young man, he had emigrated from Ireland and found work on an American merchant ship. When Congress passed a measure outlawing alien crewmen, he was "voluntarily" deported from San Francisco to Fiji with thirty-two dollars in his pocket, making him the modern equivalent of a nineteenth-century castaway. He found work as a commercial diver, fought for the British during the Malaysian Emergency, and ended up in the Gilberts, recruiting laborers for the phosphate mines on Ocean Island. Except for six months as a bouncer in a New York nightclub, he had lived here ever since, operating two boats carrying copra and dry goods between atolls and continuing a tradition of "beachcomber-trader" that is both longer and more honorable than you might think.

The Gilberts were among the first Pacific Islands to be visited by beachcombers, and by the middle of the eighteenth century many atolls had small colonies of castaways, whaling-boat deserters, and romantics. One history of beachcombers in the Pacific concludes that three quarters were seamen and most British and American, "with a rather conspicuous anarchical Irish element." Their lives were brutal and short. They destroyed themselves with drink, murdered each other, or were killed by natives. In the Solomons, several parties of shipwrecked sailors found themselves confined to small pens and eaten, one by one, to celebrate religious festivals.

"Beachcomber" was then a pejorative term, connoting indolence and irresponsibility, civilized men turning savage, "going native," and being "on the mat." Yet they were more than an exotic curiosity or a footnote to Pacific history. They introduced firearms, repaired Western machinery, and explained European customs, becoming intermediaries between trading ships and islands. In the nineteenth century, the Pacific was as unexplored a frontier as the American West, and the beachcombers were its pioneers — ones who had an effect on the natives far more benign than that of American pioneers.

Brian Orme may be as genuine a nineteenth-century beachcomber-trader as you can find in the central Pacific, not a two-year technical assistant, a slow-moving boat person, a foreign volunteer, or an anthropologist making a calculated visitation. Yet in spite of his prodigious beer-drinking, cursing, marrying, and procreating, he still cannot escape the worst of our century — or, as he puts it, "I came here for the romantic life and I've ended up computing bloody taxes and managing welfare schemes. I tell you, I'm a bloody clerk."

But he is also, by his own choice, surrounded by the equipment of a middle-class suburbanite. His living room has a wet bar, imitation portholes, and antimacassars. There is a picnic table and a hammock in the yard, carpeted bathrooms, bunk beds for the children, and modern appliances. Only the salty wind and a view of palms, ocean reef, and military scrap say Tarawa rather than a suburb of London, New York, or perhaps Montreal, where he had recently visited his sisters.

"I drove them crazy," he said without apology. "I wanted to sit in their gardens, reading books, sleeping and drinking piss. But they kept saying, 'Wouldn't you like to *do* something?' 'I am,' I said. 'I'm drinking piss, sleeping and reading. I'm in bloody heaven. I "do something" on Tarawa.'

"But that wasn't good enough, so to please them I drove into Montreal with their gray-faced husbands. Up a bridge through two tunnels, just to sit in a little box of an office all day, then come home. Next they took me to a bloody awful play and to some shithouse called Pedro's, where I drank piss and insulted their husbands. That was my fun in Montreal."

Orme was proof you could become a South Seas beach-comber and still be hurt by your children. In the last century, his twenty-nine offspring would have been close at hand, living on the next plot or next atoll, tapping toddy, weaving mats, fishing, and running his stores. Instead, they were scattered across the Solomons, Australia, and Fiji. His two eldest daughters had become sociologists in Australia, and the thought of them set him pacing the room, swearing, shouting, and jerking his arms like a puppet. "University graduates, educated women, and they both become fucking sociologists. And their husbands! Christ, one's another sociologist with a pointy little beard. Come to think of it, all my daughters' husbands look like something dragged from a dead rat's asshole.

"Last year they came for Christmas, and right away it's 'Please be nice, daddy. Please don't drink, daddy, or swear or argue.'" He affected a girlish whine: "'Be nice, daddy; be nice.' Now what the fuck does that mean: 'Be nice'? Can you tell me? I said, 'I was "nice" bringing you up. Working my ass off so you could go to Australia and become sociologists who can't find a single fucking country on a map!'

"Last year they came for Christmas and I took over an island at the mouth of the lagoon, where the fishing is good and the swimming clean. I dragged over a generator, ice chests packed with cold piss, whiskey, a tarp for shade, and thick steaks. Now they can all fish, drink piss, eat, fuck, whatever . . . but it's not good enough and they're complaining: 'It's too hot, it's too cold, the kids will get sunburned, there're too many flies.' So they came back here with their rat-assed husbands and spent a week in the house with the blinds down, watching tapes on my VCR. I stayed out there alone, drinking piss and eating the steaks. Fuck them all."

But he said this without conviction. He had been wounded. He had offered his children a desert island, good fishing, and solitude, softened by reliable shade, steak, and cold beer and they had rejected it: this, the most idealized version of a beachcomber's life he could imagine.

Orme said, "I love pulling people's pissers." Then he told stories, swearing every word was true. I heard about a drinking bout with Lee Marvin in Fiji during which they drained two bottles of vodka while Marvin confided deep secrets. I heard his analysis of the battle of Tarawa: "The tide was dry as a nun's pussy." I heard the reason for his popularity with the nuns of Abemama: "I have a tape of *The Sound of Music* I show them on my VCR, then I lecture the novitiates on the evils of drink." I heard him boast about posing for a mural behind the altar of Abemama's Catholic church. It showed heaven to the right, hell to the left, and "You'll recognize me," he said. "I'm the bloody devil."

He had leased a boat to CIA agents. "There was a referendum in the Marshalls they wanted to fiddle, so they filled my boat with so-called traditional leaders, who all got seasick. They brought fake ballot boxes, microphones big as fucking beer cans for bugging political meetings, and dancing girls from Tarawa, even though the Marshallese don't like Gilbertese dancing. The agents never took off their Brooks Brothers suits, so everyone spotted them.

He had rented his Abemama pub to the Peace Corps for a conference. "They wanted to sleep on pandanus mats, but I said, 'Fuck you, I'm not pulling bloody beds out of the rooms for you lot. The people here sleep on mats because they can't afford a bloody bed. They'd have beds if they could, and they think anyone who doesn't is a bloody idiot.' All the volunteers had this lank hair, and one was a nutrition expert. Ha! Bloody nutrition expert. This poor son of a bitch couldn't even feed himself— looked like a dead rat caught in a drain pipe. 'What can you do?' I asked. 'You can't mechanic, can't fish, can't carpenter, fix a car, build a house. You don't shave. What the bloody fuck can you

teach the people here?' The Peace Corps ought to send us a bicycle repairman, a hotel manager, a retired plumber, not these
useless assholes. The people here, they keep Peace Corps volunteers as pets."

The breeze quickened, and we moved outside to sit on
Orme's lawn furniture and piss against his palms. A daughter
brought our eighth beers, although we had thrown out a third of
the last few cans when they became warm. "Be careful out here,"
he shouted as I relieved myself. "Still plenty of live ammunition
around, and shells by the ton." Nearby, a blue shell casing poked
from the sand. "You Americans claim you recovered all your
bodies. What crap! They just found a skeleton while digging the
new telephone cable. It was big-boned, with a web belt and a
Marine Corps ring. Someone stole the ring, but they airmailed the
rest."

Orme thought Betio could expect "more fucking battles and
bloodshed if they let the Russians in." Kiribati was broke. Its export earnings barely covered its Australian beer imports, and
money was needed for the nine-million-dollar budget. Since Britain had reduced its aid, and the United States refused to force its
tuna fishermen to pay royalties, Kiribati had turned to the Soviet
Union, offering its fishing rights for a million-and-a-half dollars a
year. America's indifference to saving Kiribati from communism
had stuck Brian Orme with the job. He had encouraged opposition to the Soviet treaty by distributing to the Catholic churches
copies of a *Fiji Times* headline: RUSSIANS PAY TO KILL POPE. "I'm a
Kiribati citizen, so no one can accuse me of being an outside agi-
tator," he said with a sly smile.

His Kiribati partner, Henry, arrived with a list of politicians
who had agreed to vote against the Soviet treaty. "I handle the
whites, he handles the spooks," Orme said. Henry laughed, and
Orme's daughter Moira, herself half "spook," gave a weary smile.
Orme saw her. "You see, no one takes me seriously," he said. "It's
just the way I talk, and I can't help it — don't want to either, goddammit!"

But wasn't he taking a risk, I asked, orchestrating this campaign, challenging the prime minister to "piss in his pocket"
(whatever that meant), and making statements like "I make the
bullets and old Henry fires them"?

He looked disgusted. "Fuck me, everyone's always saying

'Orme, you make too many waves.' But I tell them, I *am* the bloody waves!"

I should not have worried. The people I asked about Orme said, "Oh, that Brian can get away with anything. He makes noise, but everyone just says 'Ach, it's just Brian again.'" "The people here are genuinely fond of him. In fact, the president likes him personally." "He loves stirring it up, but no one should underestimate him; he's cleverer than he lets on."

I agreed. For all the swearing and piss-drinking, this was a wise man, certainly wiser than if he'd never been deported to Fiji, raised those twenty-nine children, married those countless wives, or bought that pub near Equator Town.

"Remember, if you don't like my pub, I'll give you your money back," he shouted after me. "That's my policy. But I only had to do it once. Some rat's ass . . ."

But after a week at Orme's pub, far from being a rat's ass clamoring for my money back, I would happily have paid more. At last I understood the appeal of these Pacific atolls, and why Stevenson had stayed four months and Orme a lifetime. It was all in the beauty of their simple ingredients — palm trees, reef, water, and sky — and in the contrast between a black, turbulent ocean and the nearby lagoon, blue and smooth as ice. And on Abemama there was no asphalt, litter, or power lines to distract from the cloud shadows sweeping across the water; from the milky offshore skies merging seamlessly with a sun-bleached ocean; or from the racing puffball clouds or the black ones the people called "teasing showers," because all day they danced around parched Abemama, dumping their rain just beyond its reef. Orme's hotel faced a channel good for swimming and snorkeling, and its cabins were constructed of palm, pandanus mats, and the bark of the sweet-smelling uri. I liked the noise of the place: surf on a reef, men singing as they rewove the walls of my cabin, and the scratching of the hermit crabs that infested my roof; and I liked eating turtle stew by candlelight in the open dining room, all the while watched by the portrait of a man I first took for Brian Orme but who was actually Robert Louis Stevenson.

"So you've noticed," said Willy Tokataake, the young

Abemaman manager of the hotel. "Yes, they could have been twins."

Yes, they could. Both had the same narrow face, receding hairline, watery eyes, and moustache, although Stevenson's drooped. I asked if Orme had commissioned this portrait (in keeping with his fondness for "pulling pissers"), but Willy shook his head and pointed to a framed photograph of Stevenson at a banquet of Hawaiian nobility. In it the resemblance to Orme was still greater, a coincidence more spooky for the hissing gas lamps and the thatched room that might as easily have belonged to Stevenson as to Orme.

Stevenson had arrived in Abemama in 1889 on a chartered schooner, *The Equator*, hoping to alleviate his tuberculosis and find colorful material for a book. His account of four months on Abemama is a valuable record of the last moments of a traditional Micronesian monarchy. Just four years after Stevenson left, King Binoka of Abemama was dead, measles had decimated the population, and Britain had annexed the Gilbert Islands. That Stevenson and Binoka should have become friends; that Binoka, who usually prohibited white traders from landing on his island, should build Equator Town for Stevenson, and weep at his departure; and that Stevenson should call Binoka the "one great personage in the Gilberts," is not surprising when you consider that each gave the other exactly what he wanted.

Binoka was a fanatical collector of European skills, ideas, and novelties, "greedy of things new and foreign," as Stevenson described him. His palace was crammed with umbrellas, waistcoats, music boxes, spectacles, rifles, and tools — "all that ever caught his eye, tickled his appetite, pleased him for its use, or puzzled him with its apparent utility." Stevenson had packed *The Equator* with trading swag, pleasing Binoka with five-cent cigars, mouth organs, scented soap, and a bowl of goldfish, although he believed "it was by our talk that we gained admission to the island; the king promising himself (and I believe really amassing) a vast amount of useful knowledge ere we left."

In return, Stevenson found in Binoka a character as bizarre as any he had invented. Here, a decade from the twentieth century, was a tyrant who slept on a pillow stuffed with the pubic hairs of virgins; who lived among forty queens and twenty concubines, "the only master, the only male, the sole dispenser of honours, clothes and luxuries, the sole mark of multitudinous ambitions and desires"; and whose favorite expression was "I got power," which he sometimes exercised by executing those who displeased him as they walked unawares down coral pathways. Stevenson reported he was a crack shot, and "when he aims to kill, the grave may be got ready."

"You would call him lusty rather than fat," Stevenson said of Binoka, "but his gait is still dull, stumbling, and elephantine. He . . . goes about his business with an implacable deliberation. We could never see him and not be struck with his extraordinary natural means for the theatre: a beaked profile like Dante's in the mask, a mane of long black hair, the eye brilliant, imperious, inquiring. . . . His voice [was] shrill, powerful, and uncanny, with a note like a sea-bird's. Where there are no fashions . . . he dresses — as Sir Charles Grandison lived — 'to his own heart.' Now he wears a woman's frock, now a naval uniform; now (and more usually) figures in a masquerade costume of his own design. . . . In the woman's frock he looks ominous and weird beyond belief. I see him now come pacing towards me in the cruel sun, solitary, a figure out of Hoffman."

Although Willy was King Binoka's great-great-grandson, he had inherited few of the tyrant's genes. He was slight and shy, with a pretty face and long hair curled at the ends, like a Sunday-school Jesus. He never touched alcohol or cigarettes — Binoka was addicted to both — and was determinedly monogamous. Stevenson described the commoners of Abemama as having "a curious politeness, a soft and gracious manner, something effeminate and courtly." That was Willy Tokataake.

He had attended the merchant marine academy on Tarawa, afterwards crewing on a German freighter. It was a life that would have pleased his great-great-grandfather, a gorging on foreign places and novelties, but it had terrified Willy, who remembered mostly dangerous bars and aggressive whores. He recalled huge Finnish girls in Helsinki, bustling up the gangplank in winter coats, furry as polar bears and vexed to find, instead of hearty German sailors, a crew of shivering little Micronesians. They demanded vodka, and the Scottish girls wanted whiskey. The whores of Puerta Plata chased Willy. "We left the customs shed and they came running," he said. "They were all tall — perhaps they were men. They screamed, 'Come with me.' 'No! With me!'

We fled in terror. I dodged one who was running so fast she slammed into a fence. Bam! One grabbed my balls and shouted, 'I love you!' After this I stayed on board ship, watching television and going ashore only in the American ports. Those ports also had the best television, with so many channels I stayed up all night watching late movies, then the morning prayer." After two years of this, Willy had had enough. He returned home, married, and embraced Abemama. He was a booster, so anxious that I like what had once been his family estate that he drove me to all the island's attractions.

The first was a rectangle of smooth stone surrounded by black volcanic rock and bordering the ocean beach. It was known as Tetabo's Rock, after Binoka's great-great-grandfather, the first in Abemama's royal line. Before Tetabo, the island had been fractured into independent kaaingas, or extended families. In the early eighteenth century, Tetabo became leader of his kaainga, defeated rival ones, united Abemama, and extended his rule to the neighboring atolls of Kuria and Aranuka, becoming Abemama's first "master of the land." His success is attributed to his extraordinary feats of strength. Historians speculate that a glandular abnormality made him large, like the giant of a circus sideshow, and that his feats have been exaggerated over time. The legends have him slaying a hundred rival warriors by throwing a giant coconut log, stamping a hole in the lagoon reef, uprooting pandanus trees with his bare hands, and, according to Willy, "breaking off these rocks at low tide and hurling them into the sea. Afterwards he came here at dawn to make his magic and replenish his great strength." He dropped his voice to a whisper. "And now this is a very holy place." One thing was sure: Whatever had happened here had not been an act of nature. The volcanic rock had been too regularly and perfectly cleared, revealing the limestone underneath. "This strength was passed through my family," Willy said, "and Binoka's son Paul, even when he was only ten, could lift heavy buckets with his thumb. If I need help for a certain project, I come here at high tide and ask the gods for strength. My grandfather and father come also, and others who want to become strong before a sports contest, particularly wrestling matches."

"Does it work?"

"It give us strength to work hard, not to be lazy . . ."

"But the feats of strength?" I realized afterwards that there was a certain cruelty in these questions. The slight Willy was obviously in no shape to throw a giant coconut log, but, like a missionary attacking a pagan ritual, I wanted him to admit it.

His shoulders sagged. "Our men aren't strong now because the Christian churches discourage people from practicing the old magic. That is why our men can't lift canoes over their shoulders and carry them into the water as before. Our Old Men also failed to write down the magic words in a book, so the secrets of performing great feats died with them."

Tetabo was buried in a fenced plot in a nearby village. Willy slowed down as we passed it—"to show respect," he said—and finally I understood his bizarre driving style. We would be steaming along at twenty-five miles per hour when he would suddenly hit the brakes and for a hundred yards creep along at half speed. This was essential Abemama etiquette, a way of showing respect for village meeting halls, the houses of the Old Men, and sacred sites such as Tetabo's grave and the well of Tebanga.

As we peered down this narrow well, Willy said, "This had its greatest use in the early 1800s, before the Union Jack was flown. Tell me, how do you imagine the great-auntie of King Binoka drew water here for her baths?"

"With a coconut shell?"

"No, with a human skull lowered on a rope of hair. Because the well is so narrow, these heads were easily broken. My great-auntie would say, 'I need another head,' and she'd choose one from the general population."

His face was expressionless. If he saw anything horrifying or amusing in this story, he was not letting on. "When my great-auntie died, they stopped using heads, and the population was very relieved. If she had lived longer, there are many people in this village who would not be alive." He looked around, perhaps speculating which of the men asleep in the nearby maneaba or the women sweeping their yards these might be. "Yes," he said with more pride than humor, "their great-aunties' heads would have been fetching water for my great-auntie's bath."

A maneaba is the characteristic communal meeting hall of Kiribati. It is like an A-frame in design, with a gigantic roof held three feet off the ground by huge pillars. The walls are open, but the roof is low enough to afford privacy. A traditional maneaba has a frame of coconut logs tied together by sisal, a pandanus-thatch roof, and coral pillars carved by hand from the reef. Constructing a maneaba from these materials involves months, if not years, of hard labor, explaining why, as we entered the maneaba of Tebanga, Willy said, "That bastard!"

"Who?"

"McClure, the British district commissioner. At least I think that's his name, but my grandfather knows for sure. He's the one who burned down our original maneaba. This was reconstructed from its ruins." I asked when this had happened. "Oh, about 1900. We are planning to sue the British government for reparations. My brother Donald is building our case by interviewing people who as children witnessed or heard about the atrocity."

We stood in the center of the maneaba. Its thatched roof was four stories high and lost in shadows, its floor large enough to seat several hundred. Willy said it was the biggest and oldest in Abemama, but it was now in shocking condition. Its fence had collapsed, its mats were shredded, and plastic bags littered the ground nearby. "When the old Old Men were alive, it was in better shape, much better," he said, looking grim. "But the new Old Men are not as interested. They come here but don't repair it." A man awoke, stretching and scratching like a dog, then rolling back onto a ripped mat. Willy raised his eyebrows, giving me a see-what-I-mean? look. Kiribati's more worldly villages have now saved themselves the trouble of repairing a traditional maneaba by using tin roofs, concrete pillars, and cement floors, and it seems only a matter of time before this happens on this, the most traditional of the islands.

As we circled the building, Willy identified poles from the old maneaba, some charred by the British fire. One had a dog carved into its side. "My great-great-grandfather's dog," he said. "And that beam is where they hung the heads of his enemies. That is why the British, encouraged by the missionaries, burned down our maneaba. It was unfair, because by then that custom had ceased, although in Binoka's time heads hung from that pole like fruit."

Nothing remained of Stevenson's Equator Town but some stone foundations in a grove of stunted palms. Because his house and compound had been built from local materials, they had soon become indistinguishable from the usual rubble of dead palm and pandanus, although this did not deter Willy from imagining the house and its privileged view. "From where you are standing," he said, "Stevenson could see the king's swimming pond, and watch him bathe with his naked queens."

King Binoka's tomb sat on a cleared circle of coral rock that had been the site of his palace. It was four feet high, built to resemble a maneaba, and faced with slabs of coral and patched with cement. When I saw it, the sky above was clear of birds, although seabirds filled the skies elsewhere. Willy explained that any flying directly overhead fell to the ground dead. Only tufts of weed grew within a thirty-foot radius of the tomb, and within its rectangular coral border, nothing. People had tried planting grass here, Willy claimed, but nothing would grow. Later, his brother Donald told me, "The grass won't grow because Binoka's spirit is too strong. You probably think someone sneaks over at night to clear it, but I swear they don't. Everyone is much too afraid. Once my grandfather took me there and stood inside the stones. He said, 'Go on, you can touch it because you're a direct descendant,' but I refused. I'm afraid of that tomb." Willy also treated the tomb cautiously, posing for my picture by standing just outside the stone rectangle. When I urged him closer, he said, "No one but my grandfather dares go beyond that stone. When the roof needed repairing, only he was able to fix it. Everyone else refused. They know about the men who tried to rob the tomb. Afterwards one went mad, and the other was lost at sea. Miserable deaths for them, you know."

"When did that happen?" I asked. Thirty years before, he admitted, but the memory was fresh.

"What's inside that's so valuable?" I asked.

"We think it contains his favorite possessions"—in other words, his spectacles, music boxes, umbrellas, and mouth organs. "And of course there's his favorite pillow," Willy added, referring to the one stuffed with virgin pubic hairs.

As we drove back to the hotel in fits and starts, with Willy scrupulously braking for maneabas, Old Men, and other sites of historical or religious significance as yet unexplained, he said, "Everyone who visits us has read that my grandfather was a cruel man. [He meant his great-great-grandfather Binoka, but he usually dropped the "greats" in speaking, as he did when referring to his great-auntie.] But with his own hands he killed only two people. One was his wife, but he shot her because he was up to here with drink [he touched his forehead], and after it happened he cried for weeks."

"Who was the other?"

He sighed. He had hoped I wouldn't ask. "When Binoka sobered up the next morning, he felt so badly about what he had done he killed the man who stupidly handed him that gun."

Back at the hotel, Willy's unconvincing defense of his ancestor was joined by his brother Donald and his grandfather George, the current king of Abemama, a title officially defunct yet widely recognized. As they did most days, the royal family was sitting on the hotel's shaded terrace, sipping soda pop and watching the tides race through the channel while imagining the redress of ancient wrongs.

"Outsiders may see Binoka as cruel," Donald conceded. "But I don't think the people of Abemama ever considered him that, although to be fair, there was the time he had all the men from a single clan killed. But that was definitely in self-defense."

Willy nodded. "Yes, he just controlled society so his rivals would not take over. You might say he ran a sort of police state, but not a very cruel one. Well, maybe some cruelty, but that was the fault of his cabinet."

"It's the same way now," the king said. "Often the Old Men come to decisions alone, and only if it's something big do they bother consulting me. So you see how it would be possible . . ." I looked skeptical. I had read too much about Binoka to buy this. "All right, in those dark, stone-age days you had to be feared in order to rule, and to be feared you had to practice a little cruelty. It was just something a king did then — the custom of the times, if you will."

King George smiled, a delightful smile that revealed his six front teeth, gapped and stained the color of Tetabo's tombstone by the Benson & Hedges he chain-smoked down to the filter. With his wide grin, gap teeth, long bony face, and bald head he resembled a skull, but one of those jolly Halloween ones. He was closest to the cheerful Scandinavian monarchs who ride bicycles everywhere, unmistakably royal but with the common touch. He had tattoos on his arms, enjoyed dirty jokes, and sometimes used the language of a merchant seaman, which was what he had been until retiring to Abemama. He wore inappropriate clothes for a

king—shorts, plastic flip-flops, and novelty T-shirts—but his posture was superb.

The slander on his great-grandfather's good name that
pained him most was the story of the notorious "human rooster,"
who perched on the roof of the palace, making cock-a-doodle-
doo noises when he spied a pretty woman and then, I had read,
jumping down to rape her. A woman refusing to perform public
intercourse with the rooster might be put to death. "It's important
you understand the circumstances behind that rooster story," the
king said.

Donald interrupted. "Better just to say that rooster was a sex
maniac and leave it at that."

"No. Thurston should know that he was a man from another
island who came looking for work. He went to Binoka's son Paul
in secret, encouraging him to ask for a human rooster as a toy. It
was not the king's idea, not at all. That rooster took advantage of
our family." But was the story essentially true? I asked. "Somewhat true. He did live on the roof and attack women, sometimes,
but remember that in those dark stone-age days . . ."

But for all this talk of stone-age days, this history and these
grievances seemed fresh in the memories of the royal family.
Century-old injustices evoked the same passion as those of ten or
twenty years ago. "It is fortunate for the British," the king said,
"that they declared their protectorate six months after Binoka's
death. He had packed the maneaba with arms and ammunition
and sent several handpicked chaps to New Zealand for military
training. He was ready to put up a jolly good fight. Instead, when
that Captain Davis arrived, the king was Paul, a ten-year-old boy,
and the rest, as they say, is history."

I asked if in Paul's place they would have resisted. They nodded in unison. "Yes! Certainly we'd have fought!" the king said.
"And if we'd won, that bastard McClure never would have
burned down our maneaba. The British were shocked because
dried heads were customarily hung from the poles. Perhaps they
did not understand these were the heads of our enemies. We
hope to persuade Britain to pay us compensation."

"I am building a file with testimony from the old people,"
Donald said. "Soon we will present it to the British."

The king stubbed out his cigarette, hard, and pointed to the
lagoon. "And somewhere out there is our family's cannon. In

1912 the British resident used it as an anchor for one of his boats, an extremely rude thing to do."

"We've been searching for that cannon," Donald said. "It is our property, and we want it restored to us. I am collecting information from the Old Men, to help us locate it." The king beamed, pleased with his grandson's dedication. Donald wore heavy black-framed glasses and had the intense manner of a graduate student. He had attended school in the Solomon Islands and Fiji and continued his education by reading widely. His knowledge of the world was deep and broad, and his English was remarkable, sprinkled with phrases like "Mind your p's and q's."

After hearing of the perfidy of the British at such length, I was startled to hear the king say that when the Gilberts became independent, in 1979, the Old Men of Abemama had written to the British Queen, requesting that their atoll and the neighboring ones of Kuria and Aranuka either become independent or remain a British protectorate. "It was a serious request," he said, "not based on whim but on history, law, and our rights! Because we were the only one of the Gilberts with a king at the time of the protectorate, Captain Davis made firm promises that 'Whatever the people of Abemama want, Britain will honor,' or words to that effect." He leaned forward, tapping the table with his finger. "Who put all these so-called Gilbert Islands together? The white man. Before the British we were an independent kingdom. They forced us together just for the sake of administration. So we thought: Now that Great Britain is leaving, they should bloody well put things back the way they were, give us the chance to be independent. I assure you that most people on these islands would prefer to break away. We could stand on our own two feet—in a modest way, of course. After all, we're the biggest copra producer in the Gilberts, and together we have a population of over four thousand. Nauru is an independent nation, with a seat at the United Nations, and it only has six thousand. So are the Ellice Islands, with nine thousand, and they left the Gilberts at independence. That is all we asked from the queen: Either let us be independent or, if that is impossible, keep us. The Old Men composed the letter. It was handwritten, but very legible, I assure you. We never received a reply from her. None. Nothing. We wonder if she ever saw our letter."

"This warrants further investigation," Donald said. "We are doing our level best to discover what happened to our letter."

"The queen is sure to be surprised if she learns she was never shown our letter and it went only as far as, say, her foreign minister."

In the reading, the complaints of Abemama's royal family may appear quaint or even ridiculous, but they did not strike me that way at the time. These were intelligent and serious people, clinging to the touching but worthy notion that these old injustices might be righted, that compensation was possible, and that beyond their reef were people of goodwill who could be persuaded of their case, if only the proper facts were brought to their attention. When the king asked if I could reproduce their letter to the queen in a book or an article, "so we can be certain she sees it," I readily agreed. Unfortunately, neither he nor his grandsons had kept a copy. My search for Abemama's letter to the queen gave structure to days that were otherwise an agreeable succession of long walks along beaches and long talks with the king on the terrace of the Robert Louis Stevenson Hotel, where, as he cheerfully admitted, he sat "around on my bum all day smoking and talking because, quite frankly, there's not a lot for an educated king to do on Abemama."

One look at Henry Schutz, the proprietor of Abemama's largest private trading establishment, told me why he and Orme had fought. He was as huge and phlegmatic as Orme was wiry and quick. Orme prided himself on speaking his mind, but it was hard to get a straight word — or, for that matter, any word at all — out of the sly Schutz. During the long pauses separating my questions and his unsatisfactory or incomprehensible answers, he amused himself by building Australian quarters and dimes into skyscrapers and pushing them back and forth across the counter like a croupier, something made more interesting than it sounds by his hand-quivering hangover.

"The governor was impressed with our letter . . . yes, very impressed," he said. "We kept it a secret that a European helped with its composition."

"Did the European send it to the queen?"

"Who can say?"

"Did anyone on Abemama keep a copy?"

"It is possible. Perhaps I have one."

The next day he admitted to having lost his copy, or maybe he had given it to one of the Old Men who was at present on Aranuka. He promised to mail it to me, slipping my card into a drawer thick with old bills and correspondence. I thought I would never hear from him again, and I was right.

I called on Eric Bailey, the only permanent European resident of Abemama, hoping he might have helped compose the letter. He is a former British colonial officer who has chosen to pursue on Abemama a retirement combining the appearance of a beachcomber with the habits of an English pensioner. On the one hand, he goes about shirtless, wears a blue lavala embroidered with roses, sleeps in a green army tent, and lives in a palm-thatch lean-to, accepting whatever Abemama offers with the nonchalance of a hippie, a comparison he encourages by allowing his fringe of hair to grow into white tendrils that brush his sun-blackened shoulders like jungle vines. On the other hand, when I arrived at his compound to ask if, as one of Her Majesty's former administrators, he had seen the petition addressed to her by the Old Men of Abemama (he had not), I found him surrounded by the cosy clutter of an Englishman's retirement cottage. I once interviewed dozens of retired British colonial officers and policemen for a book about the British mandate in Palestine, and from those encounters I recognized the floppy gardening hat, green Wellington boots, stretching cats, and yapping dogs who ignored his shouts of "Oh, dry up! . . . Shut up, you!" There were the remains of breakfast: teacups with milky puddles, yellowing butter, and marmalade jars weighing down piles of correspondence. There was even a visitors' book he asked me to sign. "Although I usually forget to bring it out when people call," he said, explaining its empty pages.

From his boasting about "my wife's first-rate tomatoes" and her skill at "making do" with whatever grew in Abemama's sandy soil, from his many references to their joint projects ("That's the breadfruit we planted"), and from the thumbed pages of her *Good Housekeeping Guide to Good Cooking,* I expected a ruddy, big-jawed Englishwoman wearing a sunbonnet and carrying a basket and pruning shears. It was only when he said, "We didn't choose Tabiteau because, although it's my wife's home island, it's too remote, and we feared too much scrutiny from the inlaws," that, as Bailey himself would probably have said, the penny dropped, and I realized that the handsome native woman throwing coconut husks on the fire was not his servant but his wife.

Perhaps I made this mistake because they only communicated in pigdin English and Gilbertese, although their inability to exchange a complicated sentence had not diminished their affection. This was the second of two unconventional marriages for Bailey. During the war, he had married a Jewish girl while serving as a member of the Palestine police, an organization the Jews of Palestine accused with reason of being generally pro-Arab and anti-Semitic. After the Middle East, he bounced from journalism into the colonial office, serving twenty years in Africa before retiring to Suffolk to open a boutique. "That's right, a damned boutique!" he said. "Then in 1973 I left my wife and gave it to her, so I had to earn a living again. I came down to London to look for a job at the ODA [Overseas Development Administration] and ran into a friend in the hallway who said he needed a census taker for Christmas Island." Bailey lived there five years, finally becoming district commissioner and, after independence, a minister on secondment to the Kiribati government. But he had chosen to retire on Abemama, because "it's not a good idea for a chap to 'stay on' where he's served. You're always peering over someone's shoulders, meddling and making a general nuisance of yourself. Instead, we came here and started from scratch."

It still looked like scratch to me. And no wonder, since, as he struggled from his chair to give me a tour, it was apparent that despite a brave effort to straighten his shoulders he was disabled by a painful ailment, perhaps arthritis. It gave him a pronounced limp and caused the swollen veins on his legs to bulge with every step. Yet, with his wife, he had cleared this land, digging holes for his bananas while seated in a chair.

"Papaws are rather disappointing, aren't they? And my bananas really aren't doing well." He laughed, but his smile was pained. For my benefit he was pretending it was a huge joke, choosing to launch his new life during the worst drought in Abemama's written history. His tomatoes, cabbages, and peppers were stunted, and he admitted that "my cucumbers, my English cucumbers, are dying on me, and I haven't the slightest idea why, and we've had to buy coconuts for our pigs and chickens because there aren't enough on our land. But we've been lucky in other things. For example, the water table is near the surface, and . . ."

He looked around, searching for more evidence of good fortune. But his dwelling was one of few without a view of either lagoon or ocean, and without their cooling, mosquito-chasing breezes. His fishing nets lay in heaps, rotted through because his limp prevented him walking to the reef every day to pull them up. Instead, he left them there a week at a time, catching so little he was forced to barter the use of his truck for fish. A heap of empty mackerel tins showed that even this was not enough. "It's actually been something of an advantage, being too busy building things here to be able to fish every day," he said. "Now we can burn the tins and scatter them about. The iron is excellent for my wife's English cucumbers."

He showed me a pile of corroded pipes and twisted wire. "I shipped these useful bits and pieces from Christmas Island." He winked, as if there were something slightly naughty about this. Twenty-five years ago, Britain and then the United States had conducted nuclear tests on Christmas Island, later abandoning most of their equipment. Now Bailey's pigs lived in pens made from the wire mesh that he described with a laugh as "the ground mats." "Don't have the slightest idea why they needed them. Perhaps to absorb the radioactivity, but they make first-class pens, and they haven't harmed my pigs."

Not yet, I thought, stepping back and noticing for the first time how much of Eric Bailey's new life was fashioned from Christmas Island's nuclear-test refuse.

As he drove me back to the hotel, he said, "It's not the land we would have liked, you know, not a choice location, definitely not choice. But it was all we could afford, so it will just have to do."

The king and Willy did not think it would do. They admired his optimism and energy, but they feared for him. He had dug for thirty hours to plant a single stunted banana tree, a job usually accomplished in one. The king shook his head. "He is too old to be starting again, here or anywhere. Where are his children? His relatives?"

Bailey's solitary retirement had unsettled Willy. "But I can't wait to be an Old Man. It's my dream. You make decisions in the maneaba, you're important, and everyone listens to you. Every young man here wants to be called 'old,' and the Old Men are happy they're old. Only because they like young girls do the Old Men wish they were young. But that's it, just for the sake of love."

It did not seem odd to me that Bailey should be alone in his retirement, only that he was in Abemama instead of Arizona or Eastbourne. But it bewildered them. Why wasn't he the British equivalent of an honored Old Man, leaning against a coconut log in the maneaba and enjoying the tastiest tidbits at every feast? What was he doing, settling here with a native wife and growing English vegetables? They reminded me of Madame Suzanne trying to explain Lambaréné's abandoned grandparents. She only knew that in those remote bush villages a dangerous change was occurring that soon might spread. Here in Abemama, the last fortress of traditional Kiribati customs, the king, Willy, and Donald saw in Eric Bailey a similarly sinister harbinger.

Abemama has the highest copra production of any atoll in Kiribati, yet the palms surrounding Bailey's property were barren. When I mentioned this, the king said, "Ha! That's because you were seeing our lands, where the people have helped themselves to our nuts. We have this damned custom of people taking what they need from the king, which is to say if a chap wants something I have, why, he simply walks off with it."

"But it's an important custom," Donald protested. "Besides, they never take anything we're using. Usually they just want mosquito nets."

"That's nonsense, Donald. Your father lost his motorbike that way." He turned to me. "It started when the king owned everything, so if people took what he had — well, then, he still owned it." He lowered his voice. "This taking from the king is a very bad custom, and not surprisingly it is one of the few old customs to survive. People have forgotten others, oh yes, but not this one. It makes being king on Abemama a damned expensive proposition."

"But it's why people don't begrudge us our lands," Donald said, "because they know they can take our copra."

"And they certainly do." The king shuddered, "You plan on harvesting thirty pounds, and suddenly find three in your bags. Frightening!"

"But they always ask—"

"Yes, this is how they ask: They say, 'It is right and fitting for you to let me cut copra.' Or when a chap is fined, he comes and asks for copra to pay the court, and we end up paying all the criminal fines in Abemama. Or they say, 'Can I make that chair old for you?' which really means can I take it and sit on it until it collapses. It's not fair, boys. Rather than 'It is right and fitting,' let them learn the saying 'By your sweat you shall live.' This is the modern world now, and these dangerous customs must end."

"But we get free labor in return." Donald was the conservative, wanting to preserve every Abemama custom.

"Not bloody likely. That part of the custom — the king getting free labor — has been mysteriously forgotten. Who started this dangerous tradition anyway? I think it should be discouraged before the chaps have everything we own."

The king was having a grand time, laughing, rolling his eyes, showing off in front of his grandsons, but Donald was embarrassed that I should hear an attack on the old customs from the mouth of the king. He said, "But despite this, the king still has lands galore, and—"

"But for how long at this rate? I tell you, Donald, being a king on Abemama is a bum deal. You have prestige and land, that's all. No power, and people help themselves to whatever you own. No, these days it's much better to be a commoner than a king. If I was one of them I'd ask for things every day, and when I had everything that belonged to the king it would be 'Good-bye, Abemama.' I'd be off to see the world!"

Every night I dined before an audience. The waitresses set down bowls of fish or turtle stew, curried prawns, and rice, and then, joined by the chef, stood back, their arms folded, snapping gum, shifting from foot to foot and whispering, watching intently to see how much of each dish I would eat. Mosquito coils burned underneath the table, sending up spirals of smoke that made me feel like an idol. When I finished, they swept away the plates and played energetic games of darts on Brian Orme's board, keeping meticulous score. They hit the bull's-eye and clapped their hands, twirling with joy.

After dinner, Willy usually continued, in his low-key way, the family campaign to convince me that Abemama had been treated unfairly by history. One night he drew my attention to a faded photograph and said, "That's the king we had when the British annexed our island." It showed the ten-year-old Paul, barefoot, scowling into the camera and looking, with his round hat and scarf, like an organ grinder's monkey. Posed behind him were a dozen Old Men and a blond European, the first British Resident. "He never agreed to the appointment of that Resident," Willy said. "Never! The other islands, they agreed, but not Paul. That is why our legal position is different from the others." To prove this point he dragged out a mimeographed copy of "The Proceedings of HMS *Royalist*," identified as being written by Captain E.H.M. Davis, RN, May–August 1892. The document had been discovered in 1970 in an abandoned file in Tarawa by a Mrs. Romilly, stenographer to the assistant resident commissioner. An introduction summarized it as showing that the protectorate was motivated by a desire to curb the excesses of missionaries and traders, and to confiscate guns sold by traders to local kings — or, to put it another way, Europeans had annexed these islands to put an end to the criminal behavior of other Europeans.

Here is Captain Davis on the native society he found: "The standard of morality on these islands is decidedly high. Polygamy and infanticide are almost extinct . . . [the natives] are, on the whole, a peaceable and law-abiding people."

By contrast, he accused the white traders of introducing gambling, gin, and firearms, of promoting civil wars in order to sell their weapons, and of committing murder and rape. And he said of the European missionaries, "They trade, charge too much for books and forbid all dancing and singing except for hymns. . . . At nearly every island I was asked if the Queen would let them dance and sing."

Captain Davis swept through the Gilberts like a combination of Cecil Rhodes and Wyatt Earp, an empire builder and a lawman taming the Pacific frontier. He collected debts, levied fines, settled disputes, and confiscated guns, claiming that "most of the kings seemed happy to surrender the weapons bought from traders." He doggedly investigated crimes that were as much as a decade old. In one island, he "took further evidence with regard to the charge of rape proffered against Jorgenson, a Dane trading on the island." He settled a war between North and South Tarawa, drawing up a treaty and appointing the southern king ruler, since the northern one had been murdered two months earlier. Davis tracked down his assassin but let him off with a lecture. "I told him I did not think he had any reason to be proud of his exploit, having shot the King in his sleep — but I would look on it as an act of war." He was less charitable toward a native named Nantarabe, charged with the murder of a Mr. A. H. Sam, a Chinese from Hong Kong killed nine years earlier on the island of Butariari. It was Nantarabe's misfortune to have murdered a British subject. He was tried and executed at Tarawa, and just over my head, on the wall of the Robert Louis Stevenson Hotel, was a picture of him, tied to a palm tree and being shot by a British sailor, the whole witnessed by three officers in white topees.

On every island except Abemama, Davis assembled the Old Men in their maneaba, explaining the protectorate and gaining their approval to being ruled by a British Resident. Willy, who had been checking my progress through the Davis document, underlined with a finger the crucial entry: "16 July: Missed seeing Paul, King of Abemama. Said that all the other islands had asked for the appointment of a white Resident and I hoped he would do the same." It was the contention of Willy, George, and Donald that the king had never formally agreed, and that Abemama's status in the protectorate, and in independent Kiribati, was therefore different from that of the other atolls.

But more interesting than this questionable point of law was Davis's description of Abemama in 1892, which, with a few alterations, would have been accurate now. He wrote: "Three whites. . . . Population of 700: 150 Protestants. Labor: none. Marriage laws: betrothal. Exports: 150 tons of copra. Produce: Copra, pandanus, taro, breadfruit. Weapons: 100 guns in King's possession. Communication: American/German vessels. King does all the trading. Laws and customs: not known." Today, medicine has quadrupled the population and the royal family has lost its weapons, but Abemama is the same in its exports, marriage laws, and lack of salaried work, and the royal trading monopoly is being replaced by a government one.

Davis described "natives of fine physique, clean and healthy looking [and] nearly all well clothed. . . . Village is very clean — neat coral paths — maneaba large and very neat and suspended to the roof of the building was the massive platform on which Tenbinoka [King Binoka] — who weighed 20 stone [280 pounds] — was carried." Except for the platform, this could have described the villages and the maneaba I saw with Willy. You might be tempted to describe Abemama as "timeless," if that word had not already been so overused. Abemama was really more heedless — or, even better, contemptuous — of time, and it was just possible to entertain the fantasy that as long as you stayed there, you too might not age.

I rode on the back of Willy's motorbike to the Society of the Sacred Heart Mission. I wanted to convey to the sisters, as promised, the regards of Père Gustaaf. The mission was as far south as you can drive in Abemama and the closest I came to the equator in the Pacific, less than thirty miles. The tiny, neighboring atolls of Aranuka and Kuria are closer by several miles, but neither has either a king or an Equator Town.

The solar panels glittering on the rectory roof proved it was a thriving mission. "We are the first, the very first, in Kiribati to use solar power," said the mother superior, Sister Damiana Kauea. She was a jolly Hollywood nun who went barefoot and had the untroubled face of an adolescent. Her rooms were breezy and cool, with palms outside their windows and walls decorated with marvelous paper flowers. (Abemama's lack of bees makes real flowers scarce.) A novitiate brought us biscuits and instant coffee while Sister Kauea told me of her eighteen novitiates and twenty-five married couples training to be lay preachers. "Here we are rich in spiritual life. The catechists also have families to look after, but still they come here for instructions, and in increasing numbers."

In a directory of the society's missions we found Père Gustaaf's name. Sister Kauea lost her smile when I described Mbandaka's shrinking membership, and she promised to pray for them and write an encouraging letter. I said the Mbandaka mission was intersected by the equator, pointing out that her mission was almost as close. Did she know how many miles it was? No, she did not. Did anyone speak about the equator? No again. She was polite, but my questions bored her. Now that she had an American in her parlor, she wanted to discuss the U.S. Navy Seabees, even though she had been only a girl when they spent their fabled four months on Abemama, in 1944. They had erected a village of Quonset huts, introduced baseball, and built nineteen miles of road and the packed coral

landing strip on which my plane had put down, naming it
O'Hare Field after naval hero Lieutenant Commander Butch
O'Hare, the same man who gave his name to Chicago's airport,
although Abemama memorialized him first. The Seabees next
turned their attention to the mission, where for two years the
nuns had worked without medical supples, mail, or news from
outside. They stocked the mission with canned food, installed
electric lights running off a portable generator, and donated a
small library of books, a water pump, a powerful radio, and a
kerosene refrigerator, teaching the nuns to make, from canned
milk and powdered fruit extracts, the miracle of ice cream.

At the Mission of the Sacred Heart, these men were still legendary heroes. Sister Kauea had a copy of their yearbook, kept a
scrapbook filled with their letters and pictures, and described their
accomplishments as if they had occurred only yesterday. To
please her, I leafed slowly through the Seabee yearbook, admiring
their tractors and agreeing that although they were young men,
they had shown respect for the customs of Abemama. The proof
of this was a Seabee sign saying CITY LIMIT. TEKATIRIAKE. SLOW TO
10 MPH. ALL TROOPS ARE FORBIDDEN TO ENTER HOUSES.

I asked if I might see the mural Brian Orme had described,
assuming that it adorned the wall of the mission church, but Sister Kauea said it was in Tebanga. Mention of the mural made her
giggle and shake her head. The artist was a man named Kiraua,
who now resided in Tarawa. He had no training and, at the time
he painted it, had never left Abemama. "Where *did* he find the
idea for that picture? Oh my, I've been wondering ever since he
did it. We have searched our books for the inspiration, but it is
like nothing we can find. I believe it came from his soul, his faith,
but it terrifies our children. During the services they stare at his
picture of hell, and the priest has difficulty keeping their attention.
Because of that mural, the children of Abemama, they are terrified
of hell."

The little girls playing jacks with cowrie shells on the steps of
the Tebanga church confirmed this: While the ball was in midair,
they slapped hands, touched their ears, and crossed themselves
twice before grabbing a fistful of shells. The mural covered the
wall behind the altar, but the eye quickly skipped from Jesus, surrounded by six trumpeting angels, and from the Sea of Galilee,
with its Italianate villas and modern speedboat, to Kiraua's lurid

hell. Eight naked, emaciated sinners, their mouths open in screams, were being roasted in a flaming oven. Above them a man hung upside down, a green serpent coiled around his naked body. The devil was a winged goat-man with a furry white body, pandanus-grass skirt, clawed feet, tusks, and rainbow-colored wings. It was not the devil but the naked sinner he had speared who bore an unmistakable resemblance to Brian Orme — or, if you will, Robert Louis Stevenson. In fact, all the sinners in Mr. Kiraua's hell were white — or pink, after being broiled in the flames.

Back at the hotel, King George and Donald were sipping orange Fantas and contemplating the mounds that rose on the far shore of the sea channel. The king said, "In my father's time, they dug up those mounds looking for Paul's treasure. They were unsuccessful, but my grandsons are giving it another go."

Donald moved to have a better view of the mounds. "All we need is to get our hands on a metal detector and do some more excavations. We are convinced there is money there."

"When my grandfather Paul was dying, he kept asking for my father," the king said. "We think it was to tell him where the family's wealth was buried. Sadly, he died without communicating this information."

"When did this happen?"

"I think 1929, but since we lost our family tree we cannot be sure of the date." In 1963 the king had loaned this document to an anthropologist, who never returned it. The loss was serious. The king knew the names of his ancestors, but without the family tree he had difficulty placing them in order and remembering their ages at their marriages and deaths. He remembered that his father-in-law, the trader Alfred Smith, had saved King Binoka's life "sometime in the 1880s," but the actual date was on the family tree. He remembered that Smith was unafraid of the Japanese bombing and walked out under his umbrella to watch the Allies attack, but he was unsure when he had died. Given the choice, I think King George would have preferred recovering the family tree to recovering the family treasure.

Donald believed my best chance for finding a copy of the Old Men's letter to the queen lay with Joseph Lameko, a Tuvaluan schoolteacher who had lived most of his life in the Gilbert Islands. While we sat in Lameko's house, waiting for a grandson to find him, Donald whispered that his nationality explained the splendor of his furnishings. "We Abemamans like things to be more simple, and we don't need such modern possessions." The "modern" possessions occasioning this comment were an ancient sewing machine, some partitions painted mustard yellow, and a pendulum clock.

Lameko had a strong, bare chest, a handsome face, and the bearing of a Roman senator, a position similar, really, to that of an Old Man on Abemama. He had helped compose the letter to the queen. "It was written by hand," he said, "and then translated into English by an expatriate sympathetic to us." He remembered it as a simple communication—"We just asked for independence or for the Queen to keep looking after us here"—but he lacked a copy because he had been away when the Old Men signed the final version. Perhaps this had affected its reception at the palace: "Since the Queen awarded me a BEM and an MBE, it is not impossible to think that my signature could have made a difference."

He had earned his MBE in recognition of his long service as teacher and educational administrator on Abemama. The BEM had come earlier, at the time of the queen's coronation and to reward his work on Betio after the battle of Tarawa, when he led the 400-man labor corps that cleared rubble and buried the dead. It sounded like grisly work, but like many war veterans, Lameko counted it among the happiest times of his life. With a faraway look he said, "Ah, the time of cleaning up. What a good time that was, a *very* good time. The Americans had left their country to see the world, but we saw it without moving. They landed planes filled with boxes of food, kinds we had never tasted, and of course, ice cream.

"The American dead lay on our beaches like big whales. When we found one, the Americans came with a priest and a coffin. The Japanese we dumped into a bomb crater, although it was impossible to tell if some bodies were American or Japanese. We spent six months doing that until finally we were burying only bones." He leaned across his mat, whispering, "And another reason that was a happy time for us is that we found many Japanese medals and swords. I was too ashamed to sell these souvenirs, but I can't blame the other boys. The Americans paid fifty dollars for a banzai sword. We also found many watches, still ticking on their wrists."

But weren't the people of Betio upset at the devastation? Not according to Joseph Lameko. They considered it a fair price for the cartons of cigarettes and exotic food. "Our only criticism was that the Americans were too quick with their OKs," he said. "They were always saying, 'OK OK OK OK . . . Let's move!' They were in too much of a hurry, that's why they lost so many men." Which is as succinct an assessment of the battle of Tarawa as I have heard anywhere.

Willy collected us on his way back from the airport, where he had picked up mail and supplies for the hotel. As we left, Donald said I had violated a principal tenet of Abemaman etiquette by showing Mr. Lameko the soles of my feet while sitting cross-legged. "That is considered very rude, because your feet might have shit on them. The three big taboos of Abemama are shit, heads, and height. The most important is heads. You never touch someone's head, put your head physically higher than someone else's on purpose, or emotionally raise yourself above them. That's why on Abemama we discourage men from singing while cutting toddy: Since they're high above the ground, they might appear to be lording it over everyone."

"Even the word 'head' can be taboo," Willy added. "I would never think of asking someone, 'Would you care to eat a fish head?' To use the same word to describe a human head and a fish head is so unthinkable we say, "Would you care to eat the part of the fish where the lips are?'"

"See how polite we are on Abemama?" Donald asked. "We are so polite we would rather forget an injustice than fight. That's why we are known as the ladies of Abemama. It is a compliment."

Willy slowed to five miles an hour as we passed through a village. "And here is another rule of etiquette: If you wish to be really polite, you dismount from your bicycle whenever you pass someone. This is simple respect, but many younger men ignore it, although even the rudest kids walk their bikes past a maneaba."

"We are trying to teach them to behave," Donald said. "Every month we have a meeting in one of the maneabas where the Old Men and I lecture the children on history and customs.

This helps, but our problem is people becoming too individualistic and ignoring the good of the community."

As he spoke, Donald ripped open a package that had arrived on the plane. Inside were five video cassettes: *Jaws, Shogun, Death Race, The Werewolf of Washington,* and a James Bond movie. He explained he would show these movies in the village maneabas on his grandfather's VCR, charging admission. "My father did it until recently, but now I've taken over. It's a very competitive business, because several traders have VCRs." He spoke rapidly, never looking up from his cassettes. He was too intelligent not to know what he was doing, and what I was thinking—namely, that he first arrived in a village to deliver a stern talk on preserving island customs, then returned to screen just the type of movie that is everywhere the enemy of traditional culture. It was one step forward, two back.

"It's my job, my living," he said lamely. "Listen, the other traders charge children half price, but I charge them full. That discourages their attendance."

I said nothing.

"And tonight I'll show *Shogun.* I think it's the least violent."

The next morning King George was at his usual table, staring at the horizon, puffing his cigarettes and chuckling. I asked how he rated the etiquette of the average Abemaman. "First off, you must know the other islands are in a sorry state, with few customs remaining. But that's how they were even before the British—no customs, no manners." He picked a wad of old food from his teeth, spitting it onto the sand. "Whereas we are known as the most polite people in the Gilberts, perhaps in the whole Pacific. You can always pick out people from Abemama in a crowd. They are quiet and patient. In fact, we are famous for being quite harmless.

"This changing of our culture began with the war and having all those foreign soldiers here. The Japanese tortured people with electricity, even the island lunatic, although the worst thing they did was to smack some women on the head in public. This is an insult we've never forgotten, and it made the Americans very popular when they came. They affected our culture in small ways, but we were happy with them. Much worse have been the American movies. They have a terrible effect on the young, who see violence and bad manners and imitate them, even the karate."

He drained his Coke in a swallow and stubbed out a cigarette half-smoked. Just thinking about these movies had angered him. "And the men who broke into that warehouse on Tarawa, how did they learn to do that? What gave them that idea?" The king moistened his lips, as if savoring a tasty dish. "I'll tell you how . . . the fucking movies!"

He rocked back in his chair. "But people enjoy these movies, and I suppose we must give them freedom of choice, although we try to persuade them to avoid the worst."

Donald had chosen an inappropriate time to sit down next to his grandfather, with a blank poster and a felt-tip pen, to compose advertisements for tonight's movie and to solicit our advice as to which one that should be. "*Shogun* was a disaster," he said. "Too much dialogue, and people became restless because they can't understand English that well. They like action, violence, adventure. Do you know this *Werewolf of Washington?*"

I suggested *Jaws.*

"No, we've seen that too many times. I'll try James Bond and hope it's not *Goldfinger,* which we just had."

In lurid colors he wrote "James Bond!" The king rolled his eyes. "I can't imagine why you must do this movie business. It's distasteful, demeaning, and besides, you can't be making more than a few dollars a day."

"But everyone watches these films now."

"Not everyone here, thank God."

"If I didn't show them someone else would."

"Then let them. You are too intelligent to be engaged in this."

"My movies aren't the worst enemy of our culture," Donald said. "It's jealousy and competition between our people."

Willy joined us and said, "So many people have been dying with their skills and secrets that government officers are now going around interviewing everyone, trying to find out what they know before they die."

"The martial arts have been lost," Donald said. "The man who knew about them took his secrets to the grave."

"And the magical chants—"

"Navigational skills. People pretend to know the secrets of navigation, but they only know the rudiments. Every generation has less knowledge."

"Family trees are also kept secret. People fear that otherwise distant relatives will turn up to claim their lands and property."

Donald looked at his grandfather. "This is really why our culture is dying out."

"Yes," Willy said. "Cultural suicide."

"But what's causing this?" the king asked, tapping Donald's movie poster with one finger. "Is it because they find this new culture so exciting that they wish to kill off the old?"

The king was not a very convincing crusader against the evils of modern culture. After all, his VCR screened these films, and he later complained to me, "It's not good for my television, plugging it into the systems at those maneabas. Salt can easily get in the works. If you consider the depreciation on my set, then it's a losing proposition for us, showing those damned movies."

The patrons at Donald's movie were mostly boys under twelve. They sat cross-legged on the floor of the maneaba, quiet and respectful, as if in the classroom of a strict teacher. The rows of brown backs and upturned heads reminded me of a UNESCO brochure: "The third-world leaders of tomorrow learn," etc. But instead of a blackboard, their attention was fixed on the king's television.

The first film was an Australian television documentary about Kiribati. In a flat, authoritative voice, the narrator said, "Sanitary conditions are poor, and introducing toilets to the islanders has had its difficulties. People eat a diet too heavy in sugar and starch." Next, an Australian social worker asked a startled old man, "Did *you* have sugar in your coffee today?"

"But people like sugar," Donald whispered. "It's what they want."

The only bright spot in this picture of an unhappy people crapping everywhere and bloating themselves with sugar was the Australian Development Administration, which, we were told, was sponsoring a large project in Tarawa. "These workers," said the narrator, "are regarded as the lucky ones."

Donald admitted to not having previewed this documentary, and he regretted showing it. First his audience of little Abemaman boys saw Australians depict them as pathetically backward, and then the James Bond film, *Live and Let Die*, showed the standard of civilization to which they should aspire. In its opening minutes, a UN delegate died in agony as a high-frequency sound was piped through his headphones, a man was knifed while watching a parade, and another was tied to a stake and tortured during a voodoo ceremony. The credits showed a nude woman lying on a flaming skull. The hunched-over boys watched in reverent silence, little exemplars of Abemaman etiquette, as they learned about the world beyond their reef.

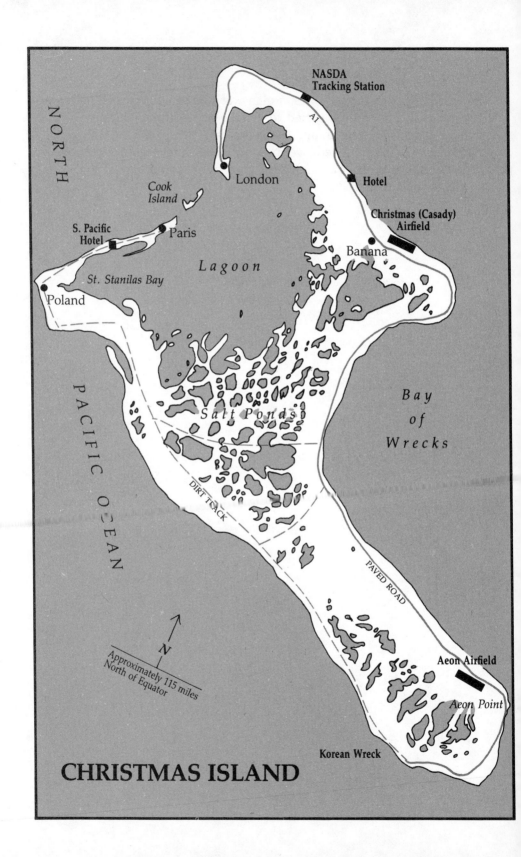

NASDA
Tracking Station

NORTH

A1

Hotel

Christmas (Casady)
Airfield

London

*Cook
Island*

Paris

Banana

S. Pacific
Hotel

L a g o o n

St. Stanilas Bay

Poland

*B a y
o f
W r e c k s*

P A C I F I C   O C E A N

Salt Ponds

DIRT TRACK

PAVED ROAD

N

Approximately 115 miles
North of Equator

Aeon Airfield

Aeon Point

Korean Wreck

CHRISTMAS ISLAND

18

I FLEW TO CHRISTMAS ISLAND ON A PLANE AS EMPTY AS THE Pacific. There were only eleven of us on this weekly flight from Honolulu, scattered like atolls across an ocean of green seats. Nine of the passengers were fishermen: four Japanese, three Japanese-Americans from Hawaii, and two Alaskans. The equatorial current stirs up plankton, making Christmas and the other Line islands a famous destination for fishermen. Ahab had followed the white whale into these waters, and the Alaskan fishermen seemed equally as obsessed with their quarry, the bonefish.

"We've been looking forward to this for a year," "Gil" said, popping his eyes like a hooked fish.

"Two years!" "Mike" corrected. "Last year they canceled the plane because we were the only passengers."

I asked where they lived. "The biggest king salmon in the world — *the world!* — was caught where we live," Mike said.

"Yes, but where's that?"

They looked amazed that this clue was not enough. "The Kenai Peninsula in southern Alaska, of course."

They were easy to confuse, Mike and Gil. They had long

faces and droopy moustaches, and they moved through the plane with the jerky gait of Keystone Cops. They crooked their fingers into imaginary hooks and cast imaginary lines. They snapped open boxes of lures and passed them around like hors d'oeuvres. The Japanese bowed and held out their own tackle for inspection. The Hawaiians moved their palms back and forth like automatic doors, measuring the length of famous catches. Mike and Gil widened their eyes and nudged ribs.

I quickly exhausted my fish stories: twenty flounder hooked in a Cape Cod harbor, a brown trout landed after days of casting through a Scottish drizzle, and the sailfish caught (mostly by the charter captain) off Acapulco. What I really remembered were hours of sunburn and seasickness, boredom and cold, disdain for the flounder, and pity for the sailfish. Seeing these stories were a disappointment, I said I enjoyed eating fish.

Gil pulled a face. "But we're going for bonefish, a sport fish. They're such terrible eating you throw them back. Besides, I never eat fish—hate the taste. Sure hope there're some steaks in the hotel freezer."

The tenth passenger was a U.S. Air Force pilot named Doug, coming to see if military aircraft could land on Christmas Island in an emergency. He had recently pulled his measuring wheel down airstrips in Honduras and the Philippines. He said, "First I ask the police if they can provide security at the airport, and it's always, 'Sure we can.' Can the control tower handle our planes? They say 'Yes.' Can the fire truck extinguish our fires? 'Of course.' Then I measure the runway."

"It sounds like the work of a day."

"Yup. Guess I'll sit in my room the other six."

From the air, Christmas Island resembled a lamb chop. The lagoon was the tasty eye; the long rib pointed southeast and was dotted with salt ponds of a chemical blue. Picture 125 square miles of Utah flats, planted with coconut palms and set adrift in the Pacific, and you have Christmas Island.

We disembarked and the sun skipped off crushed coral, exploding in our faces. We had arrived during a drought, and palm fronds drooped like thirsty tongues, blackening in the sun. The departing passengers huddled in the narrow shade of a shed marked Transit. Mike cupped his mouth, bellowing against the salty wind. "Hey! How's the fishing?"

"Great!"

"Best in the world!"

Mike and Gil almost danced into Arrivals. One of the Hawaiian fishermen took a photograph of me standing underneath a sign saying WELCOME TO KIRITIMATI [the closest the Kiribati language can get to "Christmas"]. ELEVATION 5 FEET. 119 MILES NORTH OF EQUATOR, and I helped them carry their empty ice chests to the hotel van. "This time next week," one said, "these will be heavy with fish."

Just outside the airport, a sign indicated that Poland was thirty-two miles to the left, the hotel three to the right, and London a further fourteen. We were in Banana. There were two small maneabas, a hut the size of a double outhouse with Ba-nANA HOSPital scrawled across its front, and children playing with cowrie shells in pools of shade cast by palm trees. They sat in the middle of the road, and we slowed to drive around them. Our driver had a cracked smile and a halo of frizzy gray hair, a sort of Micronesian Albert Einstein. He said London was the island's "capital," Poland was several hours' drive around the lagoon, and Paris was abandoned. "Which has the most people?" I asked.

"Banana."

But where were the bananas?

He giggled. "No bananas in Banana." In fact, there wasn't a banana anywhere on the island.

Then why the name?

"Ask the British army. They named it. You must tell us if you find out. We would like to know too."

The Captain Cook Hotel was a U-shaped building of cinder blocks and tin broiling in an open yard of sand and crushed coral, fifty yards from the ocean reef. The bar was paneled with wood that had washed ashore after the wreck of the *Aeon,* in 1909. For sixty-five years it lay untouched on the sand, surrounded by crockery and children's toys from the same ship. A woman brought me a lukewarm beer and fell asleep, her head on the counter. Fans hummed and a salt-laden wind swept through the louvered windows. On the wall were photographs of men in baseball caps, grinning and holding dead fish.

The transvestite from Tuvalu who led me to a room was tall as a Tusi and lurched across the coral pathways in spiky high heels. Being a transvestite on Christmas Island had to require devotion: Rouge and mascara were not easily purchased, and the Tuvaluan's padded bra and woolen halter must have been uncomfortable in the heat. He said there was no public transportation, not even a taxi, and so few vehicles I could not count on hitching. I took his advice and rented one of the eight white Japanese pickup trucks owned by JMB Rentals. Mrs. JMB was in the hotel to take orders. She was pretty, with clever eyes that darted like tropical fish. She quickly sized me up as a traveler on a budget and suggested "the cheap one." "It is cheap because it is old and because" — she covered her mouth, stifling a laugh — "because of the brakes."

"The brakes?"

"Yes, but nothing to worry about." An audience gathered. Someone kicked the tires of the cheap one. Einstein and the Tuvaluan chorused, "Yes, is good truck. Vroom!" They fell against its door, helpless with laughter. It sounded as if I should certainly worry.

"No, you have no worry," Mrs. JMB said, "because here there is nothing to brake for."

The Japanese fishermen waddled into the dining room wearing bathing suits and rubber reef-walkers. They bolted their food, leaving in ten minutes. Mike and Gil accelerated their forks, muttering, "We'll be out there in an hour . . . We won't be back until late, *very* late." Even though they were after bonefish, while the Japanese hoped to fill their ice chests with tuna, an unspoken competition was underway. The winner would be whoever fished the most and the Japanese had taken round one.

I walked down the road to the nearest building, the Development Office. The job of development officer on Christmas Island is one for the courageous or the foolhardy. During a hundred years of human settlement, the island's climate and isolation have wrecked almost as many economic development plans as its reef has ships. In the 1850s, Americans failed to mine guano, because the soil was too porous to bind the dung. At the turn of the century, Lever Brothers cultivated silver-lip pearl shell in the lagoon but soon abandoned the scheme as unprofitable. They planted seventy thousand coconut palms, and immediately three quarters died during a drought. A rogue French priest named Father Rougier bought the island, planting another half-million coconuts. For decades his plantation flourished, collapsing only when the Polynesian cutters accused his nephew of murder, torture, and slavery. Britain annexed the island just before the Second World War, attaching it to the Gilberts. In 1956, an airline erected a Quonset hut and a seaplane dock so its Honolulu-Fiji flight could overnight on Christmas Island. One week before the inaugural run, Britain announced it would test nuclear bombs, and during the next four years as many as four thousand military personnel and scientists lived here. In 1962, the United States and Britain jointly conducted twenty-four high-altitude tests. The military departed two years later, leaving behind a macadam road, a new wharf, and enough scrap metal, wood, and machinery to build homes, schools, and government offices for a population that grew from fifty in 1947 to twelve hundred today. The nuclear tests had proven to be Christmas Island's most successful "development program."

The Development Office stood empty, creaking in the wind. A screen door banged, reports fluttered, and metal cabinets rattled like tambourines. The documents piled on desks and chairs were stiff with salt and held down by chunks of coral. Yellowing newspaper clippings covered a bulletin board. They described sea monsters and disappearances.

I read TWENTY TON STING RAY HUNTING HUMAN PREY! The creature was two hundred feet from nose to tail and had "the wing span of a B-29." The Bikini atomic tests were responsible, perhaps. In the Philippines, it killed 150 people on a ferry. In the Marshall Islands, it claimed two fishing boats. It "exploded from the water like an erupting volcano" and was "last seen headed for the Line Islands." Someone had underlined this warning in red.

I read GIANT OCTOPUSES KILL TWO. Two Kiribati fishermen had been drowned by giant octopuses. The creatures were "at least four yards long" and "probably a result of the nuclear tests." In Kiribati, they hunt octopuses by encouraging the beasts to cling to their bodies, then floating to the surface, where a second fisherman bites the octopus between the eyes, killing it. The appearance of these vicious octopuses had prompted the Kiribati minister of natural resources to announce, "We are going to have to find another way of killing octopuses now."

Someone at the Development Office had made a hobby of the mysterious disappearances that seem to plague the Line Islands. The Second World War airport on Christmas Island was named for a young American fighter pilot who disappeared while on a routine patrol, and a British corporal had vanished during the nuclear tests, despite search parties that combed the island. The Australian manager of the copra plantation on nearby Fanning Island had only recently disappeared, perhaps a suicide, and last year a copra cutter on Christmas Island had stolen church funds and a jerry can of fuel and was never seen again.

One Development Office clipping suggested that Amelia Earhart had crashed on the Line Islands; another described mysterious events on nearby Palmyra. In 1974, an American couple had disappeared while cruising the Line Islands. Months later, friends recognized their yacht in a Honolulu marina, repainted and renamed. Fishermen from Fanning Island dragged the Palmyra lagoon and found a tin box containing teeth and bones.

Whoever had collected these stories was right: There was something spooky about these uninhabited, or lightly populated, islands floating in so much empty ocean, about pieces of sandy desert ringed by waves and overpopulated with birds, and places with so few people mysteriously losing so many. A hundred yards behind the office was the kind of empty, boiling sea where bodies might disappear while gigantic squid trod water. Waves rolled in from Ecuador like exhausted runners, flopping against a fringing reef and spewing a gasp of salt before collapsing in eddies. In the North Atlantic, water this rough comes with gray skies and gale warnings; here it was sun lit, eerie as a Hitchcock movie.

I hiked several miles over smashed coral and sharp lava. Scabs of red seaweed speckled the sand, and so many crab holes honeycombed it that every step crushed a crab home. Bird silhouettes flitted across the sand, their shadows so huge I could imagine wind gusts from their wings, and overhead tornadoes of black noddies whirled like cinders rising from a bonfire. I saw coconut husks, rusted bolts from the nuclear tests, and clamps the size of jawbones. A bird's skull rested against a plank of bleached driftwood, as if arranged for a still life. Two small orange life preservers lay several yards apart, their straps ripped open. They were the same child's size. Twins?

Swimming was impossible. The sea was rough, the reef treacherous and patrolled by gray sharks. They sounded as vicious as those at St. Paul's Rocks. Even my counterculture Pacific Islands guidebook, which encouraged risky enterprises, said, "The reefs around Christmas Island teem with fish, but gray sharks are also numerous. . . . It is recommended that divers bring a shark billy or bang stick." A midshipman on Captain Cook's third voyage, during which the island was discovered on Christmas Day 1777, wrote in his diary, "On every side of us swam sharks innumerable and so voracious that they bit our oars and rudder and I actually stuck my hanger two inches into the back of one whilst he had the rudder between his teeth."

I drove my JMB truck inland, toward what a sign described as BOATING AND BATHING LAGOON 2-1/2 M. Every few hundred yards I pumped the faulty brakes and slid into another intersection of dirt tracks left by the nuclear testers or the government copra plantation. The interior was a labyrinth of palm, heliotrope, saltbush, and abandoned military equipment. Half-tracks, steam shovels, bulldozers, and jeeps stood abandoned under yellowing palms, all slowly melting, like Black Sambo's tigers, into rusty puddles.

Now I understood why the fishing guides took CB radios and the hotel warned against driving alone. Christmas Island had more in common with other deserts than sand, scorpions, and atomic tests. It also offered the possibility of becoming fatally lost. No sooner had Captain Cook discovered the island than two of his crewmen disappeared. One survived a day on turtle blood, and the other, according to Cook's diary, "having met with a pool of clear water he went into it with his clothes on in hope of refreshing himself, but unluckily this water . . . proved no other than a pool of strong brine, by which his limbs and clothes became so stiff that he was hardly able to crawl out and in this condition he was found."

There are no hills on Christmas Island from which to take your bearings, and during the middle of the day, when the equatorial sun is overhead, it is difficult to tell east from west. Try walking a straight line toward the ocean and you are quickly turned around by hedges of saltbush. You can find the lagoon and still be lost because, unlike Tarawa or Abemama, it is chopped into a tangle of channels, inlets, and salt ponds. I learned this firsthand because my JMB truck stalled and I had to walk. Twice I took wrong turns, following dirt tracks deep into graveyards of military scrap.

In 1962, the arms talks at Geneva collapsed when the Soviets resumed atmospheric testing. In retaliation, President Kennedy announced the resumption of American tests, and Britain offered Christmas Island as a site. Within four months, an American general named Starbird had transformed it into what he described as a "gigantic outdoor nuclear laboratory." He rebuilt the British facilities, resurfaced roads, and constructed barracks for three thousand men. He was praised for a feat of logistical wizardry. Twenty years of sun and salt had transformed this "laboratory" into the landscape of a post-nuclear nightmare, a wasteland where everything had the look of being roasted in a nuclear flash, leaving as sole survivor the land crab. Jeep doors banged in the wind, hinges creaked, and the crabs scuttled through pancaked Quonset huts. You could imagine this disintegration continuing for centuries, unheard and unwitnessed.

As I walked through the ruins, I heard an imaginary Geiger counter clicking. A dinosaur of a steam shovel sat mired in salt bog, its bucket frozen in midair. Click . . . Coconuts had shattered the windshields of a line of jeeps with U.S. Army stenciled on their doors. Click . . . click. The license plates of a disemboweled Chevrolet said, For Official Use Only. Click . . . click . . . click. An observation tower lay on its side, tripods stood on concrete platforms, and blackened chimneys towered over foundations. Click . . . click . . . click . . . click. I poked my head into the back of a windowless van, seeing broken gauges and banks of lights. Earphones dangled from a hook, and wires spilled like intestines from instrument panels. Perspiring soldiers and scientists had probably been trapped in here for hours, scribbling on clipboards, puffing pipes, and cursing the heat as they waited for a van-rocking blast to set their dials spinning. Clickclickclickclickclick.

I stumbled into JMB Rentals minutes before sunset. JMB stood for John Bryden, a hulking Scotsman with a sun-scorched complexion. He was too good-natured for his size, the sort of man cowards size up as someone easily teased. The woman with the darting tropical-fish eyes was his wife, Anna. They both laughed as if they had been expecting me, and Bryden pushed a beer into my hand. His house was unfinished, a cinder-block barn open to the east. He had taken the overhead beams from abandoned bunkers and patched together his garage and workshop from other nuclear leftovers. Outside was a heap of scrap, his capital.

We drank more beer, staring out his open wall at the blackening sky. "It's not a pretty island, is it?" he said. "And as you've found, there's nowhere to swim. I tried jogging, but it's too bloody hot." He began his sentences with a Scots burr, ending them with a Micronesian laugh. "But I've been here five years, so I guess it isn't all bad." He had come to the Line Islands on contract as an agricultural officer, living first on Fanning and assuming management of the copra plantation when the Australian manager disappeared. "I preferred it there," he said. "More of a paradise, but there's no basis for a business," the "basis" on Christmas Island being the scrap and the visiting fishermen. He also had a truck and hauled cargo at the dock and airport. He repaired the island's vehicles and sold petrol from drums. In Zaïre, he would have been called a "Qaddaffi."

At every turn Bryden confounded the beachcomber myth. Instead of living on fish and coconuts, he had a freezer stocked with meat. He worked long days and filled his life with busted machinery and Hollywood films. He was more a Crusoe than a Gauguin, taking pride in the modest luxuries he could fashion from the nuclear scrap. His newest enterprise was renting videotaped movies. There were several VCRs on the island, and the maneabas sponsored weekly showings. He had bought a library of taped movies from a departing satellite engineer.

"We used to have lots more!" Anna said. "But people never return them, or they copy and rent them themselves. It's shocking!"

"Ach, who cares. They were pirated in the first place."

"But they stole *The Sound of Music*."

"We saw that at least twenty times," he said, his eyes softening. "It was her favorite and, well, I liked it too." He turned to her. "I'll erect our dish next week and we'll aim it at the HBO satellite over Kansas. They're sure to run *Sound of Music* soon."

The sun fell and mosquitoes hummed. The room darkened and we became silhouettes. Bryden sighed. "It's my fault about those tapes. But I can't bear confrontations or arguments. A few years ago we had four British technical advisers and they didn't get along, to the point of not talking. It was embarrassing to see them sitting with their families in the hotel lounge at different tables. If I wanted to speak with them, I'd have to move from table to table. I've always hated that sort of feuding and unpleasantness. Guess that's why I like Christmas Island."

Tekeira Mwemwenikiaki, the hotel's guest activities director, was the most organized, time-conscious Micronesian I met. He walked barefoot but lived by the clock. He wore a watch with an alarm, arrived early for every appointment, and scheduled the fishermen to leave at odd times like 7:55 and 4:20. He was thirty but already complaining of what sounded like an ulcer.

I was a challenge, the rare visitor who had not come to fish. "We will plan a complete week's schedule for you," he said over breakfast the next morning. "Straightaway we will drive to London to see the prison and cooperative store and to arrange audiences with government officials." He made the island's Europeans sound like a menagerie, carefully assembled to contain one of each species. There was a shipwrecked Canadian boy married to a local girl, a German-Fijian-American who exported tropical fish, the Mormon manager of the Japanese satellite-tracking station, and a Briton who had lived in the Pacific for decades, changing religions with the seasons. For the weekend, Tekeira promised a feast in his maneaba and the arrival of the twice-a-year steamer from Tarawa, a major event since everyone was expecting a relative or a friend (and since this was the only reasonable form of transportation between Christmas Island and the rest of Kiribati. The other way was to fly via Majuro and Honolulu, a four-thousand-mile journey which took several days and cost over two thousand dollars round trip.) On my last day we would drive to Paris and Poland, stopping at ground zero and the wreck of a Korean fishing boat, the point on Christmas Island nearest the equator.

Tekeira was a puzzle. One moment he was making fun of himself for not eating sashimi, saying, "I hear it's good, but to eat it is taboo to my family. See, I'm a modern man who went to school but refuses to eat fish." (Many Kiribati families believe themselves descended from certain fish, so eating these species is like eating their ancestors.) The next moment he was claiming to dislike fish because it made him fat. "Our women are too big because they eat too much fish. If I eat canned meat or chicken, why, I'm hungry a few minutes later, but when you eat fish" — he patted his stomach — "then you feel really full."

One moment he was describing the shark nets the British had strung across the bathing lagoons and the helicopters that shadowed swimmers, watching for sharks; the next moment he was saying, "Don't worry, they never attack. Just slap your feet and they run away." Then he admitted that the scar across his wrist was a shark bite.

Like everyone on this island he ended his sentences with a laugh, as if everything — too much rain during El Niño or too little now, the high price of beer or the low price of copra, or a shark bite — were a long-running joke. I mentioned that there was even more laughter here than on Abemama, and he said, "That's right! We are the happiest, friendliest people in this ocean." At first I thought it quaint, this custom of ending every sentence with a smile and a laugh. But what did it really mean? This morning the chef had laughed when he handed me a packed lunch, and I spent a moment wondering what in these sandwiches might be so amusing. Tekeira explained the laughter by saying, "It is because we know each other so well. We know everyone's habits, secrets, and history. Here, no one can fool anyone."

Tekeira had been fired from the Tarawa newspaper for writing an article critical of the government, an act either foolhardy or brave, since the government owned this newspaper, the only one in Kiribati, and he had spent years training to be a journalist. Now he wanted "to escape from the government controlling everything." He had chosen a strange place for this. Christmas Island was a frontier managed by the Kiribati government. It hoped to resettle people here from the overcrowded Tungaru atolls and it owned the copra plantation, employing most of the inhabitants as cutters. But for Tekeira, all this was outweighed by the island's isolation: "Our only contact with Tarawa is by radio, and sometimes that is impossible for days. Here we are really on our own, but I fear that will end in five years." And when that happened, he planned on moving to remote Fanning Island. It had no plane service, only two boats a year, and five hundred people. "It is paradise," he said. "You don't need money and you are really free of the government." But a moment later he was fretting about paying his son's school fees on Tarawa, then saying, "If I was lecturing the students here, you know what I'd tell them? 'Don't waste your time on education!' Ha! Look where it has put me. And next it will put me on Fanning Island." Where, I imagined, he could finally complete the tricky job of de-educating and de-Europeanizing himself.

We drove to London on an asphalt road covered with squashed crabs. Tekeira was a Buddhist about them, swerving to avoid hitting them, although the next day I learned the fishing guides often wagered which crabs their trucks would miss, so perhaps he was playing solitaire. London was a desert oasis, with palm groves, a limitless sky, and stifling silence. Every rooster, crying baby, and motorbike shocked like a fire alarm. Everywhere was proof that a satisfying life could be fashioned from coconuts and military scrap. Women baked bread in petrol drums, using coconut husks for fuel. Boys played tennis on the abandoned court of the officers' club, dashing barefoot across its crushed coral surface. Men earned wages cutting coconuts and storing copra (dried coconut meat) in warehouses still bearing signs like MOTOR POOL. People lived in cottages sided with salvaged wood and roofed in salvaged tin. Outside each was a heap of coils, sheet metal, and lumber. Most small towns have a scavenger hermit who hammers hubcaps to his walls and piles his yard with broken furniture and refrigerators. Take one of these bearded mutterers to Christmas Island and he would be in heaven.

The government offices were in the former army mess hall. The clerks went barefoot, and the wall calendar was a year out of date. Tekeira checked his watch. We were fifteen minutes early for my appointment. Or were we? The two wall clocks were set fifteen minutes apart.

While Tekeira consulted the doctor about an incipient ulcer, I visited with his friend Timaai, the assistant secretary for the Line Islands. His face and body were pear-shaped, and he wore a new earring. Like Tekeira, he had been exiled to Christmas Island because of that controversial newspaper article. He was the editor who had published it. "Tekeira and I were driven from Tarawa together," he said proudly. "But I am returning on the boat that arrives here Saturday. In actual fact, that boat has been due for several months. We are meant to have a ship four times a year, but it only comes when there is enough freight to justify the expense — twice a year, if we are lucky. That is the principal problem of Christmas Island: Our transportation is bloody awful."

I asked about the Nauru Line and the *CinPac II*. "Oh, we never count on that vessel. It is always being arrested somewhere, and the last time it arrived from Honolulu without our food supplies." He drew himself up. "That was the subject of an official protest—yes, an *official protest*!" He spluttered with laughter. "So I delivered our official protest to Island Traders. Their store is down the road. After that we ate fish and coconuts for five months. But there was a good aspect to this. Our shortage coincided with El Niño, when we were having a year of rain. The lagoon flooded, so we could stand in the road, scooping up fish in our hands. It is because of that shortage we now have a cooperative, and it has solved our food problems, we hope."

I found Robert, the manager of the cooperative store, in his warehouse, sitting on a carton of Pacific Cabin Biscuits. "Female stevedores!" he said to my first question. "That is the secret of the co-op's success." I looked confused. "They don't steal our members' orders like the men. Yes, we are built on female stevedores."

He thrust forward a ledger. "Look at this. You will be amazed. Here, use that chair. Is it comfortable? Good. We are pinching hotel chairs for the benefit of our members. Can you see it in our books? Three hundred members have joined in only six months, and we have made a net profit for them of ten thousand six hundred seven dollars and sixty-one cents Australian. But our stock is shrinking out." He swept an arm around the almost empty warehouse. "That ship from Tarawa is coming just in time to save our members from disappointment. I have ordered carefully, according to their desires." He slapped a box of cabin biscuits. "We have requested two hundred and fifty cases. Very popular. Tarawa biscuits are like cement, and members complain of needing steel teeth to eat them, but they love these Fiji biscuits.

"So what else is coming?" He checked a manifest. "Well, we pray for curried chicken." He dropped his voice. "In tin, I'm afraid. Forty cases ordered, forty cans to the case. Each member gets five curried chickens. And roast goose—tin too—thirty cases. And Mayfair, a quality beef stew!" He smacked his lips. "And thirty push-bikes, Royal Enfield from Birmingham, England. Not Chinese!" He pointed to a last carton of Ox and Palm corned beef. "This one is very speedy. My members are conservative people and prefer this one brand. We must have more. You see, sir,

when my members tire of fish and nuts, they love treating themselves to our imported delicacies."

Tekeira returned from the doctor, who had ruled out stomach
cancer and prescribed two beers, perhaps hoping it would relax
the patient. As we walked outside to the co-op members' canteen,
he whispered, "Robert is serious. He really believes in the co-op,
in serving the people. He is the closest we have"—he doubled
over in laughter—"to a Communist!"

"Some people hold back from joining our co-op," Robert
said. "But the canteen decides them. Oh yes, it pulls them right
in." The canteen was a screened-in porch with a long picnic table.
Members occupied every seat, eating slabs of fried corned beef
washed down with milky tea and smoking thin cigarettes filled
with Texas Twist tobacco. It was only ten A.M., but they were
already punch-drunk with laughter, gripped with what children
know as "the sillies." Men kicked each other under the table and
traded arm punches until, convulsed with laughter, they had to
lay their heads on the table. The tea ladies squeezed their necks.
One man lay across a bench, holding his stomach in painful hysterics.

A member said, "Here, we like to tease around."

"Now we are laughing about our president," one man translated. "He has sold our fishing rights to the Russians, and soon
the U.S.A. will pay us too. We will be a rich people." (This is
precisely what happened a year later, although the I-Kiribati did
not become rich.)

"How are we comparing?" Robert asked as we left. "You
must tell me in all honesty."

"Comparing?"

"Yes. In civilization. How are we comparing in civilization to
the U.S.A.?"

"In civilization?"

"In food? How are we comparing in that category? I tell my
members they are eating the same food as in the U.S.A."

As we waited for the prison warden to unlock the gate,
Tekeira said, "Here are our nation's very worst criminals." The
compound sat in the center of London, surrounded by a simple
fence. Prisoners could leave to fish and were able to converse with
civilians through the fence. "I have the eight most dangerous men
in Kiribati," the warden said with a proud smile. Inside I tripped

over a nylon cord, part of an unfinished fishnet. "My prisoners are wealthy men," the warden boasted. "Everyone wants to buy their nets, and they are excellent fishermen. They sell their catch to the copra cutters." And how did *they* feel, I wondered, about spending their days climbing up trees to cut coconuts while the convicts sat in this shady maneaba stringing nets?

The warden showed me a spacious room where his prisoners slept on mats, and the storeroom where their suitcases, packed with civilian clothes, awaited their release. He was like a gentleman farmer showing off his estate, and like many gentlemen farmers he was something of a bore. His prisoners' pigs were "the fattest on the island." Their papayas were "so sweet everyone wishes they could eat them." Their nets were "the best in Kiribati."

The inmates sat in a corner of their compound on coconut shells, poking a fire, like Boy Scouts toasting marshmallows. They wore blue bathing suits with yellow stripes down the side, a sort of uniform. They were the thinnest, fittest men I saw in Kiribati. They waved and threw jokes at the warden, who said, "They are here for seven to twelve years, this lot."

And what were their crimes?

He lowered his voice. "Oh, murder, rape, things like that."

He did a head count, ticking off each one by name on his sausage fingers. "Only seven!" He was momentarily panicked. "Ah, and one sweeping the post office, so I have" — he counted again on his fingers — "eight. All here! But I need four more. I have space for twelve, budget for twelve, but I only have eight. Tomorrow I get one on the boat." This thought made him happy. "Then I'll have nine, but . . . I still need three." He turned to me. "Do you know people in Tarawa? Write and tell them to send me three more, or I'll have to arrest Tekeira again."

"Oh yes, once I spent the night in jail," Tekeira admitted. "I was drunk at Ambos' Club. What a time I had with the mosquitoes here!" He pointed to the drunk tank, an evil concrete cell the size of a phone booth. On Christmas Island, a drunk suffered more than a convicted murderer.

The Cook Island bird sanctuary was a dot of land floating in the mouth of the lagoon. At times, sixteen million seabirds belonging to eighteen different species have nested on Christmas Island. They are attracted by its low rainfall, rich waters, and predictable temperatures, and by the fact that, after gliding thousands of miles on the Pacific air currents while migrating to and from Alaska, they have little choice. Alaskan plovers, I am told, can be seen collapsing in exhaustion on Christmas Island's beaches. There are also petrels, frigate birds, shearwaters and terns, tropical birds, and Edward-Lear-nonsense-rhyme birds like boobies, wandering tattlers, lorakeets, and noddies. Their populations plummeted when flashes from the atomic tests blinded them by the millions, and they recovered only to be reduced again by the El Niño of 1982, when heavy rains flooded nests and the reversal of the equatorial current decimated their food supply. Now they were returning, but in the millions rather than the sixteen millions.

The warden who took me to Cook Island admitted having little to do. The feral cats had not made it across, so man was the only predator. Islanders no longer gathered eggs, and no one hunted the birds for trophies or magical potions. We circled and crossed Cook Island single file, skirting nests and speaking in whispers. Finnish petrels were dug into the grass at the edge of the beach, like Japs in bunkers, and tropical birds sheltered underneath saltbushes, their tails resembling blood-dipped needles. Clear porcelain birds with black button eyes sat on heliotrope branches, facing away from the wind and ignoring us with the determination of a mountain gorilla. I could have easily touched these tame birds, or slapped them out of the sky.

Driving back to the hotel, we picked up Gary, the shipwrecked Canadian boy. He was walking hatless and bare-chested, with a white T-shirt flapping from his back pocket. He was coming to badger the hotel manager for a job, and the T-shirt was to make a good impression. Christmas Island is accustomed to marooned Europeans. Geography has made it the wrecking reef of European escapist dreams, the first place boat people hit after weeks of cruising to and from South America, Hawaii, or Australia, and a last chance to escape their yachts, the Pacific, or each other.

Gary was sixteen miles from Banana when we stopped, planning to walk the whole way. "Why not, man?" he said. "Got nothing else to do." We arrived to find the hotel manager on an errand, or hiding from Gary, so I spent several hours listening to his story. It was timeless, beginning with that telltale phrase "I wanted to see the world."

He had hitchhiked from his home in rural Canada to San Francisco and found work crewing on a yacht. The captain had outfitted it with oversized fish lockers, hoping to finance his trip across the Pacific by selling fish along the way. But the wind died, and their first catch spoiled before they made Honolulu. In desperation they sailed to Fanning, hoping to catch or buy the lobsters said to be plentiful there, continue to Christmas Island, and ship them back to Honolulu on the weekly flight. Fanning was Gary's first foreign culture. "Man, it was everything I'd dreamed: moonlit nights and palms," he said. "I liked it so much I began sleeping ashore. From the beach I heard people singing in the maneaba. One night they invited me to stay, and that's when I learned there's lots of love on these islands, lots and lots of love." I searched for a smirk but saw only wonder on his handsome face. "Those people were so nice, I just couldn't let them give their lobsters to that captain. They trusted us, but I knew we didn't have any money. We would have sailed away and screwed them. Our last night, I slipped ashore and told them to hide their lobsters. We left for Christmas Island with four instead of hundreds." He gave a high-pitched Micronesian laugh. "Man, was that captain pissed!"

Here Gary became vague. Their yacht, like many others, ended up on Christmas Island's reef, and the captain flew to Hawaii, leaving him marooned. John Bryden later told me this captain was "a fine man who left Gary with plenty of money." But the only way to spend plenty of money on Christmas Island would have been to buy a ticket to Honolulu, which he had not done. "Man, like, I thought I was done for when he cut out on me," Gary said. "I thought to myself, Shit, here I am on this island, all alone, without a friend, in the middle of the Pacific, with only five dollars in my pocket. Man, I wasn't looking for this life, it found me!"

The Catholic priest gave him shelter in exchange for work, and he fell in love with Tessama, a girl working in the priest's kitchen. Five months after being marooned on Christmas Island, he was married there. "These people really took me in." He sounded amazed, as if this were a first-order miracle. "So you understand what I'm saying about there being a whole lot of love on these islands. Here, man, I'm really, truly loved. This is my home now. I'm here for the rest of my life." He squinted at the shimmering coral. "Man, I could never have imagined in a million years this would be my life."

Like Patrice in Gabon, Gary had embraced the local superstitions. I heard about a stone that was a doorway to another world, and a creature that was a man while on one half of Christmas Island but a frigate bird on the other. He changed back and forth, scooting up and down the island warning of impending disasters.

"You mean things like hurricanes?" I asked.

"Nah-h-h, like if they're building their houses the wrong way, you know, facing the doorway in an unlucky direction, important stuff like that." He said this unsmiling.

Gary needed a hundred dollars a month for Marlboros, rice, coffee, and postage stamps. He had tried cutting copra, the way most men here earned cash, but found it too punishing. Seeing that people preferred tinned foods to fresh, he started canning his catch. "They lined up at my door, man," he said. "They just loved my fish. I liked eating it too. It's a nice change from fresh. But the government shut me down because I don't have a license." He tried offering scuba trips to hotel guests, but they had come to catch fish, not stare at them through a mask. Now he hoped the manager would hire him as a fishing guide. But, according to Tekeira, "whenever that Gary comes out, the manager, he hides." Finally Gary gave up and started back to London, the unused T-shirt flapping from his back pocket like a white flag.

Most evenings the fishing guides added to my collection of Christmas Island disappearances. I heard about a woman pilot who had flown solo from Honolulu in 1962 to visit her husband, stationed here during the nuclear tests. "Oh, that romantic woman!" one guide said. "She loved her husband so much she could not stand being parted."

"She crashed and her family offered a big reward," another said, "but no one found her. People looked hard. A month later soldiers discovered her plane. It was only fifty yards from the road—"

"But no body! So the family offered a bigger reward and everyone searched more, but—"

"Nothing! Not a bone."

"That poor woman, she was really in love." The guides were touched, as if this had happened last month and they had known her. Here it was again, the immediacy and involvement with an ancient story, the witchcraft of oral history.

Tekeira was skeptical. Yes, a large plane had crashed in a remote place. The wreck was near an isolated road, surrounded by salt ponds. And yes, anyone could become lost, wandering there for days. But he thought the crash had occurred earlier, perhaps before the war, and the plane had not belonged to some love-struck Air Force wife but, of course, to Amelia Earhart.

I laughed, and he said if I did not believe him I could decide for myself. He would show me the plane when we visited Poland.

After dinner we drove to London to deliver a ukulele, dance the twist, and visit a Mr. Tonga Fou, who had lived through the nuclear tests and remembered explosions illuminating the sky from Honolulu to New Zealand. At night I could finally connect Christmas Island to its place on my boyhood globe, a pinprick of light in the black Pacific. Stars sparkled like fireworks, it was bright enough to drive without headlights, and the Japanese radar dishes sat like full moons on the horizon, white and huge. During the day the frigate birds were the predators, snatching fish from the beaks of boobies and terns. Now I saw the feral cats who feasted on frigate birds and their eggs. They were black and as graceful as leopards, and I pictured their grinning mouths smeared with feathers and yolk.

We delivered the ukulele to a boy who began strumming and singing the moment it touched his hands. The dance was at the government maneaba. We arrived so early that Chubby Checkers, still popular in Kiribati, boomed across an empty floor. Tekeira locked the truck. The notorious Ambos' Club was across the street. "The men from there steal trucks and drive them into coconut trees," he explained. "Maybe we should leave now?" I refused. Tekeira was as eager to arrive early at every appointment as he was to leave the moment he did. If you did not object, you missed what you came for in the first place. A mountainous crone guarded the door, collecting admissions, fixing the boys with a chaperone's glare, and selling Juicy Fruit gum and seashell tiaras. The girls struck poses, snapping gum and puffing cigarettes. When a dump truck brought a cargo of copra cutters, they screamed and ran like rabbits, hopping barefoot over rusty cans and staring from behind palm trees with wide-open cartoon eyes. The boys swaggered until they saw the girls were not returning. Then their shoulders sagged, and they fanned out into the palms to coax them back. We left them dancing the twist.

Tonga Fou sat cross-legged on a wooden platform that served as bed, dining room, and parlor. It was lit by kerosene and moonlight, roofed in palm fronds and smelling of coconut. The surf beat against the reef, a lamp hissed, and Tonga Fou's skin glowed. He spoke while tickling his granddaughter's feet. At Tekeira's urging I opened my notebook. After Billy from Rongelap, I was prepared for stories of wasting diseases and the desecration of ancestral graveyards.

"The boys were scared," he whispered. "The army had laid blankets across the London dock, and the boys were told to crawl underneath before the blast. Oh, how they wished they could leave with us. After all, they were only teen-agers. How they envied us when we sailed away, leaving them there, under their blankets."

I was excited. This was great material. "Do any of those boys still live on the island?"

Tonga Fou giggled. "No, no, no. It was the British boys under those blankets. We were evacuated on HMS *Narvik* and spent nine months on Canton before returning home. On Canton I saw lightning and heard a *ka boom!* Then we came back and we were happy to be again with our friends, the British forces. We knew no fear because we trusted the forces. After that we took no notice of the explosions. Except the time they made us wear goggles, close our eyes, and face west, but that was fun because the children wore goggles too and, sir, imagine how amusing they looked." He rolled across his mat, holding his sides in laughter.

"Did everyone feel the same? Surely others must have—"

"Yes, some boys refused to evacuate."

(Aha!)

"They said, 'We will stay here and die with our friends the British.' Oh, those boys were devoted."

"Wasn't there anything you didn't like about the tests?"

"Well . . . yes, the problem of the weddings. The British prohibited us from taking photographs, even at weddings. We solved this by inviting the security officers to watch us take pictures."

"Were you relieved when the forces left?"

"Relieved? We were sad. Myself because I had the honor of driving them, the only native to operate military vehicles." His daughter, a veteran of these reminiscences, passed the family Bible. Pressed in it like a wildflower was his RAF driving permit. He turned on a flashlight and I saw a young Tonga Fou, framed in a halo of light.

"But not everyone drove for the forces. Are you sure everyone felt the same as you?"

"Sir, we all loved the British forces."

"And the Americans too?"

"It was sad for us when the Americans came. We had to bury so many of them."

"Because of radiation sickness? An accident?"

"Yes. Because of the Americans there were many accidents. They drank and hit the coconut trees. Or they forgot to keep left. They raced down our fine highways in their jeeps and — *kaboom!* — crashed into British boys driving on their side.

"And before the explosions the Americans took us away."

" 'Took you away'?"

"It was our choice. We could sit in the maneaba facing west or go on the American boat. I chose the boat. I thought, 'Why not? The boat is safety and comfort for the wives and children.' The sailors gave us candy and soda and showed Hollywood films. We could eat whatever we wanted. This is what people remember most about the American tests. Oh, how we ate on those American boats!

"The Americans left on June twelfth, 1964, a sad day for us because we always had such fun with the forces. We were unhappy because there were so few of us, and again we were alone on this island."

I asked others about the tests. No one else had witnessed them, but they knew about the feasts on the American boat and the British soldiers hiding under blankets. There are good reasons why the memories of the Christmas Islanders should be less bitter than those of the Marshallese. They were copra cutters on temporary government contracts who considered themselves to be residents of their "home islands" in the Gilberts. The blasts were high-altitude and without the heavy radiation that immediately sickened the Marshallese and forced them to abandon their islands (although recently an association of British soldiers who served on Christmas Island has brought lawsuits charging they were exposed to harmful doses of radiation). But if there had been any malcontents on Christmas Island, their complaints were lost forever. Such is the power of historians like Tonga Fou.

As I stood outside his house, preparing to leave, I tried for a last time to discover why they had liked the British troops so much. "All right," he said, dropping to a whisper. "I'll tell you. When they arrived we called them 'moonies' because their skin was pale as our moon. Then they removed their shirts, worked in the sun, and became dark. From a distance you could not tell them apart, our boys and the British boys. They were both shirtless, both the same color. That's when we believed, really believed, that we and the British were brothers."

The boat from Tarawa bringing the warden's ninth prisoner, Robert's corned beef, Tekeira's adopted daughter, and a new truck for John Bryden had been repeatedly postponed. The last message from Canton Island, twelve hundred miles to the west, said it would anchor Friday night and unload Saturday morning. Since then, it had been unable to contact the government short-wave radio in London, but Tekeira was convinced it would arrive on schedule and wanted to collect me at six-thirty so we could be on the dock an hour early.

"How do you know it's coming for sure?" I asked.

"Coconut news."

"But there's been no radio contact for—"

He laughed. "I promise you, coconut news." He admitted the source of this news was Philip Wilder, the half-caste tropical-fish exporter who owned the island's most powerful radio. I found Wilder in his radio shack. Mattresses and pillows covered the floor. One wall was solid with radio gear, and there were stacks of *Popular Mechanics.* Wilder had a eunuch's high voice and an oval face speckled with liver spots and freckles. He liked sprawling across his pillows like a Levantine trader. Before I could ask about the Tarawa boat, he said, "You must understand: My great-grandfather was German and I'm one-sixth American on my mother's side. One of my parents was half-Fijian, and the other was . . ." And on he went. I tend to be suspicious of people who present their family tree for inspection, particularly within seconds of an introduction. On the other hand, Wilder was a puzzling mixture. Perhaps he was tired of new acquaintances staring a second too long while examining his eyes for a slant, his fringe of hair for a kink, or his skin to see if its mahogany came from sun or pigment.

He twisted a dial with the touch of a safecracker, and I heard a burst of machine-gun fire. "Aha! The Russian 'woodpecker,'" he said. "Scrambled codes sent at high frequency. Watch now, no hands!" He threw up his arms while an automatic scanner worked across the bands. "All the latest equipment, even a Jap girl-in-a-box." He flipped a switch and a tinkly Oriental voice recited the frequencies. I heard Spanish, Chinese, the Voice of America, the BBC, and maritime communications. Wilder had spoken with the Tarawa boat, and he guaranteed that it was arriving tomorrow. He summarized the day's news: rioting in Papua–New Guinea; a hijacking in the Middle East; and the Ugandan Army running riot, slaughtering civilians while retreating from Kampala. "The world is going to hell," he said with satisfaction.

His evening entertainment was eavesdropping on maritime communications. "Here, you simply must listen to this," he said. "He's on a fishing boat off Mexico — Baja, I think. She's home in San Diego."

"How the hell am I going to pay the phone bills?" she demanded. "There are your calls to Mexico, your mother's collect calls, and the Cadillac needs three hundred dollars in repairs. John . . . John, it can't go on. Over."

"Hey, I'll work it out, babe. Over."

"How the hell can you do that? You're fishing and I'm paying a fortune in bills. There's nothing left. When are you coming home? Over."

"Fishing's great, babe. Over."

"How do I eat? How do the girls —"

"Have your pearls appraised. They should be worth —"

"Dammit, John, I'm not having it! Over!"

"I'll work it out, babe. Over."

"Work it out! Work it out!! Shit. John . . . John, the parking tickets on the Cadillac are from in front of the Safari Club. *The goddamned Safari Club!* You promised not to go there, not to see her again, and —"

"I'll work it out, babe. Over and out."

"John, when the hell are you coming back? John? John? Come in, goddammit . . ."

Mr. Wilder invited me to admire his front yard. It was heaped with choice scrap: sturdy planks, wire coils, and a collapsed radio tower. He had built his home over the foundation of the American commissary. He had hammered together the army's cast-off galvanized steel rods into an antenna. "See these steps on the back of my boat? Took them off the back of a troop transport. And know what these are? The CO_2 cartridges your country left behind. They made the soft drinks that kept your troops happy. I haven't figured a use for them, but I will.

Mr. Wilder kept his fish in a warehouse built from more scrap. "Pulled those out of a bunker," he said, pointing to the wooden supports. A splendid find!" Swimming in his wooden tanks were more striped angel fish than are pulled from Hawaiian waters in a year, and a fish native to Christmas Island that masqueraded as a clump of seaweed. He had separated his fighting fish in plastic strawberry baskets.

"I have *Newsweek* to thank for all this," he said. "Ten years ago I was one of several traders on Tarawa. Then I read in *Newsweek* that tropical fish were the most popular American pet. So, my God, it hit me! I said to myself, 'Here I am in the tropics, and there along the reef are plenty of fish.' I ordered some books, taught myself the business, and moved it here when they canceled the Tarawa Honolulu plane." And how was it going? "Oh, it's a living, sir, that's all, a living. But it sure beats selling corned beef and rice."

The boat from Tarawa was a two-thousand-ton tramp, the *Moanaraoi.* She would anchor off London four days, but no one wanted to miss the first tenders coming ashore. Saturday dawned humid and gray, with air thick as smoke and bucketing showers, but almost a hundred islanders had gathered on the wharf. For the first time I noticed forced laughter and strained expressions. And no wonder. People were greeting relatives and friends unseen for years. "She was nine when I knew her last," Tekeira said of his adopted daughter. "She's thirteen now, but I'll recognize her. I'm sure of it." He did not sound sure. There was always a chance someone had missed the boat or changed plans, meaning another six-month wait. You could not be certain until everyone disembarked. The suspense was too much for Tekeira and some men meeting their wives, and they persuaded the captain of a fishing boat to take us out to the *Moanaraoi*.

We circled her first, our men almost tumbling overboard as they waved at passengers. Those spotting wives, children, or parents whooped like lottery winners. The ship was packed with pretty girls and children, who welcomed us with plates of sea biscuits and played hide-and-seek, forcing their parents to drag them from behind rolled mats and outboard motors. The pretty girls covered their mouths and giggled as their men hugged hard. They had put on Sunday clothes and plaited their hair into pigtails. At the sight of each other, Tekeira and his daughter fell into hysterics.

The tender arrived from the dock, and despite the long journey and longer separations, there was no shoving for places. Only Tekeira remained tightly wound. All the way back to the dock he worried that the boat carrying his daughter would beat us, and later, as we all drove toward Banana, he slammed on the brakes, saying, "I saw a movie once, with Richard Burton." He shouted something at his wife, who was riding in back, holding their infant daughter underneath a rain slicker to keep her dry. "I warned her not to kill the baby," Tekeira explained. "In that movie, Richard Burton and his wife are hiding in a cellar to escape the Nazis, but she worries the baby will cry, so she puts her coat around it. When the Nazis have gone, they find the baby is smothered to death."

As I sat down cross-legged in the Banana maneaba, a woman poured Johnson's Baby Powder over my neck and shoulders, instantly solving Christmas Island's two minor mysteries: why so many people had a white frost on their bare shoulders, and why stores were so well stocked with baby powder.

"Why baby powder?" I asked. "To make us clean." "To keep us cool." "Because we have always done it." They laughed, unsure why.

The Old Men leaned against the coconut poles while their wives, daughters, nieces, younger brothers, sons, and children in great numbers sprawled behind. The maneaba's roof was tin, and the Old Men sat on strips of green linoleum. The building hummed with toddlers and the slap of bare feet as children chased one another with blue squirt guns. The dignitary at a neighboring pole (as an honored guest, I had been given one) said, "In the Abemama maneabas, mothers quiet their children. And everyone sits cross-legged and upright. Not like this!" Some of the younger men were massaging their stomachs, anticipating a buffet lunch that was heaped on trestle tables and guarded by boys with flyswatters. It bulged underneath colored scarfs, like a fat woman wrapped in a tight dress.

"Ours is not a strict maneaba," agreed the man on my other side. His name was Korae and he had the profile of a matinee idol, but he was the chief Protestant clergyman for the Line Islands. "Our dancing is not as authentic as on Tarawa, but we have more fun, much more fun!"

A choir gathered, preparing to sing by dusting themselves with more baby powder and tucking lit cigarettes behind their ears. Their songs were intricate harmonies, so well performed that even the children ceased fussing. Today was the maneaba's tenth anniversary, and these songs, composed for the occasion, celebrated its history and founders. During the singing, those sitting near the banquet tables drew closer, as if pulled by a magnet. Eyes darted to the tables and boys lifted corners of the scarfs, widening their eyes. Then the choir finished, women unveiled the platters, and Korae said, "Every month we have a feast like this. Our church is quite famous for eating."

Great creativity and expense had gone into these displays, but lacking was any appreciation for taste or appetite — my appetite, anyway. Roast chicken, lobster, or broiled fish was merely the decorative centerpiece of each churchwoman's platter, a vehicle for more popular foods. A lobster clutching Tootsie Rolls in its claws lay among bread slices smeared with green frosting from a can. Packaged chocolate-chip cookies circled a chicken like tombstones; another bird was stuffed with hard candies and surrounded by cocktail franks, arranged into blossoms. Slabs of corned beef covered sea biscuits on a bed of cold canned peas, and canned peach halves cradled meatballs. A fried fish swam through chocolate-wafer waves; another vomited canned ravioli. It was all the food I had loved as a boy and, as an adult, been taught to fear. Some of it was a mystery. "What is that?" I asked Korae.

He was shocked. "But it's *your* food!" he said. It was Spam, under a glaze of strawberry frosting.

Usually I avoided eating some suspicious local specialty by claiming an allergy, or that my stomach was unaccustomed to such a rich dish, or that it violated a religious taboo. Here these excuses were ridiculous.

"Go on, choose first," Korae insisted. I chose a chicken leg, cocktail franks, and a chocolate wafer. First the dignitaries, then the other men scooped up a bouillabaisse of these delicacies. They returned to their coconut poles, hunching like lions over their bowls, silently gorging.

"Why aren't the women eating?" I asked Korae. They were staring at their ravaged food trays, at the chicken and lobster carcasses sitting in a wasteland of Spaghetti-Os.

"Men eat first," he said between swallows. "Next women and children."

"Then why can't they eat now?"

"Because we men might want more."

More? Impossible. The men had already taken everything. And this from a man of God. I asked, "Who cooks the food?"

His look said this was a stupid question. "Women cook."

"What if they refuse?"

"If they refuse . . ." He puffed his chest. "Then we give them a good smack." But while he said this, and while he inquired about my choice of delicacies and tried to hold my eyes with his, like a magician hoping to keep you from watching his hands — all this while he was shoving food back to his wife. She slipped it into her bowl, quickly covering it with a cloth. Other men were doing the same, and everywhere children unwrapped candies passed back by their macho fathers.

After lunch, the visiting dignitaries presented gifts. One invited us to the inauguration of a maneaba next weekend. "Each family will bring a pig, so there'll be forty pigs to eat," Korae said. "Oh, yes — with us, food's the thing."

The choir performed again, this time sitting down because, as Tekeira later explained, "we were too full of food to stand." Men delivered long speeches while the audience, stretched out and holding full stomachs, dozed. Following tradition, only the Old Men spoke. (Young upstarts are told by fathers, "Who are you to speak to us? We have eaten more coconuts than you.") The last speech put the maneaba into hysterics. Korae translated. "The honored guest is asking if you will send us street girls from America to admire the equator buttons you have given us.

"Street girls?" I presumed he meant prostitutes.

"Yes, we know about the famous American street girls. Last week we saw a movie about street girls in Los Angeles."

The formal program was over, but most stayed to watch video-cassette movies on a communal television. Tekeira reported seeing *Gung Ho,* a John Wayne film about the Marine raid that preceded the battle for Tarawa, and *Tora, Tora, Tora,* a re-creation of the Japanese attack on Pearl Harbor. He said Second World War movies set in the Pacific were popular. "They're about our islands, so they make us feel important."

I simply did not know what to make of this banquet. The stern amateur anthropologist in me said this addiction to canned foods, linoleum, baby powder, video movies, and Tootsie Rolls was sad. The realist said the fact that the banquet occurred within the maneaba affirmed the strength of the traditional culture. Besides, there was a certain art in designing these colorful platters from canned food. And how could you blame anyone for enjoying the easy entertainment of a taped movie, or favoring the variety and ease of canned food over the monotony of fish and the hard work of preparing taro root? At least, unlike the way it was in Gabon, these luxuries seemed to be giving them joy.

Besides the sign at the airport, the Japanese satellite-tracking station and the new wind-profiling radar installation were the only physical evidence I could find that Christmas Island is the nearest inhabited land to the equator for thousands of miles. In a field across from the hotel, the United States National Oceanic and Atmospheric Administration (NOAA) was erecting a device to determine wind currents along the equator. Andy, from Colorado, was in charge. His laid-back cowboy act was convincing until you learned he had programmed the computer to analyze this wind data and was about to enter a Ph.D. program at MIT. He described his device as a "wind radar gun," or a "wind-profiling radar" that could record even minor and localized changes in wind speeds by measuring at thirty-second intervals the echoes produced by upper-air turbulence. "We know about the big currents," he said, "but the small ones are a mystery. Imagine the ripples a twig makes as it moves down a river. That's the magnitude of disturbance we'll be after." Until recently, no one had gauged these small, mysterious wind shifts. Now Andy's bosses in the TOGA (Tropical Ocean and Global Atmosphere) project believed this data might improve global weather forecasts, helping to predict phenomena such as El Niño. There had been a sudden growth in computer and radar stations along the equator. The one at St. Paul's Rocks that Peggy had visited was a Columbia University project; Andy worked for the University of Colorado, which had placed similar devices on the Pacific islands of Ponape and Nauru and was considering the Brazilian Amazon. In Honolulu, one of Andy's co-workers told me, "These projects are an easy way for a university to get government grants, so there's competition. Yeah, it's real hot now, equatorial weather."

I had expected a dish, or a skyline of antennas. Instead, Andy supervised six Kiribatians in red baseball caps as they cleared a field and erected 800 evenly spaced five-foot-high galvanized steel stakes and strung them with wire. John Bryden was delivering a fiberglass box to house the computers, an event that had attracted the American Mormon in charge of the Japanese satellite-tracking center. His facility bore no resemblance to this, but as the other man of technology on the island, I suppose he was a rival all the same. At least he behaved that way, wearing a cynical smile as the box slid off the flatbed truck.

He ran his fingers over its joints, hinges, and bolts. "What do you think?" I asked.

"Soon rusted," he said with satisfaction.

"Are you sure?"

"Of course, I know everything about this island." Humming and shaking his head, he zipped away in a yellow Datsun. I had dismissed as exaggeration Bryden's story of the four Europeans sitting at different tables in the hotel; now I believed it.

The preparations Tekeira made for traveling the length of the largest coral atoll in the world reminded me of those for a trip into the African bush. We packed spare parts, extra water, and a short-wave radio. Doug, the pilot, came too, because Tekeira was promising a look at the wrecked aircraft that the guides and waiters, sensing our interest and wanting to please, had taken to calling "the love plane," or "that Earhart woman's plane, perhaps." Doug's hobby was investigating Second World War crashes, so he considered spending eight hours in the back of my truck, as we

bounced around the island from Banana to Paris, a small price to
see a wreck that just might (although he laughed at himself for
entertaining this idea) be Amelia Earhart's.

She had disappeared on July 2, 1937, during a round-the-
world flight that roughly followed the equator. Her Lockheed
Electra had left Lae, New Guinea, on a flight path taking her
across the equator to a landing on Howland Island, one of the
deserted, American-owned Phoenix Islands. Her twin-engine
plane had a 4,000-mile range. The distance between Lae and
Howland is 2,500 miles, and Howland to Christmas another 1,400,
so it is not impossible that she crashed here, just extremely unlikely. A recent book by Vincent Loomis, *Amelia Earhart — The
Final Story*, has made a convincing case that she landed on Mili
atoll, in the Marshalls, and died after being imprisoned by the
Japanese as a spy.

South of Banana, the heliotrope was swallowing the asphalt
and shrinking the nuclear highway to a single lane. When it finally choked this road, no one would build another. There were
no villages, no coconuts to harvest, and no reason to come except
to see the ruins and wrecks. Ground zero was a circle of asphalt,
half a football field in diameter, with concrete squares holding
iron clamps and links of rusted chain. In a thousand years these
ruins may be mistaken for a primitive altar, or proof that Christmas Island was terrorized by giants.

"Guess they really wanted to tie them down," Doug said,
kicking the chains. "Kinda embarrassing if a balloon breaks its
tether and floats away with a nuke. Once a radar balloon came
loose from Kennedy and they had to shoot it down. Hey, too bad
we didn't bring a Geiger counter."

I saw Tekeira had stayed in the truck.

Doug was a joker. A bird's shadow flitted across the asphalt,
and he said, "Watch out, I hear there's a two-hundred-pound
booby flapping around this thing." When I brought out my camera, he said, "Hey, stand over that set of clamps and I'll take your
picture." He pointed at the tethers in the middle of the circle.
"Guess that's ground zero." He snapped two photographs.
"There. You can use those in your lawsuit when your kids glow in
the dark. Hey, don't worry. After twenty years it should be OK."
But I *have* worried, at odd moments, when I remember Christmas
Island, or read of lawsuits brought by those cancer-plagued Utah

Mormons who were downwind in the fifites. And if I ever develop a cancer, I will always wonder.

After ground zero, the road became a dirt track that curled around the long southeastern handle of the island to the wreck of a Korean fishing boat. Scattered along the beach were chunks of its wood, smelling of oil and polished smooth as sea glass. The ship sat on the reef a hundred yards offshore, making it the object closest to the equator between here and Ecuador. We saw two more wrecks. There was a Canadian yacht, the *Big Bear H,* where in a half-submerged cabin tropical fish swam thick as carp in a tank. There was the *Stratosphere,* a catamaran owned by Imelda Marcos or one of her relatives. Whoever its owners, they were sufficiently powerful that its Danish captain had been afraid to leave the island and confront them. He stayed for months, attempting to salvage it and drinking until a motorbike accident left him, according to Tekeira, "with his face scraped off on the asphalt."

Father Rougier had named Poland and its St. Stanislas Bay to honor his Polish mechanic. The town had been the center of his copra plantation and the island's largest settlement, but now its days were numbered. The British custom of closing the island's dirt tracks after heavy rains had been abandoned, allowing the copra truck to destroy the road from Banana. It was a matter of time, ten years at the most, before it became impassable. Given Kiribati's poverty, and how little Poland's copra contributed to alleviating it, no one imagined the road would be rebuilt. Without a regular boat service to London (named by Rougier because it sat across the channel from his Paris), Poland was finished. In the meantime, it was Christmas Island's Tierra del Fuego or Key West, with an appealing, end-of-the-road atmosphere. I arrived at midafternoon to find almost everyone asleep. Dogs snoozed in the road and children lay swinging in hammocks. A quarter of its hundred inhabitants were in a cool copra warehouse, curled up on sacks of dried nuts. A few men shoveled copra, but after several minutes others woke from their naps, taking over the shovels and giving the first group a chance to rest.

Poland smelled mostly of coconut, and it had one of everything: one fire extinguisher on a pole, one engine to work the one water pump, one truck that drove to London once a week, one maneaba with one man asleep inside it, one nurse, and a one-room prison with one drunk, according to the one policeman who told me, "We call our Poland village 'the calm place.'" His name was Maio, he weighed over 300 pounds, and he cheerfully admitted to being the fattest policeman in Kiribati, and maybe the fattest anywhere. When we stopped, he was sitting cross-legged and bare-chested in front of his house, absentmindedly eating cabin biscuits from a plate. He had been posted to Kiribati's Siberia because a new police commissioner in Tarawa, seeing that most Kiribati policemen were seriously overweight, had made two decisions: All fat policemen must lose weight, and new uniforms would be issued. Maio ordered the largest, which the new commissioner made sure was not very large. Maio dieted and let out every seam, but still he could not button his tunic. His commanding officer on Christmas Island took pity and transferred him to Poland, a post so remote he could go shirtless.

"But I love this Poland!" Maio said. "No family disputes, only one drunk, and I have official transport [a yellow Honda motorbike]. I have time to cut copra, so"—he lowered his voice—"two salaries. And I am famous for my toddy." He shouted, and the man sleeping in the maneaba, perhaps his prisoner, brought a bottle of sour toddy. Maio strained it into glasses. It was delicious: cool, with a fizz, and only slightly alcoholic. "The only problem with this Poland is the transport," he said. The truck skips us because of fuel shortages, and we are on our own. For weeks there are no biscuits! No Ox and Palm! No sweets! Then we must eat fish and coconuts." He made a face.

We found the love plane in a labyrinth of salt ponds, palms, and criss-crossing tracks. Its remains were scattered over fifty yards: a rusted fuselage, a wing near the road, another hidden in a palm grove, a twist of green metal, and some engine parts, all covered by the latticework shadows of coconut palms. Doug turned over a wing, and I tried moving a propeller that crumbled in my hands. "It's too big a propeller for a single-engine airplane," he said, raising hopes this might be Earhart's two-engine Electra. "But there's not enough here to really tell, and some parts have been stolen." Since the plane had crashed before this palm grove had been planted, and Tekeira swore it was less than twenty years old, it could have been either Earhart's plane or the love plane.

The mystery was partially solved when Doug uncovered another wing. It had a gun mount and a faint star, showing it to be a military plane and not Earhart's. He said the gun mount and the three-bladed propeller might indicate it had crashed during the war; on the other hand, this type of gun mount remained on many aircraft flown afterwards. The star lacked the bars that were added to military markings after 1944, yet the marking was so badly corroded that there might once have been bars, and he thought the wreck too well preserved to be pre-1944. It could be the famous love plane, or it could be the plane flown by young Casady, the missing Second World War pilot, or it might have belonged to someone else. Only one thing seemed certain: Its pilot had vanished.

After a week on Christmas Island, I was beginning to flash goofy grins and end sentences with giggles. It was time to leave. The advantage of a place with a single weekly boat or plane is that you can say good-bye to everyone at once. John Bryden was at the Banana airport hauling cargo and luggage while his wife collected the rental trucks. Philip Wilder had brought his crates of tropical fish, and Gary was hoping for his fish-canning permit. The children from the maneaba squirted their blue guns, and the Tuvaluan transvestite wore his highest heels yet. The Japanese fishermen had acquired Christmas Island laughs. They told stories about fish leaping from the water, biting them in the crotch and "leaving us sopranos."

No one checked our luggage for guns. No one showed interest in my ticket or passport. The policemen had holes in their knee socks and identical blue stains on their tunics from pens exploding in the heat. They posed for Japanese photographs, comparing their ink stains, laughing and shaking their heads at the coincidence.

The huge jet brought two fishermen from Honolulu.

"Only two passengers!" Tekeira said.

"Two is better than none," answered John Bryden's practical wife.

"That depends on who the two are," Bryden said, perhaps remembering the Palmyra Island murders.

For a week I had not heard a single argument or raised voice, not seen a child cuffed, a dog abused, or an old person mocked. There was no wealth but no poverty, and plenty of food, although for my liking it was the wrong sort. The people were as tame and trusting as the birds on Cook Island, although not as well protected, and their future probably less assured. I could not imagine what would ever bring me back, but I knew that many Wednesdays at noon I would remember this airport, these people, and walking to this plane while hearing, or so I imagined, laughter echoing louder than the jets.

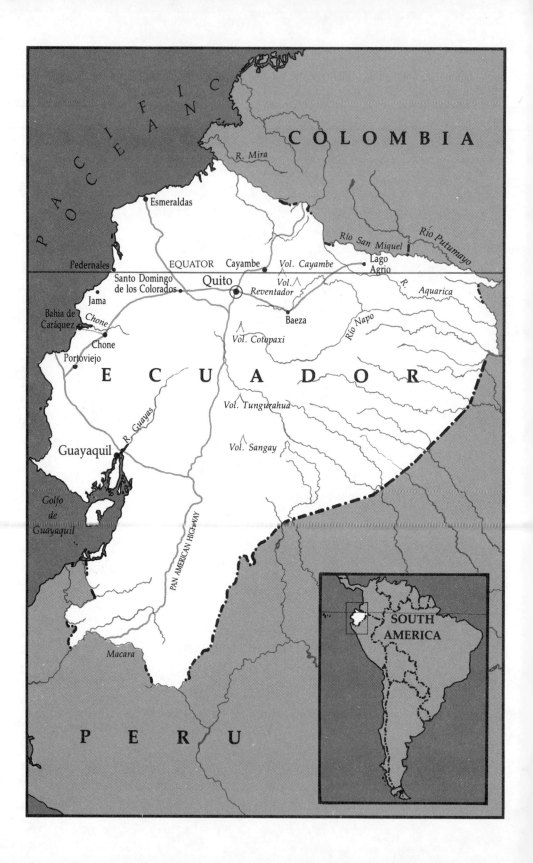

19

YOU COULD SAY THAT IN ECUADOR THE EQUATOR ALMOST killed me, or, conversely, that it saved my life. I had bought a ticket landing me on March 1 in Quito. I planned to spend three days visiting the largest equatorial monument on earth and walking up the south slope of Cayambe volcano to the highest point on the equator. On March 4 or 5 I would have taken a bus east to Napo Province and the jungle oil-boom town of Lago Agrio. This is a ten-hour trip on a road twisting thousands of feet down from the Andes plateau to Baeza. From there the road follows the Rio Quijos, brushes the base of Reventador volcano, and, cutting back and forth across the equator, runs along the Trans-Ecuadorian oil pipeline and the Rio Aquarico to Lago Agrio. Like the Trans-gabonaise Railway, this road is one of few places in the world where for any distance you can travel "along" the equator.

During the night of March 5, a powerful earthquake struck Ecuador. Its epicenter was ten miles east of Reventador, almost smack on the equator and the road to Lago Agrio. The quake triggered floods, and a wall of water swept through the Aquarico valley. Heavy rains had already soaked the hills, and whole mountainsides slid loose, ripping through jungle, snapping bridges, burying villages and highways, and cutting the pipeline, spilling oil into the western tributaries of the Amazon, where it killed fish and damaged the food supply of a hundred thousand Indians. A third of Napo Province's seventy-five thousand people lost their homes, four thousand were missing, and at least a thousand died, although Ecuador's director of civil defense said, "We will never know precisely how many died, since a lot of houses and buses have been buried under thousands of tons of mud." The earthquake had performed the work of centuries: eradicating the existence and shared memory of entire families and communities. In places there were no survivors to mourn, remember, or even enumerate the dead, and this I found as frightening as any wall of water or live burials in acres of mud.

According to one report, "Eyewitnesses report that many trucks and buses traveling the road were swept away, burying their occupants alive." In all, fourteen buses had been entombed under ten feet of mud, and, had I kept to my schedule, there was a good chance I would have been in one of them. I would have died more or less on the equator, buried in a rattletrap bus or swept downstream to pollute the Amazon, perhaps wearing one of my ridiculous buttons, and my wife, with justification, could have blamed my death on the equator. But I could also thank the equator for my survival, because at the last minute I remembered the spring equinox and postponed my trip by two weeks so I could be in Quito on March 21, when at noon the sun is hanging directly over the equator. Then I changed my mind again, deciding to start in the coastal city of Guayaquil so I could first travel north to where the equator emerges from the Pacific, and because when I said "Quito" nothing came to mind, but "Guayaquil" meant pickpockets and bananas, dripping palms, rust-streaked tramp steamers, men in white suits, and parrots.

When I arrived there, I saw mostly water. Ecuador was in the grip of another El Niño, less severe than that of 1982 but bad enough to have turned the valleys outside Guayaquil into brown lakes. The sky was gray and carpeted with storm clouds, rivers had spilled banks, and houses sat on stilts over flooded fields. I ran through a cloudburst to the terminal and drove to the city through a wall of water. Pumps pulled geysers of water from blocked drains, and roads had become ponds floating with refuse. The rain changed to drizzle, and I walked to the docks through streets smelling of diesel and insecticide. The Guayas River ran fast and brown, its current carrying whole bushes and trees, islands of water lilies, and a bloated pig.

I ate in an empty restaurant where even the ice cream tasted faintly of anchovies. The newspapers predicted disaster. The consequences of the ruptured pipeline were serious, and already there was rationing, demonstrations in Quito, and soldiers guarding filling stations. By week's end, said one headline, Guayaquil would have NO FOOD! NO GASOLINE! NO POTABLE WATER!

The next morning the rain had stopped, and I found the Guayaquil of my imagination. In the Parque Bolivar, lizards chased up cypress trunks, through an iron bandstand, and past elderly men in white suits. They were liver-spotted and sat leaning on canes, reading carefully folded newspapers. Two boys in white shirts stared into the lens of an accordion camera. On a poster, the photographer had displayed his work: dozens of blurred photographs of solemn families posed in front of the cathedral, identical to the pictures taken of their grandparents, in this same park and perhaps by this same camera. I shared a bench with a young man in despair. While working in Toronto, he had become homesick and returned to Guayaquil. Now he regretted it. He judged cities by the articles of clothing his salary could buy. Toronto was three new shirts, a sweater, and a pair of slacks every month; Guayaquil was a pair of socks.

There were no parrots to be seen along the riverfront promenade, but I found my rusty freighters, docked in a line near a statue of Bolivar. They were painted red, green, and blue, chipped and rust-streaked, and busy exchanging bananas and coconuts for Coca-Cola. The Palacio Municipal was across the street, a baroque elephant built in the 1920s to replicate a palacio destroyed by fire. Like a nineteenth-century world's-fair pavilion, it had a high glass dome protecting a center court from the elements. There were overhead fans, pigeons fluttering through girders, and cubbyhole offices stuffed with manila files and decrepit functionaries who wore suspenders. Shabby men stood in long lines, clutching bank notes and patiently waiting to pay this tax or buy that license.

Two blocks inland was a Guayaquil of multi-level car parks, computerized bank-teller machines, brisk men in black suits, narrow streets of glass office buildings, and digital clocks clicking the time as they advertised Citibank. This Guayaquil had the Unicenter, an atrium of chilly fountains, hanging plants, glass-capsule elevators, and guards in baseball caps. There was even a casino, American fast food, and video games. The graceful Palacio Municipal was where Guayaquil's citizens went to be milked by civil servants; the ugly Unicenter was where they went to have fun. It was not hard to guess which place, and which architecture, they preferred.

Guayaquil has a splendid new bus station on three levels with spiraling concrete ramps, escalators, clean rest rooms, and good snack bars. In fifteen minutes there I encountered more kindness than you might find in a lifetime at New York's Port Authority. A policeman led me to the end of a cavernous ticket hall where the Reina del Camino—"Queen of the Road"—company sold tickets to Bahia de Caráquez, the coastal town nearest the equator. A female clerk wrote my name on a manifest, patiently explaining in slow Spanish which seats were over the wheels, and which had good views. Another woman took me upstairs to the bus, and the driver insisted on putting my bag behind the last seat, instead of on top under the tarpaulin where rainstorms might soak it.

The roads outside Guayaquil resembled causeways. Farmers' shacks sat like islands in flooded fields, and clouds smothered distant foothills, promising more rain. The road wound through banana plantations and cattle ranches and fell into watery agricultural valleys. It was a slow trip because, like the Kigali Express, the bus stopped for whoever waved, and to slow down traffic every village had built bumps into the road. These obstacles also enabled gangs of boy vendors to jump aboard to sell meat pies and soda pop from plastic buckets. They had hoarse voices, bruised faces, and scabby legs, and few looked more than ten, but they all had that serious manner little boys assume when handling money. After canvassing the passengers, they squatted in the aisles to wait for the next stop, wide-eyed and, despite the heat, shivering.

It was a weekday, so most of the passengers were women. They wore white dresses and white shoes and clutched white purses. Even the smallest girls carried these purses. I watched three girls in white high heels pick their way around a black puddle to climb aboard the bus, and a quarter of a mile later we stopped in front of a hovel to leave a mother and daughter in identical white lace blouses. It was a brave choice of color in this mud-splattered countryside.

After the market town of Protoviejo, the hills steepened and the villages shrank. Showers appeared fast, clouds raced, and rainbows flashed suddenly. The air smelled of salt. We were a dozen passengers, then nine, then six. A woman insisted I move to the front to appreciate the view. We came over a rise to see the River Chone widen into an estuary resembling a Scottish loch. Hills rose on both sides, their green tops hidden in mist, and white birds fluttered like ticker tape. A heart-shaped island divided the water, a rainbow piercing its center like an arrow.

The road followed the southern bank of the Chone to Bahia. It was a dozing, end-of-the-road port, the kind from which mercenaries set out unnoticed. Wind had bent and tattered its palms, and the arcaded buildings were pockmarked, as if by gunfire. The surf muffled roosters and radios, and there were few cars. People walked or rode wobbly bicycles, and the population was polyglot, including the black descendants of shipwrecked slaves and Chinese traders. Fishing, making coffins, and moving around crates of soda pop seemed the principal industries. On both sides of the town green headlands punched the Pacific like fists. Coconut husks and blackened hunks of driftwood covered a gray ocean beach where a donkey grazed and men threw out red nets. A fishing boat, its poles out, squatted like a giant insect on the horizon. Waves broke a mile offshore, then regathered their strength to crash against the beach. With its whitecaps and incessant wind, it was a sea identical to the one off Christmas Island.

A small vacation colony filled a point of land dividing the estuary from the Pacific. Since Bahia lacked a commercial airport and was six to eight hours from Guayaquil or Quito, this resort was not much, a forlorn clutch of villas and low condominiums, deserted in the off-season except for workmen and guard dogs. Everything was walled in, locked up, or chained down, leaving little open to the breeze or the eyes of a stranger. There was no confusing where public property ended and private began, and signs identified villas as belonging to Familia this and Familia that. So here was Ecuador, with its personalismo and machismo, its preoccupation with private property and the rights, dignity, and prerogatives of the individual—particularly the male individual—and a few thousand miles out there was communal Micronesia, with its maneabas, open houses, and democratic councils of Old Men. It seemed impossible they were neighbors along the same equator.

But I was still forty miles south of where the equator first hits the western coast of South America. I had four maps of Ecuador. They agreed that the equator ran between the villages of Jama and Pedernales, but one map showed only Jama, another only Pedernales, and on a third the coast was empty. Two had roads leading inland from both villages but without a coastal highway connecting them. One showed a thin road running north to Jama and the equator from San Vincente, the village across the estuary from Bahia. My most reliable guidebook said, "After heavy rain there may be a two or three day delay before road service is resumed." I took the ferry across to San Vincente and discovered there was a bus north to Jama and along the beach to Pedernales, but heavy rains had washed out the road, canceling the bus for several days. San Vincente was smaller than Bahia, and without its paved streets, and last night's downpour had left everything up to its knees in mud: donkeys, cars, buildings, and children's legs. Trucks spun their wheels, and the girls in white hippity-hopped between rocks. I asked the woman selling ferry tickets to describe how the coast looked to the north. She yawned. "Es el mismo" — "It's the same." I bought a ticket back to Bahia. I was becoming less of an equatorial purist.

At sunset, I sat in a three-table seaside café watching the waves and deciding that if I ever needed to hide out or recover from a tragedy I would come to Bahia. The seafood was delicious and the beer served ice-cold in pewter mugs, with a side dish of banana chips. I never saw a policeman, and sending even a postcard to the United States baffled the one-room post office. It was possible to imagine that if you sat in this café or lay on that deserted beach long enough, the solstice sun would cauterize any emotional wound and the sandy wind scour away any tragedy.

The people I met seemed to have made an off-season trip to this edge-of-a-continent town for precisely these reasons. In a café, I joined two chubby rich girls with button noses and streaked blond hair. They wore T-shirts with cartoon characters and spent hours drinking beer while reading aloud the captions of paperback romances titled *Mujer de Barrio* and *Quiero Ser Mujer*, although something in this second triggered a tragic memory, causing one girl to burst into sobs.

My hotel was a white Greek-island box facing the Pacific. A pale young man sat on the terrace from late afternoon until closing. He chain-smoked and never ate, staring at the setting sun and first stars while drinking rum-and-Coke with the jerky motions of a robot. He wiped away tears, and without being asked a waiter brought fresh drinks. He was unapproachable in his grief.

A German couple and their daughter had come for a week. The daughter was a bony, raw-faced woman in her late thirties who favored cowboy boots and halter tops. She moved like a sleepwalker, and her father always walked with an arm around her shoulder. I asked why they had chosen Bahia. It was in a guidebook, they said. They were polite, but not interested in strangers. They followed a routine: sleeping late, then lying on the gray beach in skimpy bathing suits, glistening with oil, the only sun-worshipers in Bahia. The parents were always nudging their daughter to roll over, inspecting her tan lines and applying more oil, as if dark skin might heal her. At five they appeared on the hotel terrace in resort clothes and took snapshots with a Polaroid, forcing smiles and raising gin-and-tonics as the sun fell into the Pacific. The instant pictures rolled from the bottom of the camera and they passed them around, admiring them with melancholy expressions.

The early bus left for Quito with so few passengers that I had a front seat. The driver had surrounded himself with icons and crosses — eight in all, if you counted the religious medallion plugging a hole in the windshield. For much of the way, the road to Quito ran about twenty miles south of the equator. We followed the Chone river past more flooded fields and banana trees to an energetic agricultural town. It was squalid but lively, undoubtedly a better place to live than visit, and notable mostly for the contrast between the filth of its streets and plazas, and the obvious pride its citizens took in their own appearance. At every large village, more boy vendors jumped aboard. After months of tropical travel I had become accustomed to looking down at the greasy hair of child beggars and hawkers, to seeing their scrawny shoulders and upturned hands and feeling their hands tugging on my pants. But on an Ecuadorian bus I had to confront them at eye level. I had to watch as they hauled themselves up the steps and see their smudged faces as they pushed their lukewarm sodas and suspicious snacks. And from this vantage point they all looked terrified, exhausted, or vacant. In a crowded market, I can sometimes trick myself into believing that the children who sell flowers, lottery chances, and Chiclets are out of an *Our Gang* movie, dirty and unruly but having great fun. But this was too obviously unpleasant work, hauling these pails and dishes, balancing them in swaying aisles and riding thirty minutes one way, thirty the other, just to sell a few cakes. Bob in Uganda was right. They *are* a first-class marketing tool, these third-world children.

After the lowland city of Santo Domingo we climbed seventy-five hundred feet in only seventy-five miles, following a wild river studded with rocks and passing villages that looked out of the Pyrenees, with their dark stone houses, smoky fires, and roofs growing moss. Blankets of clouds obscured the Andes and mist filled the ravines, and as the bus swung around curves, climbing into denser fog and colder drizzle, I closed the window, put on a sweater, and fell asleep, believing I would miss nothing. I woke in an Oz of checkerboard farms, wide valleys, and snow-capped volcanoes. The air was cool and thin, colors vivid, shadows sharp, and the sun dangerous. In three days the spring equinox would put it exactly over the equator, and then, because this high plateau also contains the Cayambe volcano, at seventeen thousand feet the highest point crossed by the equator, nowhere on earth would it be so scorching.

In Ecuador, volcanoes up to twenty thousand feet line the western and eastern cordilleras of the Andes. These are massive mountains, with barren slopes, rounded tops, and thick bases. They stand alone, without the deep valleys and jumbled peaks that give the Alps their character. They are more colossal and intimidating than pretty, perhaps explaining why villages huddle around churches, and why Quito is tucked into a narrow valley and its colonial quarter a cozy place of claustrophobic streets and plazas, so urban that unless you gaze over the tops of the buildings or climb to the hill where a statue of a winged Virgin watches over the city, you scarcely notice the surrounding volcanoes.

After the humidity and squalid, lowland villages, Quito

seemed like another country. Its old city was unspoiled, its parks filled with flowers, and its smart Avenida Amazonas served by spotless, double-decker buses. Crime was said to be minimal, and every evening the elite staged an evening paseo past the sidewalk cafés of Amazonas, making me think of a Spanish city like Zaragosa or Granada, a high place with dry air and sudden chills. Here were the same fussed-over children, young men with jackets thrown casually over their shoulders, and olive-skinned women in white sweaters, leaning into one another like Spanish women, whispering as they walked.

Within hours I had found a hotel, hired a guide to take me up Cayambe, and called at several embassies trying to wangle a seat on a relief plane to the earthquake zone. In a bookstore I bought *Mitad del Mundo,* by Professor Humberto Vera, identified as a "distinguished professor at the School of the Science of Information of the Central University of Ecuador." It had been published in 1986 to commemorate the two hundred and fiftieth anniversary of the French equatorial expedition that had established the metric system by measuring the length of the longitudinal arc from the equator to the North Pole, a meter being one ten-millionth of this distance. Rather than a scholarly treatise, Professor Vera's book was a grab bag of equatorial exotica. It featured a blurred photograph of Samantha Ridge, "Queen of New York," standing before the equatorial monument in 1970. There were pictures of Archbishop Makarios in 1966, the Lord Mayor of London in 1972, and Cynthia Griffin, Miss Midlands of 1967. Several snapshots showed the ancient Inca festival of Inty-Raini, celebrated yearly on the spring and fall equinox, although in successive years the dancers wore different costumes and seemed engaged in entirely different rituals.

Professor Vera had strained to fill his 134 pages. One chapter described in detail the famous visit of Archbishop Makarios, even identifying the churches he had visited and the names of his official party. There was a color photograph of Professor Vera, pointing to the Greenwich meridian during a holiday in London. There was a poem to the equator — its author was Professor Humberto Vera — and there was "How to Say 'Welcome to the Middle of the World'" in nineteen foreign languages including Romanian, Finnish, Lingala, and Turkish. There were pictures of the shadows cast by the equatorial monument at different times

of year. There was a description of the equatorial diploma designed by Professor Vera and available at his store, and many
photographs of Folklore Vera, his combination souvenir shop,
post office, and equatorial museum.

One chapter listed twenty-two "Unusual Occurrences at the
Middle of the World." Here are some of them:

A person can place one foot on the northern hemisphere and
the other on the southern hemisphere. It isn't often one can
do this.

One can send a post-card from the Northern Hemisphere
and in a matter of fractions of a second it arrives in the
Southern Hemisphere. This happens on top of the equinoccial desk where the Equator Line crosses it.

You place one finger on the Northern Hemisphere and another on the Southern Hemisphere. This also occurs on the
equinoccial desk.

So far, yet so near, two persons, one in the Northern Hemisphere, the other in the Southern Hemisphere may shake
hands or embrace while they remain within their respective
hemispheres.

In 30 seconds the four hemispheres can be traversed. Anyone
can do it by walking, without need of a space capsule and in
less time than that taken by the astronauts. How is this possible? It is necessary to come to this place and that and other
feats will be demonstrated.

Being in the middle of the torrid zone a very chilling cold is
felt. Visit and experience this phenomenon between the
hours of five and six P.M.

Equilibrium: Walk over the Equator Line latitude 0-0-0 at an
altitude of 6,377.397 meters without the danger of falling.
[Underneath was a photo of "a beautiful girl walking on the
Equator Line without danger of falling. . . . . !"]

Eat equinoccial peanuts, the most delicious in the world,
raised in the sands sun-bathed with concentrated infrared
rays. Also taste the wine made from equator grapes.

You weigh less here than at the latitude from which you came! See for yourself on the special scale.

When you stand on the Equator you are traveling at more than 1,667 km per hour due to the rotation at the earth. This is the maximum velocity attainable in this manner.

Record of the crossing of the Equator: a person who visits this place can attain a record as large as he desires of crossings of the equator. If he crosses 60 times per minute we will extend a certificate certifying that he actually has done it.

Be present on the 21st of March and the 23rd of September for the traditional equinoccial feasts and participate in the official "Equinoccial Dance."

After all this, I was eager to meet Professor Vera, weigh myself on his scale, eat his equinoccial peanuts, and dance in his sun festival, even though there was something rather familiar about his mad championing of the equator—something that reminded me, ever so slightly, of myself, and that kept me from holding him up to very close, or very critical, examination.

To celebrate finding Professor Vera, and he was certain to be at his sun dance on Saturday, I went to a restaurant described as one of Quito's best. It certainly had that appearance: tables of soberly dressed Ecuadorians, a French ambience, and an extensive menu of seafood that was, I hoped, rushed up from the coast in refrigerated trucks. Eating seafood is risky in third-world countries, but I thought, What the hell? The United States imports shrimp from Ecuador, and I had already eaten in far less savory places, and besides, would these elegant Ecuadorians dine here if the kitchen was poisonous? The handsome couple at the next table were impressed that a visitor to Quito had found this place so quickly. They recommended the shrimp ceviche and fish stew. I thanked them and took their suggestions, and so began months of agony. Four hours later I was vomiting and convulsed with diarrhea, burning with fever, then chilled and chattering like a monkey. I fainted on the bathroom floor. I ate only eggs and toast, losing ten pounds, but I took enough pills so that after two days I could walk to the office coordinating American earthquake relief.

I had read in the Ecuadorian papers that American cargo planes and helicopters were carrying relief supplies to the earthquake zone and returning with refugees. And I had read that ten days earlier, in Lago Agrio, a relief helicopter overloaded with foreign journalists had wobbled during takeoff, almost crashing. They were doing their job, but I was not sure it was mine. Whatever I wrote would not appear in time to open any foreign pockets, and I have always disapproved of touring the site of a natural disaster out of mere curiosity. But, despite these reservations, I still begged for a seat on a relief flight, arguing to myself that, after all, the earthquake had ocurred on the equator, almost killing me, and like a passenger saved from an air crash by a sudden change of plans, I had a macabre interest in viewing the wreckage.

The embassy had organized a bus tour to the most accessible earthquake villages. First I was told I could go, then that demand from within the embassy was so great, with all the clerks and typists wanting to see for themselves, that I had been bumped. As a consolation, I could watch video tapes depicting the destruction along the road to Lago Agrio, the one I had planned taking. It was a cold way to see your brush with death, sitting in a swivel chair and drinking coffee from a happy-face mug while squinting at a television screen in a dark cubicle in an air-conditioned AID office in the Computec building. The video tapes had been filmed by a jiggly camera from a helicopter, with a commentator shouting over the engine. I adjusted to the blurred colors and saw cut bridges, buried highways, and flooded valleys. The villages resembled those tornado-flattened towns in the Midwest. The commentator said, "There were two settlements here . . . thirty-seven landslides on this stretch of road . . . a farm over there. Hey, here's a town covered in mud."

I asked the secretary if any Americans had died. In a matter-of-fact voice she said, "No Americans are missing, but whole Ecuadorian families are gone, and there are no survivors to miss them." The government had first announced only seventeen "official" casualties, army recruits traveling by bus, but no one doubted there were more. "Many are under only three feet of mud," she said, "so they'll turn up. Wild animals and dogs are already gnawing on what's exposed."

During my illness, President Cordero's opponents in Quito

had used the earthquake as an excuse for anti-government demonstrations. They pretended to protest the freezing of prices, gasoline rationing, and sudden shortages, but their real complaint, as
always, was against the controversial Cordero, who, because he is
a self-made millionaire from rival Guayaquil, is particularly unpopular in Quito, a city of landed gentry and civil servants. His
unorthodox style and his knack for humiliating opponents have
made things worse. He is said to have ordered a large vodka before one morning press conference, telling the assembled journalists, "I like one to loosen me up." For reasons too complicated
to explain here he has attempted to "solve" a dispute with his
country's Supreme Court by padlocking its doors, the Ecuadorian
Congress has voted to impeach his finance minister, and an elite
force of air-force commandos briefly kidnapped him after murdering a bodyguard. From all this you might conclude that President
Cordero is a *caudillo* who seized power in the usual Ecuadorian
fashion. Instead, his election in 1984 was the first peaceful transfer
of power from one democratically elected administration to another in two decades. Banana-rich Ecuador is one of several Latin
American countries that could have inspired the term "banana
republic," and forty different presidents, dictators, and juntas have
crowded its ninety-five years of independence. The most important was José Maria Velasco Ibarra, who led the country five times
and is noted for saying, "Give me a balcony and I will rule."

Following the anti-Cordero demonstrations, the Plaza de In-
dependencia had filled with riot policemen carrying submachine
guns and soldiers poking their heads from armored cars like turtles. Foreign newspapers predicted a coup, and it was unclear if
these security forces would protect the president, arrest him, or
shoot it out. I went to Quito's oldest church, the monastery of San
Francisco, to escape the soldiers and rest my churning guts. Steps
leading to the door from the plaza were pinched at the top by a
balcony. As the crowd of Friday-afternoon worshipers slowed to
navigate this choke point, they had to detour around tables from
which women sold religious medallions, icons, and votive candles.
As I tried to pass between these tables, two Indians stepped in
front of me, blocking my way. They were so short I saw only the
tops of their round hats. I stepped back and two more jammed
me from behind, trapping me in a four-Indian vise. I had expected
South American pickpockets to be subtle, their sensitive fingers

darting unnoticed into innermost pockets. But this was more like a mugging. I felt like an assembly-line chicken, wrung, hosed down, and plucked. Stubby fingers rummaged through my pockets, probing and grabbing. I struggled, but my hands were pinned to my sides. I shouted, and the votive-candle women looked away.

I chased my assailants into the church, but it was packed with Friday-afternoon supplicants: ragged people, many of them Indians and, to my eye, indistinguishable from the pickpockets. They worshiped in side chapels and filled the nave, chanting after a priest. My enemies were probably kneeling in prayer, giving thanks. The church resembled one of those gaudy Hindu temples where the faithful throw butter at statues of their favorite gods. It was adorned by baroque carvings and had time-blackened relics and a gold ceiling. It was beautiful—if your idea of beauty is wretched people kneeling in fervid prayer beneath a fortune in gold.

I will admit to not being in the best mood to appreciate the splendors of this church. I had lost sixty dollars in Ecuadorian sucres, a pocket comb, and even the handkerchief I stuffed over my money to bamboozle pickpockets. I felt like a fool. For months I had carried cash and valuables in a long pouch attached to my belt loop by a rock-climber's carabiner. It hung inside my trousers, large and uncomfortable, but in this modest Catholic city, the safest of all South American capitals, where tourists were rarely molested and women walked through public parks alone after dark, I had dispensed with it. In months of traveling through poor countries, this was the only time I lost a penny to theft or dishonesty.

The bus from Quito to the largest equatorial monument in the world said MITAD DEL MUNDO—"Middle of the World." For an hour it chugged down into an increasingly cactus-filled and desert terrain. Rocks were scattered across the last half mile of the highway. A passenger said students had come here to protest President Cordero's response to the earthquake, and these boulders remained from their barricades. I asked other Ecuadorian visitors, the bus driver, the sellers of handicrafts, and finally Professor Vera himself why the students chose to demonstrate out here. No one knew, so I was left with my own theory: that in a country named after the equator, this monument was like the White House or the Lincoln Memorial, a national symbol.

The equator monument at Mitad del Mundo is a hundred-foot-high, pink stone obelisk with a concrete globe balanced on its nose. The architecture is thirties Fascist, a structure too big, solid, and rectangular, and too much resembling a cemetery marker. It was built in 1986 to mark the two hundred and fiftieth anniversary of the French expedition and is a replica of its predecessor, a much smaller one erected in 1936 to commemorate the two hundredth anniversary of the same expedition. The new monument was large enough to hold every other equatorial sign, pillar, and monument I had seen, and it had more attractions and gimmicks than all the others combined. Nearby were planetariums belonging to Spain, France, Germany, and Ecuador; a village of souvenir stands; men with Polaroid cameras; a snack bar; a restaurant; and, under construction, a "tourist village" of white bungalows. As I arrived, workmen were wiring loudspeakers to broadcast music for the "Equinoccial Indian Festival of Inty-Raini," and schoolgirls in pink uniforms circled the monument, waving and chanting "Good-bye, Mitad del Mundo, good-bye!"

I entered the obelisk through a metal mausoleum door decorated by a bronze sun. There was an ethnographic museum on nine floors, and an elevator to an observation deck set just beneath the globe. I asked a pretty girl at the information desk if Professor Vera had arrived yet for the festivities, and she said, "Oh, I'm afraid my father's not coming. This year he hasn't received an invitation." Adriana Vera looked pained. "Perhaps it was an oversight, but you can find him at home." She pointed out a dirt road running south from the curio stalls. "It's only five minutes' walk. Please go. He loves discussing the equator."

Professor Vera's one-story villa sat on a hillside with sweeping views of the arid valley. There were lazy insects, creeping vines, dusty paths, and a maid humming in the kitchen. She pointed me to a cinder-block hut smelling of glue. A handwritten sign over the door said DESIGN AND DECORATION OF HAND-ICRAFTS, and inside Professor Vera sat hunched over a desk, sticking the word "Ecuador" in gold lettering onto the sides of wooden ball-point pens. They fitted into a desk set decorated with a model of the equatorial monument. Dozens of these models filled his work tables.

"I'm the only one who makes them," he said with pride. "It's my own design." Twenty years earlier he had moved to the equator for its dry climate. Quito was only twelve miles south, but it was considerably wetter and cooler because of its higher altitude. He had purchased the land surrounding the old monument, in a stroke gaining sole ownership of the most popular equator in Ecuador, which he soon transformed into a splendid little enterprise.

He had opened an Equatorial Museum and printed his own postcards and Official Equatorial Diploma, selling them to tourists visiting Folklore Vera, his all-in-one store, post office, and visitor center.

He had installed a scale where, for one sucre, visitors could see themselves weighing less on the equator. "You should have been here then," he said. "The tourists, they lined up in front of my scale."

He had sold the Inty-Raini, a special equatorial cocktail once drunk on the equator by the Incas, he said.

He had inaugurated a "Fast Equatorial Mail." For a fee, visitors could hand Professor Vera a letter, then watch him postmark it and race down the counter into the southern hemisphere to hand it back. "One *segundo* and their mail moves between two hemispheres. Is good business for me." He winked.

He had dug an equatorial wishing well. "I read that tourists like to throw coins into Italian fountains, then wish. So I built a fountain. And sure enough, the tourists threw in their coins to make a wish at the middle of the earth. Is very good business for me."

He had printed ten thousand copies of his book on the equator and had already sold half. He suggested we distribute one another's equatorial books. He would handle mine in Ecuador and I would sell his in America. He was completing his third equatorial work, *The Ancient Religion of the Sun on the Middle of the Earth,* which described the symbolism of the sun in native equatorial religions, and the sacrifice of virgins. "They had many fiestas," he said, "so they sacrificed many, many virgins."

He had choreographed the "Indian" dance of Inty-Raini, which was now performed at noon on every spring and fall equinox. "I thought Indian fiestas would bring people to my museum," he said, "so we had them."

"But how did you learn about these Indian dances? Did the Indians teach you?"

"Is somewhat adapted." He laughed. "Is Indian ceremony, more or less."

Five years earlier, government officials had put an end to Professor Vera's equatorial enterprises by constructing the new monument. They expropriated his land, replacing his museum and store with modern structures and compensating him with these nearby acres. He missed posing with the politicians and beauty queens who visited the Mitad del Mundo, and he detested the new monument. "It is three times the size of the old one and too big for tourist snapshots. Before, they could take pictures with the whole monument backed by snow-covered mountains. But now . . ." He gave a loud Bronx cheer.

What to make of Professor Vera? He had the trustworthy, big-featured peasant face of an Anthony Quinn, and the grin of a minor scalawag. He really was a professor at the university, and capable of dense digressions on Indian equatorial rituals and the French metric expedition. He was equally capable of batting on about wishing wells and his newest scheme, a retirement village for wealthy Americans. "They would simply love it here," he insisted. "We have the same climate as Arizona, only here is cheaper and they are on the equator. Perhaps you would care to be my sales agent in the States?"

It was 11:20 A.M. In forty minutes the sun would be directly over the monument, casting no shadow. If I was a few seconds late, I would miss it entirely and have to wait another six months. "Will you be attending the dance?" I asked, making a show of glancing at my watch.

"I'm not going this year. I have my work here." He nodded toward the unfinished curios.

"But it's your ceremony." How could I go to the Inty-Raini dance leaving behind in this dim atelier the man who, although he was reluctant to admit this, had invented it?

"I have not been invited." He pulled out a notebook. "You go without me. But first — and you have plenty of time — tell me about the other equators. I will include your research in the next edition of my book—giving you credit, of course. Where did you start?"

I described Macapá.

"What! Only a concrete line? No statue? No folklore selling?" He slapped his forehead in amazement and stared at a blank page, uncertain whether this incredible information was worth recording. "Who measured the line there?"

"I imagine the Brazilians did."

"Ha! But here have come the French, the Spanish, and the Germans. International science has proven without a doubt the equator is here. Perhaps in Macapá you were not exactly on the equator? Only here, in a country named for it, can you be sure."

I told him about the lonely rail crossing in Gabon, then checked my watch. It was 11:35.

"No restaurant in Gabon? No souvenir shops? Or sign even? Why, it can't be!" He was now writing furiously. "And the Congo?"

"I missed it."

"Zaïre?"

I described Mbandaka's rock.

"Only a little plaque?"

"And the government had removed it."

He revolved an index finger opposite his forehead. "Government there is crazy."

He was pleased that the Kenyan equator was well populated with signs and handicraft salesmen, and ecstatic when I described the impressive markers at Bonjol and Pontianak, although shocked that the Indonesians had neglected their commercial possibilities. "No post office? No telephone service? Not even a scale?" Professor Vera felt sorry for these primitives.

A boy ran into the workshop and laid an envelope on his desk. It was a formal invitation to attend the festivities. I suspected his daughter's hand.

"Aha! They insist I give a speech," he said, hurrying behind a partition and making a noisy business of splashing water and brushing his teeth. He wiped his face on a curtain and appeared, transformed, close shaven and wearing the uniform of a South American dignitary: dark suit, sunglasses, and Panama hat. He flipped fast through a file of equatorial speeches, all blurred carbons on onionskin. "No. No. Not right. Too short." He grabbed the longest and we ran for his car. It was 11:52.

We arrived at three minutes to noon. Professor Vera ran across the lawn to join other dignitaries standing on the steps of the monument. The spectators were students in school uniforms, dragged here in buses. The Inty-Raini dancers stood on a pink sidewalk running west from the obelisk. A yellow line in its middle marked the equator. They were ten young women, one for each planet and the sun. The planets wore Hollywood vestal-virgin costumes: white mini-skirt togas and yellow slave-bands around their ankles. The sun wore a yellow toga and straddled the line. None of the girls was remotely Indian, and two planets — Saturn and Mercury, I think — were blondes. I asked Professor Vera afterwards why real Indians were not recruited to perform his Indian dance. He had never considered it. "But is authentic Indian dance," he said. "So what difference who dances it?"

It began at 11:59. To the accompaniment of music from a scratchy record, the planets circled the sun, genuflecting and raising their arms heavenward. At noon they fell to the pavement, prostrating themselves. The students laughed and talked throughout, and even Professor Vera was too busy revising his speech to pay attention. For an instant I stared straight up into a dazzling sun. The combination of equator, equinox, and altitude made it feel as if I had laid my face against an electric heater. At last I could feel the effect of the equator, and, in this absence of shadow, see it too.

The Inty-Raini dancers left to whistles and obscene lip-smackings. A politician recommended morality and hard work to the students, and Professor Vera, loyally wearing one of my buttons, described the heroic sacrifices of the eighteenth-century French cartographers. Afterwards he posed for pictures in front of the monument, waving his hat in the air. Then he circulated through the curio stalls, collecting in cash the weekly royalties earned by his book. He insisted I join him for lunch. It might be years, or never, before he met another equator enthusiast. Few men shared his fascination with the equator, and he could not bear to let me go.

We drank several liters of beer and he recited his equatorial poem, then said "Welcome to the equator" in a dozen languages. One minute I heard a lecture on Inca customs, the next a crackpot explanation for the recent earthquake: "The middle of the earth tries to fly away because it's going fastest; therefore it's dangerous to live on the equator." He tried to interest me again in his equatorial retirement village. "But you could tell them it's healthier to live on the equator. We have natural springs, dry climate, water, power, telephone, everything like Arizona, only cheaper! And we equator people live longer too!"

We drove west to a bluff overlooking the monument. Professor Vera tooted his horn, and an Indian woman hobbled from a hovel on the arm of her great-great-grandson. She had two teeth and a creviced face and wore a patchwork of rags. "She is at least a hundred and thirty," he said, "perhaps more! You can describe her to Americans interested in moving here. Her name is Juana-Caiza. She will convince the wealthy Americans. Yes?"

She looked a hundred, but poverty had undoubtedly aged her more than time. Forget her precise age: It was a feat to have lived so long in these conditions. I handed her an equatorial button and she scowled. "I think she would prefer a hundred sucres," the professor said. "Most visitors pay at least that for the pleasure of viewing her."

Professor Vera had more equatorial sights to stretch out our afternoon. We drove to the Pululagua Crater, an extinct volcano at the edge of the western cordillera and the first place touched by the equator after it climbs from the coast. The crater was a green bowl, filled with Indian farms and bounded by a perpetual wall of clouds. Next I admired the former equatorial monument, now in the village of Calacali. The obelisk was the twin of the newer memorial, but only a tenth its size. Despite being the centerpiece of the plaza, it looked neglected. Professor Vera collected more book royalties from a handicrafts store and offered to buy beer. He promised the coldest, freshest, most delicious beer in Ecuador, but I was still awash with the first three liters and refused. On the way back we stopped at the side of the road to urinate. The landscape of treeless valleys and cloudy volcanoes matched the equatorial monument: massive and awe-inspiring, but not pretty.

"Imagine it is centuries ago and the Mayans are marching into this valley," he said. "For generations they have followed the path of the sun from Central America, across Panama, down the

Cordillera from Colombia. Why? Because they wish to live on the site of the equinox, at the middle of the earth."

"I thought the Indians here were Incas."

"No, my theory is Mayans, brought by the equator. They sacrificed virgins during the equinox, and their sun festivals prove they knew this was the earth's middle." He swept his arm in an arc. "Just look! Perfect for retired Americans. Nowhere will they find more healthy sun. And we have all sports, even hang-gliding!" Sure enough, members of Quito's elite had bought themselves gliders. A mile away, winged men jumped off a cliff, soaring high on the arid currents and gliding across the equator like the huge colored butterflies of a psychedelic dream.

Sight unseen, I had hired a German, "Karl," to drive and walk me to where the equator crossed Cayambe. The director of the mountain-guide service had first telephoned two other men, who had to refuse because the new rationing laws made it impossible to find gasoline over the weekend. But Karl had Peruvian plates on his Land Rover, making him exempt from restrictions. At 18,800 feet, Cayambe is the second highest mountain in Ecuador and, with its crevices and frequent avalanches, among the most dangerous. I would only be going to where the equator crossed at 15,000 feet on its southern slope, but Karl did not seem like the man to get me even this far. The spare tire screwed to the hood of his Land Rover was bald, and he had a broken finger tied in a splint, so he would be driving me up these mountain roads with one hand. He did not know Ecuador well, having driven his poky Land Rover up from Lima during the Peruvian rainy season, hoping to find clients like me. He admitted having visited Cayambe just once, and since that had been two years earlier, with friends who did all the driving, he worried about finding the correct road to the refuge. When he picked me up early Sunday morning, he complained of sleeping only four hours the night before, poor preparation for an eight-hour drive and what I hoped would be a strenuous high-altitude walk, and he looked terrible, a weasely man with the scraggly beard and hollow eyes you see in photographs of German soldiers retreating from the Eastern Front.

We had driven only ten minutes before I discovered why he looked like this: Two nights before, he had dined at the same restaurant that had poisoned me. He had chosen the deluxe sea-food platter, suffering a deluxe version of my illness. He drank tea from a thermos, shared my breakfast of biscuits and Lomotil, and said, "I'm not sure how far I can walk today." In truth, he had no intention of walking at all.

The first forty miles were along a highway climbing in and out of barren valleys. Somewhere among the gulches, canyons, and cacti, the equator crossed the road unmarked. (But coming back from Cayambe that evening, we took a parallel road on which the equator was announced by a concrete globe mounted in a fountain smeared with political graffiti. Karl chose this as backdrop for photographs to convince his parents he was prospering in South America. Handing me the Polaroid they had given him for this purpose, he posed before the only depressing equatorial marker I had seen. He fluffed up his greasy strings of hair and dragged fingers through his beard, loosening a flurry of dirt. He puffed up his chest, straightened his filthy clothes, and forced a smile. Afterwards he apologized for this show of vanity, saying the photographs were "for my many girlfriends and to show my parents I'm OK." The film was old, so the instant snapshots had a yellow tint, making him look as if, aside from everything else, he had contracted hepatitis. (I would have liked a photograph of his German parents as they shook these from an envelope.)

Outside the village of Cayambe we turned onto an unpaved and unmarked road — the one, I hoped, that climbed six thousand feet in fifteen miles to the Cayambe refuge. My guidebook described the last six miles of this road as rough, and I wanted to walk it, but Karl refused. "Unless it's damaged by the earthquake, is better for us to drive all the way," he said, opening his thermos with quivering hands. I soon discovered he was willing to take almost any risk — to slam through punishing ruts and swing around crumbling parapets, his tires spitting loose gravel — to avoid walking. And knowing how he felt, the way I did yesterday, I could not blame him. I faced facts: I was being driven to the second highest volcano in Ecuador by a sick, aging hippie who held the wheel with one broken hand while gripping his ravaged stomach with the other.

He had brought a topographical map that was useless. The equator was its southern boundary, so it showed Cayambe's peak but neither the refuge nor the road leading to it. After several wrong turns he gave a weak smile and said, "I guess is different, driving with other people and driving yourself."

Traffic was all in the other direction, with Indians walking and riding open trucks to the Sunday market in Cayambe. Karl flagged down a truckload of stone-faced Indians and shouted, *"Dondé refugio?"* The driver pointed up our road, but still Karl stopped at every crossroads, shouting the same question at ever younger and less certain Indians. They ignored us or contradicted each other. The adults wore sweaters, patched and unraveling, the kind the English reserve for gardening. At the sight of us, children fell to their knees, bowing heads and begging in a "Now-I-lay-me-down-to-sleep" pose, with their palms pressed together and tilted up.

Higher up, the farms gave way to groves of eucalyptus, meadow, and cattle. Cayambe was a cap of snow, round as a Homburg and smoking plumes of clouds. We passed the last ranch at ten thousand feet, according to Karl's altimeter, and the road immediately deteriorated to a rough track. We wound through a tundra of brown grass, white horses, and long-fingered green cactus, stopping every fifty yards to clear rocks from the road. Karl knew he could not afford a flat. At twelve thousand feet, when we were still two miles from the refuge, I left him on a precarious corner, holding his aching guts with his broken hand, spinning the wheel, and cursing while trying to maneuver between a rockslide and a precipice.

I climbed a stony valley and, once out of sight, broke out a lunch I did not care to share, two nut bars and a lime. Despite being poisoned by the same restaurant, I felt little comradeship for Karl. What good was a guide who refused to walk? The clouds and snow squalls slid away and again I saw Cayambe's snow-fields. A tongue of ice licked down the southeast slope to within yards of the refuge, a gray stone building imitating the mountain huts of the Alps. Karl picked me up when I was almost there. Perspiration soaked his shirt and he was breathing in gulps. After an hour of moving rocks and backing and filling, he had freed his Land Rover. His determination to avoid walking was heroic.

The refuge was ten years old but already a ruin. Its roof leaked, and lovers had defaced the walls with hearts scrawled in charcoal. The mestizo guard was lonely. He started chattering the moment we appeared, spreading out a map of Ecuador and running his fingers along lines of volcanoes and rivers flowing east from Cayambe into the Amazon. He said the equator was a hundred and fifty feet above the refuge. He knew this because in 1975 a visiting Spanish priest had made measurements so he could leave a statue of the Virgin on the highest point in the world crossed by the equator.

A storm rolled up from the jungle bringing sleet, horizontal rain, black clouds that turned the glacier blue, and, finally, "snow on the equator." When it cleared, Karl disappeared into the toilet, and I scrambled up a gravel hill to see the Virgin. It was a small white statue, set in a hollow with a commanding view. Beyond it the equator crossed a snowfield before disappearing into the clouds that hugged the eastern cordillera, into a wall of mist and fog so dense it was almost possible to imagine the earth was flat, and that beyond this snow and ice was its very edge, where the equator stopped.

Except for a visit to Macapá on the way home, it was here that the equator stopped for me. The earthquake had made the rest of Ecuador inaccessible, meaning I could not reach equatorial Colombia without detouring a hundred miles north through Bogotá, or equatorial Brazil without an even longer detour south through Lima. Furthermore, between the Virgin of Cayambe and José Maria's cabin, the equator crossed only jungle, narrow Amazon tributaries, and, at a deserted spot, the road from Manaus to Boa Vista.

I was sorry to miss eastern Ecuador, because it was there, with its jungle roads and towns bordering the equator, that I had hoped to take a long walk. I had traveled on jungle rivers, and driven through and flown over jungle, but except for brief excursions in Indonesia, I had not walked far into it. To be honest, though, I was not all that sorry. I was becoming superstitious. I had narrowly missed being buried alive by the earthquake, and I had contracted an illness that months later was diagnosed as amoebic dysentery. I had also confirmed what I had suspected but would not admit to myself at the beginning, that I preferred tropical islands and the towns at the edge of continents to the jungle in their middle; and that more than its flora and fauna, I was interested in the people of the equator.

*   *   *

I arrived back in Macapá nauseous, feverish, and with trembling intestines. Still, compared to many places I had been, it looked pretty good, with its confident men flashing that optimistic Brazilian thumbs-up sign. I stayed in the same hotel, and across the street the same steady wind rippled the Amazon. It was a weekday, so the soccer players were in school, and it was Macapá's rainy "winter," so what had been dusty was now overgrown. New street signs pointed toward an illusionary *centro,* and a new carnival had taken over the main square, boasting a bearded woman and a larger *avião infantil.* The dock in front of the hotel was being lengthened in a major harbor renovation program, said a sign, and I wondered if José Maria had escaped the governor's solar clock.

Sondra's house was a surprise, a Macapá outpost of the good life. It had a tile roof, flowering shrubs, and, of all things, a swimming pool. A handsome young woman with an oiled body and round sunglasses lay sprawled across an air mattress. It was Alessondra, no longer, it looked to me, a "virgem."

Sondra was much thinner and better dressed than I remembered. She squinted up, probably thinking I was a madman. Who else would come to Macapá twice to stand on its equator?

"And I'd like to visit José Maria again," I said.

"Ah, that nice man."

"Is he living in the same house?"

She had not seen him since my last visit. I was disappointed. I had pictured them becoming friends and, over cups of coffee, wondering when I would return.

Sondra's English was no better. I asked if she had finished her course.

"I still have two years."

"But you had two years before."

"I am only attending part-time, but my dream is the same: Finish my degree and go to the U.S.A. for more study of English. Can you recommend a university pleased to have me?" She appeared happier and less suspicious. Before, it was "nothing to be a woman in Macapá," but now, as we rode in the taxi to the equator, she touched my arm to make a point and admitted to liking

Macapá's heat, friendly people, and safety. "In São Paulo, no one is safe from crime, but here I never fear for my children."

"Have you translated for other travelers?" I asked.

"In truth, you were my first, and my second was only last month." A small cruise liner with 150 Germans and Americans had docked in Macapá. They had come for the equator, but Sondra had dragged them to the other sights too, including that zoo.

"And Alessondra?"

"She has a baby, but she is married, so all is OK." She smiled, a proud grandmother forgetting her battles with those boys who ran away "whoosh!"

Four months earlier, the government had transformed Macapá's simple equator into an eight-story concrete slab. A hole punched in its top represented the earth. "We have a new governor," Sondra explained, "and he made this monument. You like it, yes?" I did not. Gone was the world map outlined in aloe plants and white stones. Gone too the observation deck and the low concrete wall that had accurately portrayed the equator as a line dividing the earth and not as a pyramid, an arrow, a boulder, or an obelisk. Replacing all this was this slab. It sat atop a long building with smoked windows that could have been a turnpike rest stop.

"It is our restaurant for tourists," Sondra explained. "Here the Germans and Americans ate lunch." I looked inside. The empty rooms had chairs for several hundred. But who would dine here? Macapá is encircled by jungle and Amazon delta. Its only roads lead to Calçoene and Oaipoque, its only ferry to Belém. Still, it was impossible not to appreciate the bravado of building this place, the same bravado that has bankrupted Brazil and that says, "We are passing our lives in this Macapá, and it is more than bumpy streets, humidity, and shabby carnivals. We have our slogan: O futuro e agora — 'The future is now.' We have our equator! And now we have an equatorial palace of a restaurant!"

We climbed a flight of stairs to the roof, where the old monument with its twin obelisks and magnesium lettering had been preserved as a curiosity. The neighboring field was still an overgrown meadow, the ambitious plan for an equatorial soccer field having disappeared with the previous governor. To the east, the road running to José Maria's house was unchanged. This equatorial complex must be the "solar clock" he had worried might swallow his farm, although the only solar clock I saw was a sundial mounted on the roof.

José Maria's shack was even more forlorn and deserted than before. Boards had fallen loose, and the foliage had advanced. The same dreamy girl opened the door, but moments later José Maria was hugging me and saying, "Why, we were wondering about you only last week."

He was still bare-chested and wearing tattered shorts, but much heavier. He scolded me for using his back door. Now this shack was only for storage, as was the other one that had been their home. Here, There, and Everywhere had run away, and a snake had killed Cinderella, but he had bought new dogs. The old governor had been replaced by one who did not covet his equatorial plot. "Yes, that governor is gone, but I am still here," he said, flashing a thumbs-up. Everything certainly was thumbs up for José Maria. He lived in a sturdy new house, situated at the top of the hill to catch his unusual breeze, and his wife could watch *The Love Boat* on a still larger color television.

I handed him the Lambarené crocodile. He accepted it without complaint, placing it on a shelf between his stereo speakers and pretending not to notice when it rolled over dead on its crippled legs.

Three landscape paintings decorated his walls. They were primitives, executed in bright colors and done with wit and style. One showed a park filled with playing children, and another a snowy mountain range and a woodsman's cabin, almost an exact copy of the print José Maria had given me and I had given to Maria Lagendijk, in Lambarené. In its lower right-hand corner it was signed "José Maria."

I was amazed. "You never said you were an artist."

"It is nothing. Since you left I bought paints and canvas and taught myself. In Macapá these things are not expensive."

"But the mountains? Have you seen them?"

"There are mountains in my imagination."

He led me outside to his new project: a soccer field with flimsy goalposts bordered by piles of lumber and a half-completed pavilion. "Here I am building the motel, bar, and soccer field Marco Zero," he said. The open-air bar would be the first step, to be followed by cottages and a swimming pool. "I hope for many customers from Macapá. My friends have been begging me to build a bar, since they know it is cool on the equator. They will play soccer, drink beer, retreat from the city, and escape their problems. My wife will cook. All is planned."

"How did you pay for the wood, the new television, everything?" I wanted a better explanation than before, that living on the equator was lucky.

"Chickens," he said. "My chickens have given me all this." The government had fixed the price of chickens, and somehow — Sondra's English was not up to explaining precisely how — this had been a windfall for José Maria.

"Are you returning to visit us soon?" he asked. I gave the cowardly answer that I might come back in a year or two. He insisted I write down his address, and if anyone should visit Macapá and want to play a game of soccer or drink a cool beer on the equator, here it is: 893 Garade das Pedrinhas, Macapá, 68200 Brazil. I left through his new front gate, passing a sign saying Retiro JE. Elizabeth said it stood for "José-Elisabeth"; he said it meant "José Especial," a long-running joke. I gave them handfuls of my equatorial buttons, presents for their first customers. He hugged me twice and, standing in the middle of the road, threw me a double thumbs-up that he held until I was out of sight.

At the beginning, I had imagined the equator as a circle of monuments, the center of a shrinking green frontier, or a heavy rope connecting volcanoes, jungles, and atolls. But now I would remember it as a necklace of people, all scheming how to make the best of their "one and only precious lives." I had a sudden, but brief, urge to keep going and discover what had happened to the others. Had John found someone to buy that tusk? Were Patel's empty stores still blazing with light? Had Father Gustaaf moved his equatorial library to safety? Had Genevieve returned from Baltimore to revolutionize Rwanda? Had Muthemba found a publisher? Had Ar married his iron butterfly? Was the king of Abemema's grandson still showing violent movies? Had Tekeira moved to Fanning Island? Would I replace Archbishop Makarios in Professor Vera's next book?

To the more important questions I already knew the answers. I knew that because the population of most tropical countries is growing so fast, the earth's five billion people will have doubled in only thirty-five years. And I knew this was the main reason why every year more tropical forest is lost. So if I traveled again around the equator right away, I would find more people, less forest, more erosion, and a smaller and more moth-eaten equatorial green belt. Many of the changes would be visible. The slums of Mathere would have advanced several hundred more yards along that valley, and more tin-roofed transmigration camps would stretch across Borneo's hills. More people would be clinging to the hovels of DUD or sitting idle on the curbs of Muqdisho. The circles of cleared land dotting the road to Macapá would be closer together, and the Rwandan children begging from the gorilla-watching tourists more numerous. In fact, as you read these words, all this, and more, has already happened.

ACKNOWLEDGMENTS

DURING MY TRAVELS PEOPLE TOO NUMEROUS TO MENTION — and in some cases I fear that if I did mention them it would be no favor — invited me into their homes, guided me around, and spent hours in conversation. I am sure they will not agree with everything I have written about where they live. I can only thank them for their many acts of kindness and hospitality, and say that the impressions of the resident and traveler are often at odds, and the truest insight can be a monopoly of neither.

Many people have contributed a great deal to the preparation of my manuscript and the production of the book. I am grateful to, in Britain, Bruce Hunter, my agent, and Paul Sidey, my editor, and, in New York, Pam Altschul, Maria Epes, Cheryl Asherman, Al Marchioni, Susan Halligan, Lisa Queen, and Will Schwalbe.

I would also like to thank my wife, Antonia Bullard, for her hard work and tolerance of my long absences from home, my agent, Julian Bach, for his wise counsel, my friends Judy Wederholt and John Coyne for their unceasing encouragement, my friend Carolyn Marsh for her meticulous copy editing, and, most of all, my editor, Adrian Zackheim, for his skillful direction and inexhaustible enthusiasm.

— *Manhattan and Willsboro, New York*
March 1988